From the Writings of

Maria Mitchell

The world of learning is so broad, and the human soul
is so limited in power! We reach forth and strain every nerve,
but we seize only a bit of the curtain that hides the infinite from us.

We especially need imagination in science. It is not all mathematics,
nor all logic, but it is somewhat beauty and poetry.

We cannot accept anything as granted,
beyond the first mathematical formulae. Question everything else.

Every formula which expresses
a law of nature is a hymn of praise to God.

The habit of travelling once adopted cannot be easily given up.

The step, however small, which is in advance of the world,
shows the greatness of the person, whether that step be taken
with brain, with heart, or with hands.

For women, there are undoubtedly great difficulties in the path,
but so much the more to overcome. First, no woman should say,
"I am but a woman." But a woman!
What more can you ask to be.
Born a woman, born with the average brain of humanity,
born with more than the average heart,
if you are mortal what higher destiny could you have.
No matter where you are nor what you are,
you are a power. Your influence is incalculable.

— MARIA MITCHELL

MARIA MITCHELL

A Life in Journals and Letters

EDITED

BY

HENRY ALBERS

COLLEGE AVENUE PRESS
Clinton Corners, New York

MARIA MITCHELL: A Life in Journals and Letters
Copyright © 2001 by Henry Albers.

COVER BACKGROUND PHOTOGRAPH: "The Orion Nebula: The Jewel in the Sword," courtesy of Mark McCaughrean/ESO. Copyright © 2001 European Southern Observatory. COVER PHOTOGRAPH of MARIA MITCHELL: Courtesy of Special Collections, Vassar College Libraries.

COLLEGE AVENUE PRESS
is an imprint of
THE ATTIC STUDIO Publishing House
P.O. Box 75 • Clinton Corners, NY 12514
Phone: 845-266-8100 • Fax: 845-266-5515
E-mail: CollegeAvePress@aol.com

PRINTED IN THE UNITED STATES OF AMERICA
10   9   8   7   6   5   4   3   2   1   FIRST EDITION

Library of Congress Cataloging-in-Publication Data
    Maria Mitchell : a life in journals and letters / edited by Henry Albers.
        p. cm.
    Includes bibliographical references and index.
    ISBN 1-883551-89-7 (alk. paper)
    1. Mitchell, Maria, 1818-1889.   2. Astronomers—United States—Biography.   I. Albers, Henry.
QB36.M7 M37 2001
520'.92—dc21
                                                        2001001652

For Wilma

my wonderful wife of over 50 years

— and —

for our three children

Catherine, Christina, and Peter

CONTENTS

Maria Mitchell

ILLUSTRATIONS

Maria Mitchell

WILLIAM AND LYDIA MITCHELL. Married for nearly fifty years, William and Lydia Mitchell were the parents of ten children, including the famed astronomer. Maria was their third child, born August 1, 1818. *Below:* Mitchell home on Nantucket with a wooden ladder leading to its rooftop "walk." (*Chapter One includes enlarged details of each of the photographs below.*)

MITCHELL FAMILY

WILLIAM MITCHELL   born Dec. 20, 1791   died April 19, 1869
LYDIA COLEMAN   born Jan. 30, 1793   died July 7, 1861
married December 10, 1812

ANDREW COLEMAN MITCHELL   b. Jan. 30, 1814   d. 1871
m. Ann Elizabeth Swain, May 21, 1843

SALLY MITCHELL (BARNEY)   b. Jan. 30, 1816   d. Mar. 25, 1876
m. Matthew Barney, April 4, 1838   *(Nantucket)*

MARIA MITCHELL   b. Aug. 1, 1818   d. June 28, 1889

ANNE MITCHELL (MACY)   b. Nov. 8, 1820   d. Mar. 16, 1900
m. Alfred Macy, May 2, 1857

FRANCIS MACY MITCHELL   b. Feb. 19, 1823   d. Aug. 3, 1891
m. Ellen Mitchell, April 27, 1853   *(Chicago)*

WILLIAM FORSTER MITCHELL   b. Aug. 31, 1825   d. June, 1892
m. Charlotte Dow, Feb. 5, 1846   *(Nantucket)*

PHEBE MITCHELL (KENDALL)   b. Feb. 23, 1828   d. June 4, 1907
m. Joshua Kendall, Sept. 14, 1854

HENRY MITCHELL   b. Sept. 16, 1830   d. Dec. 1, 1902
m. Mary E. Dawes, Sept. 8, 1854
m. Margaret Hayward, 1873 (d. 1875)
m. Mary Hayward, 1877 (d. March 1902)

ELIZA MITCHELL   b. Sept. 16, 1830   d. April 5, 1833
(Twin of Henry)   *(or May 4)*

ELIZA KATHERINE MITCHELL (DAME)   b. June 28, 1833   d. Feb. 10, 1907
m. Owen Dame, July 9, 1857

Maria Mitchell

CHRONOLOGY
Maria Mitchell *(1818-1889)*

1818   Maria is born August 1st on Nantucket Island, Massachusetts. Named after her mother's sister, she is the third of ten
children.

1831   The twelve-year-old Maria assists her father as he observes an
annular eclipse.

1836   At eighteen, Maria becomes the first librarian of the Nantucket Atheneum. She continues being self-supporting for
the next fifty-two years.

1843   Maria withdraws from the Quaker religion.

1847   On October 1, while "sweeping" the sky from the rooftop of
her home in Nantucket, Maria discovers the comet which
now bears her name. For this discovery she is awarded a Gold
Medal by the King of Denmark.

1848   The celebrated astronomer is elected an Honorary Member
of the American Academy of Arts and Sciences.

1849   Admiral Charles Henry Davis hires Maria to do computations for the newly established American Nautical Almanac
at a salary of $300 a year.

1850   Mitchell becomes a member of the American Association for
the Advancement of Science.

1853   She is awarded an honorary LL.D. from Hanover College.

1853   Maria begins to keep a personal journal, a practice she continues for the rest of her life.

1857   The vigorous astronomer travels extensively throughout the
−58   United States and Europe, accepting invitations from leading
European scholars, visiting observatories, traveling to Rome
with Nathaniel Hawthorne and family, and becoming the
first woman to visit the Vatican Observatory.

1859   Mitchell obtains a new telescope with money raised by
public subscription.

1861 Lydia Coleman Mitchell, Maria's mother, dies on Nantucket. Maria and her father move to Lynn, Massachusetts.

1865 Maria Mitchell accepts an offer to become the first professor of astronomy for the newly established Vassar College. She and her father William move to Poughkeepsie, New York where they take up residence in the observatory.

1869 William Mitchell, a beloved figure on the Vassar campus, dies at age seventy-seven.

1869 Professor Mitchell leads a group of Vassar students on an eclipse expedition to Iowa.

1870 Maria receives an honorary Ph.D. from Rutgers Female College.

1873 On a summer break from Vassar College, Mitchell travels to Europe, including a trip to Russia.

1875 The Association for Advancement of Women (A.A.W.) meets in Syracuse, NY with Maria as president.

1876 In her concern to solidify women's higher education, Mitchell turns her attention to fund-raising, seeking to raise money for the Vassar Observatory.

1876 Maria presides at the A.A.W. meeting in Philadelphia.

1878 In August, Mitchell leads a party of six to observe a total eclipse of the sun in Colorado.

1881 The sixty-two-year old astronomer observes the Great Comet of 1881.

1887 Mitchell receives an honorary LL.D. degree from Columbia University.

1888 Suffering from ill health, Mitchell resigns her Vassar College professorship and returns to Lynn.

1889 On June 28, the seventy-year-old Maria Mitchell dies at home in Lynn. At her funeral on Nantucket, Vassar's President James Monroe Taylor describes her as "an impressive figure in our time."

FOREWORD

INETEENTH CENTURY AMERICA WAS FILLED with pioneers whose lives revolved around exploration and discovery. Maria Mitchell was one such pioneer, although not in the traditional sense. Her territory was the heavens, and her exploration made her a leader in the advancement of women in science. Her career in astronomy, rare for a woman in that period, stemmed from an unusual background. As a child in a large Quaker family in the sea-faring community of Nantucket, Maria received a solid primary school education. Her formal education was augmented by her job as a librarian. It was at the Nantucket library, the Atheneum, that Maria taught herself the fundamentals of calculus and higher-level science.

Maria's father William Mitchell, a prominent local banker, was an influential figure throughout her life. In his role as president of the Nantucket Philosophical Institute, he hosted a number of prominent writers and scientists of the period who visited the island. These visitors were an inspiration to Maria, and were also very useful as contacts and references for her subsequent journeys abroad.

Maria was fortunate to be on an island where women were largely self-sufficient, since their men were gone to sea for long periods. She became well-versed in the operation of key navigational devices such

Maria Mitchell

as the sextant and telescope, which she enjoyed turning towards the skies. She also received invaluable training in instruments as assistant to her father, whose diverse skills included being an instrument repairman. Like a good sailor, Maria learned the skies well, perched on a small porch on the roof of her Nantucket home. An avid observer, Maria noticed something no one else in the world had ever seen—a new comet, visible only through the telescope. Through the efforts of William and George Bond, a father-son astronomer team at Harvard, Maria was able to document her sighting, which was rewarded with a gold medal from the King of Denmark who had established a prize for such a discovery. That honor brought her worldwide acclaim.

Among those who admired Maria Mitchell was Matthew Vassar, a prominent beer brewery magnate in Poughkeepsie, NY, whose fondness for a niece prompted him to found a women's college in 1861. He persuaded Maria to become one of Vassar Female College's first professors. Typical of her modest nature, Maria at first felt that she was unworthy for the task. She went on to become one of the College's most distinguished faculty members, well-loved by her students for her dedication and teaching skills. It is interesting to note a parallel between her life at early Vassar and her childhood: just as the women of Nantucket taught themselves to be self-sufficient because of their sea-faring men, the young women first entering Vassar sought self-education at a time when many of the nation's young men were away from their families because of the Civil War.

In the early years of the College, astronomy was a course which required rigorous observations and calculations. Vassar students had to demonstrate proficiency in mathematics in order to enter Mitchell's astronomy course. Maria's own work included measurements of binary stars and planets. She was among the first astronomers to pour photographic emulsions to provide documentation at the telescope, and several hundred of her images of the sun and stars have been preserved in the Vassar archives. Maria insisted that students learn astronomy by doing astronomy, a tradition that is upheld today. By asking whether students had observed something or merely read it in a book, she imparted the importance of gleaning knowledge actively rather than passively. She was legendary for keeping young women up past curfew to make late observations, and in the late 1800s she made two cross-country trips with her students to view solar eclipses. Her first group of six students, dubbed "The Hexagon," included Mary Whitney, who succeeded Maria as Vassar's second observatory director. Maria inspired many generations of female astronomers, some of whom went on to do research at Harvard, Yale, and Chicago; in general, astronomy jobs for women were rare.

Today the field of astronomy still consists primarily of men, although the balance is slowly shifting: nearly twenty-five percent of the current generation of astronomers are women, compared with about ten percent among graduates of the 1960s and 1970s. Mitchell would have been pleased at this progress in opening up astronomy to everyone who loves it. Maria and her father lived in the original Vassar College Observatory, the first building completed on campus. Designated as a National Historic Landmark, the building's original mission is now carried on in the new Class of 1951 Observatory at the edge of campus. Her Nantucket home is also preserved as a museum, as part of the Maria Mitchell Association of Nantucket.

Maria did not initially seek to break new ground for women; she was a scientist first and foremost, but did not let inequities go unnoticed. Professor Mitchell became involved in campus politics when she realized that her salary was far less than her male counterparts. This inequity led to many exchanges with the administration and trustees at Vassar College, and paved the way for the balance that exists in the coeducational Vassar of today. For many years, Maria was active in the Association for the Advancement of Women, and presided over regional meetings. She served as an outstanding example of achievement for women, being one of the first women to be elected a member of the American Academy of Arts and Sciences and the American Association for the Advancement of Science. She also received several honorary degrees from colleges and universities.

Maria Mitchell

Henry Albers, the editor of this valuable work, was the fifth director (and first male director!) of the Vassar College Observatory, and held the Maria Mitchell Chair that was endowed in Maria's honor by her students. In 1997, Dr. Albers was awarded the first Maria Mitchell Women in Science Award by the Nantucket Maria Mitchell Association for his lifetime of dedication to guiding students in astronomical research. Following his retirement in 1990, he pursued his interest in the history of Maria and her students. That research led him to libraries in wide-ranging locales, where he searched old manuscripts to trace the history of documents and letters exchanged between Maria and her colleagues. His legacy to future generations of astronomers, and to women in the sciences in general, is this illuminating collection of Maria's diaries and correspondence, the most complete ever compiled. His insight into Maria's discourse gives us a large glimpse into the life of an extraordinary woman. Through this important historical document, we can come to know Maria as a person and understand the inspiration that America's first woman astronomer instilled in the many whose lives she touched.

Debra Meloy Elmegreen
MARIA MITCHELL PROFESSOR OF ASTRONOMY
Vassar College, April 2001

PREFACE

HEN I BEGAN TEACHING ASTRONOMY at Vassar College in 1958, I became intrigued by the life and legacy of Maria Mitchell. The college observatory, her home for more than twenty years, still contained some of the furnishings that she had used; her large telescope stood silently in its dome. One small closet held crumbling envelopes enclosing glass photographs which dated back to the 1870s—which turned out to be photographs of the sun taken by Mitchell and her students.

These astronomical photographs were the first memorabilia of Mitchell that I actually held in my hands. They heightened my interest in this famous woman and, as time permitted, I searched for all the original material I could locate.

My search has taken me through the Vassar archives, to Nantucket where she lived, and to the archives of numerous other organizations which held Mitchell memorabilia. I have gathered copies of her existing diaries, letters and articles, amassing a valuable archive of Maria Mitchell material.

In this archive one can find the extensive diaries she wrote during many periods of her life; the letters that came in to her from all over the world; lecture notes for her talks to students and to national

Maria Mitchell

organizations; her ideas about the education of women, about science and even her personal expenditures. Famous people appear in the diaries and letters, including: Julia Ward Howe, Mary Livermore and Mary Somerville; Sir George Airy and Sir John Herschel; Harriet Hosmer and Nathaniel Hawthorne. Even the Emperor of Brazil paid a visit to the small observatory on Vassar campus and this is duly recorded. The diaries are a gold mine for information about Mitchell's thinking. Her personal reflections reveal the warmth of her personality, her concern for her students and relatives, her strong belief in the education of women, as well as the creative fun she had at "Dome Parties."

Maria Mitchell believed in woman's education to the depth of her being. As one of her colleagues later reported, "However interested you might have been in woman suffrage and all the other subjects concerning the 'cause,' you felt that in comparison with this grand woman you hardly knew the alphabet. She judged everything from the standpoint 'How is this going to affect women?'"

She demonstrated by her life that women could aspire to something higher than being pleasant in the drawing room. Her students were among the best educated women of the day and several of them followed her into teaching and science. Letters and reminiscences attest to the high regard her students felt for her. Perhaps her greatest accolade, as reported by one student, was being the only member of the faculty who was never given a nickname.

My purpose in presenting this book is to offer as much of the archival material as feasible, in order to bring the real Maria back to public notice—so that a new generation can meet her. In order to present as accurate a picture as possible, I have centered this work on her own diaries; in fact, significant portions of all of her existing diaries are included here. The diaries and letters are presented with only minor editing, so that the reader may get as close as possible to the immediacy of the writer. Additionally, many of the letters that she wrote and received, illuminating various stages in her life, are also given. In a few instances I have included statements by persons who knew Maria intimately or were her students. In general, I have avoided the numerous newspaper articles and reminiscences about her life which appeared often during her lifetime and after.

Maria Mitchell was a towering figure in the growing feminist tradition of the nineteenth century. She was unique in being able to combine the roles of scientist, educator, and feminist in the forum she was afforded in her day—and her words merit our attention in the twenty-first century.

Henry Albers
FAIRHOPE, ALABAMA
April 2001

Maria Mitchell

NANTUCKET BIRTHPLACE OF MARIA MITCHELL. Born in a small room on the first floor, Maria was the third of William and Lydia Mitchell's ten children. *Inset:* On the front steps of the Mitchell's home are two young girls (Catherine and Christina Albers, *c. 1964*) holding flowers and wearing long dresses typical of the style worn by Quaker children in the 1800s.

CHAPTER 1

EARLY YEARS ON NANTUCKET

This time was noted by me. I was 12 1/2 years old.
– M.M.

HE ISLAND OF NANTUCKET lies about thirty miles south of Hyannis, Massachusetts, separated from Cape Cod by the waters of Nantucket Sound. It is a remnant of a large sandbar left behind when the continental glaciers retreated at the end of the last ice age. Because the land was not well-suited for agriculture, the early settlers naturally turned to the sea for their living. Eventually a large whaling industry grew up on the island. At one time Nantucket was the largest whaling port in the United States and its ships traveled throughout the world. The whaling industry played an indirect but important role in the life of Maria *(Mah-RYE-ah)* Mitchell.

When Mitchell was born on August 1, 1818 — the third of the ten children[1] of William and Lydia Mitchell — Nantucket was in the midst of a boom in the whaling industry. Following the great hardships brought on by the War of 1812, with its embargo on commerce and loss of ships to privateers, the peace witnessed a resurgence in whaling, and by the 1820s there were over eighty ships sailing from the island in search of whales. This growing industry brought renewed prosperity to the island and created fortunes for many of the ship owners. The boom times reached their peak in the 1840s, after which the industry slowly declined as the whaling ships began to use more accessible ports or were lured to the gold fields of California. By 1870 the whaling industry had died on Nantucket.[2]

It was during the War of 1812 that William Mitchell had married Lydia Coleman. Like most Nantucket residents, they were financially dependent on the whaling industry. In a short autobiographical sketch written for his children in 1868, Maria's father recorded that he had "earned his bread [as] a cooper and soap broiler, an oil and candle manufacturer, a farmer, a schoolmaster, an insurance broker, a surveyor, a chronograph rater, an astronomical observer for the Coast Survey…and cashier of [the Pacific] bank." He also acknowledged to his children that "pecuniarily my whole life has been a struggle, subjecting thy patient mother to much endurance."[3]

William Mitchell was a lover of astronomy. Although he had no formal training, he became a highly skilled astronomical observer. In this role he was able to earn fees by rating the chronometers of the whaling ships and by determining latitudes and longitudes for the U. S. Coast Survey. Through this work, Mitchell became well known to a large number of scientific men throughout the country and carried on a considerable correspondence with them. He was able to borrow telescopes for his work in astronomy, and his notebooks are filled with observations of eclipses, the positions of planets, and meteorological data.

In 1837, William Mitchell was appointed cashier of Nantucket's Pacific Bank. This position provided his family with a steady income for the next twenty-four years, and spared them from some of the vagaries of the whaling industry and the irregular income from his astronomical work. The family moved from their home on Vestal Street, where Maria had been born, into the top story of the bank building. William Mitchell's annual salary at the bank was $1,200 a year and his astronomical work for the Coast Survey brought in about $100 annually.[4] Although the bank position provided the main income of the family, he did not give up his astronomical interests. His daughter Phebe recalled that "a little observatory…was placed on the roof of the bank building, and two small buildings were erected in the yard for the transits."[5]

Maria Mitchell came to share her father's love of science and for many years was his colleague in astronomical work. From her father she learned how to make the astronomical observations that could be used to determine time and position. She became so proficient in this kind of work that she could rate a ship's chronometers as well as her father. Later she taught some of the young men of the town how to make these observations that were so essential to the art of navigation and a necessary skill for any sailor who aspired to be a deck officer. At one time she was even asked to set up a school to teach navigation, but declined.[6]

Julia Ward Howe, interviewing Mitchell for her book, *Our Famous Women,* asked how she had been attracted to astronomy. Mitchell replied:

> It was, in the first place, a love of mathematics, seconded by my sympathy with my father's love for astronomical observation. But the spirit of the place had also much to do with the early bent of my mind in this direction. In Nantucket people quite generally are in the habit of observing the heavens, and a sextant will be found in almost every house. The landscape is flat and somewhat monotonous, and the field of the heavens has greater attractions there than in places which offer more variety of view. In the days in which I lived there the men of the community were mostly engaged in sea-traffic of some sort, and "when my ship comes in" was a literal, not a symbolical expression.[7]

Mitchell's mother also exerted a strong influence on the development of her daughter, especially in filling her with a love of reading. William Mitchell reported of his wife Lydia: "She was an intense reader in her youth. For the use of the books in two circulating libraries she served each as librarian until she had read every volume. The substance of her reading through the day was related to her socials in the evening. ... The care of her family took the place of her books in later years, but after her children reached maturity, her reading was resumed. Dickens was her favourite author ... and nothing written by him escaped her. ... "[8]

In commenting on her younger years, Maria Mitchell recalled:

> We always had books, and were bookish people. There was a public library in Nantucket before I was born. It was not a free library, but we always paid the subscription of one dollar per annum, and always read and studied from it. I remember among its books Hannah More's works and Rollins' *Ancient History.* I remember, too, that

Charles Folger,[9] the present Secretary of the Treasury, and I had both read this latter work through before we were ten years old, though neither of us spoke of it to the other until a later period.[10]

Maria's love of reading continued throughout her life, and her letters written shortly before she died mention several books that she was reading even in her failing health.

Mitchell started her schooling when she was five or six. There are no records of those first days, but her younger sister Phebe wrote, "As a little girl, Maria was not a brilliant scholar; she was shy and slow; but later, under her father's tuition, she developed very rapidly."[11] In assessing the validity of Phebe's statement we should note that she was ten years younger than Maria; Phebe could not have known from personal experience anything about her sister's first years in school.

Many years later, Maria Mitchell recorded her own memories of those first school days in a verse that praises her teachers for instilling in her a love of books. The poem contains no indication that she was a "slow learner" or that she disliked school in any way; rather it conveys a joy in learning and love of schooling from the beginning. Mitchell wrote, "My feet were chilled ... my heart with fear was shaken," but at a smile from her teacher, "my heart had stilled its rapid beating." She continues in her praise of her teacher saying,

What though I say unto myself
The valued stores of glittering pelf
Dame Fortune may deny me
The love of books that maiden taught me
The blessings which through life it brought me
A Rothschild could not buy me.[12]

In his "Biographical Notice," Henry Mitchell also did not put much credence in the idea that his older sister Maria was slow.

The books in which her earliest notes appear[13] *are Bridge's "Conic Sections," Hutton's "Mathematics," and Bowditch's "Navigator." Some of the notices have spoken of her as backward in childhood upon her own authority; but the date of her review of the "Hyperbola" in Hutton is given on the margin and makes her seventeen, which shows that by that time she had caught up to or passed her contemporaries....*

The "Navigator,"[14] or, as the whalers were prone to call it, the "Epitome," was the text-book of all the young men fitting to be whalers; but it was quite out of the question for any of these to comprehend the mathematics that lay hidden behind the practical formulas of navigation. Maria Mitchell, however, was not content with the latter, and undertook to reach the spirit of Bowditch's precepts. This was not an easy task in those days, before Professor Benjamin Peirce had published his "Explanation of the Navigator and Almanac," and she was obliged to consult many different scientific books and the reports of mathematical societies before she could herself construct the astronomical tables.[15]

We can find indications of Mitchell's involvement in astronomy at an early age. In February 1831, an eclipse of the sun was visible along the eastern seaboard. William Mitchell made observations of the time of the eclipse to help determine the longitude of their home on Vestal Street as accurately as possible. His son Henry wrote:

These observations of the eclipse...had for practical object the determination of the longitude of the house in Vestal Street where the chronometers of the whale-ships were carried to be rated and set to Greenwich time. Mr. Mitchell came in time to be the rater of all the chronometers of a fleet of ninety-two whale ships, requiring observations on every fine day of the year. We mention this to indicate how accustomed his daughter must have been to the talk of astronomy, even as the source, in part, of her daily bread.[16]

The several pages of observations made during this eclipse are still preserved in William Mitchell's log at the Maria Mitchell Library. At a later date Maria Mitchell herself wrote in the log: "This time was noted by me; I was 12 1/2 years old. M. M."[17]

This record is the earliest we have of the astronomical activity of the young Maria Mitchell. It shows that she became her father's assistant in his astronomical work at a young age.[18] She had started as his pupil in the local school, then became his assistant and coworker in astronomical work. Eventually, as Maria's fame increased, their roles were reversed, but their close association continued until the death of her father in 1869.

Courtesy of Helen Wright / CAP Archives

WOODEN LADDER LEADING TO THE ROOFTOP "WALK" AT THE MITCHELL HOME. Maria and her father William spent many evening hours "sweeping the heavens" from the outdoor walk atop their Nantucket home. *Below:* An initialed 1831 entry in her father's log is the earliest account we have of Maria Mitchell's astronomical activity.

This time was noted by me; I was 12½ years old. M. M.

One other early record about Maria Mitchell appeared in the Nantucket newspaper on August 15, 1835:

SCHOOL

MARIA MITCHELL proposes to open a school
for Girls, on the 1st of next month, at the Franklin school house.
Instruction will be given in Reading, Writing, Spelling,
Geography, Grammar, History, Natural Philosophy,
Arithmetic, Geometry and Algebra.
Terms, $3 per quarter. None admitted under six years of age.[19]

One clear inference we can make from this short advertisement is that, even at the age of seventeen, Mitchell was sufficiently well known on Nantucket to draw students to her enterprise. A year later she gave up her school when she was hired as the librarian for the newly opened Nantucket Atheneum. Her salary was sixty dollars per year. She would not teach again until 1865, when she was appointed professor of astronomy at Vassar College. From her first little school until shortly before her death in 1889, more than fifty years later she was always employed in some capacity and was entirely self-supporting.

Over the years, many stories have grown up about Maria Mitchell; that she was a slow learner has already been mentioned. One of the most prominent stories is associated with the great fire of 1846. In July of that year Nantucket was devastated by a fire that destroyed more than three hundred buildings in the center of town. An often repeated story says that Mitchell saved the Methodist church from destruction during the great fire. At the height of the inferno several buildings were blown up to keep the fire from spreading.

As the story goes, when the church was about to be destroyed, Mitchell, sensing that the wind had changed direction, stood on its steps to prevent its destruction. The only eyewitness account we have of this event—and the role of Maria Mitchell during the fire—is found in a portion of a letter published in the *Nantucket Inquirer and Mirror* in 1874. The letter writer recalls meeting a Commodore Goldsborough who was in command of a U.S. Coast Survey ship anchored in the harbor that eventful night. The commodore informed him:

Maria Mitchell

I am now sixty-three years of age, but I remember that night as if it were yesterday. I was then Lieutenant. We went to the Atheneum; the flames were within a short distance of it when a man said to me there is a collection of articles in that museum that cannot be found in any other collection in the country. I got my men in line, and we moved the most valuable to what we thought was a place of safety; but we had to move them again, and a third time, and then many of them were lost.

The fire was then making its way toward the Pacific Bank, and as Mr. William Mitchell's family was among the few that we had become acquainted with, I ordered my men to stand by and watch the flames. They came on, and we cleared the vaults, and had the valuables removed to a secure place; then Mr. Mitchell said, if the church goes, we shall all go. Can you blow it up, Lieut. Goldsborough? Yes, said I; bring the powder and set it here; and I got my men in line and made a slow match.

Just then Miss Mitchell, the astronomer, came to the door, and asked what was in that cask? I didn't want to tell her it was powder, just then, so I said, silver; but the fire came raging on, and they all called, blow up the church! but... I thought I could see that the fire was pulling around to the north, and I cried, hold on! there's a chance to save the church! and the church was saved.

– E. V.H.[20]

There are no extant diary records by Maria from these early years on Nantucket, if any ever existed, and the amount of archival material is scant indeed. But the large amount of material which dates from 1847, when she discovered her comet, leads one to believe that other Mitchell documents may have been lost in the great fire. There is a story that Mitchell destroyed some of her diaries after the fire, but that cannot be verified.

We are fortunate that some of Maria's siblings wrote about their early life on Nantucket, filling in some of the gaps in our knowledge of life in the Mitchell household. In 1896, Phebe Mitchell Kendall included many of her own comments about their home life when she published an abridged version of Mitchell's diaries as *Maria Mitchell, Life, Letters and Journals*. Her brother Henry wrote the aforementioned "Biographical Notice" for the American Academy of Arts and Sciences; the Notice was published in 1890 and gives a good picture of Maria's early education in science and mathematics. However, it should be noted that these authors were in their sixties when they were writing about those early years; their memories may not always have been accurate.

Julia Ward Howe, in her article on Maria in *Our Famous Women*, gives the famed astronomer's view of life in the Mitchell household.

> *In this thrifty household Maria's task was what she calls, "an endless washing of dishes," which, weary as it may sometimes have been, she preferred to needlework. The drudgery necessarily entailed by narrow circumstances, was however relieved and rendered endurable by the atmosphere of thought and intelligence which gave its tone to the house.*[21]

Maria's sister Anne Mitchell Macy published a short, colorful article about a Sunday afternoon at the Mitchell home, entitled "An Astronomical Garret." Two years younger than Maria, Anne tells her niece about the house, its contents, and the importance of astronomy in the household.

> *"Aunt Anne," said my little niece Polly*[22] *one day, "was your attic at the old house full of wonderful things when you were a little girl?"*
>
> *"Our attic! Do you mean our garret? There were no attics in the days when I was young! Yes," I continued, "our garret was full of wonderful things. I can truly say no garret was ever like our garret. Except the combined flavor of salt-fish and herbs of various kinds, the air of our garret was unlike that of any which I visited ... Not a chest do I remember in our garret, not an old desk, not an old chair, yet my garret was the loveliest one to play in that ever was heard of."*
>
> *"Because it was empty?" queried little Polly.*
>
> *"It was crowded full! Your grandfather, who was my father as well, was an astronomer. Everything like a telescope, sextant, chronometer, etc., had its proper place in shed or closet of suitable nature, or on the top of the house on an outside walk. Your grandfather when a young man had given courses of lectures on his favorite topics; that was long before my day, before there were orreries,*[23] *or any of the modern facilities by which to illustrate the phenomena of the heavens. Consequently his diagrams were home-made; but as the age progressed*

Maria Mitchell

and science was a little more recognized, the home-made matters were stowed away under the eaves....

"...rolling around the garret were to me enormous balls of hard wood, once used by the lecturer to illustrate axes, poles, etc. of the different worlds; these spheres were in some cases six inches in diameter, in others a foot. One, for instance representing our Earth, was painted white, a wire running through the shortest diameter to represent the axis and extending some three or four inches beyond the poles to make it easy to handle when held up to the audience. Saturn was a yellow ball, very imposing looking because of the flat rings looking like two brims of a hat, got loose from the crown and pushed up midway; a short distance from the ball, however, a little wire kept these rings in their proper places as regard the planets and each other. Jupiter was a green globe with very black belts. All of these planets in their sundry and irregular places rolling over the garret, might seem to make the walking hazardous, but we were always on the lookout as a matter of habit.

"Under the roof one day my brother pulled forth a long strip of painted wood on which in large black letters beautifully printed were the words, 'AN UNDEVOUT ASTRONOMER IS MAD.'[24]

"It was Saturday afternoon, a stormy Saturday afternoon, and he and I unendurable in the living room had been sent to the garret where we had determined upon building a steam-boat. The 'Undevout Astronomer' as a central mast, nailed to a cross beam, just reached the floor. The diagrams, four in number, gathered around the top of the 'Undevout' and secured with a piece of braid torn from the Earth's orbit fell in draperies to the floor serving as the steam-boat awning. A portion of a whale's vertebral column, no unusual appurtenance to a Nantucket garret, formed a seat and helped to stay the flowing cloth, while Jupiter and Saturn and the Earth and the little Asteroids by their respective weights, kept the sides of the awning. It was a comely thing to look upon and we were proud of our work. Night overtook us so we planned to meet therein the next day, Sunday, and have a quiet sitting.

"The quiet took mightily therefore were we allowed with all due reference to the day of the week to repair to the garret with our books. In order to overlook this quiet our mother, in her wisdom, mistaken though it proved to be bade us leave the garret door ajar, she herself

leaving the stairway door of the next lower flight wide open into the living room, where the elder members of the family were gathered in their Sunday garb, and the baby at rest in the cradle. It was not often that this house was so peaceful, but the steam-boat had thus far proved the blessed peacemaker. My brother and myself had not spoken and it is doubtful whether a word of the books held in our left hands according to the school law had received a glance from their respective owners, so well satisfied were we with our surroundings.

"Suddenly a draught moved one of the diagrams; the braid, which, as you remember was taken from the earth's orbit, gave way and set Mars, which had lost the protruding part of its axis down the garret stairway striking Jupiter as it went and Saturn flew after Jupiter. The Asteroids, little pictures with great ears, struck by the scene rushed after the others to find what the hue and cry meant and the Earth brought up the rear. The garret door ajar was forced widely open, and in some strange way Jupiter received a blow which threw him with tremendous velocity down the next flight of stairs. Bump, bump! Whack, whack came Saturn tumbling after, whose rings seemed so many shrieking fiddles, while popping and hopping like tiny marbles flew the little Vesta, Pallas, Juno, and Ceres, distractedly aiming everywhere. All finally met in a group at the feet of our father—and he taking his Sunday nap.

"We have roused the neighbors!" said my brother.

"The sequel I will not tell you, Polly, but among the elder children sitting in the living room that memorable Sunday was your Aunt Maria Mitchell, afterwards Professor of Astronomy at Vassar College. Who knows what work those rolling planets began in their sublime ignorance!"

"Who knows??" said little Polly with a giggle.[25]

Phebe's *Maria Mitchell* includes this description of the early Mitchell household.

There was everything in the home which could amuse and instruct children. The eldest daughter [Sally] was very handy at all sorts of entertaining occupations; she had a delicate sense of the artistic, and was quite skillful with her pencil.... The girls learned to sew and cook, just as they learned to read—as a matter of habit rather than of instruction. They learned how to make their own clothes, by making their dolls'

Maria Mitchell

clothes—and the dolls themselves were frequently home-made, the eldest sister painting the faces much more perfectly than those obtained at the shops;... There were always plenty of books, and besides those in the house there was the Atheneum Library, which, although not a free library, was very inexpensive to the shareholders.[26]

Henry's reminiscence emphasizes Maria's education and scientific achievements.

In 1836...she was appointed Librarian of the Nantucket Atheneum...It was in this library that Miss Mitchell found Laplace and made a special study of Bowditch's Appendix to the third volume of the "Mechanique Celeste," which treats of the orbits of comets; and here, too, she read the "Theoria Motus" of Gauss in its original Latin form.[27] *This was at a progressive period in her father's scientific career, and his daughter contributed to his success by the most devoted assistance.*

She helped in the observations at all hours of the day or night that became necessary, and when her father was absent or lecturing or on business tours she maintained the continuity of series of observations that he had undertaken. These two enthusiasts acquired gradually quite a well-equipped observatory....The aspects of the planets, the solar spots, meteors, and auroral clouds, were observed diligently, but in 1845 when Smyth's "Celestial Cycle" (containing the Bedford Catalogue) appeared, they entered upon systematic studies of nebulae and double stars, using often the two telescopes side by side on the top of the Pacific Bank. Thenceforth they were prospectors beyond the frontiers; and routine work gave place to exciting explorations.[28]

A more personal glimpse of Mitchell is found in this extract from a poem she wrote in 1853, when she was thirty-five. Evidently not sought out by the young men of the island, she was the only one of the Mitchell children who never married.

Did you never go home alone, Sarah,
It's nothing so very sad,
I've done it a hundred times Sarah
When there wasn't a man to be had
And I've done it a hundred times more
When I've seen them stand hat in hand
I've walked alone to the door,
And they've continued to stand.[29]

Throughout her life, Maria showed an undiminished love and deep understanding of children. We find in her diaries that her nieces and nephews visited her often and, as they grew up, they would stay with her for extended periods. Phebe writes:

> Maria was always ready to "bear the brunt," and could at any time be coaxed by the younger children to do the things which they found difficult or disagreeable. The two youngest children[30] in the family were delicate, and the special care of the youngest sister [Kate] devolved upon Maria, who knew how to be a good nurse as well as a good playfellow. She was especially careful of the timid child; she herself was timid, and, throughout her life, could never witness a thunderstorm with any calmness.[31]

The following note was written many years later by one of the young people of the island, Lilla Barnard. She recalls Mitchell's kindness in showing her Venus during the daytime* using the telescope.

> ...I remembered one day in summer...Up the straight street, devoid of all shade trees, came Miss Mitchell, not as yet with the position and title of professor....As our astronomer, even then known to the whole world, turned from the street into the "cart road" that led to the enclosure, she saw the child. The ever ready smile flashed into her face, and without delaying her steps, she said "Good afternoon, Lilla; come with me and I will show you Venus while the sun shines." Her quick spoken words fell on glad ears, and the child sprang after her, believing because Miss Mitchell said so, but in utter bewilderment as she looked into the sunny sky.[32]

During much of her life, Maria Mitchell struggled with matters of faith and religion. When she was only twenty-five, she was disowned by the Friends Meeting. It is quite possible that Maria initiated this action herself as a protest against the Society that had disowned her oldest brother Andrew only a month earlier for his marriage to Ann Elizabeth Swain. The two actions are recorded on the same page in the minutes of the Women's Society. At the women's meeting of August 31, 1843, it was noted, "This meeting unites with the men's in the disowning of

---

*Finding Venus in the daytime is not as difficult as it sounds, especially using a telescope with setting circles. Without a telescope, it certainly is more difficult, but both professionals and amateurs are often able to do so.

Andrew C. Mitchell for marrying contrary to the order of our society." Less than a month later, on September 28, the minutes report: "Maria Mitchell informed us that her mind was not settled on religious subjects and that she had no wish to retain her right of membership...it is concluded to disown her from membership having the concurrence of men Friends."[33]

We should not draw the conclusion from this "disowning" that Mitchell was without religious beliefs. She unambiguously described astronomy as the "study of the works of God," and her diaries are filled with references to church services that she attended and sermons that she heard. As James Monroe Taylor, then president of Vassar College, said at her funeral in speaking of her character:

> ...*This genuineness explains also a marked feature of her religious experience. She would not use the language of faith often because it did not seem to her that she had clearly grasped the truths which came through faith. It would be a grave error to infer from this that she was not a religious woman in a true sense. She was always a seeker for truth...earnestly, honestly, she sought to fathom the mysteries of being and of destiny that press in on all, but she would not allow herself to say one word beyond what she felt she really knew.*[34]

In considering her formative years, Maria Mitchell later offered a grateful assessment of her childhood years as part of a large Quaker family growing up on Nantucket in the early part of the nineteenth century.

> Our want of opportunity was our opportunity—our privations were our privileges, our needs were our stimulants—we are what we are partly because we had little and wanted much, and it is hard to tell which was the more powerful factor.[35]

CHAPTER 2

MARIA'S COMET

*This evening at half past ten Maria discovered
a telescopic comet five degrees above Polaris.
(William Mitchell, 10 mo 1, 1847)*

ℐN 1836, THE EIGHTEEN-YEAR-OLD Maria Mitchell became
the first librarian at the Nantucket Atheneum, a position she
would hold for twenty years. As her brother Henry pointed out, she in
essence acquired a college education through the books at the
Atheneum, where she taught herself mathematics, including calculus,
and the most advanced astronomy of her day. In the evening and often
well into the night, she devoted her time to her other great interest,
searching for comets. Almost every clear night she could be found in her
small observatory on the roof "sweeping" back and forth with a small
telescope, hunting for these elusive bodies.

A comet usually appears as a fuzzy object when seen through a small
telescope. But there are many other fuzzy objects which appear in the sky
that can be easily confused with a comet.

Imagine the challenge facing young Maria Mitchell. In order to make
certain that she had actually discovered a comet, Maria had to show that
the nebulous object she spotted had changed position from night to
night against the fixed background of stars. In her day this kind of a
search demanded an intimate knowledge of the sky because available star

maps were generally very poor. Even if she did find a comet, she might not necessarily be the original discoverer because astronomers all over the world were engaged in the same nighttime pursuit. It might be weeks later that a letter or newspaper arrived with the news that someone had preceded her in the discovery.

Maria Mitchell's long hours of searching were finally rewarded on October 1, 1847, when she noticed a nebulous object, a comet, near the North Pole of the sky. Phebe reports the events of that evening as follows:

> *Miss Mitchell spent every clear evening on the house-top "sweeping" the heavens. No matter how many guests there might be in the parlor, Miss Mitchell would slip out, don her regimentals as she called them, and, lantern in hand mount to the roof. On the evening of October 1, 1847, there was a party of invited guests at the Mitchell home. As usual, Maria slipped out, ran up to the telescope, and soon returned to the parlor and told her father that she thought she saw a comet. Mr. Mitchell hurried upstairs, stationed himself at the telescope, and as soon as he looked at the object pointed out by his daughter declared it to be a comet. Miss Mitchell, with her usual caution, advised him to say nothing about it until they had observed it long enough to be tolerably sure.[1]*

Finding this comet was undoubtedly a watershed event for Maria Mitchell, changing the course of her life dramatically. Without this discovery and the subsequent award of a gold medal, she might easily have remained simply an avid amateur astronomer and librarian on an isolated island. But now the worldwide astronomical community opened to her. Her name became so well known that when she went to Europe ten years later her fame had preceded her and she was invited to the homes of many famous scientists. In the United States she was honored with the gift of a good telescope from the Women of America and also a prize of one hundred dollars from the Smithsonian Institution of Washington, D.C.

Her discovery was duly recorded by her father in his diary. As William Mitchell indicates, the comet eventually became bright enough to be seen without a telescope.

> *10 mo 1, 1847. This evening at half past ten Maria discovered a telescopic comet five degrees above Polaris. Persuaded that no nebulae*

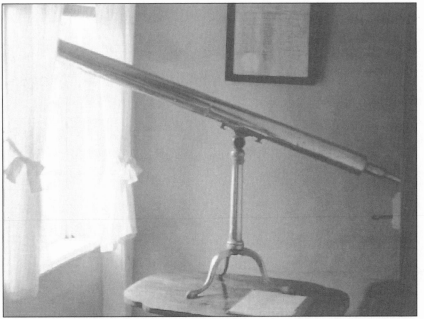

Photo by Henry Albers; Medal/diary: Nantucket Maria Mitchell Association

HISTORIC MEMORABILIA NOW PRESERVED AT MARIA MITCHELL'S
BIRTHPLACE ON NANTUCKET ISLAND. In the upstairs landing of her
home, Maria had a special nook which served as her study. It is shown
here with the "Dolland," the telescope she had been using when she discovered the comet. *Below:* Maria Mitchell's father
kept a diary and recorded her celestial spotting
on October 1, 1847. *Left:* The gold medal
awarded by the King of Denmark to Maria
Mitchell for her discovery, indicating the date
under the words *Cometa Visus*, circumscribed
by the words in Latin, "Not in vain do we
watch the setting and rising of the stars."

Maria Mitchell

could occupy that position unnoticed it scarcely needed the evidence of motion to give it the character of a comet.

10 mo 2. The object has moved toward the West and toward the pole. Diminishing its R.A.and increasing its Dec.* It seems much brighter than last night. It has no train, nor is there any increase of light towards its centre. ...

10 mo 16. Up to this time I have been absent; in the time it proves that Maria was the first discoverer in America so far as we have been able to ascertain. Its motion has been very rapid. Its approximate position this evening, 10 mo 16, at 7:05 mean solar time at Nantucket is R.A. 16h 17m 32 sec, Dec. -2° 35'.

On the evening of the sixth and 7th inst[ance] I saw it with my naked eye while at Sandwich. Again on the 15th while at Providence, it is this evening distinctly seen (in spite of a bright moon), in the position above stated, in the constellation of Serpentarius.[2]

William Mitchell wasted no time in notifying his friend William C. Bond, director of the Harvard College Observatory, about his daughter's fortuitous find. His letter to Bond was with the first mail that left the island after Maria's discovery. This letter, posted October 3, eventually established her priority in finding the comet and was instrumental in obtaining the gold medal. Other astronomers in Europe independently discovered the comet on October 3, October 7, and October 11.

I write now merely to say that Maria discovered a telescopic comet at half-past ten on the evening of the first instant, at that hour nearly vertical above Polaris five degrees. Last evening it had advanced westwardly; this evening still further, and nearing the pole. It does not bear illumination, but Maria has obtained its right ascension and declination, and will not suffer me to announce it. Pray tell me whether it is one of George's; if not, whether it was been seen by anybody. Maria supposes it may be an old story. If quite convenient, just drop a line to her; it will oblige me much. I expect to leave home in a day or two, and shall be in Boston next week, and I would like to have her hear from you before I can meet you. I hope it will not give thee much trouble amidst thy close engagements.[3]

---

*Positions on the celestial sphere are designated in the same way as longitude and latitude on the earth. Declination (Dec.), comparable to latitude, is measured north and south of the celestial equator, while Right Ascension (R.A.) corresponds to longitude and is measured eastward along the celestial equator.

A friendly note in response to her discovery came from William Bond's son George.[4] One of the few letters in the archives with "Dear Maria" as the salutation, this letter is of particular interest because there is a long-standing, but unsubstantiated, story that George and Maria were in love; he eventually married someone else.

> *Dear Maria:*
>
> *There! I think that is a very amiable beginning, considering the way in which I have been treated by you! If you are going to find any more comets, can you not wait till they are announced by the proper authorities? At least, don't kidnap another such as this last was. If my object were to make you fear and tremble, I should tell you that on the evening of the 30th I was sweeping within a few degrees of your prize. I merely throw out the hint for what it is worth. It has been very interesting to watch the motion of this comet among the stars with the great refractor; we could almost see it move....*
>
> *G. P. Bond.*[5]

William Bond reported on the comet in his diary:

> *Oct. 7, 1847. Rec'd a letter from Wm. Mitchell announcing that his daughter Maria had discovered a comet on the 1st inst.*
>
> *Oct. 8. Last evening we obtained positions of the Nantucket Comet. It is quite bright with considerable condensation of light—fills the field of the telescope with a power of 180, is distinctly seen as nebulous cluster of stars by the naked eye—moving rapidly—at rate of 6 degrees daily towards the sun.*
>
> *Oct. 9. The people examined The Nantucket Comet, Maria Mitchell's, with great interest and we compared it with the great nebula in Andromeda.*[6]

Congratulations on her discovery arrived from a variety of scientists including A. D. Bache, who was a good friend of the Mitchells and superintendent of the U.S. Coast Survey.

> *We congratulate the indefatigable comet seeker most heartily on her success; is she not the first lady who has ever discovered a comet?*[7] *The Coast Service is proud of her connection with it! Now if she determines the orbit also it will be another jewel for the civic crown. As far as to feathers and caps you eschew all others.*[8]

In 1831, Frederic VI, King of Denmark, had established a prize of a gold medal to be given to anyone who discovered a comet using a telescope. The story of the gold medal and subsequent events might be considered an early example of what in today's parlance would be called "networking." As Phebe wrote:

> Few women with scientific tastes had the advantages which surrounded Miss Mitchell in her own home. Her father was acquainted with the most prominent scientific men in the country, and in his hospitable home at Nantucket she met many persons of distinction in literature and science.[9]

When Maria's father was appointed an overseer of Harvard College and chair of the Observatory Visiting Committee, the Mitchells gained access to the academic community, especially to Harvard's president, Edward Everett. Maria Mitchell and her father were good friends of the Bonds and were welcome guests in their home in Cambridge. This network of friends stood her in good stead when Edward Everett[10] championed her right to the Danish medal for her discovery of a telescopic comet in 1847.

The rules stipulated that the discoverer notify the observatory at Altona, Denmark, or the Astronomer Royal of England by the "next post" in order to be eligible for the prize.[11] Maria Mitchell was clearly recognized as the original discoverer of the comet on October 1. It would seem that she met the necessary requirements and should easily have been eligible for the gold medal.

But she was initially denied the prize on the grounds that she and her father had not notified the authorities in Altona immediately. Other astronomers, notably George Bond, had also been denied the king's prize on other occasions for failure to follow this rule, which was probably not widely known in America. Edward Everett, with the considerable weight of his office as president of Harvard College, took up Mitchell's cause. He made the case that William Mitchell's letter to the Bonds at Harvard satisfied the rule of immediately notifying the proper authorities of the discovery. Eventually he was successful in his role as Maria's advocate. In early 1848 Everett wrote William Mitchell:

I take the liberty to inquire of you whether any steps have been taken by you, on behalf of your daughter, by way of claiming the medal of the king of Denmark for the discovery of a telescope comet. The regulations require this information of the discovery should be transmitted by the next mail to Mr. Airy, the Astronomer Royal, if the discovery is made elsewhere than on the continent of Europe. If made in the United States, I understand from Mr. Schumacher[12] that information may be sent to the Danish minister at Washington, who will forward it to Mr. Airy—but it must be sent by next mail. In consequence of non-compliance with these regulations, Mr. George Bond has on one occasion lost the medal. I trust this may not be the case with Miss Mitchell.[13]

Mitchell's father replied:

Thy kind letter of the 10th instant reached me duly. No steps were taken by my daughter in claim of the medal of the Danish king.

On the night of the discovery, I was fully satisfied that it was a comet from its location, though its real motion at this time was so nearly opposite to that of the earth (the two bodies approaching each other) that its apparent motion was scarcely appreciable. I urged very strongly that it would be published immediately, but she resisted it as strongly, though she could but acknowledge her conviction that it was a comet. She remarked to me, "If it is a new comet, our friends, the Bonds, have seen it. It may be an old one, so far as relates to the discovery, and one which we have not followed." She consented, however, that I should write to William C. Bond, which I did by the first mail that left the island after the discovery. This letter did not reach my friend till the 6th or 7th, having been somewhat delayed here and also in the post office in Cambridge.

Referring to my journal I find these words: "Maria will not consent to have me announce it as an original discovery."

The stipulations of His Majesty have, therefore, not been complied with, and the peculiar circumstances of the case, her sex, and isolated position, may not be sufficient to justify a suspension of the rules. Nevertheless, it would gratify me that the generous monarch should know that there is a love of science even in this to him remote corner of the earth.[14]

Maria Mitchell

However resigned William Mitchell claimed to be about the gold medal, Everett was not willing to drop the matter so quickly. In a letter to Denmark's Professor Schumacher he noted:

> *The regulations relative to the king of Denmark's medal have not hitherto been understood in this country. I shall take care to give publicity to them. Not only has Mr. Bond lost the medal to which you think he would have been entitled, but I fear the same has happened to Miss Mitchell of Nantucket, who discovered the comet of last October on the first day of that month. I think it was not seen in Europe till the third.*
>
> *Cambridge, 24th January, 1848.*
>
> *Post Script: The foregoing was written to go by steamer of the 15th, but was a few hours too late. I have since received some information in reference to the comet of October which leads me to hope that you may feel it in your power to award the medal to Miss Maria Mitchell. Miss Mitchell saw the comet at half-past ten o'clock on the evening of October 1st. Her father, a skillful astronomer, made an entry in his journal to that effect. On the third day of October he wrote a letter to Mr. Bond, the director of our observatory, announcing the discovery. This letter was dispatched the following day, being the first post-day after the discovery of the comet. This letter I transmit to you, together with letters from Mr. Mitchell and Mr. Bond to myself. Nantucket, as you are probably aware, is a small secluded island, lying off the extreme point of the coast of Massachusetts. Mr. Mitchell is a member of the executive council of Massachusetts and a most respectable person.*
>
> *As the claimant is a young lady of great diffidence, the place a retired island, remote from all the high-roads of communication; as the conditions have not been well understood in this country; and especially as there was a substantial compliance with them—I hope His Majesty may think Miss Maria Mitchell entitled to the medal.[15]*

It was nearly ten months before Everett was able to convey some good news to the Mitchells. On November 10 he wrote to Maria's father:

> *I have this day received a letter from Mr. Fleniden our chargé d'affaires at Copenhagen giving me the agreeable intelligence that he has received official information from Count M. the Secretary for Foreign Affairs that the King had awarded the Comet medal to your daughter for her discovery of the 1st of Oct. 1847.[16]*

In March 1849, the Harvard president wrote to Mitchell that the gold medal was in his hands. Maria Mitchell was the only American ever awarded this unique honor.

> *I have the pleasure to inform you that your medal arrived by the last steamer; it reached me by mail, yesterday afternoon.*
>
> *I went to Boston this morning, hoping to find you at the Adams House, to put it into your own hand. As your return to Nantucket prevented this, I, of course, retain it, subject to your orders, not liking to take the risk again of its transmission by mail.*
>
> *Having it in this way in my hand, I have taken the liberty to show it to some friends, such as W. C. Bond, Professor Peirce, the editors of the "Transcript," and the members of my family—which I hope you will pardon.*[17]

The prized gold medal is now in the possession of the Nantucket Maria Mitchell Association, which displays it for special events.

Following the discovery of the comet and the awarding of the gold medal, Maria Mitchell received many other honors and her name became well known nationally and internationally. Her membership in the American Academy of Arts and Sciences in 1848 was the first of the many honors bestowed upon her. Her membership certificate still hangs in the family home, although on the certificate the word "FELLOW" was crossed out and "an Honorary Member" inserted by Dr. Asa Gray.[18] This should not be construed as an anti-feminist action on Gray's part, as some have supposed. The "Honorary Member" status was awarded by the Academy, as the minutes of the May 30, 1848 meeting attest: "Miss Maria Mitchell of Nantucket, the discoverer of the comet which bears her name, was chosen an Honorary Member of the Academy."[19] This honor is formally acknowledged by her father's June 30 letter to Asa Gray:

> *I have been requested by my daughter Maria to acknowledge the receipt of thy official communication of the 29th ult.★ and that of the 5th inst. informing her that the American Academy of Arts and Sciences had elected her an honorary member of that body; and also to convey her acknowledgments for the honour thus conferred upon her, and to signify her acceptance thereof.*[20]

★ult. – ultimo: in the previous month; inst. – instant: in the current month

When the Nautical Almanac was established in 1849, Maria Mitchell was hired as one of the astronomers who computed its tables. The ships that sailed the earth from Nantucket and other ports used these tables for navigation purposes.

> *My dear Miss Mitchell,*
>
> *I am authorized by the Hon. Sec'y of the Navy to invite your business as a computer for the American Nautical Almanac directed to be prepared by the Act of Congress approved March 9, 1849. Your compensation is fixed at $300 (three hundred) for a volume, and will commence from the date of your acceptance of this appointment.*
>
> *Charles Henry Davis[21]*

Mitchell was given the responsibility of computing the tables for the planet Venus. Each position for the Almanac involved a long, careful, calculation done to a high degree of accuracy in order to determine the right ascension and declination of the planet throughout the year. She continued doing these calculations for almost 20 years. Her compensation for this work, combined with her Atheneum salary, made her financially independent.

In the summer of 1849, Maria was invited by A. D. Bache to do further work for the Coast Survey and to learn how to use its new instruments.

> *I will be glad to have Miss Maria Mitchell as an Assistant at my next station near Portland when I expect to use the zenith sector and zenith telescope. It shall be no expense to her and I will instruct and give her practice in the use of these instruments if she is willing to come. My wife is with me and we will consider Miss M. as part of my family for the nonce. Mrs. B. uniting with me in the invitation which I make officially. I will also make such compensation as we make to learners. Let me have an answer at once, I oblige.[22]*

Her father wrote to Bache after her return on the success of this excursion:

> *Henry and Maria are in fine spirits, and as to the latter, I am quite jealous of her. She has not only had a "nice time," but a delightful one. There is nothing like camp life. All this we could put up with, but there is nothing upon earth comparable to Mr. and Mrs. Bache. I*

suppose we shall have to endure it and let it go. Seriously—for your kindness to her we are much obliged....[23]

Later Maria Mitchell wrote about her experiences during that summer and again praised Bache for his helpfulness.

The training of the survey is rigidly exact, and those, who, like the above mentioned employees, come under Mr. Bache's immediate instruction, bear grateful testimony to the patience with which he listens to their difficulties, and to the willing ability with which he throws light upon the dark places.[24]

In addition to working at the Atheneum and performing calculations to be done for the Almanac, Mitchell still made time to search for comets from the observatory on Nantucket.[25] Although she was never again a first discoverer, she did find several comets before official announcements appeared. On May 19, 1849, her father noted in his diary:

Maria this evening at about 10h 30 min. called my attention to a nebulous body[26] *suspected it to be a comet, in the constellation of the Great Bear two thirds from R to Y [designations of stars] and without or left of a line connecting them. She saw it last evening the 18th but imagined it to be one of the nebulae denoted by Smyth.... The above comet proved to be one sometime since discovered in Europe by Goujon.*[27]

Mitchell herself recorded some of the difficulties she experienced while searching for comets. While this excerpt from Maria's writings sounds somewhat humorous, most astronomers would agree that using a telescope in cold weather is not always pleasant.

Accidents of Observing, Apr 10. The comet[28] looked in upon us on the 29th of March. It made a twilight call looking sunny and bright as if it had just warmed itself in the equinoctial rays. A boy in the street called my attention to it, but I found on hurrying home that Father had already seen it and had ranged it between buildings, so as to get a rough place.

It was freezing cold but we went to work in good earnest that night and the next night we could see it which was not till April. I was dreadfully busy and a host of little annoyances crowded upon me. I had a good star near it in the field of my comet seeker but what star? On that rested everything and I could not be sure even from the

Maria Mitchell

catalogue, for the comet and the star were so in the twilight that I could get no good neighboring stars. We called it theta Arietis or 707. Then came a waxing moon and we waxed weary in trying to have the fainter and fainter comet in the mists of twilight and the glare of moonlight.

Next I broke a screw of my instrument and found no screw could be bought in town of that description. I started off to find a man who could make [one] and engaged him to do so the next day tho' the next day was Fast and all the world was fasting at least from labor. But the screw was made and it fitted nicely.

The clouds cleared and we were likely to have a good night. I put up my instrument but scarcely had the screw driver touched the new screw than out it flew from its socket, rolled along the floor of the "walk," dropped quietly through a crack on to the gutter of the house roof. I heard it click and felt very much like using words unbecoming to a woman's mouth.

I put my eye closer to the crack but could not see it. There was but one thing to be done, the floor boards must come up. I got a hatchet but could do nothing. I called father, he brought a crow bar and pried up the board, then crawled under and found the screw. I took care not to lose it a second time. The instrument was fairly mounted when the clouds moved in to keep it company and the comet and I again parted.

In all observations the blowing out of a light by a gust of wind is a very common and very annoying accident but I've met with a much worse one for I dropped a chronometer. Out it rolled, out of its box and on to the ground. We picked it up in great panic but it had not even altered its rate, as we found by later observations. The glaring eyes of a cat who nightly visited me were at one time very annoying and a man who climbed a tree and spoke to me in the quietness of the small hours fairly shook not only my equanimity but the pencil which I held in my hands. He was quite innocent of any attempt to do me harm but he gave me a dreadful fright. For spiders and bugs which summer in my observatory house I have rather an attachment but they must not crawl over my recording paper. Rats are my abhorrence and I learned with pleasure that some poison had been placed under the transit house.

One gets attached (if the term may be used) to certain midnight apparitions. The aurora is always a pleasant companion, a meteor seems to come like a messenger from departed spirits and even the blossoming of the trees in the moonlight becomes a sight looked for with pleasure. And from astronomy there is the same enjoyment as a night upon the housetops with the stars as in the midst of other grand scenery. There is the same subdued quiet and grateful sensuousness— a calm to the troubled spirit and a hope to the desponding.

When a man bores me I think what a pity he couldn't be employed in constructing artesian wells, and what a fortune it is that he is in my room instead of being beneath a ship, he would certainly sink it in "no time." Counting it at half an hour a day lost to bores I have lost in 17 years, 258 days, calling the 12 hours wasted a day.

Even astronomers who are as well cared for as those of Cambridge, have their annoyances and even men as skilled as they are make blunders. I have known one of the many Bonds with great effort turn that huge telescope down to the horizon to make an observation upon a blazing comet seen there and when he had found it in his glass, find also that it was not comet but the nebulae of Andromeda, a cluster of stars on which he had spent much time and which he had made a special object of study.[29]

In a June 1851 letter to her married older sister, Maria relates to Sally M. Barney the activities of the Mitchell family. The letter shows that even though Mitchell seldom mentions family members in her diary, she clearly kept up with what they were doing.

My dear Sister,

I have this moment rec'd thy letter. Henry's address is "Gifford Village, Belknap Co., N. H." Be sure and put on the word "village." The family is as usual. The help is the colored woman—so far very good—two dollars worth, very willing quite unlike Celia. Aunt Love is again with us and "goes it."

Mother thought some of going to Q. M. [Quaker meeting] but has given it up thinking she can't spare time. (I will take the family in order.) Father has gone to meeting—nothing new about him. The only new facts about me, are that I went to the knockings last night and being very careful not to speak for fear I should offend, did a worse thing, by moving the table with the end of one finger just as the woman, only not so much, upon which the spirits spelt out that they "didn't like the company!" Fact the second—that Mrs. Dassel[30] has painted me kneeling at my telescope. It looks like Adeline Coffin and is of course not handsome. If thee was here thee would have Mitchell's painted at once. She has a head of a child of N. P. Willis that is very lovely. She has taken a room at the Atheneum and put up about a dozen pictures—very beautiful—Isabel is lovely. She has not tried to make a portrait, but a pretty picture and it is in undress. She is now engaged on Abra'm Quary—he is much flattered by it and it will be a fine portrait. I think we shall buy it or a copy for the Atheneum. Mitchell [Sally's son] could be painted for $25 anywhere from that to a hundred. She will paint Father also for herself—having made a pencil sketch—The least sketch that she makes is recognized. We like her very much and she comes in like Korcelski every day.

Where was I in the family—Oh, Anne comes next—She alternates with chills and fever as usual—gave up school yesterday and will go to Mary Ann Potter's in a week or two.

Frank went to ride yesterday morning with Emily Shaw and to the knockings last evening. Of course he was mad with me because I didn't see anything wonderful but admits 'twas a bad time. He will go up harbour on the 6th with a party which is all I know of his plans—oh no—I heard him say today that he and Whitney would marry and go to the Sandwich Isls. next Spring. Forster writes that the District have given up the school and he will take it on his own hook. Phebe rocks today and reads a new novel. She paints in Mrs. Dassel's room.

Kate was eighteen yesterday. Her presents were a pen from Frank; neck ribbon from Anne, garters from Phebe and "Bertines Method on the Piano" from me. She will commence taking music lessons of Mrs. Richter this week and will take them all summer. I "cast about" in my mind to find some employment for her and this was all I could think of, which pleases her very much. As she is of age, the elders could say nothing. She can practice daily at Phebe's piano—at which Anne and Charlotte both work now.

Andrew—he should have come first—is daily expected in Potter's vessel. Eliz'th is getting ready to move. The children all go to Cousin Lydia Barker's. I don't know whether the old lady and Robert will go to New York now or not.

Henry writes in fine spirits—has a shanty 2500 feet above the sea—an assistant a country fellow. The shanty has bunks and they sleep on boards. I think it is just the life for him—he has a home at the foot of the mountain when he desires civilization. Bouliter had just come from the South and told him he met in Charleston a Polish count who knew our family. Henry writes that Lissie Bond is very sick and that probably she will not recover. We make all allowance for Henry's dismals, but have written to ask. We saw in the paper the death of Maria Bache—eight days from Rio Janeiro, on board a steamer.

I have written very fast, a habit which I have acquired from the trembling of my hands—If I write slowly the letters show that the hand is not steady—I hope it will be legible. One item more, Aunt Maria goes to Q. M. I shall send this unpaid for the good reason that I have no money—You may take it out in ice cream when you come to Nantucket again.

Love to Matthew—I do so wish Mitchell was here to be painted.

Maria [31]

I saw the stars
in the evening of the 10th
and met them like old friends
from whom I had been long parted.

MARIA MITCHELL
Diary Entry, Feb. 12, 1855

Photo of the Orion Nebula: courtesy of Mark McCaughrean/ESO; Inset: courtesy of the Nantucket Maria Mitchell Association

MARIA MITCHELL, AVID ASTRONOMER. Maria's diaries clearly reveal her profound appreciation of her skyward explorations. On one occasion, she wrote appreciatively of the different colors of the stars, describing one pair "just east of the belt of Orion ... of different shades of red." Earlier, she had written poetically: "[F]rom astronomy there is the same enjoyment as a night upon the housetops with the stars as in the midst of other grand scenery. There is the same subdued quiet and grateful sensuousness—a calm to the troubled spirit and a hope to the desponding."

CHAPTER 3

NANTUCKET DIARIES

I am just learning to notice the
different colors of the stars.

$\mathcal{A}$S THE EXCITEMENT generated by her comet discovery began to wear off, Maria Mitchell's life settled into a new routine. Her mornings were spent doing calculations for the Nautical Almanac; in the afternoons, she worked at the Atheneum; and on clear nights she continued to search the sky for comets from her small rooftop observatory. Her sister wrote that "she cared but little for general society, and had always to be coaxed to go into company."[1] Nevertheless, she was certainly not a recluse and participated regularly in many activities on the island.

It was at this stage of her life that Maria Mitchell began to keep a diary. From the 1850s until shortly before her death in 1889, Maria regularly kept an account of her activities and her reactions to the world around her.

Her diaries reveal that Maria had an opinion on almost everything, from Wordsworth's poetry to how to raise children. A voracious reader, Maria often took the time in her diary to critique the latest books she was reading. She also recorded her joys and frustrations with astronomical observing and calculations.

Maria Mitchell

On various occasions, Mitchell attended lectures at the Atheneum and traveled to Boston to the theater. In addition to Boston, her "off island" journeys included trips to Providence and New York, offering some commentary on New York society. Throughout the diaries, an underlying note of sadness is evident. "It is a blow, sudden and severe," she wrote when one of her closest friends died. Maria was especially worried when her mother became sick; and she rejoiced openly at her recovery.

Maria's diaries are also interesting for what she did not record. There is no mention of her mother in any of the diaries until she became ill. She did not record her brother Henry's wedding in 1854, and only obliquely alludes to Phebe's wedding the previous week, noting later how lonely she is without her sister at home.

"I could cry daily at the things for which I miss her," she wrote plaintively. With the notable exception of Phebe, the rest of the Mitchell family is almost entirely absent from Maria's diaries. An occasional letter shows that she kept up with all their activities, but she does not give them space in her private writings.

The extant diaries in her handwriting begin with an entry for September 12, 1854, a month and a half after Maria's thirty-sixth birthday. She, together with Kate and Anne, were the only ones of the ten Mitchell children then living at home. By this time she had been working at the Atheneum for more than fifteen years and doing computations for the Nautical Almanac for about five years. A few entries that date back to 1853 were published by her sister Phebe.[2] They are included here even though the original diary no longer exists. The first of these entries shows that Maria was a feminist even at this time.

> Feb. 15, 1853. I think Dr. Hall (in his "Life of Mary Ware")[3] does wrong when he attempts to encourage the use of the needle. It seems to me that the needle is the chain of woman, and has fettered her more than the laws of the country.
>
> Once emancipate her from the "stitch, stitch, stitch," the industry of which would be commendable if it served any purpose except the gratification of her vanity, and she would have time for studies which would engross as the needle never can. I would as soon put a girl alone into a closet to meditate as give her only the society of her needle.

The art of sewing, so far as men learn it, is well enough; that is, to enable a person to take the stitches, and, if necessary, to make her own garments in a strong manner; but the dressmaker should no more be a universal character than the carpenter.

Suppose every man should feel it is his duty to do his own mechanical work of all kinds, would society be benefited? Would the work be well done? Yet a woman is expected to know how to do all kinds of sewing, all kinds of cooking, all kinds of any woman's work, and the consequence is that life is passed in learning these only, while the universe of truth beyond remains unentered.

Feb. 19, 1853. I am just learning to notice the different colors of the stars, and already begin to have a new enjoyment. Betelgeuse is strikingly red, while Rigel is yellow.[4] There is something of the same pleasure in noticing the hues that there is in looking at a collection of precious stones, or at a flower-garden in autumn. Blue stars I do not yet see, and but little lilac except through the telescope.

May 11, 1853. I could not help thinking of Esther [a much loved cousin who had recently died] a few evenings since when I was observing. A meteor flashed upon me suddenly, very bright, very short-lived; it seemed to me that it was sent for me especially, for it greeted me almost the first instant I looked up, and was gone in a second—it was as fleeting and as beautiful as the smile upon Esther's face the last time I saw her. I thought when I talked with her about death that, though she could not come to me visibly, she might be able to influence my feelings; but it cannot be, for my faith has been weaker than ever since she died, and my fears have been greater.

Sept. 19, 1853. I am surprised to find the verse which I picked up somewhere and have always admired

> *Oh, reader, had you in your mind*
> *Such stores as silent thought can bring,*
> *Oh, gentle reader, you would find*
> *A tale in everything*

belonging to Wordsworth and to one of Wordsworth's simple, I am almost ready to say silly poems. I am in doubt what to think of Wordsworth. I should be ashamed of some of his poems if I had written them myself, and yet there are points of great beauty, and lines which once in the mind will not leave it.

Maria Mitchell

Oct. 31, 1853. People have to learn sometimes not only how much the heart, but how much the head, can bear. My letter came from Cambridge and I had work to do over.[5] It was a wearyful job, but by dint of shutting myself up all day I did manage to get through with it.

The good of my travelling[6] showed itself then, when I was too tired to read, to listen, or to talk; for the beautiful scenery of the West was with me in the evening, instead of the tedious columns of logarithms. It is a blessed thing that these pictures keep in the mind and come out at the needful hour. I did not call them, but they seemed to come forth as a regulator for my tired brain, as if they had been set sentinel-like to watch a proper time to appear.

November 1853. There is said to be no up or down in creation, but I think the world must be low for people who keep themselves constantly before it do a great deal of stooping!

1853. I was told that Miss [Dorothea] Dix[7] wished to see me, and I called upon her. It was dusk, and I did not at once see her; her voice was low, not particularly sweet, but very gentle. She told me that she had heard Professor Henry speak of me, and that Professor Henry was one of her best friends, the truest man she knew....

She does not brighten up in countenance in conversing. She is so successful that I suppose there must be a hidden fire somewhere, for heat is a motive power, and her cold manners could never move Legislatures. I saw some outburst of fire when Mrs. Hale's book was spoken of. It seems Mrs. Hale wrote to her for permission to publish a notice of her, and was decidedly refused; another letter met with the same answer, yet she wrote a 'Life,' which Miss Dix says is utterly false....

I asked her if she did not become at times weary and discouraged; and she said, wearied, but not discouraged, for she had met with nothing but success. There is evidently a strong will which carries all before it, not like the sweep of the hurricane, but like the slow, steady, and powerful march of the molten lava.

It is sad to see a woman sacrificing the ties of the affections even to do good. I have no doubt Miss Dix does much good, but a woman needs a home and the love of other women at least, if she lives without that of man.

Dec. 8, 1853. Last night we had the first meeting of the class in elocution. It was very pleasant, but my deficiency of ear was never more apparent to myself.[8] We had exercises in the ascending scale, and I practised after I came home, with the family as audience.

H[enry] says my ear is competent only to vulgar hearing, and I cannot appreciate nice distinctions. I am sure that I shall never say that if I had been properly educated I should have made a singer, a dancer, or a painter—I should have failed less, perhaps, in the last. Coloring I might have been good in, for I do think my eyes are better than those of any one I know.

Feb. 18, 1854. If I should make out a calendar by my feelings of fatigue, I should say there were six Saturdays in the week and one Sunday.[9]

Mr. ___ somewhat ridicules my plan of reading Milton with a view to his astronomy, but I have found it very pleasant, and have certainly a juster idea of Milton's variety of greatness than I had before. I have filled several sheets with my annotations on the "Paradise Lost," which I may find useful if I should ever be obliged to teach, either as a schoolma'am or a lecturer.[10]

March 2, 1854. I 'swept' last night two hours, by three periods. It was a grand night—not a breath of air, not a fringe of a cloud, all clear, all beautiful. I really enjoy that kind of work, but my back soon becomes tired, long before the cold chills me. I saw two nebulae in Leo with which I was not familiar, and that repaid me for the time. I am always the better for open-air breathing,[11] and was certainly meant for the wandering life of the Indian.

Sept. 12, 1854.[12] I am just through with a summer and a summer is to me always a trying ordeal. I have determined not to spend so much time at the Atheneum another season. To put someone in my place who shall see all the strange faces and hear the strange talk.

How much talk there is about religion! Giles[13] I like the best for he seems like myself to have no settled views and to be only religious in feeling. He says he has no piety but a great sense of infinity. Yesterday I had a Shaker visitor and today a Catholic and the more I hear, the less do I care about church doctrines. The Catholic Priest I have known as an Atheneum visitor for some time. He talked today on my asking him some questions and talked better than I had expected. He is plainly full of intelligence, full of enthusiasm for his religion and I suspect full of bigotry. I do not believe he will die a Catholic Priest. A young man of his temperament must find it very hard to live without family ties and I shall expect to hear if I ever hear of him again that some good little Irish lassie has made him forget his vows.

My visitors in other respects have been of the average sort. Four women have been delighted to make my acquaintance, three men have thought themselves in the presence of a superior being, one has offered me 25 cents because I reached him the key of the museum, one woman has opened a correspondence with me and several have told me that they knew friends of mine. Two have spoken of me in small letters to small newspapers, one said he didn't see me and one said he did!

I have become hardened to all, neither compliment nor quarter dollar rouses any emotion. My fit of humility which has troubled me all summer, is shaken by the first cool breeze of Autumn and the first walk taken without perspiration.

Dr. Brewster[14] thinks it absurd [of] the author of the work on "Plurality of Worlds"[15] to suppose that our Earth has been singled out as the theatre for man's action, but when he comes to combat the scriptural argument he admits the possibility that as Christ's mission reached backwards to all ages preceding his coming, and forward to all future ages, it may also extend its influence to the other worlds; thus making the earth in reality the theatre of a nobler visitation than that which it experienced at (was affected by) the entrance of man.

The following entry reveals the frustrations of comet hunting. Although Mitchell had discovered a comet on September 18, 1854, she did not learn until the twenty-first that someone else had discovered it before her.

Sept. 22, 1854 On the evening of the 18th while "sweeping" there came into the field the two nebulae in Ursa Major which I have known for many a year, but which to my surprise now appeared to be three. The upper one (as seen in an inverted telescope) appeared double headed like one near the Dolphin, but much more decided than that. The space between the two heads being plainly discernible and subtending a very decided angle. The bright part of the object was clearly the old nebulae but what was the appendage? Had the nebula suddenly changed, was it a comet, or was it only a very fine night?

Father decided at once for the comet, I hesitated with my usual cowardice and forbade his giving it a notice in the paper. I watched it from 8 1/2 to 11 1/2 [8:30 to 11:30 p.m.] almost without cessation and was quite sure at 11 1/2 that its position with regard to the neighboring stars had changed. I counted its distance from the known nebula several times but the whole affair was difficult, for there were flying clouds and sometimes both nebula and comet were too indistinct to be definitely seen. The 19th was cloudy and the 20th the same with the variety of wearisome breaks, through which I could see the nebula but not the comet.[16]

On the 21st came a circular and behold Mr. van Arsdale had seen it on the 13th but had not been sure of it until the 15th on account of the clouds. I was too well pleased with having really made the discovery, to care because I was not first.

Let the Dutchman have the reward of his sturdier frame and steadier nerves. Especially could I be a Christian because the 13th was cloudy and more especially because I dreaded the responsibility of making the computations *nolens volens* [willy-nilly] which I must have done to be able to call it mine.

I try to be generous towards the man, but I am <u>not</u> <u>sorry</u> when I hear that European observers have beaten him! Father was awfully disappointed but put the notice of my having made the discovery into the paper and sent it abroad. I claim this as my third comet, though only one has been mine from the first. I made observations for three hours last night and am almost sick today from fatigue, still I have worked all day, trying to reduce the places and mean to work hard again tonight.

Sept. 25. I began to recompute for the comet with observations of Cambridge and Washington today. I have had a fit of despondency in consequence of being obliged to renounce my own observations as too rough for use. The best that can be said of my life so far, is, that it has been industrious and the best that can be said of me, is, that I have not pretended to what I was not.

Oct. 10....I seized on a pleasant day and went on to the Cape for an excursion. We went to Yarmouth, Sandwich and Plymouth enjoying the novelty of the new car-route.[17] It really seemed in some parts like railway traveling on our own island, so much sand and so flat a country. The little towns too seemed quaint and odd and the old gray cottages looked as if they belonged to the last century and were waked from a long nap by the railway whistle.

I thought Sandwich a beautiful and Plymouth an interesting town. I would fain have gone off in poetical quotation such as "The breaking waves dashed high" or "The Pilgrim Fathers where are they" but Katy who had been there before desired me not to be absurd but to step quietly on the half-buried rock and quietly off. Younger sister knew a deal so I did as I was bidden to do and it was just as well not to make myself hoarse, without an appreciating audience....

Oct. 17. I have just gone over my comet computation again and it is humiliating to perceive how very little more I know than I did 7 years ago when I first did this kind of work. To be sure I have only once in the time computed a parabolic orbit but it seems to me that I know no more in general. I think I am a little better thinker, that I take things less upon trust but at the same time I trust myself much less.

The world of learning is so broad and the human side is so limited in power! We reach forth and strain every nerve but we seize hold only of a bit of the curtain that hides the infinite from us. Will it really unroll to us at some future time? Aside from the gratification of the affections in another world, that of the intellect must be great, if it is enlarged and its desires are the same.

In a wedding on September 14, 1854, Phebe Mitchell had married Joshua Kendall. That fall, Maria recorded how deeply she missed her younger sister.

I have no sickness of heart for a long time comparable to that which Phebe's absence gives me. I could cry daily at the things for which I miss her. She had so much mind and was almost always with me, good natured and that is invaluable in the home circle.

When you are seasick and a vessel goes madly up on a wave and plunges recklessly down into the gulf below, how she shakes her sides and seems to be convulsed as if with a chuckle at your heaving indignation. What a dreary desolate feeling it gives you, as if your only friend had deserted you and turned mocker.

I have been reading Mrs. Stowe's second volume, and on the whole I think it a pretty good book. The descriptions when they are in the region of Mt. Blanc are interesting and the little anecdotes of strawberry girls and beggars are pleasant.... I think I could have written as good a book and I am sure I could have had as good a time. The best of the book is, that you can't help feeling that she had a good time and you can't help enjoying it with her. She might well be pleased to find that children in the interior of Europe knew her by reputation and loved her through her book.

Courtesy of the Nantucket Maria Mitchell Association

FIVE MITCHELL SISTERS *(c. 1849)*. Maria is in the back row at left and Kate, the youngest, is next to her. In the front row *(left to right)* are Anne, Phebe, and Sally. Another sister, Eliza, was born in 1830 but lived less than three years. Maria was probably closest to Phebe, who published a book about her famed sister several years after Maria's death. In her now out-of-print 1896 book, Phebe noted that the "special care of the youngest sister [Kate] devolved upon Maria, who knew how to be a good nurse as well as a good playfellow. She was especially careful of the timid child..."

Maria Mitchell

Whatever may be the merit or demerit of Uncle Tom, it has had a wonderful success and has won her an enviable reputation. The reputation of Uncle Tom has pushed this work on. If it was by an unknown writer, it would have no reader. I do not believe one person would get through it....

One diary entry in the autumn of 1854 gives an excellent picture of a day in the life of Maria Mitchell at this time.

Oct. 21 This morning I rose at six, having been half-asleep only for some hours, fearing that I might not be up in season to get breakfast a task which I had volunteered for the preceding evening.

It was but half light and I made a hasty toilet. I made a fire very quickly, made the "kettle" boil, prepared the coffee, baked the graham bread, toasted white bread, trimmed the solar lamp and made another fire in the dining room before seven o'clock.

I always thought that seasonal girls had an easy task of it and I still think so. I really found an hour too long for all this and when rang the bell at 7 I had been waiting 15m for the clock to strike. I came down to the Atheneum at 9 1/2 and having decided that I would take the Newark and Cambridge places of the comet and work them up I did it, getting to the three equations before I went home to dinner at 12 1/2. I omitted the corrections of parallax and aberration not intending to get more than a rough approximation to find to my sorrow, that they do not agree with those from my own observations. I shall look over them again next week.

At noon I ran round and did up several errands, dined and was back again at my post by 1 1/2. Then I looked over my morning work. I can find no mistake. I have worn myself thru trying to find out about the comet and I know very little now in the matter. I differ in computing the two sets of elements...I saw also today in the Monthly Notices[18] a plan for measuring the light of stars by degrees of illumination, an idea which had occurred to me long ago—but which I have not practised.

On the evening of the 22nd I observed Algol[19] for two hours from 7 to 9 p.m. It was faint at seven and gradually dimmed until near nine. I think was dimmer after 8 1/2 than before but at 9 it began to brighten and I being very tired gave up looking. I was sorry that I did as the "Monthly Notices" gives 9h 08m for the minimum of which I was not aware at the time. There was no sudden change at all and from 7 to 8 1/2 the change in all was not great. I saw no change of color.

1854, Oct. 23. Yesterday I was again reminded of the remark which Mrs. Stowe makes about the variety of occupations which an American woman pursues. She says it is this, added to the cares and anxieties which keep them so much behind the daughters of England in personal beauty. And today, I was amused at reading that one of her party objected to the introduction of wood floors in American housekeeping, because she could seem to see herself down on her knees, doing the waxing. Throughout Mrs. Stowe's book there is an openness which I like, no pretense in affectation, religious cant but it is honest habit and not affectation.

But of yesterday—I was up before six—I made the fire in the cellar and made coffee. Then I set the table in the dining room and made a fire there. Toasted bread and trimmed lamps. At seven I rang the breakfast bell. After breakfast I made my bed and partially swept the chamber—"put up" the room. Then I came to the Atheneum and looked over my comet computations till noon. Before dinner I did some tatting, and made seven button holes for Kate.

I dressed for the Atheneum and then dined. Came again to the Atheneum at 1 1/2 and looked over another set of comet computations which took me until 4 o'clock. I was then pretty tired and rested by reading "Cosmos."

Lizzie Earle came in and I gossiped for half an hour. I went home to tea and as soon as tea made a loaf of graham bread. Then I went up to my room and read through (partly writing) two exercises in German which took me 35m. It was stormy and I had no observing to do, so I sat down to my tatting. Lizzie Earle came in and I took a new lesson in tatting, so as to make the edge. I made about half-yard during the evening. At a little after nine I went home with Lizzie and carried a letter to the Post Office. I had kept steadily at work for 16 hours when I went to bed. ...

Oct. 27. Last night I heard Josiah Quincy Jr.[20] lecture on the Mormons. It was the first lecture of the Atheneum course. I went to the first last winter and listened with contempt to Matthew Hale Smith.[21] I had expected of a Quincy something very much above a Smith, but the distance between the two men, is not, after all, so very great.

Both lectures were anecdotal, if Quincy's was more witty it was also more inelegant. It would have made a pleasant drawing room lecture but had not the dignity desirable in a Lyceum discourse, where it is presumable something will be taught. But the fault is not with Matthew Hale Smith nor with Jos. Quincy Jr. While the community is the same and the taste for lectures the same, and the lecture going people are no more enlightened, great men will come down to the level and small ones will struggle up to it....

Nov. 14. I went down to see Ida Russell ten days ago. I was curious to see for myself whether sickness had changed her in body and spirit. I found her much the same Ida as when I last saw her three years ago, when she panted up the hills at Albany.... Ida is strong in her dislike of the "platform women" as she calls the Antislavery and woman's rights people. I told her not to speak of them with such contempt as I had always felt that when I was pushed for money, I could write some astronomical lectures and go into the cities and deliver them.[22] "Don't Maria" she said, "do anything else. Take a husband even!"

(I) What! The weak minded man such as would happen to fall in love with me?

(Ida) Well, then there's the river.

(I) Yes, as the bowl or the dagger but I don't fancy any of these things!

Ida says she is tired of farming, that the care and the labor are too much for her. That she "raises a good deal of stock" and that is another great care.

Nov. 24, 1854. Yesterday James Freeman Clarke[23] the biographer of Margaret Fuller came into the Atheneum. It was plain that he came to see me and not the Institution. I was a good deal embarrassed and made such an effort to appear as if I wasn't, that I was almost ready to burst into a laugh at my own ridiculousness.

He rushed into talk at once, mostly on people, and asked me about my astronomical labors. As it was a kind of flattery I repaid it in kind by asking him about Margaret Fuller. He said she was a very remarkable woman, that he never met any one, man or woman, who so impressed him with the truth of their convictions. That, when listening to others, he sometimes thought, "that is a good idea" but with Margaret he felt that it was not a "good idea" it was a settled fact. He said she did not strike anyone as a person of intellect or as a student, for all her faculties were kept so much abreast that none had

prominence. I wanted to ask if she was a lovable person but I did not
think he would be an unbiased judge, she was so much attached to
him....

Dec. 5. Last night I had two letters which did me good. One was
from Lizzie Earle and one from Ida Russell.

The love of one's own sex is precious for it is neither provoked by
nicety nor retained by flattery; it is genuine and sincere. I am grateful that I have had much of this in my life. I am sometimes sorry that
those who give me so much, should give it to me when it might be so
well suited to the domestic station of wife and I am humbled when I
consider that they give it to me because they know me so little—that,
living in the same town with me, they would know me better and
love me less.

I have an entirely different regard for Lizzie and Ida. I love Lizzie as
one loves a sister, I admire Ida and am jealous of her regard for others. It is something like love and less generous than that which I have
for Lizzie; which is affection. But all these affections are weak compared with what one has for kindred. The ties of blood are stronger
than all other ties.

Strangely enough, I dreamed of Ida a few nights since. I had tho't
so much of what has been said of her in connection with Whittier
that I dreamed I saw them together. I wonder if it was a glimpse of a
scene in a future state. The parlor in which I seemed to see them was
the dirty one of the Odeon House and anything but ethereal. Ida gave
a quotation from a German writer in her letter which pleased me. It
was "if we recounted all our blessings we should have no time left for
lamentation!"

I am brightening and cheering up under the healthy influences of
leisure—I have no work and am enjoying the freedom of thought
consequent upon it. Now life seems pleasant and worth the having,
when in the summer, I am dropping beneath the heavy logarithms, I
wonder that anyone wishes to live.[24]

Two classes of people can afford to dress: the rich who can gratify
every taste and the poor who have only the taste for personal adorn-
ing and can spend all they earn in its satisfaction. But take it as you
may, dress requires either money or thought. One can look well on
very little money, but there must be the thinking, planning sewing all
done by oneself and the taste which is used in selecting a ribbon
might make a colorist in an artist, and the thought spent in fitting a

dress, would be worth something to the architect, and the time spent in pulling the stitches is worth much to any of us....

Dec. 12. When I consider how many useless words are spoken, how many foolish ones, how many which isolate and provoke, how many which pollute the mouth that utters and the ears that listen, I am almost ready to condemn the use of language and to wish that mankind communicate by signs, or by pictures and certainly my commiseration for dumb people is much lessened. They have much but how much they [end of entry]

Dec. 21. I have just put down Mrs. Stowe's first volume of "Sunny Memoirs" and true to my general theory of preferring people to scenery I prefer this to the second. I read the 2nd some time since, when that was within my grasp and the first was not. All the way through the second, I felt that I could have written as good a book. I give up the idea now, I could not have written so unobjectionable a book and at the same time used so much independent judgment....

Dec. 26, 1854. They were wonderful men, the early astronomers. That was a great conception, which now seems to us so simple. That the earth turns upon its axis and a still greater one that it revolves about the sun. To show this last was worth a man's lifetime and it really almost cost the life of Galileo.

Sometimes we are ready to think that they had a wider field than us for speculation, that truth being all unknown it was easier to take the first steps in its paths, but is the region of truth limited? Is it not infinite? Is there less truth now than in the days of Galileo?

We know a few things which were once hidden and being known they seem easy. But there are the flashings of the Northern Lights. "Across the left they start and shift." There is the conical zodiacal beam seen so beautifully in the early evenings of Spring and the early mornings of autumn, there are the comets, whose use is all unknown. There are the brightening and flickering variable stars whose cause is all unknown and the meteor showers and for all of these the reasons are as clear as for the successions of day and night. They lie just beyond the daily mist of our minds, but our eyes have not yet pierced through it.

Jan. 1, 1855. A friend is not to be found in the world such as one can conceive of such as one needs, for no human being unites so many of the attributes of God, as we feel our nature requires.

In one who shall be guide, counselor, well-wisher and the like. We have therefore a circle whom we call friends, giving a name to the whole, which perhaps in its singular occupation might be used for the combination. Out of the whole circle we may make up a single friend. We love them all but we love the union of all better.

From this one, we have the intellectual stimulus of his higher nature. We become active as we see him active, we gird ourselves for labor as we see him in the struggle, we are more of a man because we know one.

From another we have the warmth of affection and our hearts grow as if in a summer feeling. We are ordered in good work, we are sympathizing to all mankind, we look at the ones of our race with a more lenient eye, for we see with the eyes of our friend.

So a third neither stimulates the intellect nor warms the heart, but he cheers us. We are more elastic and buoyant, more happy and radiating more happiness, because we know him. There are the jolly men of the earth and may the earth be jolly to them, for we could not spare them. Whatever our degree of friends may be, we come more under their influence than we are aware.

Who of us acts and speaks without an eye to the approbations of those he loves? Is not the assent of another a sort of second conscience? I may doubt about the moral right of some action but if I tell it to a friend whom I esteem and he defends it, I am at once strong in my decision. I should now battle for it with all the strength of argument which I could command, but I carefully avoid the argument which really is most convincing to myself, that he thinks. So Evil grows quickly by being kindred together. It is frightful to commit a sin alone and few do it. We prop ourselves up with accomplices, we surround ourselves with those who can down for us the uprisings of conscience.

Who of us judges a work of art and sees only with his own eyes? Who listens to a lecture and hears only with his own ears? We turn aslant as we stand before the picture to see what good judges are looking. We open the guide book to see what we ought to admire. We listen as we come out of the crowded lecture room to know what the man thinks, we not only do not condemn with our tongues if the man will not, but insensibly our judgment is inspired by that of those around us. It is not a weakness to be deplored. We were more than conceited did we rate ourselves so much above the rest of the world

Maria Mitchell

that we needed no outward aids to judgment. We were born dependent, our happiness is in the hands of others. Our character is molded by them and receives its coloring from them as much as our feeling relates the parental impress.

On a telescope, the cross hairs are very fine filaments placed at the focus of the eyepiece. The observer moves the telescope so that the star or comet is exactly centered on the cross hairs and then a position can be determined. Mitchell's cross hairs had evidently broken, and it took her three weeks to get a satisfactory replacement.

Jan. 1, 1855. I put some wires into my little transit this morning. I dreaded so much when I found yesterday that it must be done, that I disturbed my sleep. It was much easier than I expected. I took out the little collimating-making screws first. Then I drew out the tube and in that I found a brass plate screwed on the diaphragm which contained the lines.

I was at first a little puzzled to know which screws hold this diaphragm in its place, and as I was very anxious not to unscrew the wrong ones, I took time to consider and found I need turn only two. Then, out slipped the little plate with its three wires, where five should have been, two having been broken. As I did not know how to manage a spider's web, I took the hairs from my own head taking care to pick out white ones because I have no black ones to spare. I put in the two after first stretching them over pasteboard by sticking them into the little grooved lines which I found with sealing wax dissolved in alcohol.

When I had with great labor adjusted these as I tho't firmly, I perceived that some of the wax was on the hairs and would make them yet coarser and they were already too coarse, so I washed my little camels-hair brush which I had been using, and began to wash them with clear alcohol. Almost at once I washed out another wire and so another and another. I went to work patiently and put in the five perpendicular ones besides the horizontal one which like the other had fizzled up and appeared to melt away.

With another hour's labor, I got in the five, when a rude motion ruined them all again and I began over. Just at one o'clock I had got them all in again. I attempted then to put the diaphragm back into its place. The sealing wax was not dry and with a little jar, I sent the wires all agog.

This time, they did not come out of the little grooved lines into which they were put and I hastened to take out the brass plate and sat them in parallel lines. I gave up then for the day, but as they looked well and were certainly in firmly, I did not consider that I had made an entire failure. I thought it nice lady-like work, to manage such light threads and turn such delicate screws, but firm as are the hairs of ones head, I shall seek something firmer for I can see how clumsy they will appear when I get on the eyepiece and magnify their imperfections. They look parallel now to the eye but with a magnifying power every little crook will seem a billowy wave, and a faint star will hide itself in one of the yawning abysses.

Jan. 10. The older I grow the more I admire independence of character and yet the less does this characteristic belong to me and the more rare does it seem to be in the world. When we consider too, how short is life and how much shorter are the petty vexations of life, it seems strange that we should not act up to our convictions of duty and disregard what may be said of us by our fellow men. For what is my neighbor more than I, that I should succumb to his views in preference to my own? And what possible good can become to me from such submission? I cannot even please him for very possibly his expressed opinion is not his own but that of some other neighbor of whom he stands in awe.

And so we have a chain of ignoble submissions reaching perhaps around the world. I cannot suppose it arises from cowardice and I therefore suppose it comes from a still more despicable weakness—that of indolence.

Thinking is hard work and when we have come to a definite conclusion on some point, we must retrace our steps to find our thread of reasoning and perhaps we must prop its strands on the way that it need not break...and then we must bring a strong light to bear on this thread as the vision of another may not be as clear as our own, and all this is <u>work</u>, and from work we shrink.

We say then to ourselves "let us take an opinion ready-made which perhaps has been growing from the time of the Pharaohs and must come to us with all the toughness of time" and somebody, early in the world's history must have done some thinking, for there are good ideas about which have been afloat for ages and ages and if they are good in our day and adopted to it there must have been some far-reaching thought at work.

Maria Mitchell

1855, Jan. 11. Resolved—to get an hour a day at least, for study, however busy I may be during this year and to get it in the morning.

Jan. 15. Finding the hairs which I had put into my instrument not only too coarse, but variable, and disposed to curl themselves up at a change of weather, I wrote to Geo. Bond to ask him how I should procure spider lines. He replied that the web from cocoons should be used and that I should find it difficult at this time of year to get at them.

I remembered at once that I had seen two in the Library room of the Atheneum which I had carefully refrained from disturbing. I found them perfect and unrolled them. I was surprised to find how much length of web could be unrolled. I wound it around a card, but in carrying the card home in my pocket I lost a great deal from the rubbing off. Fearing that I might not succeed in managing them, I procured some hairs from Clifford's head. Clifford [a young nephew] being not quite a year old, his hair is remarkably fine and sufficiently long.

I went to work on the diaphragm Sunday morning. I made the perpendicular wires of the spider's web, breaking them and doing the work over again a great many times. Using up my stock of web and rummaging round under dirty beams and dusty rafters until I found another cocoon. The webs strained very much and the slightest breath would break one. They were so fine too that I felt afraid of my eyes but I at length got all in, crossing the five perpendicular ones, with a horizontal one from Clifford's spinning wheel.

They looked ready and I felt that I improved my mechanical efforts. After 24 hours' exposure to the weather I looked at them. The spider webs had not changed, they were plainly used to a chill and made to endure changes of temperature, but Clifford's hair, which had never felt a cold greater than that of the nursery, nor a change more decided than from his mother's arms to his father's, had knotted up into a decided curl.

N.B. Clifford may expect ringlets. I took out this diaphragm again.

Jan. 22. Horace Greeley in an article in a recent issue of the *Tribune* says that the fund left by Smithson is spent by the regents of that Institution in purchasing books which no publisher would undertake and which do no good to anybody. Now, in our little town of Nantucket with our little Atheneum, these volumes are in constant demand.

Reformers are apt to forget, in their reasoning, that the world is not made up entirely of the wicked and the hungry, there are persons hungry for the food of the mind, the wants of which are as imperious as those of the body. The claims of which upon the benevolence of the wealthy are so well founded. If these persons are denied their rightful foods they are not developed as their creator designed and they must rush down into the day laborers path, with a mental suffering compared to which physical chill is small.

Reformers are apt to forget too, that the social chain is indomitable; that link by link it acts together, you cannot lift one man above his fellows, but you lift the race of men. Newton, Shakespeare and Milton did not directly benefit the poor and ignorant but the elevation of the whole race has been through them. They probably found it hard to get publishers, but after several centuries, the publishers have come to them and the readers have come, and the race has been lifted to their level. The coral insect does not at once make an island and his first earthy deposit may not seem to the continents around of much marketable value, but by and by it decks the neck of the princess and later still the island appears and man has another dwelling place.

I do not suppose that such works as those issued by the Smithsonian Regents are appreciated by all who turn them over, but the ignorant learn that such things exist, they perceive that a higher cultivation than theirs is in the world and they are stimulated to strive after greater excellence. So I steadily advocate in purchasing books for the Atheneum, the <u>lifting</u> of the people. "Let us buy, not such books as the people want, but books just above their wants, and they will reach up to take what is put out for them."

We may in this way, form on Nantucket, a taste for the refined and elevated and might thus destroy the taste for the gossiping and adventurous. I despise a gossipy book of travels and I almost despise a book like "Roughing it in the Bush" which any one could write, who had been through the scenery and out of which only amusement is obtained.[25] No one is even the better able (that I can see) to encounter hardships, for the greater part of the hardships met and conquered need not have been met and probably are fictitious.

1855, Feb. 12. I saw the stars in the evening of the 10th and met them like old friends from whom I had been long parted. They had been absent from my eyes three weeks. I swept round for comets about an hour and then I amused myself with noticing the varieties of color. I wonder that I have so long been insensitive to this charm in the skies, the tints of the different stars are so delicate in their variety and the grouping has all the infinity of the Kaleidoscope, infinitely extended.

What a pity that some of our manufacturers shouldn't be able to steal the secret of dye-stuffs from the stars and astonish the feminine taste by new brilliancy in fashion. I found in the little bear [Ursa Minor] a pair of stars coming into the field at once, one bright red and one bright green. Just east of the belt of Orion I found a pair near together of different shades of red, one being orange-red. We call stars known to revolve about each other binary systems, but may not stars apparently very remote be binary systems.

Feb. 23. As our circle of friends narrows they naturally seem to clasp as in a closer and closer embrace. It is the sad theory in growing old, that we outlive one and another of those we love. I heard of Ida's death today. It is a blow, sudden and severe.

The year 1855 brought not only the death of three of Maria's closest friends, but also the serious, ongoing illness of her mother, causing Maria to describe it in December as the hardest year of her thirty-seven-year-old life. Phebe later explained, "In 1855 Mrs. Mitchell was taken suddenly ill, and although partial recovery followed, her illness lasted for six years, during which time Maria was her constant nurse."[26]

March 12, [1855]. What a change a fortnight has made. I have passed through a fortnight of great anxiety in nursing my Mother. I have never been a believer in a special Providence, but when I saw her recovering I felt like giving thanks to God and when anyone says to me "how is your mother," I felt like saying "Better, thank God" instead of "thank you."

The Catholic method of outward show of gratitude seems to me as absurd as before. I would have been glad to make a pilgrimage to Jerusalem to offer up on the holy sepulcher my thanks.

There came to me while in the sick room a letter from Geraldine Rivers telling me of Ida's death and one from Mr. Vinton telling me of Phebe's [his wife]. My two friends died within four days of each other. Their deaths were as different as their lives. The one struggled for life with a strong spunk and fought the battle bravely, she died in great suffering. The other yielded to the enemy without an effort and passed so gently from life to death that those around could not tell when one was exchanged for the other.

And so I have lost two women I loved as I have loved few out of my home circle. I always tho't Ida loved me more than I her and I Phebe more than she me. As is said by Taylor "Loftier minds to lower cleave, with firmer force than these to those" and Ida was my superior. She was many-sided but crystal like, every side gave a gleam of light. ...

March 20. I have had letters from Mr. Vinton. I had imagined that Phebe's death would be overwhelming to him, that he would sink like a child and need a protective arm. ... The most that I fear for him, is, that with his susceptibility to female influence, some woman whom I could not respect, may get an ascendancy over him. I feel like comforting him and yet I cannot bear to attach myself to him as I once did, for I no longer respect him as I did then. A good wife ought to be of real value to him but can he ever obtain one?

March 21. Another death today. Miss Bansey has passed through the scene which she lived in dread of. With all her peculiarities she is a great loss and we could not spare her. She has for 40 years made life at Nantucket social, she has founded clubs, given parties, brought people together and made them like each other. Many a young man can say that but for her, he had lived in entire seclusion at Nantucket. Some few married men must admit, that, but for her they had died bachelors, or married less happily.

The world is sadder to me than before. I feel as if I must be lonesome, but I thank God that my home circle is still whole. It has been a winter, which I cannot soon forget, for I have lost three friends whom I valued. I feel as if I must cling more closely to those who are left, for how, at my age, can one form new attachments.

I have held the tears just behind my eyelids for a month, not being able to cry because of the danger of affecting mother and being ready to do so, at every moment. I felt when this year came in, a sinking of the heart, as if it had more duties for me, than I could well go through with. I did not think of the many trials to which in less than three months I must be subjected.

April 18. A young sailor boy came to see me today. It pleases me to have these lads seek me on their return from their first voyage and tell me how much they have learned about navigation. They always say with pride "I can take a lunar, Miss Mitchell, and work it up!" This boy I had known only as a boy but he has suddenly become a man and

Maria Mitchell

seems to be full of intelligence. He will go once more as a sailor he says and then try for a second mate position. ... He said his Capt. with whom he came home asked him if he knew me, because he had heard of me. I was glad to find the Capt. was a man of intelligence and had been kind to him.

A letter penned by Maria Mitchell to one of her "boys"—Alexander Starbuck, author of *The History of Nantucket*—contains further insights into her life at the Atheneum and her interest in the lives of its visitors. It was written after her return from Europe in 1858.

Nantucket Aug 24th 1859
Alexander Starbuck
Dear Sir,

I meant to write something before you left us, to show to you and to others, my high appreciation of your character, but I put it off from day to day and you left before it was done. I dare say you needed no help of mine, and that you are well situated and busy enough before this time, but perhaps you will not be sorry to have me send you now my good wishes, and express to you my expectations that your manhood will make good the promise of your boyhood. It is strange to think of you as already a man, and I hesitated about the beginning of this letter, as I cannot believe you any older than when I first knew you, some six years ago.

My Atheneum "boys" have turned out wonderfully well—they were good boys at the outset or I should not have employed them, and I hope they learned no evil from me. Some information they could not help getting from the handling of good books. I think no one of them was more faithful in his duty or more industrious than you.

I suppose you have little opportunity now for practising as a penman, but perhaps the nicety of handwork that you had acquired, will help you in your new work. I carried a copy of a letter, by you, to England with me, and the penmanship called forth the admiration of Mrs. Airy the wife of the Astronomer Royal. I hope you will not lose such an accomplishment.

I should be glad to have you write to me when you can find time and tell me what you are doing and what friends you are making.

Yours very truly,
Maria Mitchell[27]

May 12. Are the myriads of new planets[28] indeed fragments, or are they truly new to our system, like the comets of short orbits?...

June 2. I have just returned from a trip to New York. I met Mrs. Dassel whom I never meet without feeling that my good angel was near me when I was thrown in her way—she is so entirely natural and yet so interesting. I found her copying a French pastille as she now takes portraits in that way.

She says she has learned some policy and keeps some money by her for the rainy days and well she may with three children and a fourth in prospect. My godchild is now three years old, very precocious and very pretty. I was struck with her resemblance to the little sister that I lost more than 20 years ago.[29] Mrs. Dassel declares that her eyes are like mine and that it was a consequence of our being so much together before the child's birth.

I met at Mrs. Dassel's, Mrs. Ripley,[30] whom I am always glad to see. She always gives me a bird's eye view of New York society in a rapid tongue-sketch. She says that in what is called society, conversation, like that one hears in New England is entirely unknown. I supposed that she gave a higher meaning to the word "conversation" than I but on my asking, she said "in Society such conversation as you have had with Ida Russell is unknown, books are not mentioned, the words you use would not be understood. In New England women talk of the Fugitive Slave Laws, in New York society, it is never spoken of and down town even, it is talked of by a very few men. I have met with the finest minds in New York but they are not in society."

I have asked myself since, how I should feel "in society." Could I understand their terms? Could I enter into their enjoyments? She told me in answer to my question "don't they talk?" that they have four subjects, the weather, dress, upholstery and the opera. Except when the first was on the topic I should have to be silent and the first is so soon exhausted. The opera is really a subject of high art and if understood must require a good deal of intellect....

One of the earliest professional honors bestowed upon Maria Mitchell was being chosen as the first woman member of the American Association for the Advancement of Science. Over the years, she often attended the Association's scientific meetings. One diary entry, as noted by Phebe Mitchell Kendall, refers to the meeting held in Providence in 1855.[31]

Maria Mitchell

Aug. 23. It is really amusing to find oneself lionized in a city where one has visited quietly for years. To see the doors of fashionable man open wide to receive you, which never opened before. I suspect that the whole corps of science laughs in its sleeve at the farce. The leaders make it pay well.

My friend Mr. Bache makes these occasions the opportunities for making sundry little wheels, pulleys and levers operate. The result of all which is that he gets his enormous appropriation of $400,000 out of Congress every winter. For a few days, science reigns triumphant. We are feted and complimented to the top of our bent, tho' complimenter and complimented must feel that it is only a sort of theatrical performance, for a few days and over, one does enjoy acting the part of greatness a while. I was very tired after three days of it and glad to take the car and run away.

The descent into a commoner was rather rapid. I went along to Boston and when I reached out my free ticket, the conductor read it through and reached it back saying in a gruff tone "It's worth nothing—a dollar and quarter to Boston." Think what a downfall! The night before and "one blast upon my bugle horn was worth a 100 men." Now one man alone was my dependence and that man looked very much instead to put me out of the car for attempting to pass a ticket that in his eyes was valueless.

Of course I took it quietly and paid the money merely remarking "You will pass 100 on this road in a few days on this same ticket." When I look back and think upon the paper read by Mr. Jones in his uncouth manner I think "When a man is thoroughly incorrect, how careless he is of mere words."

Sept. 17. A day of do-nothing. I am afraid all my days will soon be so and yet it is thus. No fault of mine. It is certain that I must either give up the astronomy entirely or put someone in my place a large part of the year. I was never more dissatisfied with my life than I have been this summer. I wish I knew what was best for me to do.

This morning Peter gave me a rebuke that I felt, he said no men loved dissipation but they were driven to it because they could not gain admittance to the society that they desired. "Just," he said, "as you say I shall not come into the Ath[eneum] in the morning, other people say young men shall not come in their circles and so the young men must go drunken."

I asked him whether women were not better than men. He said no, not in cities and that his opinion even of the women in the higher walks of life, was confirmed by the many physicians with whom he talked. Peter was serious and sensible and is full of flame and shimmers. I hope they will not prove mere chimeras for he has a great heart....

1855 Sept. 26. A few days ago the door of the Atheneum opened and Dr. Swift entered. He did so daily about 15 years ago and I sat for a moment in a state of bewilderment. Had 15 years elapsed, or had I been dreaming that time was passing and was it only another daily visit. It was really 15 years and I rose and almost embraced him. I was so glad to see him.

His hair is white but in other respects how little is he changed and his spirit is if anything more youthful. It is pleasant to see a man at near 60 as young as he is at 60. The Doctor's spirit seemed to be at great height. He recalled our old astronomy labors together and we talked very fast for a few minutes.

I saw him again in the evening and again the next day and I was glad at each time, but, the 15 years have had their work and I do not care for him as I did 15 years ago. It is dreadful to think of the lessening of affection and attachments but it is nothing to look back upon the things, and it is as certain as growing old.

I am through with my computing except a very little and now I hope for some days of earnest study. I feel constantly hurried because of the shortness of life and I have so much to do. I want thoroughly to understand the subject of perturbations[32] before I go to Europe and I feel that there is an infinitude that I do not know....

I count it among the pleasant things this summer that I received a present of a copy of "Howard's Illustrations of Shakespeare" from a man almost a stranger to me, an eccentric person, who owns a fine large Library. I had been a little civil to him, no more than I should have been to any feeble old man and I had rather set him down in my head as a miser because he bought books which he did not read, intending at his death to endow some bookless Institution. I suppose they will do more good so disposed of, but I do covet them.

He was a small thin old man of 70 very infirm and carrying his head much on one side altogether so peculiar looking that one could not but notice him. My annoyances from strangers have either not been as great this year as last, or I have learned to be callous.

Maria Mitchell

One man and one woman asked me if I was the astronomer and I do not even change color. One man offered me 50 cts. for a sight of the museum and I colored very slightly. One insisted on my giving a sketch of my astronomical labors to a party of his friends and I <u>did</u> "color" almost with indignation and declined doing it. That man I set down as a fool and I had thought it before.

The "home duties" Maria mentions in the following diary entry likely refer to taking care of her mother. Phebe, noting her sister's role as their mother's constant nurse, says: "Maria's eyes were always upon her."[33]

I have read almost nothing, except newspapers—how could I? Working 6 hours a day is as much as I can bear, with the exercise and the home duties besides. But it makes me feel miserable to perceive that I am only a money getter.

Oct. 1. I have been struck in reading Schiller with the excellence of his female characters. What I particularly noted is their simplicity of language, the peculiarity being called to my mind by the much greater ease which I find in translating what they say....

The doctrine of a future accountability for the deeds done in this life, seems to have the support of the need of our nature, for when we work with the eye of a master upon us we will be more faithful, even the best of us, than when the eye is turned away.

Oct. 31. I saw Rachel in *Phaedra* and in *Adrienne*. I had previously asked a friend, if I, in my ignorance of acting and in my inability to tell good from poor, should really perceive a marked difference between Rachel and her aids. She tho't I should. I did indeed!... It is founded on the play of Euripides and even to know the passion which Phaedra and Rachel as Phaedra, represents, must have been too strange to be natural.... She was more agreeable as the Princess in *Adrienne*. I felt in reading Phaedra and in hearing it, that it was a play of high order and that I learned some little philosophy from some of its sentiments, but for Adrienne I have a contempt.... I have always disliked to see death represented. Rachel's representation was awful. I could not take my eyes from the scene and I held my breath in horror....

The audience to hear *Adrienne* was very fine, all the Cambridge professors, the Unitarian clergymen and the divinity students seemed to have turned out. Most of the 2000 listeners were obliged to follow with the book, but it was good to know that they followed the French, for precisely as the last word was uttered on the French page over turned the 2000 leaves sounding like a shower of rain. The applause was never very great. It is said that Rachel feels this is a Boston peculiarity, but she ought also to feel the compliment of so large an audience, in a city where foreigners are so few, and the population so small, compared with that of New York. She evidently had the very elite of the city.

Nov. 14, 1855. Last night I heard Emerson give a Lecture. I pity the Reporter who attempts to give it to the world. I began to listen with a determination to remember it in order, but it was without method order or system. It was like a beam of light moving in the undulatory waves meeting with occasional meteors in its path. It was exceedingly uplifting. It surprised me that there was not only no commonplace thought, but there was no commonplace expression. If he quotes, he quoted from what we had not read, if he told an anecdote it was one that had not reached us....

1855. Deacon Greeley urged my going to Boston and giving some lectures to get money. I told him I couldn't think of it just now as I wanted to go to Europe.

"On what money?" said he.

"What I have earned" I replied.

"Bless me," said he "am I talking to a capitalist? What a mistake I have made!"

A western gentleman who meant to compliment me, said "I wish I could swap half my head for half yours."

Dec. 3, 1855. One thing in Sydney Smith[34] displeases me very much. Throughout his life he appears to have ridiculed the Quakers. They seem to have been his butt and I like him the less for it....

Dec. 16. All along this year I have felt that it was a hard year. The hardest of my life, and I have kept enumerating to myself my many trials; today it suddenly occurred to me that my blessings were much more numerous.

If mother's sickness was a sore affliction, is not her recovery a great blessing and even the sickness itself has its bright side. For we have joyed in showing her how much we prized her continued life. If I have lost friends, I have not lost all. If I have worked harder than I felt that I could bear, how much better is that than not to have as much work as I wanted to do. I have earned more money than in any preceding year. I have studied less, but have observed rather more than I did last year. I have saved more money than ever before, hoping for Europe in 1856.

On the 12th [of December] at 8 o'clock, I found a comet in Cetus. It is probably that seen by Bruhns in Berlin on Nov. 12.[35] It is round and bright and moved so rapidly that in an hour I was certain of its change of place. From 8 to 10 1/2 it had moved about half the diameter of my field of view. I tho't it varied in its light but of this I am not quite certain, as I at times changed from one instrument to another, and I cannot be certain that my eye was not somewhat affected by the size of different powers, so as to affect my judgment. I would give a good deal for it to be my own possession, because it would convince me that I was not declining in vigor.

I did not see it on the 13th on account of clouds, but on the 16th I saw it again and found it had moved about 6 deg in RA and about 1 deg S in Dec. bringing it very near alpha Ceti. I watched for it in the Transit Instrument but the clouds came up and tho' I saw the star, I did not see the comet. It looked less like a ball, more shaggy than on the 12th. I think it [is] approaching the sun because it is moving W[est]—farther from the sun than we are and near to us because it moves rapidly.

We calculate that tomorrow night it will be very near to the moon. Today it rises and down drops the mercury on the Barometer and notwithstanding Mother predicts a clearing off. I have no hope of one and must learn to wait, hard as it is.

Dec 27. Last night I looked again for the comet calling its motion 2 deg per day for the last 12 days. The wind was blowing a gale from NW and the thermometer stood at 27. I stood the lantern down on the roof and it blew over at once, and the door of the scuttle too with a loud slam and Father's hat left his head without any salaam.

I put up the comet seeker with a good deal of difficulty, but the night was very clear and I wanted at least to make an effort. Father very coolly told me that to prevent myself from being blown off the house, I had only to lie down, whenever a flare of wind came upon me. I did not need to do this however. It was a cutting air which I felt afraid to breathe and my fingers soon became useless from the chill, so I swept 40 minutes and descended. I saw no comet. If I did not look at its old place and see that it was not there and if I had not called Father to such I should think my senses had deceived me, for it is plain that at no other place in the U.S. has it been seen....

1856, Jan 9. A terrible storm came up on the night of the 5th. It began to snow about four in the afternoon, the wind being high at NE and the barometer slowly falling. But the thermometer was up to 32 and I told the little boy who consulted me as learned in those things and who was anxiously hoping for sledding that it would without doubt be a heavy storm. But it might be only of wind and rain. It steadily increased and snowed all the evening so that the 27 persons who came to the Atheneum reminded me of the lines "Miller, miller musty troll" for they shook showers of snow flakes like pollen from their cape and hats.

When I left the Atheneum at 9, I was startled at the height of the wind and the blinding clouds of snow which went past me. There were many prayers in the shape of sighs went up that night "for those who go down upon the sea in ships." It stormed all night. I heard the gates blow to, the bricks fall from chimneys, and at length something went from the observatory which I hoped was only a chair. It was a night too noisy for sleep and the morning bro't no relief in that respect.

We did not go out to church and no bell rang to call us. Only the Friends held a meeting and that but half the day. Father found the observatory door was blown open and everything was covered with snow. I feared that I had lost my notes.

On shovelling away a snow drift they came out bright and perfect, only changed for the better by the washing they had received. It was a storm to enjoy when it was over, for the deep cuts were very picturesque and the work of making them was inspiring.

Everybody seems to like to clear away snow. It is the only kind of architecture and sculpture which some men reach and the cutting away of the snow is to them like the cutting away of marble to the artist. I wonder they don't attempt arches to their gateways, and domes to their porticoes. The effect would be charming in a week of intense cold. All the papers speak nowadays of the beauty of the frost covered trees glittering like a Briareus in diamonds.

Maria Mitchell

The diary entries for 1856 end with Mitchell's observations of the storm of January 9. There are no more diary entries for that entire year; but Maria kept a record of the extraordinary winter of 1857 in a separate diary she labeled "Journal of the Hard Winter."

1857 Jan 22. Hard winters are becoming the order of things. Winter before last was hard, last winter was harder and this surpasses all winters known before. We have been frozen in to our Island now since the 6th. No one said much about it for the first two or three days. The sleighing was good and all the world was out trying their horses on Main St.—the race-course of the world. Day after day passed and the thermometer sank to a lower point and the minds rose to a higher, and sleighing became uncomfortable and even the dullest man longed for the cheer of a newspaper. The *Inquirer* came out for a while, but at length had nothing to tell and nothing to Inquire about and so kept its peace....

Inside the houses we amuse ourselves in various ways. Frank's family and ours form a club, meeting three times a week and writing machine poetry in great quantities. Occasionally something very droll puts us in a roar of laughter. Frank, Ellen and Kate I think are rather the smartest, tho' Mr. Macy has written rather the best of all.

At the next meeting each of us is to produce a sonnet on a subject which we drew as in a lottery. I have written mine and tried to be droll. Kate has written hers and is serious. I am sadly tried by this state of things, I cannot receive papers from Cambridge and am out of work; it is cloudy most of the time and I cannot observe and I had fixed on just this time for visiting Phebe. My trunk has been half packed for a month.

Jan 23. Foreseeing that the thermometer would show a very low point last night, we sat up until near midnight when it showed 1 1/2 below zero. The stars shone brightly and the wind blew fresh from WNW. This morning the wind is the same and the mercury stood at 6 1/2 below zero at 7 o'clock and now at 10 a.m. is not above zero....

There are about 700 barrels of flour in town, it is admitted that fresh meat is getting scarce. The streets are almost impassable from the snow drifts. There was no ice in our lodging room last night and the thermometer in the sitting room was above 40 showing that the house is not easily chilled.

Kate and I have hit on a plan for killing time. We are learning poetry, she takes twenty lines of Goldsmith's "Traveller" and I twenty lines of the "Deserted Village." It will take us twenty days to learn the whole and we hope to be stopped in our course by the opening of the harbor. Considering that Kate has a beau from whom she cannot hear a word, she carries herself very amiably towards mankind. She is making a pair of boots for herself which look very well. I have made myself a morning dress since we were closed in.

Last night I took my first lesson in whist playing. I learned in one evening to know the King, Queen and Jack apart and to understand what Kate, my partner, meant when she winked at me....

I bought a copy of *Aurora Leigh* just before the freezing up and I have been careful, as it is the only copy on the Island, to circulate it freely. It must have been a pleasant visitor in the four or five households which it has entered....

I have no fear of scarcity of fuel or provisions. There are old houses enough to burn. Fresh meat is rather scarce...We have a barrel of pork and a barrel of flour in the house and Father has chickens enough to keep us a good while. There are said to be some families who are a good deal in suffering for whom the Howard Society is on the look out. I gave an old quilted petticoat to the society last week and mother gives very freely to Bridget who has four children to support with only the labor of her hands....

Jan 26. We left the mercury 1 deg. below zero when we went to bed last night and it was at zero when we rose this morning. But it rises rapidly and now at 11 a.m. it is as high as 15. The weather is still and beautiful...

Our little club met last night each with a sonnet on a subject drawn by lot from a basket full. I did the best I could with a very bad subject. Kate and Ellen rather carried the honors away but Mr. Joseph Mitchell was very taking. We kept the house warm all the evening with the mercury steadily at +3. Our crambo playing was rather dull all of us having exhausted ourselves on the sonnets. We seem to have settled ourselves quietly into a tone of resignation in regard to the weather. We know that we cannot "get out" any more than Sterne's starling and we know that 'tis best not to fret. The subject which I have drawn for the next poem is "Sunrise" about which I know very little.

70

Maria Mitchell

Kate and I continue to learn twenty lines of poetry a day and I do not find it unpleasant, tho' the "Deserted Village" is rather monotonous. We hear of no suffering in town for fuel or provisions. I think we could stand a three months siege without much inconvenience as far as the physicals are concerned.

Jan 26. The ice continues and the cold. The weather is beautiful and with the thermometer at 14, I "swept" for an hour and a half last night comfortably....

Jan. 29. Now all is changed, the roads are slushy and the water stands in deep ponds all over the streets. There is a dense fog, very little wind and that from the East, the thermometer above 36.

For about twenty years, the book-loving Maria Mitchell held the position of librarian at Nantucket's Atheneum. Her letter of resignation, although undated, was probably written in 1856. At that time she was still doing her computational work for the Nautical Almanac. Whether she resigned her position owing to the pressure of caring for her mother, or in anticipation of her trip to Europe, she does not say. Whatever the case, the thirty-eight-year-old Maria would start a year of traveling the following March.

Nantucket, Oct. 20 [1856]

Mr. E. G. Kelley

Will you say to the Trustees of the Atheneum that I wish to resign my position as Librarian on the 1st of Nov. up to which time I have supplied the place.

Having had this step in view for some years, I have caused to be prepared a catalogue of the books in the order in which they stand, which may be found in two bound volumes....

Yours,

Maria Mitchell[36]

CHAPTER 4

TRAVELS IN AMERICA

One peculiarity in travelling from East
to West is that you lose the old men.

$\mathcal{I}$N THE SPRING OF 1857 Maria Mitchell traveled to the West and
South of the United States as governess to Prudence Swift,
daughter of H. K. Swift, a banker from Chicago. There are no letters in
the archives that shed any light on how Swift settled upon Mitchell as the
chaperone for his daughter; nor are there details about how they decided
upon the extensive itinerary which eventually included a trip to Europe
on a grand tour.

It is also worth noting that there are no surviving letters from Prudence to Mitchell after the European trip. Maria's diaries contain scant
mention of her traveling companion, yet the arrangement seems to have
been an amicable one. Prone to criticism, Maria voiced no complaints
about her young ward.

Why Mitchell accepted this position with the Swift family is not
entirely clear. For some time, she had wished to go to Europe for a year
and had been saving her money for such a trip. Perhaps the arrangement
was a way for her to do so with minimum expense to herself.

In any event, Mitchell traveled to Chicago in the spring of 1857 to
pick up "Prudie," having first stopped at Niagara Falls and Meadville,
Pennsylvania. With Prudie and her father, Maria went to St. Louis by
train to embark on a Mississippi steamboat for the trip down to New

Maria Mitchell

Orleans. From there, the two ladies traveled alone across the South to Charleston, South Carolina making various stops in between before slowly wending their way northward. They visited Mammoth Cave and then Richmond, Virginia. The diary entries stop just after a visit to the Natural Bridge in Virginia.

BEFORE SHE COULD START on what was to be a year of travel, Mitchell first needed to obtain a leave of absence from her work for the Nautical Almanac. Initially, the Secretary of the Navy would not grant permission for such an extended leave, as a letter to Mitchell from Charles Henry Davis, superintendent of the Almanac, reveals.

> *Cambridge, Oct. 21, 1856*
> *My dear Miss Maria;*
>   *The Secretary does not say you shall <u>not go to Europe</u>; he says you cannot, if you do go, retain your connection with the Almanac. I am very sorry for your disappointment, <u>very</u>; if it depended on me, you should have a suite of apartments with a carriage, a hussier, and a valet de place, waiting your arrival in all the principal cities in Europe.*[1]

Once again Mitchell's network of friends came to her assistance. Joseph Henry, director of the Smithsonian Institution, interceded on her behalf. He alludes to the situation in the postscript of a letter dated February 13, 1857 to William Mitchell:

> *The Secretary of the Navy is in such bad health that I have not been able to have an interview with him and therefore have done nothing relative to the reversal of the opinion as to the visit of your daughter to Europe. I have called twice on the Secretary for this purpose but have not been able to obtain an answer.*[2]

Eventually a compromise was reached. Maria Mitchell was permitted to retain her position with the Almanac while she went on her trip—provided she took her work with her and sent in the results of her calculations as usual.

Mitchell started the diary of her western trip in Erie, Pennsylvania after a brief stop in Meadville, Pennsylvania. She had stopped in Meadville to visit her married sister, Phebe, whose husband, Joshua Kendall, taught at the theological seminary there.

March 2, 1857. I left Meadville this morning at six, on a stage-coach for Erie. I had, early in life, a love for staging, but it is fast dying out. Nine hours over a rough road are enough to root out the most passionate love of that kind. Our stage was well filled, but in spite of the solid base we occasionally found ourselves bumping up against the roof or falling forward upon our opposite neighbors. Stage-coaches are, I believe, always the arena for political debate. Today we were all on one side, all Buchanan men, and yet all anti-slavery. It seemed reasonable, as they said, that the South should cease to push the slave question in regard to Kansas, now that it has elected its President. I do not believe myself that a new slave state can be formed. When I took the ride out to Meadville on the "mud-road," the stage was full of Fremont men, and they seemed to me more able men, though they were no younger and no more cultivated.

Tonight I am at Brown's Hotel in Erie, a little bit homesick, but not more than I expected to be. I knew there was so much to be gone through but I trust that I shall live yet to take care of the old folks at home.[3]

Her visit to Chicago was mentioned in a short newspaper item by the *Democratic Press* of Chicago.

A Distinguished Visitor—Miss Maria Mitchell of Nantucket has been spending several days in Chicago as the guest of Gen. H. K. Swift. Most of our readers will remember that Miss Mitchell is confessedly the most distinguished lady mathematician and astronomer in the U.S., and probably among the fair cultivators of the higher mathematics she has no equal in the world of science, Mrs. Somerville alone excepted.[4]

I believe anyone might travel from Maine to Georgia and be perfectly ignorant of the route, and yet be well taken care of, mainly from good-nature in every one. I found from Nantucket to Chicago more attention than I desired. I had a short seat in one of the cars, through a night. I did not think it large enough for two, and so coiled myself up and went to sleep. There were men standing all around. Once one of them came along and said something about there being room for him on my seat. Another man said, "She's asleep, don't disturb her." I was too selfish to offer the half of a short seat, and too tired to reason about the man's being, possibly, more tired than I.

Maria Mitchell

I was invariably offered the seat near the window that I might lean against the partition when I sat with a gentleman, and one gentleman threw his shawl across my knees to keep me warm (I was suffering with heat at the time!). Another, seeing me approach Chicago alone, warned me to beware of the impositions of hack-drivers; telling me that I must pay two dollars if I did not make a bargain beforehand. I found it true, for I paid one dollar for going only a few steps.

One peculiarity in travelling from East to West is, that you lose the old men. In the cars in New England you see white-headed men, and I kept one in the train up to New York and one of grayish-tinted hair as far as Erie; but after Cleveland, no man was over forty years old.[5]

The prairie does not please me, it is brown and desolate looking and with the broad lake stretching out from it, one might easily imagine himself on Cape Cod looking upon the ocean except that the prairie around Chicago is flatter than any part of Cape Cod. The little towns of Ohio are very pretty and look as if they might be clean....

I have walked about in Chicago. I no longer think it like up-town New York for the streets have been so much raised that it more resembles a city which has been visited by a severe snow storm and whose sidewalks only have been cleared off.... The book stores are beautiful to look at, as pretty as those of New York and Boston but the literature is less solid and every thing seems young, nothing seems profound....

A Chicago musical audience is like everything else in Chicago—youthful, young lads and young misses sit beside you and a man of 40 is an old man. I suspect there is a good deal of surface life in the city and little of quiet home happiness for the men, as money seems to be the great aim of the whole community. There are said to be a good many men worth more than half a million.

March 10, 1857 Chicago....I cannot believe in the beauty of the prairie. Seen as I see them, covered with snow, they are dreary in the extreme....

Our engine was uncoupled and had gone on for half a mile without the cars before the conductor perceived it. The time from Chicago to St. Louis is called 15 1/4 hours, we made it 23. No trains between Hyannis[6] and Chicago are now running at any violent rate, 20 miles in 40 minutes was our fastest and that on a level plain. If the prairie land is good farming land Illinois is destined to be a great state. If its people will think less of the dollar and more of the refinements of social life and the culture of mind it may become the great state of the Union yet.

March 12. Planter's Hotel, St. Louis. So far I am not much interested in St. Louis. It is more finished than Chicago, and the streets are very good....

March 13. St. Louis.... We went upon the levee this morning and for miles the edge was bordered with the pipes of steamboats standing like a picket fence. Then we came to the wholesale streets and saw the immense stores of dry goods and crockery.... Altogether St. Louis is a growing place and the west has a large hand and a strong grasp....

The voyage on the Mississippi River started smoothly enough but immediately encountered difficulty: the steamboat ran aground on a sandbar the first day.

March 19 1 1/2 p.m. We came on board the steamer *Magnolia* this morning in great spirits. We were a little late and Prudie rushed on board as if she had only New Orleans in view. I followed a little more slowly and the Brigadier General came after in a sober and dignified manner. We were scarcely on board when the plank was pulled in and a few more minutes and we were afloat in the Mississippi. The *Magnolia* is a large boat, with a good-natured commander. Fortunately for us almost no passengers, Prudie and myself being the only ladies. We had therefore the whole range of staterooms from which to choose. Each could have a stateroom to herself and we talked in admiration of the pleasant times we should have watching the scenery from the stateroom window or from the saloon, reading, etc.

We started off finely. I who had been used only to the rough waters of the Atlantic coast was surprised at the little jar and the steady gliding motion of the boat. I saw nothing of the mingling of the waters of Missouri and Mississippi of which I had been told, perhaps I needed some one to point out the difference.... We exalted in our majestic march over the waters, I thought it the very perfection of travelling and wished all my family and all my friends were on board....

Here we are, five hours out and fast aground. We were just at dinner, the Captain making himself agreeable, the dinner showing itself good when a peculiar motion of the boat made the Captain heave a sigh, he had been heaving the lead all the morning. "Ah," he said,

Maria Mitchell

"just what I was afraid of, we've got to one of those bad places and we are rubbing the bottom." I asked very innocently if we must wait for the tide and was informed that there was no tide felt in this part of the river.

Prudie turned a little pale and showed a loss of appetite. I was a little bit moved but kept it private and ate on. As soon as dinner we went out to look at the prospect of affairs. We were close on land and could be put ashore at any minute. The Captain had sent around a little boat to sound the water and the report brought back was of shallow water just ahead of us, but more on the right and left. While we stood on the deck a small boat passed us, a sailor very gleefully calling out the soundings as he threw his lead. "Eight and a half, nine." But we are still now at 2 pm high and dry. They are shaking the boat and making efforts to move her. They say if she gets over this there are no more places for her to meet. I asked the Captain of what the bottom is composed and he says of mud, rocks, snags and everything. He is now moving very cautiously and the boat has an unpleasant tremulous motion.

March 20. Mississippi River. Latitude about 38 degrees. We are just where we stopped at noon yesterday. There is no change and of course no event. One of our crew killed a possum yesterday and another boat stopped near us this morning and seems likely to lie as long as we are on the sand bar. We read some from Shakespeare after breakfast this morning and then betook ourselves to the wheel house to look at the scenery again. While there a little colored boy came to us bearing a waiter of oranges and telling us that the captain sent them with his compliments. We ate them greedily because we had nothing else to do. Our boatmen work steadily to try to get us off the bar. They carry ropes to the trees, on the bank in hope of warping the boat around so that she shall lie across the stream. She lies perfectly still and I slept as soundly last night as when at home. I only wished there could be motion enough to keep me awake. The water is not deep enough to sink the boat if there were snags near, but the bottom is said to be soft.

March 21. Still on the sand bar, no hope of getting off. We heard the pilot hail a steamboat which was going up to St. Louis and tell them to send us a lighter and I suppose we must wait for that. The weather is charming as can be. The mornings are cool and the noons are warm. The Captain let us go ashore yesterday but there was so little to be seen after we got there and it was too warm to ascend the hills. We cut our names on the trees, picked up pebbles and came back. We begin to think it a long time to lie here and dread the warm weather that we may find at the South, if we get there at all. It's my private opinion that this great boat won't get off at all, but will lie here until she petrifies. I have made up my mind to be patient for a season but there comes a time when patience is no longer a virtue and I would be glad now if Mr. Swift would take passage in the first steamer that goes by bound for the south.

March 24. We left the steamer *Magnolia* after 4 days and 4 hours upon the sand bar, near Turkey Island. Upon seeing the *Woodruff* approach we left in a little row boat and it seemed at first as if we could not overtake the steamer, but the Captain saw us and slackened his pace. Prudie and I clutched hands in a little terror as our little row boat seemed likely to run under the great steamer but our oarsmen knew their duty and we were safely put on board the *Woodruff*. We found her even more stylish than the *Magnolia,* full of passengers, with a good Captain and good regulations.

Today the river banks began to show signs of verdure. On the west bank we saw a tree in bud and wheat looking very pretty. The banks are very changing and at times we seem to be too much surrounded by land to creep out and we go through some narrow defiles where it seems to me that we had better not meet a boat. This morning we had a heavy clap of thunder. I thought it was some movement of the boat machinery but finding myself whole in the legs and arms I determined to sleep a little longer.

March 25. We stopped at Cairo at about 8 o'clock this morning. Mr. Swift, who went on shore, says it's a good business place and has about 2000 inhabitants....

The travelers observed a partial eclipse of the sun from the steamboat. They used a simple device—a piece of glass covered with soot from a candle flame—as a filter to cut down the light enough to prevent the sun's rays from harming their eyes.

March 26. Yesterday we count as a day of events. It began to look sunny on the banks especially on the Kentucky side and Prudie saw cherry blossoms. We remembered the eclipse and Mr. Swift having brought with him a broken piece of glass from one of the windows of

Maria Mitchell

the *Magnolia,* I smoked it over a piece of candle, which I brought from room No. 22 of the Planter's House, St. Louis, and prepared to observe the eclipse. I expected to see the moon on at 5:20 but as I had no time I could not tell when to look. It was not on at that time by much, but in 10 minutes after, was so far on that I think my time cannot be much wrong. It was a little cloudy, so that we saw the sun only 'all flecked with bars' and caught sight of the phenomenon at intervals. We were at a coal landing at the time and not far from New Madrid....

The 25th was also our first of night steam boating. After passing Cairo the river is considered to be safe for night travel and our boat started on her way about 8 1/2. She had been out only about half an hour when a lady with me playing cards, threw down her hand and rushed with a shriek into her stateroom. I perceived then that there had been a peculiar motion to the boat and that she suddenly stopped. Mr. Swift went forward and ascertained that one of the paddles had caught in a snag but there was no harm done. It made us a little nervous however, still we slept well enough. As I look upon the river I wonder that boats are not continually snagged, little trees are sticking up on all sides and sometimes we seem to go over a meadow and to push away rushes. A yawl, which was sent out to sound yesterday, was snagged by a stump which was high out of water, probably carried on to it by the current. The little boat whirled, round and round and the men were plainly frightened, for they dropped their oars and clutched the sides of the boat. They got control however in a few minutes and had the jeers of the men left on the steamer for their pains....

March 30. We stopped at Natchez before breakfast this morning, and, having half an hour, we took a carriage and rode through the city.... The Captain's daughter assures us that we shall reach New Orleans either tonight or tomorrow morning....

Seven days after boarding the *Woodruff* the party finally reached New Orleans.

March 31. We are at length in New Orleans, and up three flights at the St. Charles, in a dark room, at the pretty price of three dollars a day.... The peculiarities of the city dawn upon me very slowly. I first noticed the showy dress of the children, white waists and fancy skirts—then the turbaned heads of the black women in the streets, and next the bouquet-selling boys with their French phrases.

April 2. New Orleans. This morning we went to the French market. The French character of the city was shown in the narrow streets through which we passed intended only for foot passengers, very narrow. The sidewalks meeting in the middle of the street except for the separation of the gutter. ... The French market was not clean enough to suit us ... We passed through Jackson Square and saw the monument and looked at the flowers, then went on to the Spanish Cathedral. ...

April 3. New Orleans. This morning we went to a slave market. It looked on a first entrance like an Intelligence Office. Men, women and children were seated on long benches, parallel with each other, all rose at our entrance and continued standing while we were there. We were told by the traders to walk up and down the passage between them and talk to them as we liked. As Mr. Swift passed the men, several lifted their hands and said to him, "Here's the boy that will suit you. I can do any kind of work." Some advertised themselves with a good deal of talk. The men talked freely of what they could do and boasted that they could ride a horse bare back, break a horse, drive two in hand, etc.

I perceived that no two spoke to Mr. Swift at once tho' three different persons begged him to buy them. One woman pulled at my shawl and asked me to buy her. I told her I was not a housekeeper. "Not married?" she asked. "No." "Well then get married and buy me and my husband." I told her when I was married I should probably be rich enough to buy them all. There was a girl among them whiter than I, who roused my sympathies very much. I could not speak to her, for the past and the future were too plainly told in her face. I spoke to another, a bright looking girl of 12. "Where were you raised?" "In Kentucky." "And why are you to be sold?" "The trader came to Kentucky and bought me and brought me here." I tho't what right had I to be homesick when that poor girl had left all her kindred for life, without her consent.

I could hold my tongue and look around without much outward show of disgust but to talk pleasantly with the trader I could not consent. ... We have visited several cemeteries, Protestant and Catholic. They do not bury the dead in New Orleans, but place them in vaults above the earth ...

April 6.... The yellow fever is the terror of the land. I did not understand the magnitude of this scourge until I saw how it reached to every heart. The old residents fear it, the new ones tremble before it. Those who have been many years unharmed would give a large sum I was told, to be made sure of safety by a slight attack.

April 7. I happened one day while Miss Swift's hair dresser was brushing her hair to look up from my book and ask this colored woman if she was a slave. "Yes" she said. "And does your master let you earn money by dressing hair for yourself?" "Yes. I earn all I can and I pay her $6 a week." "For which" said I, "you have from her food and your clothing." "Oh no. I have nothing from her. I keep house with my husband, he belongs to another owner who is very kind. My mistress owns me only she promised her father when he died that she would not sell me only to myself." "Then you will buy yourself." "Yes. I am trying to, but if I pay her six dollars a week that is more than half what I earn in the busiest season and she asks $700 and I cannot get so much." I remembered where I was and said nothing. ...

The party spent a week in New Orleans and then resumed their journey. It appears that Mr. Swift bid the women adieu in New Orleans and returned home to Chicago. Mitchell's diary makes no mention of Prudie's father during the remaining two months of their journey; she writes in May of going with Prudie into the Mammoth Cave "without a gentleman as protector," noting that "if two ladies travel alone they must have the courage of men."

Following their week-long hiatus in New Orleans, Mitchell's diary picks up again after they had left Mobile, Alabama, on their way to Georgia.

April 9, 1857. Steamer *St. Charles,* Alabama River. We started yesterday from Mobile at about 5 o'clock. Like all travelling on the river boats we find this still and pleasant. ...

April 11. Slavery. Every one of the South introduces its "peculiar institution" into conversation. They talk, as I expected Southern people of intelligence to talk, they lament the evil or say "it is upon us, what can we do? To give them freedom would be cruel. The Northern agitation exasperates us; we are human and cannot bear such intermeddling with our domestic affairs. If we come north we see vices peculiar to the north, we let them alone." Two old ladies, spinsters apparently of 60 years, opened the subject to me on the boat. They said "only let us alone! We admit that it is the scourge of the land." I find it hard to convince them that the rabid abolitionists are well-meaning people and I say to them, "I do not believe in sending missionaries to the Heathens, perhaps the Heathens would say 'let us alone.'" Southerners fall back upon the Bible at once. There is more of the old-fashioned religion at the South than at the North; that is, they are not intellectual religionists. Their leading denominations are Methodists and Baptists and there is a good deal of the old-fashioned piety. They are shocked by the irreligion of Massachusetts and by Theodore Parker.[7] They read the Bible and can quote it, they are ready with it as argument at every turn. I am of course not used to the weapon and withdraw from the fight....

I say to those to whom I talk that I think the Union cannot last. They say we need each other, that the north needs the south as much as the south the north. Mr. Low thinks more because of the cotton interest. Toleration of the North and kindly feeling towards it are very marked. They wish the northern man and woman would come south and see them as they are.... One argument which three persons have bro't up to me, is the superior condition of the blacks now to what it would have been had their parents remained in Africa and they been children of the soil. I make no answer to this, for if that is the argument, it would be our duty now, to enslave the heathen nations instead of attempting to enlighten them....

So far, I have found it easier to travel without an escort South and West than North; that is, I have more care taken of me. Every one is courteous too in speech; I know they cannot love Massachusetts, but they are so careful not to wound my feelings. They acknowledge it to be the great state in education, they point to a pretty village and say "Almost as neat as a New England Village."

April 15. Savannah. I am disappointed in Savannah. Indeed so far I may say all the Southern cities disappoint me....

April 20. Savannah....Everywhere one thing is admitted, that Massachusetts educates her people better than do the other states. Everywhere Yankee energy is acknowledged, but nowhere is Massachusetts loved out of its own borders and its own people. There seems to be a feeling that its people are assuming, self-righteous and obsti-

Maria Mitchell

nate. I can see the self control practiced in my presence, when the state is named...

Charleston April 23. This place has a look of a city somewhat like Boston in its narrow streets but unlike Boston in being quiet as is all the south.... We left Savannah at about 6 p.m. and in nine hours were at the wharf of Charleston....

The "reading" matter of different parts of the country differs widely. Peculiarities force themselves upon you. At the west, maps of Kansas and Nebraska thrust before your eyes everywhere. At the South Miss Murrays letters are in every book store, tho' you may ask in vain for Mrs. Browning's poems. But everywhere Boston and New York are the standards of excellence. Boston seems to me more talked of at the South than New York. It was evidently the admiration of the South for its education and the horror for its irreligion....

April 28. Charleston. Nothing can exceed the hospitality shown to us. We have several invitations for each day and calls without much limit....

April 29.... Charleston is full of ante-revolution houses and they please me. They were built when there was no hurry. They were built to last. They have lasted and they will last yet for the children of their present possessors....

May 1. It does not follow because the slaves are sleek and fat and really happy, for happy I believe they are, that slavery is not an evil....

May 3. I asked Miss Pinckney today if she remembered George Washington. She and Mrs. Poinsett spoke at once "Oh yes, we were children," said Mrs. Poinsett....

May 9, 1857. Nashville. We left Charleston, its old houses and its good people, on Monday and reached Augusta the same day.... and for the Augusta House, I can only give this advice to its inmates: "Don't examine a black spot upon your pillow case, go to sleep at once and keep asleep if you can." We left Augusta at 5 o'clock at night, travelled all night and reached Atlanta at about four in the morning, took a room and went to sleep.... From Atlanta to Chattanooga where we passed one night and were off at 6 o'clock in the morning for Nashville.... we were tired and hungry when we reached Nashville. The City Hotel is a respectable place....

May 11. Mrs. Fogg of Nashville took us to call on the widow of Pres. Polk. We found her at home, tho' apparently just ready for a walk. She is still in mourning and tells me that she has not travelled fifty miles from home in the last 8 years....

May 14. I was a little doubtful about the propriety of going into the Mammoth Cave without a gentleman as protector, but if two ladies travel alone they must have the courage of men. I called the landlord therefore as soon as I arrived at the Cave house and asked if I could have "Mat" who I had been told is the best guide now that Stephan is so much unwell. The Landlord promised Mat to me for two days. After dinner we made our first attempt.... We clambered over heaps of rocks, we descended ladders, wound through narrow passages, passed along chambers so low that we crouched for the whole length, entered upon lofty halls, ascended ladders, crossed by bridges over a yawning abyss. Every nightmare scene that I had ever dreamed of appeared to be realized. I shuddered several times and was obliged to reason with myself to assure me of safety.... The star chamber is very pleasing. It is one of the elliptical rooms, the ceiling apparently immensely high. When you look up you are for a moment under the impression that it is night, for above you is a dark blue vault studded with stars. It is the reflections from numerous points of your own little light....

May 18. Today we retrace our steps from Nashville to Chattanooga....

May 24. Lynchburg. We left Knoxville without having seen it. We were not well treated at the Lamar House... We left, taking tickets to Lynchburg, upon the supposition that this place was the point from which to start for the Natural Bridge....

May 25. Buchanan, Virginia. We came today from Buford's Depot to this place, eleven miles by stage....

May 27. There is this great difference between Niagara[8] and other wonders of the world, that is you get no idea from descriptions or even from paintings. Of the Mammoth Cave you have a conception from what you are told, of the Natural Bridge you get really a truthful impression from a picture. But Cave and Bridge are in still life, Niagara is all activity and change. No picture gives you the varying form of the water or the change of color; no description conveys to your mind the ceaseless roar. So too the ocean must be unrepresentable to those who have not looked upon it. We went to the Natural Bridge yesterday. We took a carriage to ourselves for the day and were driven at a very moderate pace, for all is moderation here, a distance of about 11 miles....

May 29. Richmond. We came here from Lynchburg in 8 hours on a warm day, for all days now are warm in Virginia. We came to the Exchange Hotel and for 24 hours we remained in quiet to rest... After dark, on one of our stage coach rides, we stopped at Blountville for supper. The Hotel did not promise much from the outside, but we had a good room and sat down to a good table. I looked around with complacency upon its abundance, tasted its good coffee, broke bread and asked for butter. "We have none" said the waiter, "it can't be had in this part of the country." I looked at the milk and I said to the Landlady "Why can't butter be made in this country?" "Oh," said she, "we have it usually but have not now for five days. Blountville is the county town and the lawyers were all here last week and they've eaten up all." "How large is your population?" asked Prudie. "Three hundred," she replied. We looked at each other in amazement. The county town has 300 people, how few people have the other towns!

Mitchell's southern diary ends with the two travelers conversing in the Blountville dining room on that warm May day in 1857. For two months, Maria did not take up her journal again—until late July, when she and Prudie were aboard a ship in the Atlantic Ocean bound for England.

From a letter she wrote later, we know that Maria stopped in Washington, D.C. to visit her brother Henry sometime prior to her transatlantic journey. While in the nation's capital, the thirty-eight-year-old Mitchell also visited the Smithsonian director, Joseph Henry, to obtain letters of introduction from him for her time in Europe. She also undoubtedly thanked him for his assistance in getting permission to take a lengthy leave from the Almanac. As there is no mention of Prudie during this two-month period, we do not know if she stayed somewhere with friends or accompanied Mitchell back to Nantucket.

CHAPTER 5

ENGLAND AND SCOTLAND

There are four great men whose haunts I mean
to seek and on whose footprints I mean to stand:
Newton, Shakespeare, Milton and Johnson.

OLLOWING THEIR TRIP through the South, Maria Mitchell and
Prudie sailed for England aboard the steamer *Arabia*. While in
Great Britain, they visited observatories and universities, and saw the
sights from London to Scotland. The journey was a great success—until
Prudie's father was ruined in the panic of 1857. In the middle of November, Prudie needed to return home, having seen only England and Scotland; Mitchell stayed abroad by herself, completing the tour she had
originally planned. After watching her "young friend" set sail for the
States on November 11, Maria remained in England for a short while,
then went to Paris, and on to Rome for the winter. As she had hoped,
Mitchell stayed for nearly a year in Europe—from the time she sailed
from New York on July 22, 1857 until her return home to Nantucket in
the middle of June 1858.

One of the goals Maria had set for herself was to visit the European
observatories and meet the famous astronomers whom she knew only by

name. In this she was eminently successful. There was hardly an important observatory she did not visit nor an important astronomer she did not meet. Letters of introduction were an absolute necessity to be accepted in Europe, so Mitchell took care to obtain the best possible references. She obtained letters from the Bonds, Joseph Henry, Bache, Edward Everett, and others before she set forth.

She became good friends with Sir George Airy,[1] the Astronomer Royal for England, and her correspondence with the Airy family continued for many years. Mitchell and Prudie stayed overnight with the Airys at the Royal Greenwich Observatory on several occasions. They were guests at Collingwood with Sir John Herschel and his family. Sir John, the only son of Sir William Herschel, the discoverer of Uranus, was the foremost naturalist in England at the time. In Cambridge she was a guest of the Master of Trinity College, William Whewell, an important natural philosopher. He was one of the few persons she met to whom she seems to have taken a dislike. "There was a tone of satire in Dr. Whewell's remarks which I did not think amiable," she wrote in her diary.

Wherever they went the two travelers were welcomed into the homes of famous people. Apparently there was something in the personality of this independent New Englander that struck a pleasant chord in her new British acquaintances. The letters and diary entries indicate that they were not simply being "polite" but developing genuine friendships with her.

THE FOLLOWING LETTER from her friend George P. Bond to Sir George B. Airy is typical of the letters of introduction Maria carried with her in Europe.

Oct. 15, 1856

G. B. Airy, Esq.

I have the honor of introducing to your acquaintance Miss Maria Mitchell, daughter of the Hon. Wm. Mitchell of Nantucket. Miss Mitchell is just setting out on an extensive European tour in the course of which she is desirous of visiting the principal observatories of the old world. To the advantages of a refined intellectual culture she adds an extensive acquaintance with mathematics and astronomy and is herself an experienced and accomplished observer. She will value highly the privilege of a visit to Greenwich without which indeed she would scarcely think the objects of her journey to be obtained.[2]

Before launching on her European trip, Mitchell sought to learn more about the difficulties that two women might face traveling in Europe without a male escort.

Nantucket, Mass. June 28 [1857]

My dear Miss Dix,[3]

I expect to leave for Europe in the *Arabia* on July 22d. Can you do anything for me, in the way so common, of giving good advice. I will try to be more mindful of it than recipients usually are. I expect to travel with a young girl and without gentleman and shall be most grateful for any information as to any peculiar trials which may be thrown our way.[4]

Maria's extensive diaries about the European trip begin on July 25, nearly two months after her final diary entry from Virginia. Her intervening time on Nantucket would have been filled with preparing for her sister Kate's wedding to Owen Dame on July 9, and watching over her mother, who was now quite ill; Maria mentions neither circumstance in her diary. During this time, she probably also tried to do some of the computations for the *Nautical Almanac* so that she would not have as many computations to do while she was in Europe. Her diary[5] starts when they were three days out at sea on the *Arabia*.

Steamer *Arabia*. July 25, 1857

We have been three days on the sea; it is neither as dreadful as I feared, nor as interesting as I hoped, but very monotonous. Eating is the great business of our lives, and even if we feel quite wretched, we go to table.

July 26th. We are now on the "Banks" and have had fog for two or more days and what is worse, for two or more nights. But as there is very little motion to be perceived, we do not feel uneasy and should forget there was danger, were it not for the constant blowing of the "whistle" to warn the fishing vessels.... Our voyage has been good thus far, and if the still weather continues we shall consider ourselves very fortunate.

Monday, July 27th. It is still foggy. Last night between nine and ten o'clock, the boat suddenly stopped. The stewardess told us it was for the purpose of sounding.... We have good fare, but as there is only one cow, our milk is scanty. Those who go up to breakfast early have the milk of the cow; the late risers have preserved milk which is very poor. Just now, lunch time (eight bells) the sun comes out.

Tuesday July 28th. The fog has been less today but the wind has increased; it is cloudy and looks like a storm. Even with two shawls on, I find it too cold to be on deck; the ladies cabin is kept too much shut up.... I considered it a proof that I am a good sailor, when I said "I will go on the house-top and look at the weather this morning" instead of "on deck." Mother Carey's chickens [storm petrels] were seen yesterday and a brig was seen today.

Wednesday July 29. I learn today that we did not stop a few nights since merely to sound, but because we found ourselves close upon a vessel, so close that one could have jumped on board....

Friday, July 31. They say that we shall see the coast of Ireland tomorrow, and every heart rejoices, for tho' the passage has been very fine, we are weary of our close quarters and long for the sight of green fields, and indeed of any object of any kind to look upon....

Saturday Aug. 1. We were called early this morning with the cry of "Land." I sprang up, hurried on my dress and went upon deck; but no land could be seen on account of the fog. After breakfast I went up again and we were close upon it. There lay old Ireland, a mass of black-looking rocks and soon we saw Cape Clear and enjoyed the refreshing sight of green fields.

August 2, 1857. We have landed in Liverpool and are at the Adelphi Hotel. The voyage is over, and altho' a remarkably fine one, no one of the hundred passengers by the steamer *Arabia* would be willing to turn around and go back, even with the assurance of an equally good time.... We passed the Custom House examination with little trouble. My trunk was not opened, as a friend who was known to the Officials mentioned that I was connected with the United States Government. Tobacco and reprints of English works, are the most asked for by the Officer; even the Ladies are asked if they have tobacco....

August 5. I did not send my letter to Mr. [Nathaniel] Hawthorne[6] until yesterday, supposing that he was not in the city. But when Mr. [James] Martineau[7] called, he asked me if I had seen Mr. Hawthorne, said he had not yet left, and that he would be a great loss to Liverpool when he did. I sent my letter at once; from all that I had heard of Mr. Hawthorne's shyness, I thought it doubtful if he would call, and I was therefore much pleased when his card was sent in this morning. He was more chatty than I had expected, not any more diffident and not any less awkward.

He remained about five minutes, during which time he took his hat from the table and put it back once a minute, brushing it each time. The engravings in the books are much like him. He is not handsome, but he looks as the author of his works should look; a little strange and odd, as if not quite of the earth. He has large bluish gray eyes; his hair stands out on each side, so much, that one's thoughts naturally turn to combs and hair brushes and toilette ceremonies as one looks at him.

August 8. We left Liverpool this morning at ten o'clock and taking a slow train, we did not get to Manchester till noon. Our room at the Hotel was secured in advance, and we went off at once to the art exhibition. We spent six hours in the Gallery and I came away having seen only very few; the collection is immense....I could not believe as I stood before these fine paintings that I beheld the original works from which I had seen so many engravings....

August 12. Today we left Worcester and left it with regret, for we had made pleasant friends and the town itself is one of interest. For the first time I felt that I was in a land which had a "past," for I saw a Cathedral; we could not enter it, as it was undergoing repairs.... We visited the China works for which Worcester is celebrated and saw the process of making Chinaware...I looked over the shoulder of a little girl, who painted blue stars on a white cup.... She told me she was 13 years old and earned a shilling a week by working many hours every day....

August 13. I begin already to notice the difference between the home training of English and American children. The former are better bred, especially their table manners are better. In general English children do not come to dinner with the parents; sometimes they come in with the fruit, sometimes they are at table during the first courses and go off when the fruit comes on. The differences seem to be made by the school house of the children. I cannot find that English girls go to school; they seem to have Governesses, the boys go to school....

We are in "lodgings" in London. Last night the mere idea that we were in London, kept us from sleeping. When I did fall asleep, I had a distressing dream that I went home, without seeing the famous city. It is difficult to believe that we are so far away from home.... We find ourselves the only lodgers, with a housekeeper and servant to attend to us; besides a military tailor, never seen, who is the landlord.

We ordered breakfast at 8 1/2; we rose at 9 and ate the cold toast. We pay 2 1/2 guineas a week for three rooms; a handsome parlor with a really elegant sideboard, a handsome piano, out of tune, a lounge and easy chair; thirteen large oil paintings and seven vases of wax flowers, a bedroom containing four mirrors and a dressing room which we turned into another bedroom. Our drawing room looks out upon Cork St. but one window at the corner gives a side glance upon Burlington Gardens, and in the distance sees Regent Street. We came in at 4 p.m. yesterday and ordered tea. The Housekeeper said "Shall I get a half pound of tea, shall I get cream, will you have cake" and when we called for lights she said "Will you have tallow, wax, or those only partly wax." Our tea was brought and when I had made the tea, the rest was put into the side-board, the key of which was put into my hands. We had beefsteak for dinner and the piece left comes on tomorrow for breakfast. We have the use of table linen free of charge, but we pay for the washing. We buy our own soap, we pay extra for the Piano, and besides, the servility of the housekeeper and chamber maid, shows that they expect handsome fees.

We went out as soon as breakfast and we walked for hours on Regent St. looking in at the shop windows. The first view of the street was beautiful, for it was a misty morning and we saw its length fade away, as if it had no end....

August 14. London. We have been out for a drive. We drove for three hours and found no end to the buildings and to London. The driver asked where he should go and I told him to the Strand, for I had heard more of that street than of any other, and then I said "To St. Paul's, one of the palaces and Hyde Park." The Strand seemed to me narrow, St. Paul's seemed large and the Park immense....

August 15. Westminster Abbey interested me more than I had expected. We went into the chapels and admired the sculpture when the guide told us we ought and stopped with interest sometimes over some tomb which he did not point out. I felt a little sad when I came to the tomb of Mary Queen of Scots; it is said that her son removed her body to this place 25 years after her execution. I stepped aside reverently when I found I was standing on the stone which covers the remains of Dr. Johnson. It is cracked across the middle. Garrick lies by the side of Johnson, and I thought at first that Goldsmith lay near, but it is only a monument, the body is interred in Temple Churchyard. You are continually misled in this way, unless you refer at every minute to your guide book; and to go through Europe reading a guide book which you can read at home, seems to be a waste of time.... The base of Newton's monument is of white marble... the remains are not enclosed within. [A]s I stepped aside, I found I had been standing upon a slab marked "Isaac Newton" beneath which the great man's remains lie....

August 17. Today we have been to the far-famed British museum. I carried as "open sesame" a paper given to me by Prof. Henry asking for me special attention from all societies with which the Smithsonian [is] connected.... The art of printing has brought us incalculable blessings, but as I looked at a neat manuscript book by Queen Elizabeth copied from another, as a present to her Father I could not help thinking that it was better than worsted work!... Nothing makes me more conscious that I am on foreign soil than the constant recurrence of associations connected with the executioners block. We hung the Quakers and we burned the witches but we are careful not to remember the localities of our barbarisms. We show instead the Plymouth Rock or the Washington Elm.... Thus far England has impressed me seriously; I cannot see how it has ever earned the name of "merrie" England.

As soon as she had sent around her letters of introduction, Mitchell was involved in a new network of friends and acquaintances who made sure that she was invited to many homes. The following letters are typical.

18 August 1857

Dear Miss Mitchell,

Admiral Smyth[8] joins me in rejoicing to learn that you are so near and we hope you will soon gratify us by a visit here with your companion. I fear you will find London what we call empty, everybody that one cares to see is sure to be in the country and even at the public institutions, the Directors and assistants are mostly away on leave. Mr. and Mrs. Airy, however, have recently returned to the Royal Observatory at

Maria Mitchell

Greenwich from a tour in Scotland and of course you have introduction to them. Indeed, your name alone is sufficient. Pray tell me what your plans are so that we may consider how we can be most use to you and how we can have most of your company. ... A. Smyth[9]

> *Royal Observatory, Greenwich, 1857, August 17*
> *Dear Madam,*
> *I have received your card accompanying Professor Bache's letter. The pressure of business, partly accumulation during my absence and partly incidental to Mondays prevents me from having the pleasure of paying my respects to you today. If circumstances permit I will wait on you tomorrow but as I have on my hands some special references from the Government, I am not certain that I can do so.*
> *In the meantime, permit me to say, first that I shall hope to have the honour of seeing you at this place and shall be glad to learn your convenience of time, secondly that I shall be glad to learn in what way I can assist you either in London or in any other part of Britain.*
> *G. B. Airy*[10]

> *I need not say that we shall be most happy to receive your young companion with whom my daughters will be much interested in becoming acquainted. We hope that you will be able to stay all night with us, as it would not be comfortable for you to return late in the evening to London. ...After our early dinner my daughters will like to show your young friend the prettiest points of view about Greenwich Park and Blackheath.*
> *Richarda Airy*[11]

In addition to general sightseeing and visits to leading observatories, Maria Mitchell made it a priority while in England to visit places associated with famous persons. With Prudie in tow, she set out to find them.

August 19. There are four great men whose haunts I mean to seek and on whose footprints I mean to stand: Newton, Shakespeare, Milton and Johnson. Today I told the driver to take me to St. Martin's St. where the guide book says that Newton lived. He put me down at the Newton Hotel, but I looked in vain to its top, to see anything like an Observatory. I went into a "wine shop" near and asked a girl who was pouring out a dram, in which house Newton lived. She pointed not to the Hotel, but to a house next a church, and said "that is it, don't you see a place on top, that is where he used to study nights." It is a little oblong-shaped observatory, built apparently of wood and much blackened by age....

Next, I told the driver to take me to Fleet St., to Gough Square and to Bolt Court, where Johnson lived and died. Bolt Court lies on Fleet St. and it is but a few steps along a narrow passage to the house, now a Hotel, where Johnson died. But you must walk on farther through the narrow passage, a little fearful to a woman, to see the place where he wrote the dictionary.... a great city always draws to itself the great minds and there Johnson probably found his enjoyment.

August 20. Yesterday we went to London Bridge and stopped for a few minutes at St. Paul's where we mean to go again....I have had exceedingly kind notes from Mr. Airy, Mrs. Airy and Mrs. Admiral Smyth and today Mrs. Airy called and I was at home. She is a quiet woman; no English woman is other than quiet, and very simple in manner. She was also very simply dressed, a common straw bonnet, a dark silk dress and straw colored gloves. I should not have thought to look at her twice, but I felt drawn towards her at once because she was so unpretending. She tells me that Mr. Airy's study is the drawing room and that the children may even dance without annoying him.

Mitchell carried with her to Europe a prized possession: one of the first photographs ever taken of the stars. The use of photography in astronomy was being developed by the Bonds at Harvard, and they were anxious to acquaint other astronomers with this new method of doing astronomy. Mitchell gave the Bonds' photograph to Sir George Airy during her first visit. She then wrote to William Bond, seeking assurance that she had done the right thing.

1 Burlington Gardens, London

My dear Mr. Bond,

I hope I have done all right about the photograph of the stars! I spoke to Mr. Airy about it and he at once desired me to put it into his hands. I felt that I could do no better and today he expressed himself so warmly about it, that I am persuaded I did just the right thing. He said "I am delighted with it and it is a great step. You Americans are much ahead of us in some things, the 'go ahead' is worth something.

Maria Mitchell

I shall write to Mr. Bond, &c." Will you write me a line to say it is all right?...[12]

August 25. Today we took a cab and drove to the National Gallery...August 26. To the Picture Galleries yesterday, to an Iron foundry today...August 27. We took St. Paul's Church today and spent nearly two hours in it....

September 1, 1857. We have just returned from Sydenham and a visit to the Crystal Palace.[13] The trains run very often, from London Bridge to the Palace, the 1st class carriages are very comfortable and the time occupied is only 15 minutes....I was lost in the immensity of the building and separated from my party. Knowing my own inability to find my way to them, I sat down in the Alhambra court and waited to be called for. It was a full hour before Prudie found me. She had judged that I would sit down and wait to be found, but had not, until some fruitless searching in the other parts of the building, remembered my admiration for the Alhambra.

September 3. We have been three weeks in London "out of season" but with plenty of letters; at present we have as many acquaintances as we desire. Last night we were at the opera; to night we go out to dine and tomorrow evening to a dance, the next day to Admiral Smyth's. The opera fatigued me, as music always does. I tired my eyes and ears in the vain effort to appreciate it. Mario was the great star of the evening, but I knew no difference.

One little circumstance showed me how an American with the best intentions may offend against good manners. American-like we had secured good seats, were in good season, and as comfortable as the very narrow seats would permit us to be, before most of the audience arrived. The house filled and we sat at our ease, feeling our importance and quite unconscious that we were guilty of any impropriety. While the curtain was down, I heard a voice behind me say to the gentleman with me, "Is the Lady on your left with you?" "Yes" said Mr. R. "She wears a bonnet which is not according to rule." "Too late now" said Mr. R. "It is my fault" said the attendant, "I ought not to have admitted her, I thought it was a hood." I was really in hopes I should be ordered out, for I was exceedingly fatigued and should have been glad of some fresh air on looking around, I found that only the "pit" wore bonnets.

September 4. We have been to the Bank of England, dragging our already four-weeks-wearied feet through aisles nearly as long as those of the Crystal Palace and up and down narrow stair cases....

September 6. We left London yesterday for Aylesbury. It is by railroad, two hours, like all railroads in England, it runs seemingly through a garden, in many cases flowers are cultivated by the roadside. From Aylesbury to Stone, the residence of Admiral Smyth, is two miles, two miles of stage coach riding. Stage coaches are now very rare in England and I was delighted at the chance for a ride.... We found the stage coach crowded; the driver asked if we were for "St. John's Lodge" and on my replying in the affirmative gave me a note which Mrs. Smyth had written to him, to ask for inside seats. The note had reached him too late, and he said we must go on the outside. He brought a ladder and we got up. For a minute I thought "what a height to fall from" but the afternoon was so lovely that I soon forgot the danger and enjoyed the drive. There were six passengers on top.

Aylesbury is a small town and Stone is a very small village. The driver stopped at what seemed to be a cultivated field and told me that I was at my journeys end. On looking...I saw Mrs. Smyth and her daughter coming towards us. It was a walk of about 1/8 mile to the "Lodge" a pleasant cottage surrounded by a beautiful garden.... At Admiral Smyths I saw some excellent photographs of the moon, but in England they have not yet photographed the stars.

September 7. My confidence in the strength of English government increases. For the upper classes England is a happy country as America is for the lower. England is governed, America is not....

September 10. Today I presented myself at Burlington House, asked for the rooms of the Royal Society[14] and when I found them, I asked to see any relics of Newton which they might have....

September 12, 1857. I took the outside of the stage coach from Windermere to Ambleside, a distance of six miles and well may one do so; he is repaid the trouble of climbing by the succession of magnificent views he comes upon. Windermere lake was on our left and beyond the mountains so mingled with the clouds that I could scarcely tell where mountains ended and cloud began. The coach wound through a highly cultivated region and I felt the truthfulness of the expression "Smiling plains" as applied to England....

Maria Mitchell

September 13. We have spent the Sunday in ascending a Mountain. I have a minute route marked out for me by Professor Airy who has rambled among the lakes and mountains of Cumberland and Westmoreland for months at a time and who says no man lives who knows them better than he does. In accordance with these directions I took a one-horse carriage this morning for Coniston waters in order to ascend the hill called the "Old Man." The waiter at the "Salutation," Ambleside, which we make headquarters, told me I should not succeed if I made the attempt, as the day was not fine, but I have not travelled six months without learning that a waiter is not always disinterested in his advice. When the waiter said it would be raining therefore, I borrowed his umbrella, and we set off in an open carriage. It was a ride of 7 miles, up hill and down dale among hills and around ponds (lakes they call them), in the midst of rich lands and pretty mansions, with castles occasionally and once a ruin.

Arrived at Coniston Hotel, the waiter said the same that the waiter had said at the "Salutation." "It is too cloudy to ascend the Old Man." But as soon as he found that if we did not ascend we did not remain at Coniston, it cleared off amazingly fast to the waiters eyes, and the ponies were ordered. I thought at first of walking up, but having a value for my feet and not liking to misuse them, I mounted a pony and walked him rather than walk myself. ...

September 14. ... We determined to take a carriage which could be an open or closed one as we chose, and to set off for a ride of some seven or eight miles, to the Langdales, Great and Little, to Grasmere and back to Rydal Mt. ... This guide said patronizingly to us, "You Americans speak very good English, better than the French or Germans." I laughed to think that a man who never in his life spoke the language that Addison wrote, whether it be English or not, should compliment me on my language. He himself did not understand when I spoke of a storm, he called it "stum" and a hut he called "hoot." ... Grasmere is a sweet village and we stopped to look at Wordsworth's tomb in the church yard. ... If you suggest it to the driver, he will stop again and show you a wretched little cottage, just aside from the road where Wordsworth and Coleridge once lived together. ...

Sept. 25. We reached Edinburgh between ten and eleven last night; the hour at which we reached Savannah when travelling in the slave states. ...

Sept. 27. Prof. [William Piazzi] Smyth and his wife called on me today....I asked of course about the Edinburgh Observatory. Prof. Smyth tells me that it is upon a very small scale. Herr Struve says that an observatory should be simply a case to hold instruments; the Edinburgh Observatory is a Grecian temple....

Sept. 29. I dined last night at Prof. Smyth's at 6 o'clock....They also told anecdotes of Dr. Wm. Keith Murray, an amateur astronomer, who amuses himself by showing the celestial objects to the common people and even goes so far as to put up printed placards inviting the people to come in a certain evening and see certain phenomena....The good science comes of course mainly from the established observatories, but the amateurs have an enthusiasm which is charming, and certainly the good they do in uplifting the masses must be great.

Sept. 30. Yesterday, being out for a drive, the coachman told us that Rosslyn Chapel was only an hour off so we told him to drive to that place. By his driving it was two hours off and we reached it so late that we had little time for seeing it. The ruins of the chapel are beautiful. so are all the ruined chapels we have seen....

October 1. No place that I have yet seen in Europe has interested me like Abbotsford; no palace has held such royalty. I sat down in the chair which Sir Walter Scott had occupied, and I almost felt his presence; his power I had known nearly all my life....It was rather a sad visit as all such visits must be and the clouds came up and the wind howled when we came out and we climbed the ascent to the road where we had left the carriage, I had half a mind to sit down and cry, perhaps because the "wizard" was dead, perhaps because I was a little homesick.

October 1. (#2) We visited Melrose Abbey by daylight and of course we felt obliged to visit it by moonlight, as our guide book quoted the passage by Sir Walter Scott

> *If thou wouldst view fair Melrose right*
> *Go visit it by pale moonlight*

and yet Sir Walter admits that he never went by moonlight because he thought he could see just as well by daylight! It's a fine old ruin; I thought Rosslyn beautiful, Melrose is magnificent! The pillars are immense; one aisle is perfect still and is beautiful from its fine curves....

Oct. 2 We left Edinburgh yesterday for Melrose and Dryburgh Abbey, and returned today....

Oct. 4. I met last night at the house of Professor Smyth, a little party of very cultivated people. They were at tea when I entered; I was announced by the servant and Mrs. Smyth rose to receive me....I was soon seated near an old gentleman, Dr. Maclaurin, as I afterwards learned, the author of the article "America" in the *Encyclopedia Brittanica.* He entered into conversation with me at once and Robert Chambers[15] who sat near, joined in it....Robert Chambers, the author of the "Vestiges of Creation" is about 50 years old; perhaps more; a noble looking man, with some good looking young ladies his daughters....

Sir Wm. Hamilton[16] the Astronomer Royal for Ireland, is no observer but a most excellent mathematician. When he was at one time giving a lecture on "Quaternions," a subject so difficult that no one understood him, he told in such an interesting way the difficulties that he encountered, that, when he came to describe the final triumph, the audience clapped their hands with enthusiasm, "As they would have clapped Charles Summer for an Abolition lecture" said Prof. Smyth.

October 14, 1857. It is not difficult to find the house[17] where Shakespeare was born, for there is a sign upon it, telling you twice of the fact, and even the little children in the streets know it...I found myself looking into the children's eyes to see if they appeared to be conscious of their noble birth, in being townspeople of the world's wonder; and they are fine looking children....In the church we read the Epitaph so frequently quoted.

October 16th. Yesterday, Mrs. Flowers took us in her pony basket to Hampton...

October 16, 1857. Anne Hathaway's cottage stands as it stood in Shakespeare's days. The entrance of the middle house, for the low cottage seems to be made up of three houses, is the same as it was when Shakespeare visited it, a young lover....

We were fortunate in being in Warwick on market day. An English town is peculiarly English at such a time. The irregular bit of land called the "square" fills up early in the morning with market wagons, whose horses are taken out; when the wagons at once become shops, not only for farm produce but for all cheap articles, toys, flowers and dry goods. I have never seen buyers but there are always groups of common people around, running from one wagon to another, gossiping and laughing at Punch who is always of an English crowd. Today the townspeople roasted an ox. First, they built a fireplace on the square then they put in a long grate and made a fire; then the ox was put upon a spit before it, raised high enough for a man at each end, to turn it without stooping; then a pan was placed underneath to catch the gravy. It is a custom observed twice during the year, and is probably made to "pay" as they sell the meat in slices....

[N 42] Oct. 20, 1857

My dear Miss Mitchell,

I hoped to find you at home, and settle in a few minutes what I have come for. We hope that you and Miss Swift will come to us tomorrow, to stay a few days. M. de Struve[18] is with us from Pulkova and we wish you so much to come and meet him. He also would like particularly to meet you.... Though I am sorry for the interruption of your journey, yet I was wishing you could meet Struve. He has one of his sons with him....

Richarda Airy[19]

October 22, 1857. We have just returned from the fourth visit to Greenwich, like the others, twenty four hours in length. We go again tomorrow to meet the Sabines. Herr Struve, the Director of the Pulkova Observatory is at Greenwich with his son Karl. The old gentleman is a magnificent looking fellow; very large and well proportioned; his great head is covered with white hair; his features are regular and handsome. When he is introduced to any one, he thrusts both hands into the pockets of his pantaloons and bows. I found that the son considered this position of the hands particularly English. However, the old gentleman did me the honor to shake hands with me and when I told him that I brought a letter to him from a friend in America, he said "It is quite unnecessary, I know you without."* He speaks English very well; the son speaks it very badly.

Herr Struve's mission in England is to see if he can correct the trigonometrical surveys[20] of the two countries. It is quite singular that

---

*If "Herr Struve" was not simply being polite, both his statement and Mrs. Airy's letter suggesting that the renowned Russian especially wanted to meet Mitchell, indicate that the American astronomer was widely known in Europe, even prior to her visit.

he should visit England for this purpose so soon after Russia and England were at war; one of his sons was an army surgeon in the Crimea. ... Mr. Airy says its a very good thing to have got up a reputation for being ill-natured as he has. He says the consequence is "no one has things just as he wants them and then if he happens to do a good-natured thing he gets immense credit for it."

Five visitors remained all night at the Observatory. I slept in a little round room and Prudie slept in another at the top of the little jutting out curved building. Mrs. Airy said "Mr. Airy got permission of the Board of Visitors, to fit up some of the rooms as lodging rooms." Mr. Airy said "My dear love, I did as I always do; I fitted the rooms first and then I reported to the Board that I had done it."

October 23. Another dinner party at the observatory consisting of the Struves, General [Edward][21] and Mrs. Sabine, Prof. [Baden][22] and Mrs. Powell, Mr. Main and ourselves, more guests coming to tea. Mrs. Airy told me that she should arrange the order of the guests at table to please herself; that, properly all the married ladies should precede me, but that I was really to go out first, with Mr. Airy.* To effect this, however, she must explain it to Mrs. General Sabine, the lady of highest rank. So we went out, Prof. Airy and myself, Prof. Powell and Mrs. Sabine, General Sabine and Mrs. Powell, Charles Struve and Prudie, Mr. Main, Mrs. Airy and Mr. Struve.

General Sabine is a small man, gray haired, sharp featured, about 70 years old. He smiles very readily and is chatty and sociable at once. He speaks with more quickness and ease than most of the Englishmen I have met. Mrs. Sabine is short, plain, very agreeable and not a bit of a blue stocking. Prof. Powell is fat and lazy looking, Mrs. Powell was over-dressed. Mrs. Sabine under-dressed. General Sabine not knowing it was an "occasion" was in an old coat. ... Mrs. Airy looked at me significantly when Mr. Airy forgot to carve, or helped to pudding too hastily. ... The dinner was soup, fish, chicken and saddle of mutton, side dishes were beef Oliver, i.e. rolls of fried and stewed beef, apple tart, and plum pudding and jellies and tarts next, bread and cheese next, pears and grapes next, and then the ladies left the room and the gentlemen remain over their wine, but not long, for Mr. Airy does

---

*Leading such a distinguished group of guests in to dinner on the arm of the Astronomer Royal of England must have been one of the high moments of Mitchell's stay in England. The usual protocol called for single women to be at the end of a line; this would have put Maria behind everyone, had Mrs. Airy not decided that she should go in on the arm of the Astronomer Royal.

not like it and Struve hates it. Then, before tea, others dropped in from the neighborhood, and the tea was served in the drawing room, handed around informally, the first come, first served.

The panic of 1857 began to impinge on the travels of the feted astronomer and her young companion. When Prudie's father went bankrupt, Mitchell was forced to navigate a new course of action amidst this unexpected turn of fortune. Should Maria immediately sail back home with Prudie, or should the two part company at this unforeseen juncture?

A letter to her father reveals some of Maria's thoughts about her present circumstances and options, including her clear desire to continue her travels. At the same time, she also expresses her abiding concern that her family may need her support in caring for her ailing mother.

Oct 30.

[Letter to her father]

We have just got a letter from Guion of Liverpool, saying he knows a family about to sail for America on the 11th in the Atlantic and I shall order a passage at once for Prudie and unless you say come, I shall stay. But I hope if there is any reason that I should come, your next letter will say so. I shall retain enough of the Swift money to bring me home and shall simply say to him that I have a balance in my hands. Legally, I suppose I could have held the 1000 dollars which I drew from the Bank, and morally I had a right to one half as it was given for our joint expenses.

I hope you will write to me on this hand and don't worry about me as long as I am well. I shall at once look out for a party to join for Paris and Rome. If my own family are safe and you don't need me, it would be folly to turn back when it is only a week's journey to Rome. I shall not go alone to Paris, I hope I may go with English people, because I am sure of their refinement. If I have to wait a month it will be nothing, as I can take a room high up and do my computing. The newspapers are more cheerful about New York affairs. I shall try to see Paris, Rome and Berlin, but not St. Petersburg, indeed, having seen Struve it is not so important. Don't worry. I may come on the next steamer, even if I don't come with Prudie.

[no signature]

As it turned out, Maria did procure passage for Prudie on the steamer from Liverpool on November 11, while she remained in Europe

Maria Mitchell

until the next June. But before Prudie set sail for America, Maria arranged a visit for the two of them to Cambridge University.

November 1. Our first knowledge of Cambridge was the entrance to Trinity College and the Masters Lodge. Dr. [William] Whewell[23] the Master is a stately man of about 50, noble in figure, and courteous in manner, with the appearance of patronage in his manner, so common among the English. He asked us at once to lunch and we sat down to cold fowl and tongue. The "Master of Trinity" chatted freely with Mrs. Airy and occasionally turned to me, but I was not pleased when at one of these times he said "'go the whole hog' as you say in America." After lunch we went to the Observatory....

At 6 1/2 we went again to the Lodge to dinner. We were a little late and the servant was in a great hurry to announce us, but I made him wait till my gloves were on, tho' not buttoned. He announced us with a loud voice and Dr. Whewell came forward to receive us. The drawing room had a group of guests, some standing, some sitting, some of whom spoke to me at once without a separate introduction. Dinner was soon announced and I had the honor of being handed down by the Master. It took a little time for him to arrange the guests, for they are very particular to place a lady and gentleman alternately and Mrs. Challis exclaimed when her husband attempted to sit near her and it was found the chairs were not quite regularly placed and the like, but all being arranged, the Master rushes through a grace with American precipitancy and we seated ourselves.

Dr. Whewell spoke to me of the American poets and to my amazement declared Emerson to be a copyist of Carlyle in his prose and of Tennyson in his poems. He said Longfellow was the most popular poet in the English language for he was more easily understood than Tennyson. He was quite shocked at my preferring Mrs. Browning to Mrs. Hemans and said she was so coarse in *Aurora Leigh* as to be disgusting. I told him we had outgrown Mrs. Hemans, and he asked me if we had outgrown Homer, to which I replied that they were not similar cases.

I had been told that the English did not consider Irving as an American, but I was not prepared to hear the question of a lady, "Do you consider Irving as belonging to your country?" "Certainly," I replied, "he was born and brought up there." "Yes, but his father was born in Scotland." "All our grandfathers were born in England or Scotland," I replied. Altogether there was a tone of satire in Dr. Whewell's remarks which I did not think amiable.

After dinner more guests came, and more. [W]e had coffee as soon as dinner, in a little room and tea later in the same room. The guests going in as they chose. Prof. [Adam] Sedgwick[24] came early, an old man of 74, already a little shattered and subject to giddiness. He is said to be very fond even now of young ladies and when younger made some heartaches, for he could not give up his Fellowship and leave Cambridge for a wife, which to me is very unmanly. He is considered the greatest geologist in England and of course they would say in the world, but to me there was something unmanly in his appearance....

There was, as there is very commonly in English society, some dresses too low for my taste, and the wine drinking was universal so that I had to make a special point of getting a glass of water and was afraid I might drink all there was on the table. I think no one but Prudie and myself took a drop. The servants stood in array just outside of the dining room door as we entered all in livery, one in red vest, red breeches, white stockings and drab coat. Before the dessert came on, saucers were placed before each guest and a little rose water dipped from a silver basin into them, and then each guest washed his face, thoroughly dipping his napkin into the same. The gentleman next me, Prof. [Robert] Willis,[25] told me that it was custom peculiar to Cambridge and dating from its earliest times. The finger bowls came on with the fruit as usual, I saw that the dinner was ordered by Dr. Whewell but that he knew little about it, for he admitted that he didn't know what the dishes were....

Nov. 1. The Cambridge Observatory has the usual number of meridian instruments, a mural circle and a transit, but it has besides a good equatorial of 20 feet focal length, mounted in the English way...While I was looking at the instruments, Mrs. Airy came in to the equatorial house, bringing Mr. [John Couch] Adams[26] (the rival of Leverrier), another short man, but bright looking, dark hair and eyes and again the thick voice, this time with a nasal twang. Mr. Adams is a merry little man, loves a game with children and is a favorite with young ladies.

There is no doubt that the Airys were a great help to Maria Mitchell on her European trip. Moreover, the friendship between them lasted for many years. While his daughter was still in England, William Mitchell wrote to the Airys, expressing his thanks for their assistance. Sir George replied.

Maria Mitchell

1857, November 13.

William Mitchell, Esq.

It has been a great pleasure not only to myself, but also to Mrs. Airy and other members of my family, to make the acquaintance of Miss Mitchell; and a great pleasure to have rendered her any petty services; and now it is a matter of deep gratification to receive your kind expression of the sense in which you have received the trifle assistance that we could give Miss Mitchell.[27]

As previously noted, Prudie Swift returned home in mid-November, after being in Europe nearly four months. There is no further mention of Prudie in the archives, except a letter in 1862 to Maria Mitchell from Mrs. Airy in which she writes:

I have often laughed at your tribulation in having her for a travelling companion when your eyes became open to the attraction which there was about her and how startled you were when she admired in her turn some youth's eyes! I hope she is happy in her married life. I can hardly fancy her with the cares of a mother upon her.[28]

The day after Prudie left England, Mitchell was in London, trying to make final arrangements for her visit to Paris.

London Nov 12 [1857]

Prof. Rogers,

I returned to town to day, having been to Liverpool to see my young friend set sail, which she did only yesterday—and therefore with many thanks I can decline your kind offer. I leave town again tomorrow for a short visit and shall probably be here on Monday–Tuesday and if you are not too much engaged I should be happy to have a call from you. I wait only a suitable escort to proceed to Paris—If you know of any one about to go, who would be willing to protect a lady and one trunk, I would be glad if you would give the information.[29]

Nov. 26, 1857

My dear Miss Mitchell,

...believe that you take away with you my sincere attachment and truest wishes for your health and welfare and that you may have an enjoyable and a useful journey.

Yours most truly,

Richarda Airy

P.S. Shall Mr. Airy write a letter to M. Leverrier [Paris Observa-
tory director] to introduce you? I forgot if you said you had any letters to
him. Mr. Airy would write direct to Leverrier, himself at Paris by post.[30]

[Calling Card]
Miss Mitchell and Miss Swift
Mrs. Baden Powell at Home
Wednesday Nov 25 [1857] 9 o'clock
6 Stanhope Street, Hyde Park Gardens[31]

November 26th. A few days ago, I received a card "Mrs. Baden
Powell at Home Nov. 25th." Of course I did not know if it was a tea-
party, a wedding, or a soiree, so I appealed to Mrs. Airy. She said "It's
a London rout, I never went to one, but you'll find a crowd, and a
good many interesting people."

I took a cab, and went at nine o'clock. The servant who opened the
door passed me to another who showed me the cloak-room. The girl
who took my shawl numbered it and gave me a ticket, as they would
at a public exhibition. Then she pointed to the other end of the room,
and there I saw a table with tea and coffee. I took a cup of coffee,
and then the servant asked my name, yelled (shrieked) it up the stairs
to another, and he announced it at the drawing room door just as I
entered.

Mrs. Powell and the professor were of course standing near, and
Mrs. Admiral Smyth just behind. To my delight, I met four English
persons whom I knew and also Prof. Henry B. Rogers who is a great
party man.

People kept coming until the room was quite full. I was very glad to
be introduced to Professor Stokes, who is called the best mathematician in England, and is a friend of Adams. He is very handsome—
almost all Englishmen are handsome, because they look healthy; but
Professor Stokes has fine black eyes and dark hair and good features.
He looks very young and innocent. We spoke of Prof. Peirce,[32] said he
had heard "Adams speak of him, not very pleasantly." It is evident
that Prof. Peirce has made enemies of himself rather than friends on
this side.

Stokes is connected with Cambridge, but lives in London, just as
Professor Powell is connected with Oxford, but also lives in London.
Several gentlemen spoke to me without a special introduction—one

Maria Mitchell

told me his name was Dr. Toynbee and he was a great admirer of Emerson—the first case of the sort I have met. Dr. Toynbee is a young man not over thirty, full of enthusiasm and progress, like an American. He really seemed to me all alive, and is either a genius or crazy—the shade between is so delicate that I can't always tell to which a person belongs! I asked him if [Charles] Babbage[33] was in the room, and he said, "not yet," so I hoped he would come.

He told me that a fine looking, white headed, good featured old man was Roget, of the 'Thesaurus;' and another old man in the corner was Dr. [Neil] Arnott,[34] of the 'Elements of Physics.' I had supposed he was dead long ago...Afterwards I was introduced to him. He is an old man, but not much over sixty; his hair is white, but he is full of vigor, short and stout, like almost all Englishmen and Englishwomen....

I asked him if Babbage was in the room, and he too said, "Not yet." Dr. Arnott asked me if I wore as many stockings when I was observing as the Herschels—he said Sir William put on twelve pairs and Caroline fourteen!

I stayed until eleven o'clock, then I said 'Good-by,' and just as I stepped upon the threshold of the drawing room to go out, a broad old man stepped upon it, and the servant announced 'Mr. Babbage,' and of course that glimpse was all I shall ever have!

During her four-month stay in England in 1857, Maria Mitchell wrote many letters to keep her family informed about her activities overseas. A few of her more noteworthy comments are presented here.

London, September 1, 1857.

My dear Phebe,

...Mr. Ransom is here now and I have asked him to take me and Prudie to the Theatre tomorrow night. We shall hear Mario and I don't care a bit about it. What a pity that I have to hear him. I remember one night I heard Pawdi....

I consider the future is doubtful about my travels that I am very concerned in order to be able to fall back on my own resources at any moment, if I choose. Nobody could have done better than Prudie has since we have been in England, but she thinks her Father and Brother may come at once so there will be a little "talk" if they attempt any interference or expect me to travel with them.

We take French lessons of Madame de Laplace, who comes to our room at 6 1/2 whenever we want her and stays an hour for 96 cents. She talks no English, so I have to use my miserable French. She corrects me constantly in my grammar, almost never in my pronunciation and understands all that I say of course....

Mrs. Airy says that the honor of a knighthood has twice been offered to Mr. Airy, that he declines it because he can't afford to live in any better style, that "as Lady Airy, she must not ride in an omnibus, and that is so economical."

Edinburgh, Sept. 30.

My dear Father,

...Nothing is more provoking than the ignorance of the English about Americans. I really doubt if they would know who Benjamin Franklin was, if I should speak of him. They are really too full of their own greatness to perceive that there is another great nation. Mr. Airy understands that the Bonds are astronomers, but I dare say Mrs. Prof. Smyth never heard of them, tho' of course Prof. Smyth has the transactions. And yet, no observatory has such instruments as Harvard....

October 8. Thursday eve, Edinburgh.

My dear Father,

We left on Tuesday the 6th for the Lakes of Scotland, waiting till 12 o'clock for the mail to come in from London....I shall probably not see Mrs. Somerville as she is in Algiers unless I should think it <u>politic</u> to go a very long journey....

I shall not see anywhere, half that I ought, as a whole year would not be too much for Great Britain and I am already thinking what I will do, when I come <u>again</u>.

I want to know a few things from thee. When I go into a new country and the currency is changed is it better for me to begin a new account in that currency or to keep to the pounds and shillings....I am likely to have a courier recommended to me by the Lassalls...and I have written to engage him for the 1st of Nov. I shall draw some money as soon as I get to London as I need everything. It is very cold here, the first cold I have known since last March you know....

Maria Mitchell

Nov. 14. Collingwood

My dear Father

This is Sir John Herschel's place. I came last night just at dusk, and was very warmly welcomed, first by Sir John and next by Lady Herschel. Sir John is really an old man, old of his age 66, as old as Mr. Bond, whom he resembles. I found a fire awaiting me in my room, and a cup of tea and crackers were at once sent up....I had expected to find Sir John a despot, like Mr. Airy and Dr. Whewell, but to my surprise he is gentle, and very simple, and tells funny little anecdotes (so do Airy and Whewell) and is one of the domestic circle, joins in all the chit-chat....But I am continually mortified by anecdotes that I hear of the "pushing" of Americans....

My Dear Phebe,

...When Mrs. Airy, Christabel and I arrived at Dr. Whewell's we were of course tired, just from the cars. He received us in his drawing room and even Mrs. Airy stood for some time, until he asked us to sit. We all dropped into chairs at once. These things are really ludicrous to me. Everybody laughs at my strictures upon Whewell and they all say that he is not tolerated by many people on account of this imperious manner. I call it want of good manners, I told Lady Herschel that I was half tempted to fight a battle with him, he was so severe upon American writers....

Just as I was coming away [from Collingwood], Sir John bustled up to me with a sheet of paper, saying he thought I would like some of his Aunt's[35] handwriting and he would give it to me....I am hoping to get to Paris next week. Nov 23rd about. I shall wait no longer for escort. I have had just what I intended in England as to society.

CHAPTER 6

FRANCE AND ITALY

I am in Rome!

ROM LONDON, Maria Mitchell headed to Paris in late November of 1857. Anticipating further memorable visits on the European continent, she was proudly carrying with her letters of introduction from the new friends she had made among British scientists.

After more than a month in Paris, Mitchell traveled to Rome with the Hawthorne family, on whom she had called in Liverpool. During her eventful three-month stay in Rome, Maria lived near the Hawthornes and they were often together on sightseeing trips.

Mitchell left Rome in the middle of April and traveled back to England, stopping along the way in Florence, Vienna and Berlin. In each city she met with well-known astronomers and other prominent personalities. For Maria, the most memorable meeting was with Mary Somerville[1] in Florence. For years, Mitchell had admired this famous self-taught scientist; their visit in Italy made a deep and lasting impression on Maria. Many of Mitchell's later lectures are filled with references to this meeting, and during her years of teaching at Vassar, Maria kept a bust of Mary Somerville in her study.

Mitchell's diary[2] commences as she prepares to cross the English Channel in late 1857.

November 30th. France did not burst upon me suddenly as I had hoped. We[3] took the route from Folkestone to Boulogne, and when

Maria Mitchell

we arrived in Folkestone the sea was awfully rough, so we decided to stay all night. Then we must stay all day, for there was no boat.... We took the steamboat at Folkestone at six o'clock for Boulogne and had a rough passage, a good deal more rolling than I had on the Atlantic. Then we thought it best to stay at Boulogne till morning. We landed in the dark, and as I had been a good deal sick, I forgot that I was in "la belle France" till the chatter of foreign tongues in the wharf, roused me.

...But we came into Paris in the dark. I came to the Boarding School, and was met by servants who chattered away like parrots but they understood "*eau chaud*" [hot water] and "*feu*" [fire], two very important considerations, for France seems to me the coldest country I ever knew....

I went to breakfast this morning. Two long tables of pretty girls, some American, some English and the others French, all between twelve and sixteen, and all pretty. The coffee was excellent. The milk was dipped with a ladle out of a pewter bowl as large as the largest punch bowl I ever saw. Bread and butter were all.

The lady to whom the Herschels obtained a letter is Mrs. Power; she is sister to Francis Horner[4] and aunt to Lady Lyell.[5] She tells me to stay where I am even if I think it high, as the boarding houses of Paris are not reputable. Here she says I am safe, but that at a boarding house I must not speak to any one. She says I am fortunate in having lost the young lady, that she would make improper acquaintances without knowing it. That I am not, if I keep among scientific people, in so much danger, but that the caution cannot be too great, and she tells me to trust nobody. She says I must make a written agreement with Madam Coulon, my landlady, and to look out for impositions everywhere.

December 2nd. I spent all of yesterday in seeing the outside of Paris. First in a carriage, then on foot, then in carriage again; from ten in the morning till ten at night I was sightseeing. It is really a magnificent city. Edinburgh is picturesque but Paris is splendid. The streets like the Champs Elysees and Rue Rivoli are beautiful now, and in summer must be charming....

December 3rd. No Frenchman or woman makes way for you in the street, it is not their business, you must move away from the loaf of bread on the man's head, a yard or two long, or it will hit yours as it passes.... Still the French have a charm, especially those of the lower classes, in their good nature....

December 7th. In Paris you have room to look at things. In London you have not. You can, from London Bridge, have a little view of St. Paul's but where anyone who sketched it has stood, it is not easy to see. In Paris, space is given for seeing. You can admire the Church of the Madeleine from all around. So, at Versailles, you see the palace from the magnificent grounds as a whole. A building in London is seen by corners.

December 8th, 1857. I have been more than a week in Paris, and have seen nothing, because there is so much to see....I went into Church St. Eustace, and also into Notre Dame....Coming out of Notre Dame, Mr. L. asked me if I would like to stop in at "La Morgue." I had a vague idea that it was a place where dead people were placed, and I said "yes." It is a space, enclosed by iron fence within which are inclined [planes] on which persons who are found dead are placed for the purpose of permitting their friends to recognize them. There was an immense crowd looking in, and I pushed through supposing I should see only the [planes].

To my horror I saw a young woman, and I turned away with a shudder. It must have been a person in full vigor, young and handsome, her face was full of color, and there was no appearance of death. There was drapery thrown around her. I turned away at once, but I shall never lose the impression, it haunted me at night.

On Wednesday, December 9, Mitchell paid her first visit to Urbain Leverrier,[6] director of the Paris Observatory. A decade earlier, both Mitchell and Leverrier had the rare distinction of being recipients of royal medals for their astronomical discoveries.

December 9th. I sent my letters to Mons. and Madame Leverrier and according to what I was told of the etiquette of Paris, I wrote a note and asked when I might call. They replied at once, and I suppose called, but that I don't know, and they gave me eight o'clock in the evening, therefore. I took a cab and went. It is an immense distance from Rue Tronchet where my rooms are, but I arrived, and then it was an immense distance to Madame's rooms for the observatory is very extensive.... When I entered, three gentlemen and one lady bowed, and two children stopped their noise and looked at me. As I had among other charges made to me, been told not to offer to shake hands, I kept my hand to myself. Of course the lady was Madame Leverrier, and I soon discovered which was Leverrier by the red ribbon he wore, which I know meant something, I don't know what.

Maria Mitchell

The Leverriers speak English about as well as I do French and we had a very awkward time of it. He spoke to me a little and then talked wholly to one of the other gentlemen. Madame was very chatty. ... I don't believe I shall be very intimate there.

Dec. 14th. I am beginning to know something of French ways.

1st. The French keep no fires. They have a little fireplace, they burn a little wood, a little coal but they really do not keep a warm room. If you call on a lady in the morning, she receives you in a cold room. She is wrapped in a shawl, and shivering, you are wrapped in a cloak and shivering. ...

2nd. Wood is exceedingly dear. Accustomed as I have been to a great fire, I built one in my rooms of the American kind the first day I took rooms in Paris. It cost me more than forty cents that day. ...

Despite her "awkward" and inauspicious introduction to the Leverriers, Mitchell was soon invited back. On December 14, the director's calling card was delivered, bearing a message in slightly awkward but more than passable English:

> *M. LeVerrier presents his hommage to Miss Mitchell, gives her the assurance she can visit the observatory when she pleases. Begs her to be so kind to come and drink tea this evening, he would be happy to make her himself acquainted with some instruments and particular dispositions, then he desires to present some of his assistants to Miss Mitchell, his astronomers would be most happy to be acquainted with her.*

December 15. I went to Leverrier's again last evening by special invitation. Four gentlemen and three ladies received me, all standing and bowing without speaking. Monsieur was, however, more sociable than before, and yelled out to me in French as though I were deaf. ... About ten o'clock M. Leverrier asked me to go into the observatory, which connects with the dwelling. ... With his bad English and my bad French we talked but little. ...

After my walk in the observatory I came back to the drawing room and they gave me a cup of tea. I took two swallows and I thought it was best to take no more if I was to get home straight. It tasted like rum and I suppose had brandy in it. There was no taste of tea. I came back in a cab, for miles alone, but had no fear, for I know there were soldiers at every turn. The city is as quiet as Nantucket.

December 17th.... I have met with one instance of French trickery but only one. That was, however, glaring and provoking and it came from women, and from women holding a most responsible position. It was such as I do not believe could have happened in America. The women were the proprietors of a young ladies boarding school, of which I was parlor boarded. They were men in character, and almost men in appearance, hard, selfish, and I believe unprincipled. Always smiling politely upon me, I yet felt that I hated them. There was no very great cruelty towards the young girls, but I was hungry all the time, though I presumed to "ask for more" at the table. The food was not bad, but the bread was sour...I was afraid from my eagerness to be helped, that I should become vulgar in my manners, for hunger forgets the lessons of etiquette.

December 18th. I have today been to Père la Chaise.... I came upon the tomb of the Comptesse Rumford by accident....For that of [noted French astronomer] Laplace I sought. It is an obelisk-shaped tomb, with an urn on the top. On the front are his name and titles, on the sides the title of his works, "Systemme du Monde," "Proba-bilities," "Mechanique Celeste," on the back those figures. I suppose the moon is above the tides, the whole is wretchedly done....Besides the tombs already named I found that of Galois.[7]...

December 25th. Paris is just preparing for New Year's....

Jan. 11th.... All the early observatories of Europe seem to have been built as temples to Urania, and not as working chambers of science. The Royal Observatory of Greenwich, and the Imperial Observatory of Paris, and the beautiful structure in Calton Hill, Edinburgh, were, at first, wholly useless as Observatories. That of Greenwich had no steadiness, while every pillar in the astronomical temple of Edinburgh, though it may tell of the enlightenment of Greece, hides the light of the stars from the Scottish observer. Well might Struve say that "an observatory should be simply a box to hold instruments."

In his own journal, Nathaniel Hawthorne recorded his meeting with Maria Mitchell in Paris on January 9, 1858. It was the day she had asked to join the Hawthorne family on their trip to Rome.

January 9. This morning Miss [Maria] Mitchell, the celebrated astronomical lady, of Nantucket called. She had brought a letter of introduction to me, while consul; and her business now was, to see if we could take her as one of our party to Rome, whither she likewise is bound. We readily consented, for she seems to be a simple, strong, healthy, humored woman, who will not fling herself as a burden on our shoulders; and my only wonder is, that a person evidently so able to take care of herself should care about having an escort.[8]

Notwithstanding Hawthorne's "wonder," Maria Mitchell headed for Rome in the company of the renowned author and his family in early January.

January 13, 1858. We left Paris at 11 a.m. for Lyons. We had a monotonous ride of about eleven hours, in rainy weather, over the level lands of France which though green for this time of year, are not very interesting....

I amused myself by talking to the little Hawthornes [Una and Julian], and we all aired our French by putting our heads out of the window when the train stopped and calling for "*de l'eau froide.*"

Most travellers in Europe put up the bits of bread and sugar left at their meals for the lunch of the days of travelling, and candles for the evening. The Hawthornes had a considerable supply of lumps of sugar. I had bread and candle ends. Julian Hawthorne, whose appetite was like that of most boys of eleven, had soon exhausted the paternal stock and I offered my store. Mr. Hawthorne's dry sarcasm burst forth as he saw it. "Don't do it," he said, "Julian is a bottomless pit."[9]...

We stopped in the evening at the Hotel de Provence in Lyons....I was at once struck with the brightness of the stars and Mrs. Hawthorne called to me from her room to come and look at them. Orion and Sirius were more brilliant than I had ever seen them....

January 15th. The route from Lyons to Marseilles was more interesting than that from Paris to Lyons....Still the wearisome nature of twelve hours in an enclosed carriage was not overcome. We reached Marseilles at 11 p.m. and slept before we had seen the Mediterranean....We are at the Hotel d'Angleterre. Mr. Hawthorne is so thoroughly impractical and so unable to speak any other language than English, that Miss Shepard transacts all the business and settles all the bargains.

January 18. Before I left Marseilles I took a carriage and with Miss Shepard and the Hawthorne children visited the best parts of the city and then the seaside.... On Sunday morning [January 17] at 8 o'clock we left Marseilles for Genoa and Leghorn, uncertain what our further destination would be. Mr. Hawthorne's indecision is so great that the termination of our journey together is very uncertain. ...

January 19 This morning early the boat stopped at Leghorn (Livorna) and I found in going on deck that we were in an amphitheater of masts. There was a long discussion of the question whether we would land at Leghorn and go by land to Florence, or keep on to Civita Vecchia and Rome. I dared not speak on the subject. The passengers who came on board last night are to stop here and they tried to persuade Mr. Hawthorne to stop also.

Mr. Hawthorne wavered this way and that as one or another spoke. At length Una said, "Papa, Miss Mitchell wants to go to Rome and so does Miss Shepard and so do I," and that decided him for Rome. And so the luggage which had been taken up from the hold was ordered down again and with light hearts we went ashore for the day....

I entered Leghorn with little feeling of interest; I left it with less.... We stopped at Civita Vecchia early in the morning. With a good deal of talking and hesitation, we decided to take a *vettura* [coach] for Rome and we were to leave at 10 o'clock and they promised to reach Rome in eight hours....

Nothing can be more dreary than the day passed between Civita Vecchia and Rome, in a *vettura*. Had Mr. Hawthorne been as agreeable in conversation as he is in writing, it could not have made the day pleasant. If he spoke between the two towns, I did not hear him. Even the children ceased to be animated, there came on a drizzling rain, we had no food and were all quite devoid of enthusiasm when we entered Rome in the darkness of midnight. Julian Hawthorne wished that St. Peter's dome was all one mutton chop and that he could eat it. Dark as it was when we entered we caught sight of a colonnade of pillars which Mrs. Hawthorne declared at once was St. Peter's.

January 21. I was awakened early this morning by Miss Shepard who had found her way to the Bankers and persuaded the porter to give her the letters belonging to our party, before the Bank was open. I had no letter, so I dressed at once and rainy as it was I strolled out to see Rome.

We are at the Hotel Spillman and I went on to the Piazza di Spagna, the principal street of modern Rome, at once. It was much as I had

Maria Mitchell

expected, indeed Rome was more like my dreams of it than any other city I had seen, dark high stone houses and running fountains. I took a carriage after breakfast and with Una Hawthorne, we drove to the Coliseum. It was the Coliseum as I had imagined it, but larger. We walked within for a few minutes but hurried back to the carriage to escape the shower.

In Rome, Mitchell embraced a hectic schedule of sightseeing for nearly three months. Each day found her in some new place as she visited all the well-known tourist attractions. Her overflowing enthusiasm in the early days of her Rome adventure is clearly evident in this fragment of a January 24, 1858 letter[10] to her sister Phebe.

I am in Rome! I have been here four days, and already I feel that I would rather have that four days in Rome than all the other days of my travels! I have been uncomfortable, cold, tired, and subjected to all the evils of travelling; but for all that, I would not have missed the sort of realization that I have of the existence of the past of great glory, if I must have a thousand times the discomfort.

I went alone yesterday to St. Peter's and the Vatican, and today, taking Murray[11] [a guidebook], I went alone to the Roman Forum, and stood beside the ruined porticos and the broken columns of the Temple. Then I pushed on to the Coliseum, and walked around its whole circumference. I could scarcely believe that I really stood among the ruins, and was not dreaming! I really think I had more enjoyment for going alone and finding out for myself. Afterwards the Hawthornes called, and I took Mrs. H. to the same spot.

January 22....I found some good rooms, No. 60 Bocca di Leone, and taking Miss Shepard with me to make the bargain, I engaged them. Miss Shepard began to talk Italian with the man who owned them, upon which he said, "Perhaps you speak English." His wife, who is to be my servant, is a short dark Italian woman of very pretty face. The rooms are three in number, a large parlor with a very small fireplace, a large bedroom and a room between the two which might be used as a dining room. All are clean and well furnished. For the use of these I pay $20 a month; to the woman I pay a dollar a week. She is to take care of my rooms, get my breakfast and wash my dishes. My dinner is to come from a trattoria.

Jan. 23. I have just returned from my first visit to St. Peter's. One is awed at first at a gallery like that of the Vatican and a little struck dumb with the immensity of St. Peter's and does not know if he likes it or not....

Jan. 24. I took my map today and my guide book and found the Roman Forum....It seemed to me as if I dreamed and as if these proofs of the existence of highly cultivated people so many centuries ago could not be actually existing except in my recollections of what I had read....I was not sorry to be alone for I felt the solemnity of Rome and it seemed to me that a conception of time and of the world's age was born, filled my mind for the first time in my life....

Rome. Jan. 26. Customs. Manners and customs differ in every place....You buy apples by the pound and hooks and eyes by the ounce. Not having a very definite idea of weight, I bo't a pound of one and was surprised at the small amount, an ounce of the other and found I had hooks and eyes enough for the rest of my life....

Jan. 27. Today I have been on the top of the Capitol to look at the portion of the city....While one is imagining the scene when Hannibal and his army occupied the plains among the Alban hills and besieged Rome, he is annoyed by the Guide thrusting his palm into his musings and by the unpleasant reflection that he must pay a fee....

Jan. 28. St. Peter's grows upon one like Niagara; and is indeed the only work of art in the world comparable to it. Its space can be measured only by the fatigue of the visitor. He goes on and on, never suspecting that he is making a long march, until he sets down for a little rest and finds that he is utterly exhausted....

Jan. 29. Today I have been to the museum of the Vatican. The different apartments are in themselves well worth a visit, but I directed my steps at once to that of the Apollo Belvedere, which stands alone. The figure is one of great beauty, almost too effeminate for manly beauty....I sat down in the room of the Apollo and read Byron's description. I find a poet like Scott or Byron helps me very much to a sense of the beauties of nature and art. A poet seems to have a keener perception of the characteristic charm. No one can look at the statues and paintings of the Vatican without feeling their superiority to all that they have seen before....

Jan. 30. Mrs. H[awthorne] tells me that Mr. H admits that in the character of Zenobia he felt Margaret Fuller's presence. She says that he writes wholly from inspiration and stops when the inspiration fails and that he so succumbs to the character which he portrays that he

Maria Mitchell

cannot tell if it will turn to good or ill in the end. She says no one loved Margaret Fuller, but all admired her, that Mr. Hawthorne felt her need of woman's refinements and was disgusted....

Jan. 31.... I went to French theatre in the evening, which shows that I relax in my morals like others, when I am away from home....

Feb. 1. I called on Miss Hosmer's[12] studio today. ...

Feb. 5. After the courtesy of all the crowds in the streets of Paris, the manners of the Italians do not please me....

Feb. 6. The Carnival sports began at 2 o'clock today. I had no window or balcony seat engaged so I was obliged to content myself with looking into the Corso from one of the side streets....

Feb. 9.... Now in the last days of the Carnival the streets leading to the Corso are like one bed of flowers for the baskets of bouquet literally border the sidewalks....

Feb. 10.... Carnival. I have just returned from the Corso and from a day of looking at the festivities of the Carnival. They did not really begin until 3 p.m. and they ended before six....

Feb. 11. Today has been the masking day and tho' it rained some all through the afternoon, the crowd was great and the pelting incessant....

In the next weeks Mitchell visited a wide variety of Roman sights, including the Pantheon, the Baths of Caracalla, the Borghese Gallery, the Barberini Palace, the Spanish Steps, the Temple of Minerva Medica, and the Piazza del Popolo. Besides making many return visits to the galleries at the Vatican, she also visited numerous artists' studios.

March 3. A chapter might well be written on the Americans abroad.... An influenza is now prevailing. The winter has been colder than ever known by records of the Collegio Romano for 100 years.... I am working to see the Observatory of the Roman College, but it is a Jesuitical Institution and they say only the special permission of the Pope can effect it....

March 8, 1858.... When I returned to my room I received a call from an old priest. As he left no card, the Italians I was told do not, I have not yet learned his name but he is the Director of the Observatory at the Capitol. As I talked no Italian and he no English, the conversation was maintained in bad French on both sides....

EUROPEAN TRAVELS. During her lengthy sojourns overseas, Maria Mitchell was welcomed in every major astronomical center in Europe. *Top:* The historic letter from the Cardinal Secretary of State granting Maria permission to visit the Vatican Observatory in 1858, with "benign pontifical consent." *Right:* Urbain Leverrier, director of the Paris Observatory, whom Mitchell visited several times. Mitchell and Leverrier had the rare distinction of being recipients of royal medals for their astronomical discoveries. Leverrier's computations led directly to the discovery of Neptune, although J. C. Adams, whom Mitchell had met at the Cambridge Observatory, had done similar calculations at an earlier date. *Below:* A portion of Maria Mitchell's diary entry exclaiming, "Cambridge is beautiful—but it has no trees except those in parks."

Maria Mitchell

March 15, 1858. Today an eclipse of the sun was to come off, and with Mr. B and the Westons I went to the Observatory of the Capitol to look at the phenomenon.... The old gent speaks no English, but the bad French of both of us made a language. He had placed three telescopes of ordinary mounting in a terrace which overlooks the Forum, and as it was very cloudy, we looked at the magnificent views of the Alban and Sabine Mts. instead of looking at the Eclipse.... A good many visitors were around and to my amazement some half dozen young men suddenly formed into a line and Prof. Calandrelli presented his pupils, who gracefully lifted their caps. They were fine looking fellows of about 16 and they all smiled as they greeted me and were evidently pleased at being noticed....

Eventually Mitchell obtained permission to enter the Vatican Observatory. As far as we know, she was the first laywoman ever to do so. Even the renowned Mary Somerville had been turned away. Maria wrote of her mixed feelings in a letter to her father.

I am working to get admitted to see the observatory, but it cannot be done without special permission from the pope, and I don't like to be "presented." If I can get permission without the humbug of putting on a black veil and receiving a blessing from Pius, I shall; but I shrink from the formality of presentation. I know thou'd say "Be presented."

On March 22, 1858, the following letter, written in Italian[13] by Cardinal Antonelli,[14] arrived from the offices of the Vatican.

In the desire to be of service to the estimable offices of Your Excellency, the undersigned Cardinal Secretary of State has not failed to request from the Holy Father the necessary permissions so that Miss Mitchell will be permitted to visit the Astronomical Observatory situated in the Roman College of the Jesuit Fathers. Having obtained, as was needed, the benign pontifical consent, the writer makes haste to inform Your Excellency that the proper form has already been sent to the most reverend Father General of the Jesuit Fathers, so that Miss Mitchell can be admitted to visit the said Observatory. As is proper, the present writer informs Your Excellency's office that he has set [for the visit] the 9th of next month, in the meanwhile he confirms to you sentiments of his distinct high regard.

G. B. Antonelli.[15]

The best description we have of Maria Mitchell's historic visit to the Vatican Observatory is found in a lecture she gave at Vassar College many years later. We are fortunate that she wrote down many of her college lectures.[16]

Collegio Romano. There was another observatory which had a reputation and was known in America. It was the Observatory of the Collegio Romano and was in the monastery behind the Church of St. Ignatius. Its Director was the Father Secchi, who had visited America and who was well known to the scientists of this country....

Returning one day (March 8, 1858) from a drive, I met two priests descending one of the upper flights of stairs. As my rooms had been blessed once and holy water sprinkled upon them, I tho't perhaps another process of that sort had just been gone through, and was about to pass them when one of them, accosting me, asked if I was the Signora Mitchell, changing his Italian to good English as he saw that I was and introducing himself as Father Secchi....

Father Secchi had bro't with him negatives of the planet Saturn, the rings showing beautifully, altho' the image was not more than a half inch in size. I was ignorant enough of the ways of all Papal Institutions and indeed of all Italy to ask if I might visit the Roman Observatory. I remembered that the days of Galileo were days of 2 centuries since. I did not know that my heretic feet must not enter the sanctuary, that my woman's robe must not brush the seats of learning.

The Father's refusal was seen in his face at once and I felt that I had done something highly improper! The Father said that he would have been most happy to have me visit him, but he had not the power, it was a religious Institution. He had already applied to his Superior and he was not willing to grant permission, the power lay with the Holy Father or one of the Cardinals.

I was told that Mrs. Somerville, the most learned woman in all Europe, had been denied admission. And that the daughter of Sir John Herschel, in spite of English rank and of the higher stamp of Nature's nobility, was at that very time in Rome and could not enter an Observatory which was at the same time a monastery.

If I had before been mildly desirous of visiting the observatory, I was now intensely anxious! Father Secchi suggested that I should see the Cardinal Antonelli in person with a written application in my hand! This was not to be tho't of! To ask an interview with the wiliest Cardinal...

In the course of this waiting I told my story to a young Italian gentleman, the nephew of a Monsignor, a Monsignor being next to a Cardinal. He assured me that my permission would never be obtained by Mr. Carr. After a fortnight waiting I rec'd a permission written on parchment and signed by Cardinal Antonelli. When the young Italian next called, I held it up in triumph and boasted that Mr. Carr had at length moved in the matter. The young man coolly replied, "Yes, I spoke to my uncle last evening, to speak to Cardinal Antonelli and to urge the matter, but for that it would never have come." There had been red tape and I had not seen it!...

At the appointed time the next fine day, and all days seemed to be fine, we set out on our mission. When we entered the church, we saw far in the distance Father Secchi standing just behind a pillar.... Through long halls, up windy staircases...we reached at length the Dome and the Telescope....We looked at Venus with a power of 150 but it was not poor, Jupiter was beautiful and in broad daylight the belts were plainly seen. With low powers, the moon was charming, but the air would not bear high ones, Father Secchi said he had used a power of 2000 but that 600 was more common....

The spectroscopic method of observing starlight was used by Secchi as early as by any other astronomer. By this method the starlight is analyzed and sunlight is analyzed and the two are compared....I should have been glad to stay until dark and look at the nebulae but the Father kindly informed me that my permission did not last beyond the daylight which was fast leaving us and conducting me to the door he informed me that I must make my way home alone. "But we live in a civilized country," said he. "Doubtful," thought I....

Whenever she delivered this particular lecture, Mitchell always included something about women's rights.

We smile at the tho't that a Roman Observatory would not permit a woman to cross its threshold, yet how many boys' colleges today are open to women, <u>except</u> <u>to</u> <u>walk</u> <u>through</u> <u>them</u>. The Collegio Romano was not alone an Observatory or a college, it was also a religious institution, it was a monastery, it was so for them—a church. How many pulpits [are] open to the American woman today? Really the world dares not today trust the lessons of nature or believe in the presence (soul teaching) of woman....Do you know of any case in which a boys' college has offered a Professorship to a woman? Until you do, it is absurd to say that the highest learning is within the reach of American women....

The visit to the Vatican Observatory was followed by the activities of Holy Week, in which Mitchell was an active participant.

March 28. Palm Sunday. At 7 1/2 this morning, in black dresses and black veils we drove to St. Peter's, tickets in hand to see the ceremonies of the day....

April 1. The ceremonies of Holy Thursday are the washing of the feet of the disciples by the Pope, serving them at table and the Miserere in the Sistine chapel. I attempted only the first and tho' I went early and obtained a good seat, the crowd was so great that I suffered from the bad air....

April 3. Now, in the Holy Week, even the lowest classes of people and the lowest order of merchandisers puts on holiday dress....I was surprised today by the Padrone's opening my door to permit a priest in white robe and a boy, to bless the room. The ceremony consisted in throwing holy water, upon which I involuntarily laughed. My Padrone, good naturedly said "Never mind, it won't hurt you."...

April 4. I set out about 10 1/2 for St. Peter's, having heard that the benediction would be about noon. I found the narrow streets leading to St. Peter's crowded for miles....

On Easter Sunday we could not leave St. Peter's as soon as we desired, on account of the immense crowd, so we sat down under the pillars of the colonnade to wait....

April 6. The Holy Week was not wholly over, until the fire-works had been displayed from the Pincian Hill....

A comparison between Mitchell's diary and a modern tour book of Rome shows that she saw most of the important sights before she had to leave. But a letter to her father on May 4 reveals that she was becoming jaded with her travels. "It is time I came home," she wrote, "for the keenness of my appetite is over." Nevertheless, she continued her sightseeing up to the last minute, as any typical tourist would do.

It is interesting to note that Hawthorne alluded to Maria Mitchell in *The Marble Faun,* which he wrote while in Rome:

A needle is familiar to the fingers of them all....the woman's eye that has discovered a new star turns from its glory to send the polished

Maria Mitchell

little instrument gleaming along the hem of her kerchief, or to darn a casual fray in her dress.[17]

April 10. At the last moment before leaving Rome, I did a little more sightseeing. I went to the Baths of Caracalla....

April 12. We left Rome at about 8 1/2 not with tearful eyes, as every one had told me I must, but with laugh and jest and a *vetturino* crowded full of trunks and bags and human beings.

The road lies through the Piazza del Popolo and we looked at St. Peter's again and again after we had got outside and it was impossible for me to remember that I was looking my last without a feeling of regret, but yet the regret at leaving places is nothing compared to those of leaving people and Rome has been to me, more a home than any other place in Europe....

April 15. We started off at 8 o'clock this morning under a bright sun and the bracing influence of a cold wind. Our first stopping place was Assisi.... There were two churches built one above the other and under the cellar of one St. Francis is buried.... The next stop was one of interest. It was at the door of an Etruscan tomb which was found only a few years since.[18]

April 16. We began to "do" Perugia at 10 o'clock this morning, having a good-looking guide who talked French....

April 17. Our route from Perugia this morning lay at first through a cattle fair, where pigs and oxen were plenty....

April 18. The route was tame at first, or else we had become accustomed to it. I rode on the outside the first few hours. ...

April 19. Florence, via Mandota 6307. I have just returned from a call on Mrs. Somerville. I was surprised to see her trip into the room and speak with the vivacity of a young person. She is said to be 77 and looks about 57. Her husband entered first and immediately commenced conversation....

When Mrs. Somerville came in I told her that I had heard that she was very busy and she told me that her new edition of the "Physical Geography" was now in press in London, but that of the "Physical Sciences" she had not yet received the proof sheets....Dr. Somerville says at first she concealed her studies for at that time the study of mathematics hurt a woman's character but that Playfair encouraged her to pursue them....

April 20. Mrs. Somerville told me that an English gentleman named Joule had advanced the idea of late that heat is motion and that she has enlarged on this in her book and she gave me various anecdotes illustrative of this doctrine. She remarked also that the science of magnetism had made strides in the last few years....

April 21. This morning was given to the Pitti Palace and its gallery. I had tho't the Uffizi must be the finer when I visited it yesterday, but the Pitti is really elegant in its apartments and worthy to be a Ducal residence....

The sun set over Carrara and the ruddy light fell richly upon the mountain tops, softened into a purple by the mists. I never saw a lovelier sight and I left it with regret, knowing that I looked my last.

April 22. A day of doing nothing....

April 24. Mrs. Somerville met me as I entered, told me that she was glad to see me and had expected me....

April 28. From Ferrara to Padua by post the horses being changed every 8 1/2 miles....

April 29. We have run about Venice in gondola all day. To the Cathedral of St. Marks, to the great palace and over it, to the prisons and to the Bridge of Sighs...

April 30. The passage from Venice to Trieste was 7 hours long and the sea was rough. For the first time I found myself where my language was not spoken; but I was easily understood when I tried German....

May 2. I left Trieste at 5 1/2 a.m. for Wien (Vienna). The omnibus conductor who went to the station with me, took care of my luggage, bought my ticket and told me where to go for the carriage....

From Trieste to Vienna is 24 hours by the ordinary train. I reached Vienna at 5 1/2 in the morning and found the Hotels all full. I drove from one to another and at length discouraged, I asked a Landlord who spoke good English to tell me the hours when a train would start for Dresden. He seemed to see that the case was desperate and told me he would give me a room...

Sunday, May 2, 1858, Vienna.

My dear Father,

I write just a line to say I am safe thus far and am obliged to wait here through Sunday, as I cannot rise my passport until tomorrow for Berlin. I tried to do it at Venice but could not....I am the more eager to get on to Berlin, as I have had no letter since Anne's of March 24th....I'm in a great hurry to get home but not a bit homesick....

I have written to the Barings to take my passage for the last of May so I hope I shall reach London safely by May 20. I never felt so well-satisfied with what I have done for Prudie, as since I have seen Mr. Cameron and his young companion....I don't remember that I ever said a disagreeable word to Prudie when anyone else was present....[19]

Berlin, May 4.

My dear Father,

I arrived at 10 this evening, 26 hours from Vienna....You will know how well I am by my writing tonight after 26 hours in the cars, and you will perceive that I am no coward, when I arrive at 10 o'clock and select my hack man, in a strange city.

So far, I feel that nothing is easier than to travel in Europe alone. When I get out of the cars, I rush up to a soldier and ask (in German) "What I shall do" and he sends me to a hack man and the hack man gives me a number and tells me to call a porter and so on. Frequently I have consulted several soldiers before I get on much, as I never hesitate to do it, indeed an armed man is getting to be my delight. I shall come home decidedly in favor of a standing army....

I think of staying in Berlin a week, then going to Cologne, then to Rotterdam, thence by steamer to London then a few days in London...and then to Liverpool. I mean to be in London May 20 and I have written to the Barings to retain letters.[20]

May 6. [Berlin] I received a note from Prof. [Johann] Encke[21] and went to the observatory.

May 7. Today Prof. Encke showed me the tower, formerly the Observatory.

Berlin, May 7, 1858. [Alexander von] Humboldt[22] had replied to my letter by a note, saying that he should be happy to see me at 2 p.m.... There was a clock in sight, and I stayed but half an hour....

Having been nearly a year in Europe, I had not kept up my reading of American newspapers, but Humboldt could tell me the latest news, scientifically and politically....It was singular that Humboldt should advise me to use the sextant; it was the first instrument that I ever used, and it is a very difficult one. No young aspirant in science ever left Humboldt's presence uncheered...

May 7. I think I am not well because I perceived myself to be spiteful and cross and do not rejoice in the good fortune of others. I hope I may not become envious as I become old; an envious old maid is more than an old maid simply....

May 12. How do we know that our minds and our bodies are connected now. I have a spiritual life, is it less a spiritual life now than it will be after the body has decayed? Is my soul now in my body? It acts in company with the body, but it also acts separately from it, for my thoughts are now in Boston now in New York, wherever I have been they come again.

The body cannot travel over again, without it pays in time and money and fatigue for the duplication of its journey, but the mind can always whence the bodies stops. It can also anticipate the steps of the body but here it is feeble and we call it imagination and sometimes the body when it travels finds no such lands as the mind have promised.

In France and Italy I longed for sweets, in Berlin it seems to me that even the graves have sweets.

May 17. I left Ostende at 6 1/2 p.m. May 16 and at once lay down upon a settee, the only resting place provided for such passengers and resigned myself to my fate. I was very sick for four of the six hours passage....

We reached Dover at midnight and as I had not strength to lift my bag I asked the Captain to give me a guide to the custom house. He called to a gentlemanly looking man who at once appeared to accompany me. I told him if there was a refreshment room in the route to take me there first and we stopped at a moderate looking house and he told the landlady that I wanted some refreshment. He said "What will you have madam? Brandy and water?" I told him some bread, butter and a cup of tea.

After this the man came and told me that the luggage was at the Custom house. I went with him and saw it examined. "If the train is made up," he said "you can at once go into the carriage." I found that "making up a train" means putting the carriages together and I was alone from Dover to London so few people go in 1st class carriages.

May 20. I heard Charles Dickens read "The Cricket on the Hearth."...

Maria Mitchell

May 21. I heard Chs. Kean[23] in *King Lear* and it was a wonderful piece of acting. I have seen no one else but Rachel who acted when standing still....I felt in listening that I had never read Lear before—that it was Lear and not Kean who was before my eyes.

May 22. I heard "Boots of the Swan" as represented by Robson, the best English Comedian. I could not enjoy it much.

May 24. I went to Greenwich for the last time and spent the night. I returned at 2 p.m. May 25th to London....

June 3, 1858. We came on board at 9 a.m., a company so merry that one saw at once they were Americans returning home and not Englishmen leaving.... The Misses Guion left me, and I ascended onto the ship, but I could not feel lonesome, for I was going home. I had even no feeling of regret as we left the land, though I knew that I bade it good-by forever....

June 8. We have kept on safely but not very pleasantly....I tried to make the Captain say that he could not give us breakfast on Thursday morning, but he says he would not like to put us ashore with empty stomachs. As we pass within 30 miles of Nantucket, I asked him to put me ashore to which he replies that I ought not to live there, if I can't go the long way around by New York.

At the end of her year abroad, Maria Mitchell had one final item of business—to finish paying her accounts. The Nantucket traveler often kept a record of her expenditures in her diary, but she does not seem to have recorded them all. A letter from the bank in London gives some indication of her travel expenses, though not the length of time covered.

> *London, 13 August 1858*
> *William Mitchell Esq*
> *As desired by Miss Maria Mitchell we beg to wait on you with the annexed statement of account shewing a balance of £96 of your debit of 31st Inst. which may be settled with our Agent G. Ward of Boston if found correct.*
> *Baring Brothers, Co.*

CHAPTER 7

FROM NANTUCKET
TO VASSAR

The whole enterprise is magnificent—
so much the greater is the responsibility of those who
mingle their hands in the work, and especially the first hands.

$\mathcal{T}$HE PERIOD IMMEDIATELY FOLLOWING her European tour must have been extremely difficult for Maria Mitchell. In addition to the general letdown most travelers feel when they return to the everyday world of work and cares, she also came back to a sick mother and a lonely home. In the winter of 1861, she wrote a friend, "If the holidays are sad days to you, they are no less so to me."

All her brothers and sisters were now married and had established their own households. Of the two sisters she felt closest to, the youngest, Kate, was now Mrs. Owen Dame and living in Boston, and Phebe (Kendall) was living in Meadville, Pennsylvania. Later, the Kendalls moved closer, first to Rhode Island and then to Cambridge, where Joshua Kendall established a small private school. Only Sally (Barney) and Anne (Macy) continued to live on Nantucket after getting married. Her four brothers had all married years earlier; none lived nearby. The home which had once echoed with the sounds of ten children must have been very lonely indeed.

Maria Mitchell

The care of Mrs. Mitchell fell on the shoulders of her lone single daughter living at home. Phebe reported:

> In 1855 Mrs. Mitchell was taken suddenly ill and although partial recovery followed, her illness lasted for six years, during which time Maria was her constant nurse. For most of the six years her mother's condition was such that merely a general care was needed, but it used to be said that Maria's eyes were always upon her. When the opportunity to go to Europe came, an older sister came with her family to take Maria's place in the home; and when Miss Mitchell returned she found her mother so nearly in the state in which she had left her, that she felt justified in having taken the journey.[1]

One bright event during this period was a gift of money from the Women of America that enabled Mitchell to purchase a new telescope. She obtained a five-inch telescope with an equatorial mounting, skillfully made by Alvan Clark.[2] The mounting allowed the user to point the telescope directly at an object using its known position; or, if the telescope were pointed at an object, such as a comet, its position could be read directly from the setting circles.

The new telescope was much better than any Maria had previously owned. She began at once to use her new prize and soon spotted a new comet, although she was not the first discoverer. This telescope is used today at the Loines Maria Mitchell Observatory of the Nantucket Maria Mitchell Association.

SOON AFTER HER MOTHER'S DEATH in 1861, Mitchell and her father moved to Lynn, Massachusetts. Julia Ward Howe wrote:

> From [her] small salary... Miss Mitchell had been able to lay up money enough to make at this time the purchase of a small house in Lynn [on Essex Street], valued at sixteen hundred and fifty dollars. In this house she now resided for some years with her father, to whom had been granted a pension of three hundred dollars per annum. Maria was now able to earn five hundred dollars yearly by computations. The pair lived comfortably on their own resources, "only," says Miss Mitchell, "we were obliged to keep a girl, for I, having to support myself by computing, could not do housework."[3]

Behind their new home the Mitchells built a small observatory where Maria continued her astronomical observations. The move to Lynn enabled them to be close to Kate and her family, as well as to join more regularly in the activities of Boston's scientific community.

It seems quite likely that both father and daughter had been secretly hoping to leave Nantucket for some time. There are indications in several of the letters that they had grown tired of their life on the isolated island. In an 1885 letter Maria wrote, "I don't like Nantucket but I do like the people." Mitchell had apparently outgrown the insular life of Nantucket and needed the broader world of Boston and beyond.

THERE IS NO DIARY RECORD of the time between Mitchell's return from Europe and her departure for Vassar College. We can however follow her life at this time through the many letters she wrote and received from numerous friends.

Maria Mitchell left England on June 3 and was probably back on Nantucket by the third week in June. She wasted no time in returning to her astronomical research; by the end of June she had found a comet.

> *Cambridge, July 13, 1858*
> *Hon. Wm. Mitchell*
> *I was happy to receive your note announcing the discovery of a comet[4] by your daughter. I hope she is all the better and wiser for her triumphant visit to Europe....*
> *Joseph Lovering[5]*

> Sept. 2, 1858. Nantucket
> My dear Mr. [William] Bond,
> I am very much obliged to you for the observations on the comet. What a troublesome creature it has been! Father intends to have some copies of the report printed, but not published, and he will send you one; he supposed that you had seen it. I am afraid the Dudley affair[6] will lower the climate put upon science everywhere, so many more people hear of a quarrel than ever hear of the quiet steady working of established institutions. It's a great pity....
> Kate is settled in Boston at 148 Harrison Avenue. She would be much pleased to have any of you call. I hope to visit her in October, and shall then do myself the pleasure to call on Mrs. Bond and Selena and have a talk on the glories of Old England.
> Maria Mitchell[7]

Maria Mitchell

The idea of raising money for a telescope for Maria Mitchell seems to have been first mentioned by Dr. Charles F. Winslow, who wrote to Mrs. Joseph Willard of Boston on April 19, 1849:

> *Your letter in reply to mine touching the telescope was received just as I was about to step on board this ship to embark for Chagres. I was very much gratified to find that the plan struck you so favorably and that you were going to concert with Pres. Everett of Harvard College upon the best means of effecting so desirable and laudable an object.*
>
> *I am glad I happened to think of it, for I am sure it will be the means of extending research and discoveries in the sublime departments of the universe and of unfolding new wonders among the starry worlds. Miss Mitchell has been obliged to make her observations with inferior instruments, but with a new and perfect one I am quite sure her patience and genius will yet add greatly to her reputation as an astronomical observer and will afford you and her other admirers great satisfaction for your patronage and generous mark of respect for her talents.[8]*

Several years later, the idea of honoring Maria Mitchell with a new telescope was mentioned again in a short note in *Emerson's Magazine* in 1857. The effort was spearheaded by Elizabeth Peabody.

> *A Boston friend writes us that the ladies of that city have it in con-templation to start a subscription paper for the purpose of raising $3000 to purchase a telescope for the distinguished and truly noble woman who has devoted herself with so much zeal to the pursuit of science. This sum will purchase an instrument much larger than the one now owned by Miss Mitchell, and will greatly facilitate her studies.*
>
> *We sincerely hope something of the kind will be done, and it will be a most womanly tribute to one of the most gifted and deserving of her sex. In Europe Maria Mitchell would command the interest and receive the homage of the learned and polite, in the most accomplished circles, while in America so little prestige is attached to genius and learning that she is comparatively unknown. ...*
>
> *We need a reform here, most especially, if we would not see American society utterly contemptible. In relation to our country woman, Maria Mitchell, of whom we have before spoken in the United States Magazine, we will receive and send to their destination any sums left for the above purpose at this office.[9]*

The fund-raising was successful, and seven months after returning from Europe Mitchell wrote to William Bond for advice about the telescope she was having made by the renowned Alvan Clark. She obviously wanted to get the very best instrument and accessories she could for the money. This letter was written just two weeks before Bond's death.

Nantucket Jan. 15th 1859

My dear Mr. Bond,

I am expecting to see Mr. Alvan Clark in about ten days and before I have an interview with him, I wish to ask you a few questions, hoping it will not be troubling you too much. First about the micrometer for my telescope. Having economized by taking a five inch glass instead of a six, I am not disposed to let any economical considerations come into its accessories. I want to make the best of measurements. The question is then—will Mr. Clark's micrometer made on a plan of his own, read the accuracy which he claims for it?...[10]

In a letter to Mitchell, Elizabeth Peabody recalled how she had missed the opportunity to look through the Harvard telescope.

May 6th, 1860

My dear Miss Mitchell,

The last steamer brought this letter for you from Una [Hawthorne], which I am glad to send on to you. And if she can get no other escort to Nantucket I shall be tempted to be escort myself. I used to be familiar with the Nantucket Steamboats as far as Naushon and often thought of going on to the larger island but lacked the attention which now the whole heavens makes upon me through your self....I never saw Mr. Bond at all and I do not know his sons. So I shall probably never look through the Telescope, But I mean to look through yours....

Elizabeth P. Peabody[11]

After the telescope was finished, Mitchell embarked at once on several research projects. In an encouraging letter, Admiral William Henry Smyth, whom she had met in England, recommended the observation of binary stars as suitable for her new telescope. Mitchell later published a record of her studies of binary stars in the *American Journal of Science and Arts*.[12] The micrometer she had mentioned in her letter to William Bond would have been used to measure the relative positions of the two stars in a binary system. Admiral Smyth's advice in his letter to Maria Mitchell remains valid today in scientific inquiry.

> *25-7-'59, St. John's Lodge*
>
> *... We are much pleased to hear of your acquisition of an equatorial instrument under a revolving roof, for it is a true scientific luxury as well as an efficient implement.*
>
> *The aperture of your object-glass is sufficient for doing much useful work, but, if I may hazard an opinion to you, do not attempt too much, for it is quality rather than quantity which is now desirable.... Now, for your purpose, I would recommend a batch of neat, but not over-close, binary systems, selected so as to have always one or the other on hand....*
>
> *There is, for ultimate utility, nothing like forming a plan and then steadily following it. Those who profess they will attend to everything often fall short of the mark. The division of labor leads to beneficial conclusions as well in astronomy as in mechanics and arts.*
>
> *W. H. Smyth*[13]

Despite the acquisition of her "true scientific luxury," the sadness and loneliness of Maria's Nantucket life are drearily evident in this letter to a friend, as is her concern about the impending national conflict.

Nantucket, Jan 4, 1861

My dear Kate [not her sister],

If the holidays are sad days to you, they are no less so to me. My Mother is increasingly feeble and the dread of loss is as great a source of suffering as loss itself.

I have abandoned my pleasant sitting room, and spend my time in her room, studying in a corner, when I am enough easy in mind to touch a book at all—figuring when it is a duty to figure. There is the painful peculiarity in her illness, of occasional wandering of the mind, and I remember with great anguish the gradual decline of your Aunt Anne. My Mother will scarcely live long enough for that. We try to be cheerful and to keep up her spirits and I go out sometimes in the evening, but we do not leave her alone a moment.

What a sad period it is for the whole country! I really never thought that these things could get so far. We may as well meet the trouble now as postpone it for a few years. I hope we may not have civil war. As for the praying in <u>public</u> of this day, may our President do it himself; most of us have other things about which to concern ourselves. Two American ensigns are hoisted at our wharves in honor of the day, that is all.

Our winter is duller than usual. If there is any society I am wholly out of it, so much so, that as I look around on the audience at a concert, it is almost an assemblage of strangers. Doubtless there are parties and dances and tea drinkings, but our circle becomes smaller and smaller. We have a Whist club but it numbers only eleven persons and it has not yet met.

Emily Shaw is in Boston and even she, who sees everything of the rosiest color, writes letters of croaking. Can it be that we are all old? Our Kate says she is not. She expects a newcomer[14] in April, the only thing expected in our family.

I think you don't know that [sister] Phebe's in Bristol. I wish you would go and see her. Mr. Kendall teaches the Normal School. You can find them at Mrs. Winkley's near the school, where they board.

Maria Mitchell[15]

Maria Mitchell's sixty-seven-year-old mother died on July 7, 1861. None of Maria's letters or diary entries mention this sad personal event. Soon after Lydia's death, Maria and her father determined to leave Nantucket to live in Lynn. Before leaving, however, they made sure that they would have a variety of telescopes to continue their astronomical observations.

> *Coast Survey Office*
> *September 7, 1861*
> *Wm. Mitchell, Esq.*
> *Your letter of September 4th has been received. I shall be glad if you will take the instruments with your effects to Lynn, and make observations as occasion may require for the survey. It would be as well to send the repeating circle to the office for storage as [it is] of no value in observing now a days.*
> *A. D. Bache[16]*

Maria Mitchell

Maria Mitchell was also looking for other employment possibilities, as the following two letters indicate. "Troy Female College" was probably Troy Female Seminary, founded by Emma Willard in 1821.

> *Cambridge Nov. 29th 1861*
> *My Dear Miss Mitchell,*
>
> *I am sorry that I can give you but little information respecting the situation at the Troy Female College of which I spoke to your Father. I saw the Principal for only twenty minutes or there abouts and from what he said of the Institution supposed that it was either newly started, or had just received a large accession of funds. He mentioned an Observatory as in contemplation and spoke of individuals who would probably give largely for such an object and then inquired particularly (without any suggestion) of your qualifications.*
>
> *Should they really contemplate anything of the kind, I have no doubt your chances would be second to none, saving one condition. There was a flavor of New England "Orthodoxy" in the conversation which made one suspect you would be required to relate your "Experiences" before entering upon your professional duties.*
>
> *G. P. Bond*[17]

Notice that in her 1863 letter to the Smithsonian director, Mitchell was already referring to her small facility in Lynn as an "Astronomical Observatory." No copy can be found of the circular she mentions which apparently advertised public lectures she may already have been giving.

> Astronomical Observatory, Lynn, Aug. 26, 1863
> Prof. [Joseph] Henry,
>
> I do not know that the engagement of lecturers for Lyceum readers, etc. comes in among your many duties, but as it is possible I take the liberty of asking your attention to a circular which I enclose. If it is quite out of your line of usefulness I hope you will excuse me.
> Maria Mitchell[18]

A newsy summer letter catches us up on a variety of goings-on and health concerns in the Mitchell household, including a menacing whooping cough. Sally Barney, Maria's sister, was still living on Nantucket at the time. Sally's son Mitchell[19] had been visiting his grandfather and aunt in Lynn, perhaps to receive tutoring in mathematics from Aunt Maria.

July 15.

My dear Sally,

I am very glad to have the pattern for the drawers. I shall return the specimen by Mitchell as I understand how to make them.

[Niece] Maria's little dress fits nicely and I tell Kate the two children won't suffer, if they have no other dresses for the winter. All that Maria's is wrong, is in being too large around the waist. I am sorry to hear that Aunt Maria's cough has not gone. Father thinks he has the whooping cough. He coughs incessantly, but is pretty well. He has been to Boston today.

Tell Aunt Maria to stick to the Doctor's medicine and use a plenty of it. I am ready to pay the bill. I wish I could send you some currants as I have a great many. We have very few cherries. I had to pay 38 cts. for hdkf, but I think they are nice looking, almost as nice as Father's.

I think Mitchell is all right in his algebra. He can't stand an examination in Trig but I don't believe he will have a rigorous one. Father has seen the Prof. and will give him a letter to them.

I don't wonder Anne is frightened about Fanny's whoops. Willie's was dreadful and yet Phebe says he had it very light because he was out every day. Dr. Flanders says after they vomit, two weeks will use it up and Phebe says after 4 weeks there is no fever and no danger of infecting others.

Father doesn't whoop but he sounds as if he were choking. People do sometimes have it twice. I hope Andrew won't have it. He never had it when a child of course. I don't think Father has it. I haven't a doubt that suspicious vessel near Nantucket was after Fanny Macy. What else could they want. Henry Barnard spent the night of the 4th here.

Tell Mary I think he is beautiful. Also as thou gads about, please to thank Mary Anne Mitchell for a book she sent me, I shall write a note of thanks some time.

We expect to go to Cambridge for [the Harvard] Commencement, all of us.[20]

Maria Mitchell was considered the preeminent mathematician in a family which had no lack in that department. Even though her brother

Henry was a fine mathematician and scientist, he was obviously stumped by a cubic algebraic equation that he could not solve; he appealed to his older sister for help. Reading between the lines of her response to Henry reveals that Maria was now better at mathematics than her father.

[Dated by someone as 1864]

My dear Henry,

I have begun to read upon cubics—the labor of solving such an equation as thine will be very great. I think it is possible because that of a simple equation $X^4 + X^3 + X^2 + X$ is. I shall keep on reading today.

But I would suggest this—as no one will ever work out that formula—if it conveys a truth, the truth can be told in words and the mathematical air which a formula puts on in a paper, will have no effect upon the learned and never be noticed by the vulgar—I simplify the equation a little by [a series of equations in a derivation] which runs regularly from X^4 to X. I will continue to read, as I have always wanted to get hold of "Sturm's Methods" and "Horner's Methods" and various other cobwebs in the corners of old Algebras, but I don't believe it will pay.

Father says he is afraid of thy brain if thou works this too much.

M. M.

Will Nanty [Henry's wife] come here before you go to Washington?[21]

WHILE MARIA MITCHELL and her father were adjusting to their new life in Lynn, Matthew Vassar was launching his "Magnificent Enterprise" in Poughkeepsie, New York. Vassar's project was nothing less than the establishment of the first U. S. college exclusively for women—based on the principle that women should receive the same education, with the same standards, as that offered in men's colleges. In February, 1861 he had presented to a newly selected Board of Trustees the funds and securities—valued then at more than $400,000—to start Vassar Female College.[22]

Rufus Babcock, one of the original trustees, initiated a meeting with Maria Mitchell to decide whether she was suitable to fill the astronomy position at the new college. He wrote to Mitchell on Nantucket to set up an interview, not realizing that she was living in Lynn.

Babcock was very close-mouthed about the purpose of his interview, and the first letters do not indicate that Maria was being considered for a faculty position. In fact, Mitchell totally misunderstood the purpose of the meeting, thinking Babcock wanted only to obtain her views on women's education.

The Vassar trustee even went so far as to obtain letters of recommendation without Mitchell's knowledge. In his letter of October 15, 1862, three months after the initial meeting, Babcock finally told her that he was "decided in regard to the desirableness of your being suited to fill the Chair of Astronomy."

We are fortunate that most of this correspondence was preserved. The letters give an excellent picture of how Maria Mitchell came to be hired by Vassar College even though the president, the Rev. Dr. John H. Raymond, LL.D., found her less than "indispensable" to the goals of the college.

There was a nearly three-year interval between the first correspondence and her eventual appointment as professor of astronomy. The long delay was partly due to the fact that construction of the college buildings was slowed by the war, but there was another crucial reason: many people both in and outside the college were adamantly opposed to women being professors.[23]

Dr. Milo Jewett, the first president of Vassar College, was against the idea of women professors; he and Matthew Vassar eventually fell out over that and other issues.[24] Jewett was replaced by Raymond, who was president when the college accepted its first students.

Dr. Raymond was also less than enthusiastic about women professors, but he did not push the issue. Fortunately, Matthew Vassar held firm to the concept that a woman's college should employ women professors. In 1864, he wrote to Sarah J. Hale: "My desire is now and always has been to make our College, not only a College to educate Women, but a College of instruction by women."[25]

Of the original eight Vassar professors, two were women, Maria Mitchell and Dr. Alida Avery. At a February 23, 1864 board meeting,

140 *Maria Mitchell*

trustee Nathan Bishop "suggested that [as] the Committee on Faculty & Studies had already concluded that no sectarianism would be allowed to influence their selection and that in all cases where women could be found equal to the positions they should be preferred."[26]

> *Warren, R. I. 21st August 1862*
>
> *Miss Maria Mitchell*
>
> *Respected Friend,*
>
> *Let me briefly explain the occasion of my writing as the intimate confidential friend of Mr. Vassar, the generous founder of Vassar Female College, Po'keepsie, N.Y.*
>
> *I have been designated by him to put myself in communication with yourself in regard to the interest of that Institution. He has learned with interest and satisfaction that you have indicated some willingness to cooperate in making the college a blessing to American women and to the cause of science.*
>
> *Most of the details in regard to its arrangement and Professors yet remain to be definitely settled and the founder has solicited me while sojourning a few weeks in New England to obtain if possible a personal interview with you to give and receive much more full information on this subject than can easily be communicated by the pen.*
>
> *I now write to ask whether in this season at hand you can be found at home at Nantucket this day week, or if not whether you can be at Providence at the Commencement of Brown University one week later. Indeed if this last would be convenient to you it would suit me better as I have no other motive for visiting your somewhat out of the way side of the ocean than to enjoy such an interview with yourself.*
>
> *Will you, therefore, grant me the favor of as early an answer to this inquiry as practicable addressed to me at this place?*
>
> *One reason for preferring a meeting with you in Providence a fortnight hence is that we might then meet with Dr. Tobey Geo. Newton of New Bedford, Stephen Chase of Salem and perhaps other Friends well known to you I presume and whom I have long been permitted to reckon among my intimate associates. Hoping _soon_ and favorably to hear from you I am with respect*
>
> *Rufus Babcock[27]*

Babcock wrote a glowing report to Matthew Vassar about his initial meeting with Maria Mitchell.

Patterson N. J. 8th Sept. 1862

Hon. M. Vassar

...Harriet will return to Po'keepsie this day week. By her I will send to you a formal Report addressed to you for the Exec Com if they care to look at it, in regard to my visits to Miss Maria Mitchell and to Cambridge [Harvard] University.

In regard to the former, I will merely say at present, that it was fortunate I visited her as I did. For we were entirely in error in the supposition that she had applied for a place for herself in Vassar College. She only wrote a letter of inquiry[28] for a brother-in-law, now in Meadville, Pa., whom she knew to be a very competent Astronomer and who was getting but an inadequate support.

Finding, however, that we did not need to engage teachers in the Vassar College, at present, she took no further steps in the case and our inference, naturally enough, was that she was seeking to connect herself with our Institution. I had a long and very interesting conference with her and her venerable father—the result of which I hope may be to our advantage.

She is by far the most accomplished astronomer of her sex in the world I have no doubt. And but few of our manly sort are anywhere near her equal—in her loved and chosen pursuits. She has moreover a breadth of culture I was by no means prepared to expect. She has travelled a year in Europe with the best facilities of access to all the learned; and yet with all this refineness she is as simple minded and humble as a child.

I think I left her very much enamored with the noble enterprise of our founder, and disposed to come to his aid, in the magnificent enterprise to which we all think he is worthily devoting his time, his thoughts, and his accumulated fortune.

With all the rest, Miss Maria is not such a poor miserable "blue-stocking" as to know nothing else but astronomy. The day I spent with them their domestic was absent—and Maria prepared dinner and presided in all the housewifery of their cosey establishment without parade, and without any apparent deficiencies.

In her astronomical observatory, fitted up at the back end of her garden she is still more at home, handling her long and well adjusted telescope with masterful ease, accuracy and success. She furnishes all the astronomical calculations for the Nautical Almanac, at the stipulated pay of 500 dollars a year. This she can probably take with her to Po'keepsie, if we shall be so fortunate as to secure her services.

Knowing too, that she is too independent or of too much shrinking modesty to apply for the situation, and specially that we should not expect her to be going about to hunt up recommendations of her friends for the place, I have myself obtained 3 testimonials as good and high as New England can furnish. All these I will lay before you with my report. She reads German and French in order to perfect herself in her science, and I was interested to find that her estimate of the schools for Female Education in Europe agreed substantially with my own. The truth is they have no such Institutions as you are founding nor any considerable approximation to it....

R. Babcock.

Expenses incurred in the above services for the College, Seven and a half dollars.[29]

Babcock obtained three letters of recommendation in support of appointing Maria Mitchell to the faculty of the new college. Besides the letter reproduced here, there was one from Benjamin Peirce,[30] professor of mathematics at Harvard, and one from Alexis Caswell,[31] president of Brown. All three letter writers were friends of Mitchell.

State Normal School

Salem, M[as]s. Aug. 30, 1862.

Rev. Dr. Babcock,

I should consider the Trustees of the Vassar Female College eminently fortunate, if they could secure the services of Miss Maria Mitchell as Professor of Astronomy.

Her distinguished scientific attainments, her liberal literary culture, the remarkable successes & honors which she has already attained, her signal industry & zeal in the promotion of science, her frankness & ease of personal communication, her acquaintance with the institutions & savants of our own & other lands, & her beautiful simplicity & benevolence of character, unite in commending her as preeminently fitted for this

*position in an Institution so nobly endowed, & from which so much is
anticipated for the cause of education & the progress of mankind.*

Alph^s. Crosby [Principal][32]

In August, Babcock finally admitted to Maria Mitchell the reason for
his visit.

Po'keepsie 15th Oct. 1862

Miss Maria Mitchell,

*You may have thought it somewhat strange that I have so long
delayed in writing you after the very pleasant reception you gave me at
Lynn in August. But it has so happened that I have not seen our noble
patron Mr. Vassar since our interview till the present weeks.*

*Let me however, confess myself, fully and frankly. The result of my
visit to Lynn left, on my own mind an impression so decided in regard
to the desirableness of your being suited to fill the Chair of Astronomy
in the Vassar Female College that I at once determined to have no feasible effort on my part untried that might conduce to that end.*

*I conferred with Principal Crosby of the Normal School, Salem
and said to him, and subsequently to Prof. Peirce of Cambridge and
Prof. Caswell of Providence, that I feared you had not desire enough to
be considered a candidate for appointment in our Institution to move one
finger in furtherance of your appointment.*

*Therefore I had determined to ask of each of them such a letter to
me, setting forth the conviction of your fitness, as they might be willing
to give. Each of them, most cordially furnished such a letter as giving
me entire satisfaction. You were not to know anything of this. But it has
occurred to me that possibly you might hear such a part or perversion of
what I have thus done as would give pain to your sensitive nature and
therefore I have made a full confession.*

*My Report to Mr. Vassar, accompanied with the testimonials of the
above named gentlemen have given him and our Executive Com. the
highest satisfaction. So that the way is all open now for a direct negoti-
ation with you so soon as our President, Mr. Jewett, shall return from
Europe.*

*Mr. Vassar also, to whom I had written something of your honoured
father, to whom you attribute so much in making you what you are, and
from whom very properly you would not consent to be separated, has
inquired in a very kind considerate manner whether something might not*

be assigned him in promotion of our great object. I cannot therefore but hope that the way will be open for such an arrangement as will be altogether satisfactory to you in all respects....

In regard to our plans for <u>prosecuting</u> Astronomical science, I very much fear that I too strongly implied that we would do little in this regard. Whereas my hope certainly would be, that you, as our Professor of Astronomy would be placed in a position certainly not less favourable (I would hope more so) for the prosecution of the science as that you now occupy. For certainly we cannot but desire our young ladies minds to be fed from living springs—rather than from a reservoir. I cannot but hope, therefore, that the best needed facilities would be furnished you for continuing your investigations.

Then in regard to salary—What I named to you was very crude, the mere first thoughts of <u>one</u> of a committee of 7 members—and hinting at a sum so small was rather from a too ardent wish to save as much as possible from the income of our permanent endowment to be appropriated to scholarships for meritorious but indigent young ladies.

Prof. Peirce of Cambridge volunteered the remark that he has no doubt you could retain the scientific work for the Nautical Almanac as long as you pleased and that coming into our Institution would be no interruption or hindrance. So that with that, I have no doubt our Trustees would make up a support which would be very handsome and even without it quite adequate.

But I have scribbled on very freely to a length which I fear will weary you....

With the tender of sincere respects for your venerated father and of sincere esteem for yourself, I am,

Rufus Babcock[33]

Babcock's letter took Mitchell completely by surprise. But she wasted no time in responding to his unexpected news that she was being considered as a candidate for a professorship at Vassar.

Lynn Oct. 23, 1862

Dr. Rufus Babcock,

Not a word of what you wrote me had reached me before. I supposed that the whole plan of the College was so incomplete, that no further steps had been taken. I can but be gratified that you should think me fitted to fill so responsible a position and that the gentlemen you name, whose good opinion I so much value, should be willing to speak well of me.

The copy of the "Proceedings of the Trustees" came to hand the next day after your call. I have read it with great interest....

The whole enterprise is magnificent—so much the greater is the responsibility of those who mingle their hands in the work, and especially the first hands. I think I said about all that I need say, in our long and open talk—at this stage of the proceedings, if the subject is pursued and the thoughts of Mr. Vassar and Com. still turn towards me for the Astronomical professorship, I should hope to see you again.

In the meantime I should be glad to have you keep me informed (so far as you think proper) of the progress of the arrangements in all departments.

With my best wishes for the success of the whole work, I am yours very respectfully

Maria Mitchell[34]

The first letter which Mitchell received directly from Matthew Vassar must have been very welcomed, especially since he informed her of his unequivocal view that she was the most qualified person to be professor of astronomy.

> *Oct. 29, 1862.*
> *Miss Maria Mitchell*
> *Dear Madame,*
>
> *I have on several occasions had the pleasure to hear your name mentioned at the Annual Meetings of the Board of Trustees of V. F. College as the most suitable person to fill the important Office of Professorship of Astronomy and an increased interest has been manifested since your interview with Dr Rufus Babcock, whom has been quite desirous that our Institution should avail itself of your valuable services in that department.*
>
> *You will please to excuse me when I say as the Founder of the College that I feel the deepest anxiety for the successful occupancy of that Professorship, and believe there is no one in our Country can better insure it than yourself.*
>
> *No official appointments in the Institution has [sic] been made other than the Presidency & Professorship of Chemistry—nor will there be*

until Professor Jewett returns from his professional European tour next Spring.

We are progressing finely with our College building it is receiving its roof and the whole Edifice will be completed within the time contracted. viz.: 1 June 1864—

In a few days I will send you a copy of the New Englander containing an article on our College Enterprize. I have not seen it as yet, but I have heard it well spoken of by others—

I am dear Madam

Yours very respectfully,

Matthew Vassar [35]

Lynn Nov. 22, 1862

Matthew Vassar Esq.

Dear Sir,

I have delayed acknowledging the receipt of your very kind letter of Oct. 29, supposing that the copy of the *New Englander* of which you spoke, would reach me. It does not arrive, and I take the liberty of mentioning it, supposing it has miscarried.

In common with every intelligent person in the country I have watched with great interest the progress of your enterprise, and have rejoiced in the belief that a solid education would be afforded to American women—such as they have never yet known.

Dr. Babcock sent me a copy of the proceedings at the meetings of the Trustees. If it is quite convenient to you I should like to have another; I have friends at a distance who would like to know more than they can through mere newspaper items.

Maria Mitchell[36]

Poughkeepsie November 25th, 1862

Miss Maria Mitchell

Dear Madam,

I am just in receipt of your letter of the 22d inst. and owe you an apology for my remissness.

I now send you the copy of the "New Englander" with a few Pamphlets of the Proceedings of the Board of Trustees at their first meeting, which I trust will reach you in due course of mail.

I am very happy to learn that you are taking so much interest in V. F. College Enterprize by watching its progress, &c. This day completed the roofing, our Edifice is now enclosed from Storms & Winds—during the winter we do all works that can safely be done at those seasons; There is every prospect of completing the whole Edifice by the summer of 1864.

I have the pleasure to inform you that President Professor Jewett will be home by the 1st previous. The state of the Country & Exchanges have induced him & several other Americans to shorten their journeyings.

I shall at all times be happy to hear from you.

Truly Yours,

M. Vassar[37]

The facility envisioned for astronomy instruction is described in several reports of the Vassar board of trustees given below.[38] With the new telescope, Mitchell would be able to do first-class astronomical research, especially on the planets. Regrettably, when the observatory was completed it became obvious that the telescope lens was not accurately finished and the mounting was inadequate. Both of these problems were to vex Mitchell throughout her career at Vassar and seriously curtail the usefulness of the telescope.

The problems may have been due to the untimely death of Henry Fitz, the telescope maker, before the instruments could be completed. Making a good telescope is not easy; the assistants who took up the task were probably not as capable as Fitz in the art of telescope making.

April 6, 1863 Pres. Jewett is turning his attention toward an Observatory. He has purchased through other parties of Henry Fitz of New York: Achromatic Telescope Object Glass; 12 inch aperture, 12 3/8 inches diameter. Cost of mounting to be about $2500. Only 4 larger glasses in the country.

June 30, 1863 The first essential is an Observatory equipped with equatorial telescope, transit instrument and meridian circle; sidereal clocks and chronograph, filar and ring micrometers to fit the equatorial. The Observatory must contain equatorial room, transit room, prime vertical room, library and lecture room. The roof of one wing should be finished for star tracing.

For Vassar College to open its halls without this important auxiliary in the study of the works of God would be unworthy of its grand and beneficent design and reflect dishonor on its munificent Founder.

We have purchased of Henry Fitz the object glass at the unparalleled low price of $1,600. The telescope complete will cost only $4,100 and when finished will rank with those of Hamilton College and Michigan University, exceeding in size and power the celebrated instrument at Cincinnati imported by Prof. Mitchell [no relation] from Munich, and much superior to those in Washington City, and West Point, and at Portsmouth, Amherst and Williams Colleges, and second only to the famous telescope at Cambridge.

November 9, 1863. News received of the death of Henry Fitz who was to mount and furnish the telescopic object glass. (Learned later that his contract would be carried out.)

Mitchell's own appraisal of how the department would function and how she would approach her teaching is contained in the following letter to Babcock. Babcock seems to have made several suggestions to Mitchell to which she responded. To the suggestion that she work full-time by taking a part-time position at Vassar and continuing her work for the Nautical Almanac, Mitchell replied that her teaching would be a full-time occupation. She did keep her Nautical Almanac position at first, but in a few years gave it up as too time-consuming.

The salary question addressed in the letter proved more difficult. Although the salary suggested by Babcock would have been adequate, he really had no say in the matter. Mitchell's view that she was "not worth it," if true at the time, changed rapidly after she was at Vassar; during her career at the college, she engaged in a long-running battle with the trustees about the low salaries of the women professors.

Lynn, March 18, 1864

Rev. Rufus Babcock,

Your note of March 14th is very gratifying. My Father's comfort is of the utmost importance in my eyes.

I have had no correspondence with the President of Vassar Female College, and I have known nothing of the plan for an observatory, except what I have gathered from newspaper items. But I take it for granted, that in the event of my becoming connected with the

Courtesy of J.J. Sinnott

THE ORIGINAL VASSAR COLLEGE OBSERVATORY AS IT APPEARS TODAY. When the first trustees of Vassar planned the new college, a central part of their vision was establishing a first-rate observatory. The Vassar Observatory was the second building initiated on the new campus, and the first one completed prior to its opening in 1865.

The original Vassar Observatory is now a National Historic Landmark.

College, I shall have the use, in time, if not at the outset, of at least one good astronomical instrument, in working order, not only for the instruction of the pupils, but for other scientific investigations, if the educational interests of the college will admit of it or, if I do not find a good instrument, that I shall be allowed to take my own.

Of the three suggestions which you make, I incline to prefer the first. Do you not think it will be best, if I enter the College at all, that it be for the full term?

I do not fancy half-way work, and would rather make myself useful in an institution, than to be a mere outside appendage. I should have no objection to the popular course of lectures you suggest; (I assume that they are for pupils and not for a miscellaneous audience) but I should hope, in time to find students who would tax my utmost powers, and it will be strange if Vassar College does not bring out some girls who shall go far beyond me.

I should have little faith in my having any success in other departments than astronomy, but I suppose in such an Institution the professors would work together and help one another if it became necessary. Of course the highest <u>applied</u> mathematics must come into my department.

I have no fear that there will be too little work. If the pupils are few, there will be observatory work. Vassar Female College is even now one of the landmarks of the Earth; its Latitude and Longitude must be accurately determined.

I do not suppose the present state of the financial affairs of the country, is to be taken as the normal condition of things, and I had not thought of so large a sum ($1500) as you say the President supposes I shall require. I do not believe I am worth it!

But you will please consider that I shall give to the College probably the last of my working years. I feel that I ought not to throw upon relatives, however willing, the support of my old age. Henry Ward Beecher says "Hard work does not kill a man, but worry does." Would it be wise in me to accept a difficult and responsible position, and have the additional "worry" of a painful economy, in view of the future?

Besides — would it be right in me, to lower the standard of pay for other women, by accepting a small salary? On the other hand, I feel that my want of practical experience as a Teacher, should have its proper weight, in the consideration of the value of my services. I must be a learner as well as a Teacher.

What I said to you about women as astronomical observers was probably this — The perceptive faculties of women being more acute than those of man, she would perceive the size, form and color of objects more readily and would catch an impression more quickly. Then, the training of girls (bad as it is) leads them to develop these faculties.

The fine needle-work and the embroidery teach them to measure small spaces. The same delicacy of eye and touch is needed to bisect the image of a star by a spiders-web, as to pierce delicate muslin with a fine needle. The small fingers too come into play with a better adaptation to delicate micrometric screws. A girls powers of steady endurance of monotonous routine is great. The girl who sits for two hours at the piano, might just as well take two hours at the telescope. I believe it would be better for the health even, that a girl should spend some time in the open air in the evening— the good air of out-doors being always better than the bad air in-doors. I think as observers in any department of natural science they would be excel-lent. I do not believe however, that when it comes to the most pro-found investigations of the problems of the universe, they would be found very good philosophers. But how few men are?

I do not mark my letter "confidential" preferring to leave it to your judgment. May I trouble you to thank Mr. Vassar for the copy of the Poughkeepsian containing his remarks, with which I was delighted.

Whether Vassar Female College be a "success" or not, a great step which must have a long train of good results, has already been taken.

With thanks to you for your kind interest in my affairs and for your good opinion

Maria Mitchell[39]

In a letter written to his niece on April 30, 1864, William Mitchell summarized the situation:

If we go to Vassar College we shall not change our home. Lynn will still be the resting place. The correspondence with the Trustees has been received in these parts.

> *Maria has told them what she will do and what only and it is for them to say whether she is worth what they will have to do to secure her services. They offer the most comfortable quarters that imagination could devise but their expenditures, already reckless cannot continue to pay large salaries. Their edifice and its furnishings will not fall much short of a half million of dollars.*

Mitchell did not burn all her bridges, keeping her position with the Nautical Almanac in case the college failed. The early years of Vassar College were financially very difficult, so her caution was well justified. She worked for the Nautical Almanac until 1868.

Confidential [no date]

Rev Rufus Babcock,

I do not understand from the sketch you send me, of the Astronomical Instruments, how much has actually been done, towards the Observatory. I suppose not much as yet. The instruments must be good judging from the size and the makers; the expense of mounting such, will be great. I would suggest to you (aside from any consideration of myself) if only one instrument is set up, that it be the Equatorial. If it is a good article of that size, (and Mr. Fitz made very good glasses), it will be capable of doing a great deal of work—there are not many larger ones in the world.

I forgot to say to you in my last, that, in case of my having such an appointment as I can accept, I shall try to make an arrangement with my Nautical Almanac employers, to retain the work, but not to do it myself. I am afraid to throw it up, as, if I fail in Poughkeepsie, no other such institution—that is—no place of instruction, will open its doors to me.

But as I am sure that I am not strong enough in body or mind to do two kinds of work well, I should employ some one to make the computations, using of course the whole pay of the Almanac for that purpose. That is, of course, rather premature planning, but I thought you would perhaps like to know it.

Maria Mitchell[40]

Almost three years after the first contact Mitchell was finally offered a position at the college at a salary much less than first suggested by Babcock. She was now ready to embark on a new career as professor of astronomy.

For twenty years Maria had been librarian at the Atheneum; for about fifteen of those years, she had also been a computer for the Nautical Almanac. Her new career gave her the opportunity to present her views on education and women to a wider audience than ever before.

> *Stonington, Mch. 4/65*
>
> *My dear Miss Mitchell*
>
> *Would you accept an appointment as "Professor of Astronomy and Superintendent of the Observatory," in Vassar College at a salary of $800 per annum, with board for yourself & father, and some hope of an advance after the first year, if the finances of the College justify it? ...*
>
> *J. H. Raymond[41]*

A second letter from President Raymond only a few days later at least presents his position honestly but it must have tempered her pleasure at receiving the position.

> *Boston, Mch. 7, 1865*
>
> *Miss Maria Mitchell,*
>
> *I intend to recommend your appointment on the terms named in my previous note. Whether the Committee will endorse my recommendation or the Trustees adopt it, will depend (I presume) on the question whether they think the finances of the College will warrant the expenditure for an object which, however <u>desirable</u>, I cannot conscientiously say I consider <u>indispensable</u> to the main object of the institution.*
>
> *J. H. Raymond[42]*
>
> *April 12, 1865 Fifteen votes were cast for Miss Maria Mitchell as Professor of Astronomy who was declared duly elected.[43]*

In spite of President Raymond's assessment that she was not "indispensable to the main object of the institution," Maria Mitchell was finally hired by Vassar College.

> *Vassar Female College*
>
> *Poughkeepsie, N. Y. April 14, 1865*
>
> *Miss Maria Mitchell*
>
> *I have pleasure in apprising you that upon your compliance with certain permanent and general conditions and regulations established by*

Maria Mitchell

the Trustees of Vassar Female College you are elected Professor of Astronomy in this College.

These conditions will be forwarded to you as soon as they can be prepared for that purpose unless you should prefer to visit this place and confer personally with the President & other College authorities resident here.

C. Swan, Secretary[44]

In 1915, President James M. Taylor and Professor Elizabeth Haight had this appraisal of the hiring of Maria Mitchell:

This "costly luxury" was secured and Maria Mitchell came to Vassar at the opening as professor of astronomy to bring it the distinction of her name, the stimulus of her intellect, and the vigor of her personality.

The observatory still holds the traditions of her life there: her famous dome parties to her student friends, her outspoken discussions of life and education, her intense interest in the peculiar problems of woman's training and status, her unwearying mental activity. It was a great boon that a college for women should have had a woman of such mental and personal caliber to assist at its founding. The keynotes of her character were sincerity and an eager passion for truth, and she helped impart these qualities to the life of Vassar in its pioneer days.[45]

CHAPTER 8

VASSAR COLLEGE, 1865 to 1873

I never look upon the mass of girls
going into our dining-room or chapel without
feeling their nobility, the sovereignty of their pure spirit.

*O*N JUNE 3, 1861, GROUND WAS BROKEN for the construction of the first building of Vassar Female College. The massive five-story building would contain classrooms, a library, museums and laboratories, as well as living accommodations for students and faculty. Except for the observatory, situated a short distance to the northeast, the entire college was housed in what was aptly called Main Building. A few months after the official opening on September 26, 1865, the college changed its name to simply Vassar College, partly because Sarah Josepha Hale, editor of *Godey's Lady's Book,* led a crusade to have the word "Female" stricken from the name.[1]

At that time there were no admission requirements as presently understood. Instead, interested students came to the campus, were interviewed, and took exams to see whether they had the necessary background for the college course. If not, they could enter "preparatory" classes.

When the college opened its doors in 1865, there were eight professors, of whom two were women, and twelve teachers, of whom ten were women. The "Lady Principal" was Hannah W. Lyman. As Vassar's first astronomy professor, Maria Mitchell had a newly built observatory—where she lived, taught, and did her astronomy research.

Maria Mitchell

WILLIAM MITCHELL DESCRIBED the first days of the college in a letter to his nine-year-old grandson Willie, son of Phebe Kendall. Eight years later, Willie would accompany his aunt on her fascinating trip to Russia. In the 1865 letter from his grandfather, the "dear boy" gets a good dose of astronomy, as well as a picturesque tour of the new college.

Poughkeepsie, N. Y.

9th mo. 24, 1865

My dear boy,

Twenty days have past since the date of thy very nice and acceptable letter. Twenty times this old earth on which we live has turned completely over on its imagined axis. In that period by this motion of the earth only; thou hast moved more than three hundred and eight thousand miles. But this is not thy greatest journey. By the motion of the earth toward the point at thy right hand when thou stands facing the sun, thou has moved thirty one millions of miles in the same period.

All this is perfectly true though we do not perceive it. It is not manifest to the senses so directly as is a journey to Boston; but it is as manifest to the understanding. But I have said enough about these matters for this time. At the head of this sheet on the opposite side is a very correct engraving of Vassar College. The Observatory is not in the picture, but is situated a little back of the College building and a little at the left where thou will see a cross (X). We take our meals in the college but we otherwise live in the Observatory which is very near.

The grounds in front are quite as pretty as they are represented in the picture and they extend all around the building and at quite a distance from it. In our passing from and to the Observatory we go through a beautiful lawn in a meandering graveled path like that in your garden and the distance is about 500 feet. These paths in the afternoon, especially those around the Observatory are frequented by the young ladies in their promenading and to rest they frequently take seats on the steps of the Observatory which command the most picturesque views. Besides the stately college and its ground we see at the left the Highlands of the Hudson and at the right the [Shawangunks] and the Catskill mountains.

During the four days since the opening of the college, crowds of people have been into the Observatory, consisting chiefly of the students

1865

"MAIN BUILDING,"
VASSAR COLLEGE.
Upon moving to the
newly founded Vassar
College in 1865 with his
daughter Maria, William
Mitchell, *right,* expressed
his delight at the "stately
college" which had be-
come their new home.
During the next several
years, William Mitchell
would become a "main-
stay" on campus. An
avid astronomer for
much of his life, he was a
continual inspiration to
Maria. Both father and
daughter lived in the
new college observatory,
visible at the far left of
the engraving above.

and their parents and friends who have accompanied them to the college. Aunt Maria was most of the time in the college, meeting them as they arrived shewing them the college with the other professors, while I took care of them at the Observatory shewing them the instruments and describing them. The first day I found I had talked steadily from 8 o'clock in the morning till six at night except the dinner hour. In the evening my throat was much swollen, but the second day there were fewer, and now there are only twenty or thirty a day.

It would delight thee to see all the pupils and teachers take their meals. The dining room is large, new and beautiful. The tables and all their furniture are new—all the chairs are alike. Imagine then three hundred young ladies each standing behind her chair with her left hand upon it awaiting with all the Professors and teachers the arrival of the President. When he comes in (and his place is close to the door) and draws his chair back, three hundred chairs are moved, think what a clattering. Being seated, the tick of a little dinner bell is the signal for perfect silence which continues for about a minute, then the President reaches for his napkin, an example which is followed with electric speed by all the hungry girls.

The college with its nine hundred windows makes a beautiful shew when the gas is all lighted. But I have scarcely room to send my love to thy father and mother or to say that I am affectionately thy Grandfather.

Write me often.[2]

Frequent visitors, curious about the new college and its observatory, came to the campus to see for themselves; many arrived unannounced for a visit to the observatory. Mr. Mitchell whimsically recalled a typical visit in a letter to his brother Peleg.

This is something like the style. A vigorous rap at the door, Maria goes and meets "a six footer." "Are you Miss Mitchell?" "Yes." "Is that your father?" "Yes." "Is he a clergyman?" "No." "I see he wears a white cravat." "That's his privilege." "I have been through the college and thought I would like to see the observatory. Can you show me the instruments?" "Yes. It is pretty cold in the dome, we shall be compelled to be brief." "Certainly Madam." I should have been the victim if I had not had lumbago. Often in this way we entertain persons introducing themselves, whom, we afterward find, we should be glad to know.[3]

After a year of teaching experience at Vassar behind her, Maria Mitchell recorded her own impression of the college—and its second year's opening—with her usual candor.

1866. Vassar College brought together a mass of heterogeneous material, out of which it was expected that a harmonious whole would evolve—pupils from all parts of the country, of different habits, different training, different views; teachers, mostly from New England, differing also; professors, largely from Massachusetts yet differing much. And yet, after a year, we can say that there has been no very noisy jarring of the discordant elements; small jostling has been felt, but the president has oiled the rough places, and we have slid over them.

Miss [Lyman] is a bigot, but a very sincere one. She is the most conservative person I ever met. I think her a very good woman, a woman of great energy... She is very kind to me, but had we lived in the colonial days of Massachusetts, and had she been a power, she would have burned me at the stake for heresy.[4]

Yesterday the rush began. Miss Lyman had set the twenty teachers all around in different places, and I was put into the parlor to talk to "anxious mothers." Miss Lyman had a hoarse cold, but she received about two hundred students, and had all their rooms assigned to them. While she had one anxious mamma, I took two or three, and kept them waiting until she could attend to them. Several teachers were with me. I made a rush at the visitors as they entered, and sometimes I was asked if I were lady principal, and sometimes if I were the matron. This morning Miss Lyman's voice was gone. She must have seen five hundred people yesterday.

Among others there was one Miss Mitchell, and, of course, that anxious mother put that girl under my special care, and she is very bright. Then there were two who were sent with letters to me, and several others whose mothers took to me because they were frightened by Miss Lyman's style.

One lady, who seemed to be a bright woman, got me by the button and held me a long time—she wanted this, that, and the other impracticable thing for the girl, and told me how honest her daughter was; then with a flood of tears she said, "But she is not a Christian. I know I put her into good hands when I put her here." (Then I was strongly tempted to avow my Unitarianism.) Miss W., who was standing by, said, "Miss Lyman will be an excellent spiritual adviser," and we both looked very serious; when the mother wiped her weeping eyes and said, "And, Miss Mitchell, will you ask Miss Lyman to insist that my daughter shall curl her hair? She looks very graceful when her hair is curled, and I want it insisted upon." I made a note of it with my pencil, and I happened to glance at Miss W. The corners of her mouth were twitching, upon which I broke down and laughed. The mother bore it very good-naturedly, but went on. She wanted to know who would work some buttonholes in her daughter's dress that was not quite finished, etc., and it all ended in her inviting me to make her a visit.[5]

1871....I never look upon the mass of girls going into our dining-room or chapel without feeling their nobility, the sovereignty of their pure spirit.[6]

In an early assessment of her life at Vassar, Mitchell expressed her pleasure with the college and her facilities for teaching astronomy. Less than three months into her first year of teaching, Maria wrote a glowing report to Caroline H. Dall[7] about her students, the observatory, and her eagerness to pursue astronomical studies there.

Dec. 9, 1865

...In my own department these are the circumstances. I am wholly in charge of an excellent observatory. No one has yet asked me what I was doing or what I intend to do. It is furnished with a good telescope (so far as I can judge on so short an acquaintance) and with an excellent meridian Inst[rument]. I regret that I was not in this position ten years ago. I think I could have done a great deal of good work. Whether there are years enough before me now is of course uncertain. [She was 47 years old.]

I have a class of pupils, seventeen in number, the youngest 16 the eldest 22. They come to me for 50 m. every day. I am no teacher, but I give them a lesson to learn and the next day the recitation is half a conversational lecture and half questions and answers. I allow them great freedom of questions and they puzzle me daily. They show more mathematical ability than I had expected and more originality of thought. I doubt if young men of that age would take as much interest in science. Are there 17 students in Harvard College who take

Mathematical Astronomy do you think? So far, in my class I have been allowed to do as I please, whether I always shall I do not know— We are very fortunate in our President. He is a man of good solid mind and very kind to every one.[8]

In an undated memorandum—probably written as part of her annual report to the president—Mitchell outlined what she taught in her early years at Vassar. From her description of the curriculum, we learn that she conducted a rigorous and mathematical course. Spherical astronomy, no longer emphasized in contemporary astronomy courses, was an essential part of the training of an astronomer in Maria's day. Notice that Professor Mitchell did not give what today we would call a "survey course" in astronomy. For many years, she resisted giving this kind of course.

The astronomical course begins with the Junior year, although a few familiar lectures on astronomical subjects are given to the Sophomore class.

As the instruction in this Department is conducted, as far as possible, on a mathematical basis, students who elect the study must have passed a satisfactory examination in the required studies of the mathematical course. In the first year of the astronomical course, students are taught from text books and by lectures the simple problems of spherical astronomy, the most ready methods of finding latitude, longitude and time and to compute Lunar Eclipses. They are instructed in the use of instruments, small telescopes and a transit instrument are put into their hands, which they are encouraged to use freely in their intervals of leisure. They can, if they choose, engage in the routine work of the observatory, and are allowed some practice with the meridian circle. Written examinations are given at intervals of six weeks.

Students who elect astronomy for a second year, use as a text book Chauvenet's *Spherical Astronomy,* taking up the subject of solar eclipses and that of least squares. Their final examination includes the prediction of a solar eclipse by the most rigorous method, for the latitude and longitude of the observatory. These students are allowed some practice with the equatorial telescope.[9]

It did not take long for Mitchell to realize the inadequacy of her accommodations and the telescope. She and her father lived in the observatory, but there was no separate room for her. Her sleeping quarters were in the room that also served as her parlor for receiving guests. During the day her bed was converted to a sofa, so there was obviously little privacy. To make matters worse, the room also served as an entrance to the telescope dome *and* contained the astronomical clocks used by the students for their work—at any time, day or night. Not until November, 1875 did she get separate sleeping quarters, an event which elicited a lighthearted poem from one student entitled, "Miss Mitchell Sleeps in a Bed."[10]

Just prior to the Christmas break of her first year at Vassar, Maria expressed concern about her living accommodations. In the first of many letters seeking "greater domestic comfort" in the observatory, she wrote to Cyrus Swan, a trustee of the college.

Dec 19 1865

Will you, in our absence, have the goodness to look into the Observatory and see if some arrangements can be made for greater domestic comfort? The prime-vertical room is an excellent summer lodging room, but is not fitted for winter. Besides being extremely cold, it is so far from my Father's lodging room that, in a high wind, I cannot hear him if he calls to me. I think a lounge or a portable bedstead might be used in the clock-room, if I could have servants to carry it backwards and forwards, so that my class (who use that room) should not be incommoded by it.

Will you also, for the sake of the comfort of the old gentleman, have more coal put into the Obs[ervatory]. "He dies a thousand deaths in fearing one" by freezing and the sight of a large quantity of coal seems to keep him warm.[11]

Less than a year later, Mitchell had clearly discerned the slow pace of decision-making at the fledgling college. "Our faculty meetings always try me in this respect," she recorded in her diary on October 31, 1866. "We do things that other colleges have done before. We wait and ask for precedent. If the earth had waited for a precedent, it would never have turned on its axis?" Undaunted, Maria continued her quest for improvements—expressed again in this letter written at the end of her summer vacation in New England.

16 Green St.

Lynn Mass

Aug 28 1866

...Can you do something before my return, to make the base-
ment room of the Observatory more presentable? In spite of my
efforts to keep all the visitors in the upper room, they invariably
finish a call by descending to see the old gentleman. I hope to do
something in the way of furnishing myself, can the college improve
the walls? If the college cannot, can you give me permission to
paper or paint at my own expense? The walls still show the impress
of the dirty hands of the workmen, with a few additional auto-
graphs of servants, &c.[12]

Three years after the opening of the college Mitchell was still trying to obtain decent living quarters at the Observatory. She voiced
her concern in another summer correspondence from New England.
It was yet another of her pleading, yet good-humored, letters to the
college president.

Lynn July 8, 1868

My dear President [Raymond],

My habit of grumbling has become so chronic, that I felt disposed,
as I put your note down, to fret, that three such tasteful persons as
yourself, Miss L[yman] and Miss A[very] had not settled all my
domestic questions for me, and acted as upholsterers.

If you had done it, I haven't a doubt I should have fretted at that.
And the weather is quite too warm for such active exercise as a fit of
extra fretting! I want—in the room in which the clock is [Mitchell's
parlor], four or five respectable chairs, and a lounge or sofa. If you ask
what I mean by respectable, I reply "I do not know."

I am as ignorant of furniture as of music. I want such a state of
things in that room, which is the one into which the families of
Trustees come, that those families shall not reproach me in regard to
my "style,"—which has happened in two cases. There is a lounge
already in the room—(my only bed for two winters) which I wish to
remove into my Father's room. That is, if new furniture goes into the
clock room, the old furniture goes into the other rooms.

The Observatory was not built for a dwelling house and its radical
defects in that direction cannot be overcome—it was beautifully
planned for an Observatory.[13]

Maria Mitchell

A lively exchange of letters between Maria and Vassar's president took place in subsequent years. Still vigorously pursuing her quest for improved facilities for astronomy, the intrepid professor added her concern about the lack of astronomy books deemed necessary for her teaching and research. Although there was a growing bond of mutual respect and affection between Professor Mitchell and President Raymond, she didn't hesitate to write him strongly opinionated and animated letters.

Lynn July 29 [1869][14]

My dear President Raymond,

You complain of the shortness of my note about Miss Coleman. I rejoice at it for plainly you read it through! When I left you I put into your hands a long letter. I mourn over its length, for evidently you did not read it!

In that, I told you what I wanted done, and now you ask me what it was! I have written to Prof. Farrar[15] what I wanted done to the Observatory to make it more comfortable. But I am sorry that you did not urge the matter for me, because Prof. Farrar and I differ some in our opinions, about household comforts and Observatory needs. I could not expect you would, with all your cares.

But I am sorry you could not read the letter <u>once</u> through! I can read yours several times, even while making wearisome computations!

Will you be good enough (if you've got as far as this) to let me know if there is any hope that the College will buy me the books that I want? If not, I must beg, borrow and buy, before I return to the College. I dare not repeat the brain struggle of the last year; it is suicidal to attempt to solve the problems of the universe, without a knowledge of the facts and reasoning which are on record. I think I can afford to buy some books and I know that I can beg some.

Will you then, please tell me at once, if there is <u>no</u> hope? I do not believe anyone in the college is more unwilling than I to trespass upon your time, and to harrow and worry you with my grievances, but they have ceased to be mine, when they are shared by all the students in my department, and a cause of open complaint. If the College can not do for my department, I must do for it myself.

Maria Mitchell[16]

President Raymond replied at once, offering his good-natured view of the situation *and* promising change.

> *Vass Coll, Aug. 5, 69*
>
> *My dear Miss Mitchell,*
>
> *I did, 'pon honor, read your paper "through"—and with interest and sympathy and a determination that, if I had any influence on the new powers, something should be done. But I did not charge my mind with the details, and remembered it, as the time I wrote you, as a conversation. In recalling the fact subsequently, I looked for the paper, but could not find it—and think I must have passed it with the documents accompanying my Ann[ual] Rep^t into the Secretary's hands.*
>
> *But, n'importe, you have written to the New Sup—beg pardon, the Local Agent—and I have talked with him—and he promises me the changes shall be made—and I hope you will have a more comfortable home.*
>
> *As to the books, there is "hope." You shall have them! I wish, while you are so near the Hub, you could find out the best (cheapest) way of buying them such as you need, and whether there are copies obtainable advantageously there abouts now. We hesitate about giving the order for such books to an ordinary book importer like the Appletons—and yet that may be the best thing to be done.... So the world still moves—a little—not excluding V. C.*
>
> *Affectionately,*
>
> *J. H. R.*[17]

When Maria Mitchell arrived at Vassar, she assumed control of the Observatory's new twelve-inch refractor, which was then the third largest telescope in the nation. If it had been in good working condition, this telescope could have been used to measure double stars, a very fruitful astronomical work at the time, or to study the features on planets such as Jupiter, Saturn, and perhaps Mars. It was not adapted for photography and so was mostly used for visual observing. Mitchell may have had a spectroscope to use and could have perhaps emulated the work of Father Secchi whom she had visited in Rome in 1858. But she encountered severe difficulties.

The telescope's lens had not been ground accurately and so could not reveal the detail that it should have. The drive mechanism was faulty

Maria Mitchell

MARIA MITCHELL AND MARY WHITNEY IN THE DOME OF THE VASSAR OBSERVATORY. Mary Whitney was a member of Mitchell's first class at Vassar. She succeeded Mitchell in 1888 as observatory director.

It is apparent from this photograph how difficult it must have been for Mitchell, or anyone, to use this telescope. In order to observe an object, the telescope had to be pushed by hand to the correct position, as read from the dials of the telescope, while standing on the step ladder. With no motor to slue the telescope around, it needed to be pushed by hand; a clock mechanism would permit the telescope to follow the stars.

The device attached to the end of the telescope appears to be a micrometer for measuring double stars. A set of stairs just visible behind Whitney could be moved around the telescope on tracks so that the observer could climb up to look through the telescope.

so that a star would constantly drift across the viewing field instead of remaining fixed in position. These considerable defects would have made both visual observing and the use of a micrometer extremely difficult. Moreover, the dome was immense, as it needed to be for such a large (i.e. long) telescope. The opening slit in the dome through which observations were made was too heavy for Mitchell to open single-handedly. As the stars rose and set, the dome had to be rotated, something else she could not do by herself.

All of these problems made it extremely difficult to observe with this telescope. Professor Mitchell tried to have these serious flaws corrected, but it was a long, slow, and expensive process. Dr. Benson Lossing, a noted historian and one of the first Vassar trustees, was probably the most sympathetic to her difficulties.

> *Lynn, July 12, 1868*
>
> *Benson J. Lossing Esq.*
>
> *I have yours of the 9th authorising me to make the contract with Alvan Clark for the improvements to the telescope. I shall go to see him tomorrow.*
>
> *Can you not alter the point in regard to the time of completing the work? I am afraid it will not be possible to make Mr. Clark promise, before seeing the condition of the glass, to regrind it in so short a time, especially if he has other work on hand. May I not say Christmas? Mr. Clark is so thoroughly reliable, that if he finds the glass less imperfect then I suppose he will say it. His reputation is valuable to him, and he will be careful not to risk it, by a judgment which scientific men will debate.[18]*

The following month, Mitchell wrote a long letter to President Raymond detailing the first steps in correcting the lens of the telescope:

> I am desirous to have you know the progress of the movement about the object glass of the Equatorial telescope...I came here with Mr. Clark on Wednesday the 19th [of August 1868]...Mr. Clark and Prof. Lyman spent the evening in testing the object glass. They agreed exactly in their opinion of its defects and both said I had not over-rated them. I asked Prof. Lyman if I had been wrong in declaring the glass faulty in definition and he replied "you could not have

told the truth had you said any thing else." ...The errors are those of curvature. I went with him to Mr. Lossing and today Mr. Lossing has made a contract with him, to do the work for a sum not exceeding $500....[19]

By November 4, she could happily report to Lossing that "the definition of the glass is more improved than I had any hope of."[20]

Mitchell's triumphs and frustrations regarding her facilities carried over into her ideas about what the ideal college and observatory should be. The opening of Cornell University offered her an excuse to write Ezra Cornell,[21] urging advances in women's education, adequate telescope facilities, and freedom from "sectarian bias." Apologizing for the length of her confidential letter, Mitchell assures Cornell that it is sent with "wholly disinterested motives," "written in the hope of doing my small bit of good to a great undertaking."

Vassar College

Mch. 10, 1868

Ezra Cornell, Esq.

I am much gratified at the views expressed in your letter, and wish to say some things to you, which I must request shall be considered confidential in relation to the "woman" subject and, indeed to the whole. I have no fancy for the agitation on the subject, the bad taste always shocks me. But the reasoning on the subject of woman's rights, and their claims, seems to me logical, and in time it must prevail. I consider Vassar College the best institution in the world of the kind; it is not of the right kind.

When I was last in Boston I asked Dr. Hill, Pres't of Harvard College, "How soon will girls enter Harvard College" and he replied "The most conservative member of the Faculty says 'in 20 years.'" (It is my opinion that if you remove the zero from the number of years, you will be nearer the truth.) I also asked Prof. Peirce, the Math. Professor, "If a girl knocks at your class room door and asks for admission to your class what will you do?" He replied "I couldn't turn her away and I wouldn't."

I should like that an Institution starting on so broad a foundation as Cornell, should take the lead in that respect. You perceive, if you lead, you must step quickly, for the world moves.

Next, your President in his speech declares that the Institution is to be free from sectarian bias. <u>Can</u> you keep to that? I have never yet seen in a College, freedom in religious subjects. The College of Ann Arbor is, I suppose, the free-est, but even there I suspect, altho' I do not know, they would ask what religious views a Prof. held, before they elected him. Can you elect a professor, without asking that question? I believe that the cause of true religion is hurt every day, by those narrow lines of distinction on unimportant points.

Lastly, of the Observatory. I take the liberty of asking you to aim at <u>perfection</u> in the instruments and not at <u>size</u>. Our telescope is 12 1/2 inches object glass—and a very imperfect glass. A perfect glass of half the size would do better work. The air and climate are not good enough in our Latitude for very large instruments. There is a limit to the increase of telescopes which nature has set up, and unless glasses or climate improve, it is of no use to expect to gain much by mere <u>size</u>.

I feel that I should apologize to you for so long a letter. I have written in the hope of doing my small bit of good to a great undertaking; as I have no girl to be educated and no friend wanting a position you must give me credit for wholly disinterested motives. May you be prospered at every step in the long path on which you have entered.

Yrs.

Maria Mitchell

Best regards to Mrs. Cornell[22]

Mitchell's religious sensibilities had always tended toward a self-described "Unitarianism," but her concern about "sectarian bias" grew at Vassar to be something more than an instinct for personal religious freedom. Dogma of any kind, she believed, had no place in an educational setting and she used her diaries to record her reactions to the sermons she heard.

Dec. 18, 1866. We heard two sermons: the first in the afternoon, by Rev. Mr. A., Baptist, the second in the evening, by Rev. Mr. B., Congregationalist. Rev. Mr. A. took a text from Deuteronomy, about 'Moses,' Rev. Mr. B. took a text from Exodus, about 'Moses' and I am told that the sermon on the preceding Sunday was about Moses. It seems to me strange that since we have the history of Christ in the New Testament, people continue to preach about Moses.

...I am more and more disgusted with the preaching that I hear!...Why cannot a man act himself, be himself, and think for himself? It seems to me that naturalness alone is power; that a borrowed word is weaker than our own weakness, however small we may be. If I reach a girl's heart or head, I know I must reach it through my own, and not from bigger hearts and heads than mine.[23]

January 3, 1867 Meeting Dr. Hill at a private party, I asked him if Harvard College would admit girls in 50 years. He said one of the most conservative members of the Faculty had said within 16 days that it would come about within 10 years. I asked him if I could go into one of Prof. Peirce's recitations.[24] He said there was nothing to keep me out and that he would let me know when they came....

Maria Mitchell did in fact attend Dr. Peirce's recitations at least once. Since she had known him for many years, this encounter was probably not as abrasive as it seems from reading her diary.

At 11 a.m. the next Friday I stood at Prof. Peirce's door; as the Prof. came in I went toward him and asked him if I might attend his lecture. He said "Yes." I said "Can not you say 'I shall be happy to have [you]" and he said "I shall be happy to have you," but he didn't look happy, perhaps because he was himself remarkably en dishabille. It was with some little embarrassment that Mrs. K[endall] and I seated ourselves and she says I colored when 16 young men came into the room.

After the first glance at us there was not another look, and the lecture went on. Prof. Peirce had filled the blackboard with formulae and went on developing them. He walked backwards and forwards all the time thinking it out as he went. The students at first all took notes, but gradually they dropped off until perhaps only half continued. When he made simple mistakes, they received it in silence, only one, that one his son, a tutor in college, remarked that he was wrong. The steps of his lesson were all easy but of course it was impossible to tell whence he came or whither he was going....

The recitation room was very common looking, we could not tolerate such at Vassar....I asked him if a young lady presented herself at the door if he could keep her out and he said "No and I shouldn't." I told him I would send some of my girls.[25]

During a June 1868 gathering of the Vassar trustees, the founder of the college died suddenly. Later, Rufus Babcock recorded his eyewitness account of Matthew Vassar's last moments on that memorable June 23 day: "He was reading from the eleventh page when he failed to pronounce a word which was upon his lips, dropped the papers from his hand, fell back in his chair insensible, and died..."[26] Despite being with him at the college for three years, Maria Mitchell does not allude to this tragic event anywhere in her diary.[27]

FOR NEARLY TWENTY YEARS Mitchell had been doing computations for the Nautical Almanac, a job she retained after being hired by Vassar. After three years at the Poughkeepsie college, she was forced to acknowledge that she could not continue to work for both the college and the Almanac.

In giving up the Nautical Almanac work, she was not only inexorably tying her future to Vassar College, but foregoing an appreciable salary.

"I do not feel sure that it will be for the best," she wrote on September 22, 1868, "but I am sure that I could not hold the almanac and the college, and father is happy here." Indeed, as she wrote later, "I tell Miss Lyman that my father is so much pleased with everything here that I am afraid he will be immersed!"[28] (Matthew Vassar and most of the trustees were Baptists.) Her reasons for making a wholehearted commitment to Vassar were not simply practical; they were deeply grounded in her growing commitment to women's education.

> Oct. 15, 1868. As I predicted, we had a practical sermon, "What ever you do that do with all your might," excellent in its lessons, adapted to human beings, with no theological bias in it.
>
> (Resolved) In case of my outliving Father and being in good health, to give my efforts to the intellectual culture of women, without regard to salary. If possible, connect myself with liberal Christian institutions, believing as I do that happiness and growth in this life are best promoted by them and that what is good in this life is good in any life.[29]

Maria Mitchell

A group of Mitchell's first students, dubbed "the Hexagon" by her father, became quite close to both Mitchells. In a letter to President Raymond's daughter Mary, Mr. Mitchell once observed that some Vassar students "had, in a manner, adopted us as stepparents."[30] In addition to being beloved father and mother figures for the astronomy students, both William and Maria Mitchell served as their confidants.

A letter from Maria to the college president, written after a typical gathering of students at the observatory, captures a glimpse of the camaraderie which had developed at Vassar.

[c. 1867]

My dear President,

The young ladies who rush over to the Obs. and tell me all they know, think that you alluded to me, tonight, in speaking of someone who told you of all your faults. I assure them that I could not be the person, for not only do I not know all, but if I undertook to tell all that I do know, it would take all the time I have and none would be left to tell them of theirs.

M.M.

P.S. Miss [Clare] Glover asks me if I intend to say "Yours respectfully."[31]

William Mitchell, buoyed by a holiday visit from five of his daughter's Vassar students, recalled in a letter of January 18, 1869:

On Christmas day we were visited by Miss Glazier, Miss Glover, Miss Whitney,[32] Miss Blatchley and Miss Storke of the astronomical class.... We had a cheery and jolly time of it. I almost forgot my age and my infirmities.[33]

Maria first alluded to her father's "infirmities" in a letter she wrote to Benson Lossing. Mr. Mitchell had enjoyed remarkably good health for over seven decades, but the beloved seventy-seven-year-old man would fail rapidly during the first few months of 1869 at Vassar.

Tuesday

My dear Mr. Lossing,

I shall probably not see you this evening, as my Father is not well and I do not like to leave him. Nor do I believe I can accept your invitation for tomorrow evening, which I should much like to do, were my mind free from care about him. I do not suppose he is alarmingly ill, but he is decidedly feeble.

Yrs,

Maria Mitchell[34]

My dear Miss Morse

Father had a good night (thank you for asking, which you would if I saw you) and so I don't feel so much like taking to the dagger or the bowl or the pond as I otherwise should.

M.M.[35.]

William Mitchell's waning health becomes a growing concern for his fifty-year-old daughter. Eight years after her mother's final illness, Maria is again called to care for a dying parent. In late winter, she writes to her sister with news of their father's health.

Saturday, Feb. 27. [1869]

My dear Sally,

Father is slowly gaining. I get up now only once in the night and go down to him. He sleeps five or six hours very quietly. He is very much wasted but is cheerful now. The despondency was the worst symptom. While he had no appetite, Sarah Swain sent him some delicious bread and new butter and he ate cake by cake of the bread as long as it lasted and dreamed of it nights. His appetite is a little better. He has today some looseness of the bowels but it seems to be rather a good thing for him. His mind is as clear as ever.

M.M.[36]

Thursday, Mch. 4

My dear Sally,

Father seems better again today and the Doctor thinks it merely a "flurry." But he is so feeble that any "flurry" is a serious thing. He has been up an hour today, has eaten a little dinner in bed. I slept in his room last night and shall whenever it is necessary.

MM.

I cannot write often as I am much crowded.[37]

Maria Mitchell

On April 19, 1869, William Mitchell died in Poughkeepsie. Maria was now alone for the first time in her life.

A consoling letter to Maria from a sibling (unsigned, but probably from her sister Phebe) expressed the Mitchell family's profound loss. The letter, voicing concern that Maria may be "worn out," offered the grateful reminder that "it is a great thing to have had him so long and enjoyed him so much."

> *Cambridgeport, Tuesday*
> *My dear Maria,*
>
> *We received the dispatch last night, of course we expected it, and every ring of the bell for a week had set me to shaking, but after all it is a shock, and of course it would be at anytime. I don't think we could bear it any better ten years hence. It is all the more of a loss that he was so bright and clear and that he was so little of a sufferer.*
>
> *But I feel most of all about Kate. We felt so glad all day that no dispatch came and when [?] read us the dispatch sent in the morning it was so cheering to know positively that he was still living that I think Kate went off feeling quite sure that she should see him again. My heart ached for her all night, but she was entirely unfit to go before, there was not the slightest question about it, and if she had gone before the probabilities were that she would have a fit of illness as soon as she got there.*
>
> *Andrew was here this morning, he was afraid that the dispatch had not reached me. He says he is surprised that he lasted so long, he will go on to Nantucket on Thursday. I shall go too. I am glad that they will hear of it at Nantucket before we all go on. I was afraid that they would have no warning at all. I had intended to go on today, I thought I might be of some use and I felt so much for Anne, but having the children here of course I gave it up, and after all, I don't know that it would do any good.*
>
> *Travis and May are just as sweet as they can be, and obey their mother's directions implicitly. What a comfort it is that father was so serene and patient! I enjoyed my visit to him extremely, it seems so strange, when I knew then that he was marked with death. I am so glad that I saw him then. It is not at all likely that any of us will live to his age, and preserve so much serenity and sweetness, but it is a great thing to have had him so long and enjoyed him so much.*

MARIA MITCHELL AND HER FATHER AT VASSAR COLLEGE *(c. 1867).* With the Observatory as their home, William and Maria Mitchell were a special duo in the early days of Vassar College. Taking delight in his informal role on the new campus, Maria's father often gathered with students at the Observatory outside of class, including a regular Sunday evening get together.

For more than fifty years, Maria's father was a constant support to her; when he died in the spring of 1869, she was alone for the first time in her life, finding his loss "incomprehensible." Immediately after his death, one of her sisters wrote a consoling letter to the grieving Maria, offering the grateful reminder that "it is a great thing to have had him so long and enjoyed him so much."

Maria Mitchell

We are all afraid that thee will be worn out and sick. I hope thee will be able to keep up and bear it as well as possible. I can't help thinking that he being in such a beautiful frame of mind must help thee and that was why I hoped Kate would get there in season. She has depended so much upon it, and I am afraid had a presentment that her desires were to be thwarted. I have made up my mind that she and Sally will come on together tomorrow as I suppose Sally could not take so long a journey as that from Po'keepsie to Nantucket without a night's rest. I told the little girls this morning that Grandfather would never be sick any more, and that is what comforts me, that the weakness and fatigue are over, and the clear mind free from the feebleness of the body.[38]

One obituary notice reported that when Mr. Mitchell's casket was carried from the Vassar observatory:

...the professors and teachers and the three hundred students gathered at the observatory and in heartfelt sorrow for the dead, they attended the carriages to the lodge.[39]

William Mitchell was buried on Nantucket Island next to his wife. After attending the funeral on Nantucket, Maria traveled to Lynn, where her sister Kate still lived. Before returning to Vassar, she needed a few more days to adjust to this "incomprehensible" new chapter in her life.

Lynn, Ap. 25 1869

My dear President,

I am not sure I told you how long I must be away from the College. If I took only the Sunday's rest, it would be possible for me to reach the Obs. by Tuesday, but I feel the need of more than one day of quiet, before I enter upon the new and incomprehensible life before me, and as the birthday comes so soon, I think of stopping with the little children until Thursday, and so getting to the College on Friday.

It is probable that one of my sisters will come with me, for a little stay, of a week perhaps. I am sorry to give Miss Lyman even the little extra care of a new person at table, but she will perhaps feel the less care of me.

If you have notes of the remarks made on Tuesday evening, to the students, will you save them for me? I shall take such pleasure in collecting all those things for the sake of the grandchildren, and I shall value very much whatever you may have said.

I cannot express to you my gratitude of the kindnesses and attentions which were bestowed upon my Father during the last year. I am afraid I must ask for myself in the future more and more patient endurance from those around me.[40]

INFLUENCED BY HER FATHER'S EXAMPLE, Maria Mitchell always believed that her students should be doing meaningful scientific work. To that end they counted meteors during meteor showers and had published their results; they observed with a transit telescope to determine the local time for the college; they went to Iowa (and later Denver) to observe a total eclipse of the sun and make scientific observations.

For many years, Professor Mitchell's students wrote a column for *Scientific Monthly* about astronomical phenomena of the month. Later, they took photographs of the sun each clear day; several of these photographs still exist.

One student wrote in the college newspaper about the observations Mitchell and her students made of one of the great meteor showers of the nineteenth century. They counted about 3800 meteors, with 900 occurring in one hour between 2:00 and 3:00 a.m. The newspaper reported:

> *"Hope deferred maketh the heart sick!"[41] For years, Nov. 12th and 13th have beguiled us into "sitting up for meteors;" and always the heavens have returned our gaze in eternal fixedness, or impenetrable cloudiness.*
>
> *We had lost all faith in meteors, and looked upon a shower as a myth of the ancients, or as an inverse action of the special sense of vision, on the part of some blind believer. Our scoffing, however, is forever silenced: for have we not seen a shower and quorum-magna-pars-fui'd. On the evening of Nov. 27th, Miss Mitchell's attention was attracted before dark, by a large meteor in the zenith. On her way over to tea, seeing ten or more, she thought it advisable to watch further developments, and called in the aid of two of her students.*

The Astronomical course begins
with the Junior year, although a
few familiar lectures on Astronomical
subjects are given to the Sophomore
class.

In the instruction in this Department is conducted, as far
as possible, on a mathematical
basis, students who elect this study
must have passed a satisfactory
examination in the required studies
of the Mathematical course.

In the first year of the Astronomical course, students are taught
from text books and by lectures
the simple problems of Spherical
Astronomy, the most ready method
of finding latitude and longitude
and Time and to compute during
Eclipses. They are instructed

**MARIA MITCHELL'S HANDWRITTEN DESCRIPTION OF THE ASTRON-
OMY CURRICULUM SHE TAUGHT AT VASSAR COLLEGE.** She writes:
"The astronomical course begins with the Junior year, although a few
familiar lectures on astronomical subjects are given to the Sophomore
class…the instruction in this Department is conducted, as far as possible,
on a mathematical basis…" *(See page 161 for further details.)*

They were soon joined by three others, and from twenty minutes past six to a quarter of nine, seven hundred and ninety seven meteors were counted. Only for half an hour of this time was there a perfectly organized watch, one to each quadrant of the heavens, so it is safe to say that there were double the number reported. The climax seemed to be from half past six to half past seven...[42]

Mitchell's trip to Iowa to observe the total solar eclipse of August 7, 1869 was officially associated with the expedition of Professor Coffin, superintendent of the Nautical Almanac. She was accompanied to Burlington, Iowa by several of her past and present students, who made careful observations of the eclipse. Also joining her was her sister Phebe, who painted a picture of the eclipse. Three months prior to the event, the Vassar student newspaper announced the Iowa expedition.

May 1869. Some of our eager astronomers are talking of going out West to observe the total eclipse of August 7th, 1869. It seems to be settled that Professor Maria Mitchell and "The Hexagon" of last year will go, and possibly others will join the expedition.[43]

R. W. Gilder, editor of *Hours at Home,* asked Mitchell to write an article about the eclipse. In a letter to Maria just a week prior to the eclipse, he eagerly anticipates publishing her work.

July 30, 1869
Miss Maria Mitchell,
I am most glad that you are going to "try" and very sure that you will "succeed." "Cloudy" or not cloudy we want the article. If this eclipse can't be seen, why then you have the range of all the eclipses that have happened to write about, apropos to the occasion! You will be kind enough to notice by the last letter, the time by which we would like to receive the article.[44]

Mitchell evidently met Gilder's deadline. Her article, excerpted below, was published in the October 1869 issue of *Hours at Home.*

The eclipse expedition to Iowa, taken by Maria only three months after her father's death, had one especially remarkable feature: it was made up entirely of women. Maria alludes to this noteworthy fact at the end of her lengthy article. She begins the piece by explaining how the observer obtains the time of the beginning of the eclipse.

The time at which an eclipse will occur is always calculated by astronomers some years before, and a variation from that calculation in the actual appearance of the phenomenon is a hint that something is wrong. Not that there is an error in the calculations, for, given certain data with regard to sun, moon, and earth, and the predictions will be unerring. But the data may be wrong; a deviation if computed from observing time is a fingerprint to the astronomer; it means something. ...

Having no chronograph arrangement with me, I was obliged to depend on the counting of seconds[45] by an assistant. The assistant counts aloud the half-second beats of the chronometer; and the observer, with the eye upon the point to be watched, and the ear intent on the assistant's voice, awaits the event....

At length all was ready. The observers were at the telescopes; the regular count aloud of the half seconds began. Every observer tries to do the impossible. He tries to notice what is technically called "the first contact." He tries to note the exact instant when an unseen spherical body appears to touch a seen spherical body; that is, he tries to see a point infinitesimally small, and to mark a division of time which the ear cannot measure.

At a certain second and part of a second, the moon, all unseen, was expected to make itself visible. But the moon was not up to time! There were some seconds of breathless suspense, and then the inky blackness appeared on the burning limb of the sun. All honor to my assistant, whose uniform count on and on, with unwavering voice, steadied my nerves! That for which we had travelled fifteen hundred miles had really come.

We watched the movement of the moon's black disk across the less black spots on the sun's disk, and we looked for the peculiarities which other of partial eclipses had known....

Light clouds had for some time seemed to drift toward the sun; the Mississippi assumed a leaden hue; a sickly green spread over the landscape; Venus shone brightly on one side of the sun, Mercury on the other; Arcturus was gleaming overhead, Saturn was rising in the east; the neighboring cattle began to low; the birds uttered a painful cry; fireflies twinkled in the foliage, and when the last ray of light was extinguished, a wave of sound came up from the villages below, the mingling of the subdued voices of the multitude.

Instantly the corona burst forth, a glory indeed: It encircled the sun with a soft light, and it sent off streamers for millions of miles into space! And now it was quick work! To see what could be seen, to make notes, and to mark time, all in less than three minutes, knowing all the time that narrow limitation!

Describing the end of the totality Mitchell wrote:

...another strangely shaped figure rushed out as if from behind the moon, and instantly the sun came forth. All nature rejoiced, and much as we needed more time, we rejoiced with Nature, and felt that we loved the light.

Finally, she cannot resist calling attention to the ability and dedication of her assistants.

Smyth says: "The effect of a total eclipse on the minds of men is so overpowering, that if they have never seen it before they forget their appointed tasks, and will look around during the few seconds of total obscuration, to witness the scene." Other astronomers have said the same. My assistants, a party of young students, would not have turned from the narrow line of observation assigned to them if the earth had quaked beneath them....Was it because they were women?"[46]

ALTHOUGH 1869 WAS MARKED by the waning health and eventual death of her father, the year also brought heartening and memorable moments for Maria Mitchell, in addition to the successful summer expedition to Iowa. She became one of the first women elected to the American Philosophical Society. At the 1869 meeting in which Maria was elected, Elizabeth C. Agassiz of Cambridge and Mary Somerville of England also received this same exceptional honor. Previously, the only woman elected to the Society had been Ekaterina Dashkov, in 1789.

In comparing Mitchell's 1869 response to her Society election with her response two decades earlier to her election to the American Academy of Arts and Science, a significant change is evident. In 1848, the twenty-nine-year-old Maria had asked her father to write to the

Academy to acknowledge and accept the honor on her behalf. Twenty years later, the fully established professor exhibited far more confidence, serenely expressing her self-reliance. From Vassar, she wrote an October letter of acceptance to the American Philosophical Society.

> Observatory
> Oct 22, 1869
> Chs. B. Trego, Esq.
> I have your circular of Oct 15, informing me of my election as a member of the American Phil. Society of Philadelphia. You will please accept my thanks for the honor conferred upon me. Will you have the goodness to inform me if a complete set of the publications of that society can be obtained?
> Maria Mitchell[47]

With an eye toward getting her students involved in making weather observations, Mitchell wrote to her friend, Professor Joseph Henry, of the Smithsonian Institution:

> Do you still keep up a series of Meteorological Observations at different points? If so, will you tell me if they are such as my students could make, and do you furnish instruments? I have a barometer and thermometer, but since my Father's death have kept no daily records. I should be glad to do so if I knew the best method.[48]

She received an immediate answer:

> *We should be much pleased to place your college in the list of Meteorological observers and to send you blank forms and instructions. The observations are such as can easily be made by young pupils and I think the keeping of these records will be a pleasant and instructive service[?] of regular and systematic in habits.*
> *Joseph Henry.[49]*

While teaching at Vassar, Mitchell also continued to give public lectures far beyond the Poughkeepsie campus. She reviewed her seasonal lecturing invitations in a May 1870 letter to President Raymond; and, in a letter nine months later to her sister Sally, Maria noted the pleasant travels afforded by her lectures, observing that her lecture fees amounted to more than her Vassar salary!

May 16 1870

President Raymond,

I have made no engagements to Lecture another season, but as I have in prospect several invitations, I wish to ask how much time is allowed to a professor for that purpose? I have been away two days in the last eight months (by leave) and have missed four recitations. Is it probable that [I] could have more time allowed, another year?

I believe in the little lecturing that I have done, I have worked well for women and for the College, and, if with no gain, with no harm, to myself. I am not sure that I shall be willing to Lecture at all, another season, but I want the freedom to do so, if I choose.[50]

Feb. 4 [1871]

My dear Sally,

Anne Maria[51] wants thee to give or lend her that cameo pin. She thinks that she would like to wear it. I have been to Phil[adelphia] again, and to Baltimore and really enjoyed it. I found in Baltimore some very nice schools. I met the family of Ephraim Gardner at one of my lectures.

Of course I have made some money, but I have charged too little. So, now, just as I have no applications, I have raised my price. It is a very easy thing to do, as, for an audience of 250 I do not need to raise my voice at all....

I feel very independent at Vassar because I find that even at the rate I have charged in lecturing, it pays better, a great deal than Vassar. Of course it is not _desirable_ business. I _stood_ for the first time in Baltimore and found it just as easy.

I am glad Henry has gone to Nantucket. I hope he will keep himself busy—it is the only way. If he lets himself sit down and think, he will be in danger of a life-long harm.[52] I suffered so much after Mother's death that I know what a weak state one gets into. Phebe writes that Willie is getting along nicely.

We are having examinations. I have actually had one this morning! Prof. Farrar _poked_ the girls. We had no visitors except a few of the Teachers and Profs. Mine was at 8 o'clock in the morning—so I got through early. Then, I have to go around as Committee to other examinations and it's pretty fatiguing business. I went in to six of them yesterday and I go to two or three today.

Forster's address is 116 N. Eleventh, Phil.[53]

Maria Mitchell

Just prior to her Christmas break in 1870, Mitchell wrote to Alfred Stone, a prominent architect in Providence, Rhode Island. She was seeking to arrange a lecture topic and date, in response to his invitation to speak in Providence.

Dec 16, 1870

Alfred Stone,

I have a Lecture on the Seven Stars of the Great Bear, which I shall be pleased to give before your "Union." I shall probably be in Boston from Dec 22 to Jan 3d and can come down to Providence in that time, or (what I should prefer) stop at Providence on my way to Po'keepsie, and Lecture Wednesday Evening Jan 4. I have never spoken to an audience of more than 400, and am therefore glad that your hall is a small one.

My charge to a Lyceum is $50. I charge $20 to a school, and should be glad to make some engagements in schools in and around Providence.

Maria Mitchell

My address after Dec. 21 is 81 Inman St., Cambridgeport, Mass.[54]

Although her letters reveal that Mitchell had many animated exchanges with President Raymond, her overriding respect for him and her deep appreciation for his value to the college are consistently evident. In fact, many of her letters reveal her heartfelt affection for the president, including this largely tongue-in-cheek 1870 correspondence.

Obs. Jun. 11

My dear President,

Supposing that you can at this time have nothing on your heart, head or hands, I send you two pamphlets.... That of Gov. Washburn I send, because he is one of the Mass. Board of Education and is watching Vassar with great interest—and—I want you to think of him at least five minutes, as a Trustee for Vassar.

MM.

Part 2nd

(Affectionate and Emotional)

I have learned, only last night, from Miss Lyman, that Ann Arbor was looking toward you. Of course, you won't kill us outright, by thinking for a moment of such a thing!

You are just where you can do the maximum of good, which no other could do as well—and what except to do good, can any one desire? If you should do such a horrible thing as to go, I apply now for the first vacant professorship—Greek or anything. But you won't think of such a thing!...

I submitted to my title twenty four whole hours, after which I announced that the joke was old, and have resumed the brief one of M. M.[55]

In regard to the outcome of Maria's specific references in this 1870 letter: President Raymond did remain as Vassar's president; Governor Washburn was not appointed a trustee; and, Miss Lyman, whom Maria had called a "bigot" when she first came to Vassar, was now viewed by Mitchell more favorably. In fact, Maria acknowledged to one of her nieces that both she and Miss Lyman had changed their views and had come to think much more alike during their first four years together at Vassar.

The "title" she refers to whimsically in her letter to President Raymond was undoubtedly her honorary Ph. D. from Rutgers, awarded in 1870, thus dating the June letter. In all her correspondence, Maria is never addressed as "Dr." nor does she sign herself that way. Her usual signature is a simple "MM."

Nov. 23 [1870]

My dear Lizzie [Williams, '69],

...And you are so all over a radical, that it won't hurt you to be toned down a little. And in a few years (as the world moves) your family will have moved one way and you the other, a little and you will suddenly find yourselves on the same plane.

It is much the way that has been between Miss Lyman and myself. Today she is more of a Woman's Rights woman than I was when I came here, while I begin to think that the girls better dress at tea time (tho' I think in that subject we tho't alike at first) so, I'll take another example.

I have learned to think that a young girl better not walk to town alone even in the day time. When I came here I should have allowed a child to do it. But I never knew much of the world, never shall, nor will you. And, as we were both born a little deficient in worldly caution and worldly policy, let us receive from others those lessons, do as well as we can, and keep our hearts unworldly if our manners take on something of those ways.[56]

Feb. 28, 1871
Saturday 2^h 30^m p. m.
My good natured President,

I want to hear you preach tomorrow, and I also want to see the moon pass over Aldebaran. Can't you let me do both? Will you stop at eleventhly or twelfthly? Or, why need you shew us all sides of the subject? The moon never turns to us other than the one side we see, and did you ever know a finer moon?

If I could stop the moon and do no more harm than Joshua did,[57] I wouldn't ask such a favor of you, knowing, as I do, what a difficult thing it is for you to pause, when you are once started, and knowing also, that I never want you to do so — except this once. Yours with all regret, even if it doesn't appear

— M Mitchell.[58]

A September 1871 letter indicates one way in which financial aid was obtained in the early days of Vassar College. It also reveals another side of Mitchell's character, as well as her thoughts on what was important in a Vassar student.

Sept 20, 1871
My dear Miss [Dorothea] Dix[59]
Yours of Sept 11th and a later one not now at hand, have been received.

I have brought to the college with me a young girl of 18 years whose case seems so nearly to fit the requirements which you mention that I hope you will permit me to draw on you for funds with the intention of using them for her.

Her health is perfect—her abilities fine—her character good. She is the daughter of parents who can almost educate a daughter, but who have a goodly number of sons and daughters who must share equally. I expect she will take the college aid of $100 and I have another $100 for her. I need therefore $200. If you should be willing that I should draw for this, I think it would pay good interest.

The girl's faults are that she is a little brusque, and forward—a little over free—but it is the freedom of innocence. Our College will tone her down quickly.

You will perceive that in seeking out these girls, and bringing them here, I am working for the College, as well as for the girl. I am anxious about the class of girls who will come here. We do not want the forwarding and thoughtless who abound and I am trying to improve the class.

I beg that you may not feel [?] in this matter. And if you do not feel equal to $200, and feel quite free to the amount of $100 I will raise the remaining $100 myself.

I sincerely hope you will make me a visit at the Observatory. My accommodations are scientific rather than domestic, but I will try to make you comfortable. As a College we are far from perfect, but we are sincere and earnest workers for what we think to be the best, and we shall gratefully receive any suggestions you may make.

Maria Mitchell[60]

Mitchell established a popular annual tradition at the Vassar Observatory—the "Dome Party." Held at the end of each year, the large observatory dome was decorated, and tables were set up for eating, either breakfast or lunch. For the parties Mitchell wrote short, mostly humorous, verses about each student who attended. The idea of writing these personal verses evidently arose at the first dome party, when the group realized that it was the birthday of Anna Mineah, Class of 1870. Anna reminisced about the occasion many years later.

The party included both astronomy classes of that year.... We were invited to come early—and it was quite light as refreshments of ice cream, strawberries and cake were served by two of the college maids as we sat at small tables in the dome room.

Afterwards Miss Mitchell gave us reminiscences of Caroline and William Herschel, and spoke of her own love of poetry and rhythm (She once gave me a copy of Whittier's "My Triumph" saying she would rather have written that than discovered a comet.) and proposed a game of crambo....

At the reading that written by Miss Mitchell fell to my lot...I remarked to my neighbor that I should keep that as a souvenir of Miss Mitchell, as a gift for my birthday. Gertrude [Mead] at once cried out

Maria Mitchell

"Oh, Miss Mitchell, it is Anna Mineah's birthday!" Of course con-
gratulations followed. Then consternation, when Miss Mitchell com-
manded that each one should write me an ode.[61]

By the opening of the college year in 1872, Mitchell was well established in her new career at Vassar College. She looked forward to the
new academic year, which began on September 23, noting:

Everything seems to open favourably for the coming year...to make
us comfortable. President and Lady Principal [were] in more than
usual health and the house [was] full of students. All is promises.[62]

Maria took her role as a Vassar professor very seriously, as she
recorded on September 26 of the same year.

My classes came in today for the first time, 25 students, more than
ever before. Fine, splendid looking girls. I felt almost frightened at
the responsibility which came into my hands, of the possible twist
that I might give them.

By this time, however, the college was not her only concern.

My first small worry is not collegiate. I have been asked to sign an
appeal to women to electioneer for Grant. The Republican party of
men has heartily endorsed [the] Suffrage movement and I would
gladly work for those Republicans, but cannot work for any political
party and cannot go into politics. Probably they can work as well
without me. Wendell Phillips says that the first Woman's rights
meeting was held in Worcester in 1848. It was small, but the call for
it was signed by R. W. Emerson and wife. Dr. Howe favored it but
Mrs. Howe did not. Theodore Parker laughed at it. Mr. Phillips
thinks that Greeley has never been in favor of women.

Sept. 30. Small worry No. 2 is an invitation to lecture to the Young
Men's Christian Association. I can't do it, but I wish I could! If I were
not connected with the College, I would give them a moral lecture.
As it is I shall probably decline the lecture but offer an evening with
the moon to about 50 (write this). Wrote to Indianapolis that I would
come for $100 in February.

Putting our feet firmly on the unchangeableness of math law. That
2 + 2 are 4 is certain throughout the universe as are Right and Wrong.

Following this reflection, Maria penned notes for an article on women in science, including this summary of her philosophy.

It is better to be peering in the spectroscope than on the pattern of a dress. It is better to crack open a Geode than to match worsteds. It is better to spend an hour in watching the habits of an insect than in trying to put up the hair fantastically....I have been asked why should girls make astronomical observations when there is no work of that sort to be done. It is not to be sure as likely as that they should cook. Women have been called upon to navigate ships, the utility of a study is not its claim to value.

Over the years, the honors given to the esteemed Maria Mitchell grew significantly. Sorosis, an organization of women founded in 1869, soon made Mitchell an honorary member, and she often attended their meetings.

> 185 Renseu St. B*klyn*
>
> June 8th, 1871
>
> My Dear Madam,
>
> I have the honor to inform you that at the last regular meeting of the Sorosis, you were elected an honorary member of the society. The last business meeting of the season will be held on Monday, June 20th, at Delmonico's. The next regular social meeting is on the first Monday in October. It will give us all much pleasure to welcome you among us, and we hope that next Autumn you may find time to give us that gratification.
>
> Kate Willard[63]

> Oct 22, 1872.
>
> Miss Maria Mitchell,
>
> Sorosis gives a Reception to Miss Emily Faithfull[64] on Monday Nov. 4th at twelve o'clock in Delmonico's parlors. We anticipate a large gathering of members resident and remote as well as many guests from home and abroad. The Ex[ecutive] Com[mittee] desires to express the sincere wish that you may find it convenient to be present with us—and also to favor the Club with a few remarks.
>
> A. C. Fletcher[65]

190 *Maria Mitchell*

Maria Mitchell did "find it convenient" to be present at the November Sorosis meeting, as she colorfully recalls in her diary.

1872. Nov. 4. Sorosis.

Lunch was at noon, but it was noon neither mean nor apparent [a reference to mean solar time and apparent solar time] but a Sorosis noon.

Some 100 guests arrayed themselves around tables or around the walls of the room. Mrs. Wiler presided at the central table with Miss Faithfull on her right and Jenny June Croty on her left. At the same table were Dr. Emily Blackwell,[66] Dr. Mary Putnam[67] and Mrs. Bullan of the Revolution....A question for discussion then came up whether most good would be exerted by Sorosis if it had a special aim or aimed only at a general expression of views....

At this time, there was a remote possibility that Mitchell would leave Vassar for another institution. She received a letter from the president[68] of Swarthmore College in early December 1872, indicating his personal interest in having her on the faculty of the Pennsylvania school.

> SWARTHMORE COLLEGE
> 12 Mo. 4 1872.
> Prof. Maria Mitchell
> Thine is at hand. I should be willing to apply to your Board if that is the best way, or do anything which thee would advise to secure thy services for Swarthmore. Of course I could do nothing officially until the Board has acted. I mean our Board. I will bring the subject to their notice at their meeting in the 5th month. Hoping to see the time when thee will be closely connected with Swarthmore, in name and reality.
> Edward Magill.[69]

Vassar College was quite protective of its lady professor, as the following letter to Swarthmore's president testifies. It appears that Vassar's president and trustees felt that the college had the right to decide where Mitchell could work and with whom she could be professionally associated. Whether or not Mitchell knew of this letter is not known, nor is the reason for the long gap between the two letters.

Vassar College
June 15th, 1874
President Magill,
    Your note of the 4th inst. addressed to the Trustees of this College, was submitted to the Executive Board, and I am authorized to communicate their reply. "With a great sum" have the Board obtained the valuable services of Prof. Maria Mitchell (engaging her whole time), and the prestige of her name, for the benefit of the college. While they will not refuse their consent to her occasionally delivering lectures elsewhere, for her own advantage and that of others, they think it but right that she should always do it as the Vassar College Professor of Astronomy, and do not see how they can consent to have her published as Professor of Astronomy in another institution.
    Trusting that, on reflection, this decision will commend itself to your approval, as fair and right, I am
    J. H. Raymond, President.[70]

MARIA MITCHELL WAS a regular participant at the meetings of the Woman's Club in Boston. The following interchange, which took place at one of those meetings, must have reinforced for Mitchell how little men's views on the role of women had changed.

1873. Jan. 3. In Boston, Woman's Club rooms. Mrs. Howe called the meeting to order and proposed a question as to popularizing science and made a few remarks. Asking Prof. Peirce at the end what he thought, Prof. Peirce said he was not prepared on such a question. That he felt that each one should follow his own bent and his had been to pure math and he had refused to go into calculation of Life Insurance probabilities even when urged on ground that it was more useful.

He introduced the subject of Mrs. Somerville and then went on to talk of women. He said had Mrs. Somerville been a man she would have been distinguished, that she was not original, that women were not generally, that the scientific men found sympathy from women, as they were receptive and appreciative, that scientific men did not read one another's book... that women were the educators of men and should be satisfied with that.

Mrs. Norve said no human being could be satisfied with being a means only and not an end, that every person was a means and an

Maria Mitchell

end. Dr. Hodge asked Prof. Peirce if Marie Agnesi[71] was not original in science and he said, "Yes, she is the one exception."

It seems to me if, in 1800 years with every advantage some 12 men have been original in science, and if with every disadvantage one woman has been, the woman's mind must be truly wonderful.

Dr. Hodge said that in Literature women were not original. Mrs. Cheney suggested "George Eliot?" and he said he could not see that she was and then someone asked who was and [he] replied "the novelist Scott." Dr. Hodge said he didn't know how women could possibly study much beside music, if they must give 4 hours a day to that.[72]

In the winter of 1873, Mitchell was invited by Vassar alumnae in Indiana to deliver a lecture there. The *Vassar Miscellany* passed on the following report of the event:

> On the evening of February 12, 1873, Prof. Mitchell delivered a lecture at Masonic Hall, Indianapolis, Indiana. We clip the following notice from the Indianapolis Sentinel, of February 13th.·
>
> "The reputation of the lecturer and the distinguished position which she holds as an educator, gave a guarantee which drew out an appreciative audience in full force. Miss Mitchell came before it as a teacher filled with the inspiration of science.... She said that she had chosen the constellation of Ursa Major as her subject, because on account of its proximity to the north pole, it never passes below the horizon of this latitude, and is a group of stars which claims the interest of all...."[73]

1873. Feb. I found in Indianapolis a gushing hospitality which was very pleasant to receive if you did not accept all its offers. I was asked to spend a week in several different families. Then I found an interest in science and was amazed to find that they readily paid me $100 and asked me for another Lecture at the same price. I was sorry I could not go into their schools to see if there was really a taste for solid learning....[74]

A Vassar student, Helen Marshall, had accompanied Mitchell on her trip to Indianapolis. Nearly sixty years later, Marshall recalled the journey in a note she wrote for the Maria Mitchell Association. Her report offers further insights into Mitchell's character.

That trip to Indianapolis in mid-winter with Miss Mitchell I remember very distinctly. She offered me the opportunity to go with her and naturally I was delighted when my father sent the check to cover expenses. My family and Miss Mitchell's were friends from "way back." Naturally as a student I was somewhat in awe of Miss Mitchell but a remark she made as we were about to get on the train at Albany somewhat staggered me. "If my shawl drags, I want it to," she said. I made no reply but naturally resolved it might drag all the way from the east to the west coast of U.S.A. if she preferred....

We were entertained at the home of one of the Vassar girls and with the hearty greeting evidently usual with the lady she threw her arms around Miss Mitchell's neck and gave her a resounding kiss. Inwardly I was tickled for I knew nothing could be more offensive to Miss Mitchell than such a show of affection on the part of a stranger....

Miss Mitchell's brother, Frank and his wife, came from Chicago, their home, to be with her for a day or two and we all had a very enjoyable time.... On the return trip we again skirted the southern shore of Lake Erie, frozen as far as we could see, and stopped over a day and night at Niagara Falls....

Now for the vindication of Miss Mitchell's character, which was always under all circumstances just, as well as generous. As we were on the way from Albany to Poughkeepsie, she suddenly turned to me and said "I want to apologize to you." "For what?" I said. "You know when we started I said to you if my shawl drags I want it to. I did not know what kind of person you were and thought you might be like so many of the girls who torment me by looking after me until I want to be let alone!" Wasn't that lovely?...

Helen Marshall[75]

By this time, Mitchell was involved in a wide range of activities. In the early 1870s, she published two articles on the satellites of Jupiter in *Silliman's Journal,* edited a new edition of Guillemin's "Wonders of the Moon," and began to prepare an article on "The Higher Education of Women" for the Association for the Advancement of Women. She also attended many lectures on campus and commented in her diary on nearly every one.

Maria Mitchell

In a letter to her friend Joseph Henry we can also read the first indications of her need for more money for the observatory. Fund raising would gradually come to consume more and more of her time at Vassar.

1873. March. There was something so genuine and so sincere in George MacDonald[76] that he took those of us who were <u>emotional</u> completely, not by storm so much as by gentle breezes. His Lecture on Tennyson was not systematic or methodical, although I perceive Miss T. tries to consider it as artistically got up. But it was conversational, he established a kind of acquaintance with his audience and he seemed to talk with them and seemed to establish a mutual good understanding. What he said wasn't profound except as it reached the depths of the heart, his very <u>ego</u> seemed to be a pleasant kind of ego-ism.

Some of his bits were good. He said, "A poet must have a large heart." Now none of us would dare say we had a large heart. The most we should dare to say would be "I think my heart is larger than it used to be." We were so captivated by the man, that we forgave his Scotch accent, said nothing about his saying "fust" for first and omitting the "r" generally....

The Woman's Mission. A church gathering has been started in Boston. At which women officiate. I attended one on Sunday, April 20, 1873....

Vassar College, Mch. 30, 1873

Prof. Henry,

I cannot refrain from sending you a line of thanks for your letter to the "Committee of Arrangements" which I have just read in the *Popular Science* monthly. I thank you most cordially for these "three things essential to well-constituted college" and I wish to ask you if there is any way by which endowments can be obtained. Our endowments at Vassar are wholly buildings and apparatus and we Professors are crowded with tutor's work.

Do you know of any rich men or women whom I could influence to bestow something upon the Observatory? We have good instruments, but I am receiving several classes daily, and am working at night without air. You perceive how difficult it is to accomplish anything for science! My only consolation is that I have fine noble

"THE HEXAGON," 1868. These six students were Maria Mitchell's first astronomy class at Vassar. Dubbed "The Hexagon" by her father, the class included: Mary Whitney *(seated at the table)*, Sarah Louise Blatchley, Sarah Glazier Bates, Clara Glover Ginn, Mary Rebold Kennedy, and Helen L. Storke. These students were close to both Mitchells, even visiting the ailing Mr. Mitchell on Christmas Day in 1868, who recalled gratefully, "We had a cheery and jolly time of it. I almost forgot my age and my infirmities."

Encouraging her students to be active in their astronomical studies, Professor Mitchell was legendary for keeping them up past curfew to make late observations. She also made two cross-country trips with students to view solar eclipses.

Maria Mitchell

women among my students, whom I am training to open their eyes to the wonderful revelations of nature, and to receive the lessons into their hearts.

Maria Mitchell[77]

> *Washington, D.C., April 4th, 1873*
>
> *My dear Miss Mitchell,*
>
> *The receipt of your letter of March 30th has given me much pleasure though I am unable to give you an affirmative reply to your question as to a knowledge of any patron of science ready properly to endow your establishment with the means for original research.*
>
> *I indulge the hope however, that with the advance of higher education in our country the value of abstract science will be better appreciated and that college endowment will be made with other views than ostentatious architectural display, etc. You have the means of disseminating correct views on this subject through the wealthy and intelligent young women now under your instruction and I doubt not you properly improve the opportunity thus afforded....*
>
> *Joseph Henry*[78]

> *Columbia College, President's*[79] *Room, June 23, 1873*
>
> *Miss Mitchell,*
>
> *...The purpose of this letter is to inquire whether you would be willing to prepare for us a proper article [on astronomy] to be substituted for the present one. I will send you the plate proofs of the present one if you desire them, but I beg you will not take it as a model. You may treat the subject entirely on your own plan and introduce graphic illustrations if you wish....*
>
> *For this assistance, if you are willing, to render it, we desire to offer liberal compensation. For an article of the length of the present one furnished by the middle of July, we would willingly give fifty dollars; but if you extend it to a length equivalent to twenty or twenty five pages of Silliman, we will give for it one hundred dollars. I would even be willing to say that we will give one hundred dollars, without regard to length, provided the article is one to which you are willing to attach your name.*

*All our principal articles are signed by the contributors, I send you
a list of their names to which I should be very happy to be permitted to
add yours.*

Respectfully,

F. A. P. Barnard[80]

[From an article by Mitchell on Saturn, 1873]

The specialist can never believe that his subject is narrow; to him
it widens and widens. When the theological professor said to the
astronomer that his department was the Old Testament, the
astronomer replied, "So is mine, with the difference that mine is
older." On the other hand, when the astronomer boasted to the
entomologist that his department covered the whole earth, the entomologist said, "Insects do."

We are fortunate that many of Mitchell's class lectures can still be
found in the pages of her notebooks and other memorabilia. It is apparent from the following lecture that she felt it important to raise the students' consciousness about issues beyond astronomy. Her ideas about
women and their education are well articulated here.

I do not hold these women [Mary Somerville, Harriet Hosmer] up
to you as examples in their specialty. I am far from thinking that
every woman should be an astronomer or a mathematician or an
artist, but I do think that every woman should strive for perfection in
everything she undertakes.

If it be art, literature or science, let her work be incessant, continuous, life-long. If she be gifted and talented above the average, by just
so much is the demand upon her for higher labor, by just that amount
is the pressure of duty increased. Any special capability, and sense of
peculiar fitness for a certain line is of itself an inspiration from God,
the line is marked out for her by His finger. Who dare turn from that
path? And if she be of only moderate capacity, the duty of using to
the utmost her power for good is still upon her. The Germans have a
proverb "Life is not a pleasure journey, but partly a battlefield and
partly a pilgrimage."

Think of the steady effort, the continuous labor of those whom the
world calls 'geniuses'. Believe me, the poet who is "born and not
made" works hard for what you consider his birthright. Newton said

his whole power lay in "patient thought" and patient thought, patient labor and firmness of purpose are almost omnipotent.

Let me give you an instance, from my own observations. The telescope maker Mr. Clark, who has just improved the glass of our telescope, stands over such a glass eight hours a day, for six months, patiently rubbing the surface with a fine powder. It is mere manual labor, you will say. But at the end of that six months he has made a glass which reveals to the world heavenly bodies which no mortal eye ever before saw.

You know that Archimedes said "Give me a place to stand on and I will move the world." The man who makes a glass which penetrates into space farther than was ever before reached, moves the world in space. The step, however small, which is in advance of the world, shows the greatness of the man, whether that step be taken with brain, with heart, or with hands....

Are we women using all the rights we have? We have the right to steady and continuous effort after knowledge, after truth. Who denies our right to life-long study? Yet you will find most women leave their studies when they leave the schoolroom. You have heard many a woman say "I was very fond of Latin when I went to school but I've forgotten all I knew" or "I used to love mathematical studies but I don't know the first thing now." Now if Latin was worth studying in youth, it is worthy of study in middle life. If needed for discipline in youth, it is needed as culture later....

We have another right, which I am afraid we do not use, the right to do our work well, <u>as well as men do theirs</u>. I have thought of this part of the subject a good deal and I am almost ready to say that women do their work less thoroughly than men. Perhaps from the need of right training, perhaps because they enter upon occupations only temporarily, they keep school a year, they write one magazine story, they keep accounts for a few months for some uncle, they take hold of some benevolent enterprise for one winter, when it's "all the rage."

The woman who does her work better than ever woman did before helps all woman kind, not only now, but in all the future, she moves the whole race no matter if it is only a differential movement, it is growth. And this seems to me woman's greatest wrong, the wrong which she does to herself by work loosely done, ill finished, or not finished at all. The world has not yet outgrown the idea that woman are playthings, because women have not outgrown it themselves.

No man dares say that Mrs. Browning was not a poet, that Rosa Bonheur is no painter, that Harriet Hosmer is no sculptor, and, altho' you may be neither poet, painter, nor sculptor, your work should be the best of its kind, nothing short of the highest mark should be your aim.

I would urge upon you earnestly, the consideration of this one of your wrongs, a wrong if it come to you of your own doing. Whatever apology other women may have for loose, ill finished work, or work not finished at all, you will have none. When you leave Vassar College, you leave it the best educated women in the world.

Living a little outside of the college beyond the reach of the little currents that go up and down the corridors, I think I am a fairer judge of your advantages than you can be yourselves, and when I say you will be the best educated women in the world, I do not mean the education of textbooks and classrooms and apparatus only, but that broader education which you attain unconsciously, that higher teaching which comes to you all unknown to the givers, from daily association with the noble-souled women who are around you.

The ideas, the thoughts which have grown into this College are your inheritance from all the ages. Guard it and treasure it and develop it as you would any other inheritance. Moral influences are more permeating than physical and in the material world....

You and I think a great deal about our rights! I have thought more on that subject since I have been in Vassar College than in my whole life before. For myself it is of little consequence; for you, who have long lives before you and to whom new responsibilities are sure to come, it is of great moment.[81]

As documented in chapter seven, Maria Mitchell was paid an annual salary less than that received by the male professors when she arrived at Vassar College. The trustees felt that this arrangement was justified because she received free room and board for herself and her father.

The ensuing dispute over Mitchell's salary went back and forth for years; it was apparently never resolved to everyone's satisfaction. The first designation of Mitchell's salary is shocking.

Maria Mitchell

May 18, 1865 The salaries of professors fixed at $2000—they to pay rent, fuel and lights. Miss Mitchell $800 with rooms and board for herself and father.[82]

In 1865, the items of rent, fuel and lights would clearly not make up the $1200 difference in salary. Two years later, the situation had actually deteriorated—with the salary differential now being closer to $1700.

June, 1867. Resolved that we recommend the following officers for reappointment for the next college year, at the cash salaries named below: J. H. Raymond, Pres. $4000 and perquisites; H. W. Lyman, Lady Principal, $1800 and home; C. J. Farrar, Prof., $2500; S. Tenney, Prof., $2500; M. Mitchell, Prof., $800 and 2 homes [rooms for herself and her father].

Often joined in her early salary protestations by female colleague Alida Avery, Mitchell communicated her concerns regularly with the Vassar administration. An 1870 letter expressed their request succinctly.

May 16, 1870

President Raymond,

We desire to call your attention to the fact, that, after nearly five years of what we believe to be faithful working for the good of the College, our pay is still far below that which has been offered at entrance, to the other professors, even when they have been wholly inexperienced. We respectfully ask that our salaries may be made equal to those of the other professors.

Maria Mitchell

Professor of Astronomy

Alida C. Avery

Professor of Physiology and Hygiene.[83]

Eventually the trustees raised the salaries of Mitchell and Avery, but they also raised the charges for room and board—so much so that the two professors immediately protested. It is difficult to imagine what the trustees were trying to do by their action; it certainly made their two female professors quite unhappy. The dispute went back and forth for many years and the basic argument of "equal pay for equal work" was never settled satisfactorily.

After the death of President Raymond in 1878, Maria Mitchell presented a summary of the salary dispute in a letter to trustee Benson J. Lossing. It reveals that the two women professors were so upset at their situation that they considered resigning from the college.

> July 3 [c. 1879]
>
> Dr. Lossing,
>
> Yours of the 1st is received. If I were at Vassar I could send you the note of the Ex[ecutive] Com[mittee] in regard to the charge for Board at Vassar College. As it is I remember so much as this: When the vote for equal payment had passed the Board, the Ex. Com. sent a note to Dr. Avery and myself, charging us $16(?) a week for board. We were astounded and we wrote a respectful note asking them to itemise the prices of different points in the "board" that we might economise. (I had tho't I could live by myself and buy my meals.) They replied that they declined to "itemise." At the next meeting of the Board, it was voted to return to Dr. Avery and myself all over $400.
>
> The "speak to Dr. Lossing" was of a prior date. At the time that Dr. Avery and I were fighting for all women, for it was more the general than the special injustice that reached us. I often said hard things to Dr. Raymond. I felt that his timidity led him to wrong us. I told him, one evening, that Dr. Avery and I had made up our minds. She would leave in June; I would leave also, but not so immediately; I had no profession, but I should in June begin to look around for opportunities to lecture, and as soon as I could feel safe for a year, I should go.
>
> I assured him that the plan was matured and that it was not mere talk. He appeared to be much disturbed, and after a few minutes, he said "Now, you are not to tell of this hint which I give you— "write to Lossing." It was in Dr. Raymond's office. I rose at once and said "Thank you; all I wanted of you was that information; I didn't know to whom to write."...
>
> Since Dr. Raymond's death I have felt it almost a duty, to tell that the hint came from him. It is right that it should be known that he

Maria Mitchell

was with us all the time. And altho' I do not think it was quite right not to stand boldly forth it was not his way to fight if he could help it. When he fought, he fought to the bitter end—without a question his various conflicts shortened his life. "We shall not see his like again."

Thanks for your good wishes for myself and thanks for your vote on the monied question in the name of all women. I hope you and your family are as comfortably cool as I am, by the sea. We had a thunder squall last night at sunset which reminded me in its clearing off, of that which we saw from your piazza.

Maria Mitchell[84]

A brief note in Vassar's student newspaper in 1873 offers interesting information about Mitchell at this point in her career. First, she is now giving "Popular Astronomy" lectures to the students, which she had resisted for years; second, her traveling itinerary included a return trip to Europe, a land she had wistfully "bade good-by forever" fifteen years earlier.

> *July 1873. During the past semester, Professor Mitchell has given the Sophomores five lectures on Popular Astronomy....Professor Mitchell sailed for Europe, June 28. She will return early in the autumn.*[85]

At this point in her life, Mitchell was financially secure. In addition to her salary at Vassar, she received significant fees for her lectures and articles. Her brother-in-law, Matthew Barney, handled her investments. She saved a substantial amount over the years, and spent significant money on books and travel, as well as in gifts and charitable contributions. A February letter to Matthew Barney reveals the charitable (and discerning) side of Mitchell's character.

Feb. 23 [no year given]

My dear Matthew,

I had been there before your letter came. I had $20 which I didn't know what to do with. I never gave away so much as I have this year, $100 (that included Christmas presents). I mean to give about $300 a year but you see I have got ahead of my allowance. As long as my health lasts, I can afford to give, but when I live on my income, I shall be mean enough! I am just having a job done at the *Inquirer* which I pay for, but it is really not for myself.

I enclose $5. If it will do, I should like for some of it to go to Mary Ann for the gingerbread and the rest to Charles Chan; say, at least $2 and perhaps $3 to Charles Chan. I feel very sorry for him and remember how nicely he broke into Aunt Maria's house for me and he always asked after Mother.

Do not worry about M. Cary! She has two sons, and besides, I have confidential letters from her when she feels very needy! Poor woman. I pity her very much, but I do not feel in the way she wants me to, and she gets very little out of me.

I think Henry would gladly do a little for Charles Chan. Is not Margaret, his wife, alive? Give my regards to both,

MM[86]

CHAPTER 9

EUROPEAN TRAVELS, 1873

The habit of travelling once adopted cannot be easily given up.

$\mathcal{I}$N 1873 MARIA MITCHELL took time out from her regular duties to go on another transatlantic voyage. She planned to revisit some of the people and places she had seen in Europe more than a decade earlier; her 1873 itinerary also included a trip to Russia. Mitchell had actually hoped to visit Russia during her earlier visit to Europe, but time constraints had forced her to put off that leg of her 1857 journey.

The Pulkova Observatory, near St. Petersburg, was one of the most important observatories of the nineteenth century. It had been directed by the famed Wilhelm Struve, whom Maria had met during her 1857 visit to England. Upon Wilhelm's death in 1864, his son Otto became the Observatory's director. Pulkova was one of Maria's specially chosen destinations for the summer tour of 1873.

At the completion of her 1873 European itinerary, the well-traveled Mitchell could boast (had she so desired) that she had been welcomed in every major astronomical center of Europe of the day.

By this time Maria Mitchell was a celebrated feminist leader and a well-established professor of astronomy at Vassar College. Her diary reveals her changing priorities regarding the sites and people she chose to visit. She had become much more interested in fostering women's education than in seeing new telescopes, and she visited as many educators as scientists.

Setting sail in the company of her sister and brother-in-law, Phebe and Joshua Kendall, and their son Willie, the fifty-four-year-old Maria Mitchell looked forward to her three-month trek through Europe. By prior agreement, the foursome planned to separate when they reached Scotland. Willie, at age seventeen, would be his aunt's traveling companion to Russia. The four would then reunite in Switzerland and travel back to the States together.

Mitchell's 1873 passport description provides a written "snapshot" of the vigorous American astronomer.

> AGE: *54 years;* STATURE: *5 feet, 5 1/2 inches;* FOREHEAD: High;
> EYES: Dark; NOSE: Straight; MOUTH: Medium; CHIN: Square;
> HAIR: Grey; COMPLEXION: Dark; FACE: Round.
> *(Issued) 23 day of June, 1873.*[1]

June 28, 1873 Steamer *Castalia.*[2]

We have been two hours and a half out and just begin to roll a little. Had a poor sort of lunch, but got a cup of tea and some ice. State room 47 good window in it which we can open. We are allowed a small trunk in the cabin, all others are lowered into the hold. About 100 cabin passengers, all respectable looking....

June 29. I began to be sick[3] when we were 5 hours out, went to bed at about 5 p.m. had toast and tea at 7 p.m. went to sleep and slept until morning very nicely. Most of the passengers did the same. Waked and was sick. Found most of the passengers followed my example, on deck for some hours, weather good. Did not go to breakfast or to lunch, live on toast and tea, slept at noon....

8 a.m. June 30.... We are regular at our meals now, but Willie does not enjoy much. We had expected that he would get the most out of the voyage.

Mrs. Corneau tells me that the slats on the upper berth in her room broke last night and her eldest daughter came down upon her, just as she was nursing the youngest, fortunately although all were hurt, the bruises were not serious....

Maria Mitchell

July 1. 1 p.m. Mr. Read (the officer who makes the observations) says we shall be off Cape Race tomorrow and that the promise of fine weather is good. He says he takes altitudes of the sun to regulate his chronometer, but not lunar distances. He must use the old problem of Bowditch, "To find the time at sea and regulate a watch" and he must find his Latitude first and he gets his hour angle from the three sides of the triangle.

July 1. 6 p.m....We are crowded now at meals as every one is well and we think we perceive the supply of luxuries to be smaller, but the fare is good and we rush when the bell rings....

July 6. I was very sick all day.

July 7. No longer sick, but weak from want of food.

July 8. (Tuesday) a.m. We had a very hard night last night....

July 10. A good night and the cry from the young people early in the morning of "Why are you not up, we really see green fields." and we looked out of our port hole and there were beautiful green fields sloping down to the water and seemingly close to us.

July 11th. The coast of Ireland on the right and then the coast of Scotland on the left and then the coast of Scotland, on both sides as we entered the Firth of Clyde, charmed us completely and we wore our eyes out with looking...

July 11th. Noon. We are at the Waverly House in Glasgow, a Temperance House. Good enough, not <u>very</u> dirty. We hope it will not prove expensive.

July 11....Expenses Simple breakfast 1s[hilling] with meat 1.9s; Simple tea 1s; Dinner 2s; Lodging 1s.

July 12. The ride from Glasgow to Edinburgh is through tunnels and gardens. You emerge from the one to revel in the bloom of the other....

July 13. Strolled around Edinboro' in the morning, stopped in at Giles Church where John Knox once preached and walked around the Castle. The whole party is now at Darlings Hotel. We find it good but fear it is too expensive. (Breakfast 2s; Dinner 3, tea 1.6; Apartment 2; Attendance 1s;) total 9s4 or nearly $3 a day....

Edinburgh to London. The second class cars are well cushioned and are in small compartments. When I started an old lady and her daughter were with me, they said they were from Scarborough. ... It is a mark of the times that no one <u>ridicules</u> the idea of women's studying anything now.

It was 9 1/2 hours from Edinburgh to London and I went at once to the house of 4 sisters named Balcannon; they could not take me in but put me across the square into the house of Mrs. Richardson.

I am to pay 6s6d for room, breakfast and tea, both of these are to be meals with meats, for dinner, if I choose to take it, I pay 2s if I take it every day and 2s6d if I take it only occasionally.

Thursday July 17. Mr. Airy's. I went to Greenwich and arrived about 11 a.m. I had for years had misgivings about Mrs. Airy but had heard nothing. When the servant said "Lady Airy is not yet up" I knew she must be ill. Christabel came into the room and I said "Do you know me." She paused a minute and said "Miss Mitchell." Annot came in and I said "and do you know me?" She paused a minute and said "Miss Mitchell." And then Sir George Airy came in and the welcome was so hearty!

And later I saw Mrs. Airy wheeled out in a chair, a wreck and a ruin! And so tenderly cared for by all! She had been so good to me 15 years since, and was so full of vigor, that I could have cried at the sight.

She appeared to be very glad to see me, but said nothing, continuing to hold my hand and smile. And I found the girls had had such a hard life. One or the other sleeps in the room with her and they are up every night. She is fed like a child. Death of course will come as a relief for all. The girls were lovely and so careful of their mother. Sir George, as he is now, had improved with age and looks strong and vigorous. ...[4]

1873, July 21. ... Cambridge. We took an exceedingly hot day for a visit to Cambridge. I had lots of letters but could find no Professors at home. I found a lady, Miss Clough of Merton Hall, who keeps a house for a few young ladies, who study in Cambridge, under the Professors, most of them intend to be teachers. Miss Clough is about my age. Her ideas are in harmony with those of Miss Whitenholm and Mrs. Crudelius. But she is doing good work. She <u>leaves to the Professors</u> the decision of what studies are <u>suitable for women</u>.

Maria Mitchell

I seem to have come to Europe to visit the graves of my old friends, for Whewell and Sedgwick I knew 15 years ago. I stood at old Mrs. Maurier's grave and I would rather have stood at that of Lady Airy than have seen her as I did. Whewell and Sedgwick were intimate. Sedgwick has died this year, Whewell died of an accident some years since.

Cambridge is beautiful—but it has no trees except those in parks....One thing is certain, Girton College has sat itself down before the University of Cambridge in siege and the little woman Miss Davies has obtained a quiet power that is very effective. ...

From London, Maria and her nephew Willie headed for Russia to visit the renowned Pulkova Observatory.

1873 Ostende, July 26. The passage of 5 hours from Dover to Ostende was beautiful, not a ripple on the water. We are now in a most luxurious sleeping car for Berlin....

Sunday, July 27, 1873. Düsseldorf. We are detained here waiting for a midnight train....At Aix la Chapelle we got out and got our trunk out and went to a small quiet Hotel which was nice and clean....

July 29. En route for St. Petersburg and we are told that we keep this car right through. We have sleeping car thus. The lady's toilette is round and into that the Conductor locked me this morning and off the cars started. It was 4 a.m. and happily light. I found I could open the window and get air and there was a very comfortable arm chair, but I was distressed about Willie who could not know where I was.

After an hour I put my head out of the window just as Willie did the same. He was as delighted as I was. When the next stopping place came the Conductor was at hand at once and let me out. I found Willie had been much alarmed, had no idea I was on the train and had picked up my bag, with the intention of starting back for me. We have decided that we are to go on to St. Petersburg if we get separated and wait for the other party to come up....

Maria's trip to Russia was the subject of various lectures that Mitchell would later present. Fortunately, she wrote out the text of these lectures, which now provide us with revealing insights into her view of transatlantic traveling in the nineteenth century.

The habit of travelling once adopted cannot be easily given up. If you are in London you must go to Paris, or Paris you must certainly get on to Geneva. You cannot go home without Rome and it is "see Naples and die." But it does not end with Naples, it is only 24 hours across the Mediterranean and you are in Africa, besides you meet some friend who says "Have you been in Constantinople" and when you answer with mortification "No" he says "What! Come to Europe and not see Constantinople!" Of course you feel that you must go to Constantinople.[5]

1873 July 30. Wednesday. A slight unpleasantness at Eydkuhnen. Certainly I never in my life expected to spend 24 hours in this small town, the frontier town of Prussia! We came on finely from Berlin to this frontier town and here we got out and I asked the Conductor what I should do about luggage, and he told me we went on a little further before we met the inspector. We went on about a mile farther and came to the Custom House.

As we had been told that the fine car we occupied alone went on to St. Petersburg without change, we had felt much at our ease and had scattered our small luggage about freely.

Imagine our consternation when an official entered and <u>seized</u>, literally, every small article and rushed out, we following! He took cloak and bag and book and even a handkerchief which Willie had washed out in a small bowl (which I carried in my bag) and which he had hung out by a hole in it, upon a nail to dry. He also took passports!

We followed and saw our trunk land in the custom house on one side, and our divers small things on the other side of an immense room. Willie stood by one and I by the other and then we both stood together by a small collection of cloak, book, bag and ragged handkerchief (Wierzbolow). After some 20 minutes two officials came to me and holding my passport in hand told me that I could not go on without the <u>visa</u> of the Russian official, that I must go back to Eydkuhnen and remain 24 hours and start again!

One of the officials took the passport and told me he should keep it and get the visa for me, that I could leave my trunk but take my

Maria Mitchell

small luggage. When I stopped to ask explanations he motioned me into the returning car, clapped the door to and we were off, returning on our track....[6]

We were arrested on the frontier. We meekly asked how far we were to go and were relieved when we found that we went back only to the nearest town, but that the passports must be sent to Konigsberg, 60 miles away, to be endorsed by the Russian ambassador, and that might take some days.

Willie was very much inclined to refuse to go back and to attempt a war of words, but it did not seem to me wise to undertake a war against the Russian Government. I know our country does not lightly go into an "unpleasantness" of that kind....

We went back to Eydkuhnen, a little miserable German village. Happily our passports were back in 24 hours, and we started again, but we perceived another little dilemma. Our trunk had been registered for St. Petersburg and to St. Petersburg it had gone ahead of us and of the small heap of things thrown down promiscuously at the Custom House the whole had not come back to us. It was not very important. I learned how to wear one glove instead of two, or to go without. We had the ordeal of the Custom House to pass again but once passed and told we were free to go on it was like going into a clear atmosphere from a foggy one.[7]

July 28 and 29. You know it the moment you are in Russia. The buffets become excellent, one at Eydkuhnen and one a mile off but in Russia, are very different. But if buffets become better the law becomes at once poorer and the civilization lower. ...

Aug. 1. St. Petersburg is exceedingly strange. It is as if we had dropped down upon another planet....[8]

It was summer. The temperature was delightful, about like our October....Especially I noticed the excellence of the thermometers and I naturally stopped to read them.

Figures are a common language, but is was clear that I was in another planet. I could not read the thermometers, I judged that the weather was warm enough for this to be 68. I read 16...

But I came to a still stranger experience. I dated my letters Aug. 3 and went to the Banker's before I mailed them to see if there were letters for me. The Banker's little calendar was hanging by his desk and

PORTIONS OF MARIA MITCHELL'S TRAVEL JOURNALS. Occasionally, Maria would include a sketch in her diary to illustrate the topic at hand. *Above,* she depicts a peasant dress in a description of a day of travel in Russia. *Below,* a portion of her journal dated July 21, 1873 in which she writes while in Cambridge, England, "I seem to have come to Europe to visit the graves of my old friends."

the day of the month was on exhibition in large figures. I read July 22. This was distressing! Was I like Alice in Fairyland? Did time go backward? Surely I had dated Aug. 3. Could I be in error 12 days? And then I perceived that 12 days was just the difference of old and new calendars. How many times I had taught students that the Russians still counted their time by the "old style" but had never learned it myself.

And so I was obliged to teach myself new lessons in science.... When the thermometer stands at 32 in St. Petersburg water does not freeze as it does in Boston. On the contrary it's very warm in St. Petersburg, for it means what 104 does in Boston. And if you leave London on the 22nd of July and are 5 days on the way to St. Petersburg, a week after you get there it is still the 22nd of July! And we complain that the day is too short![9]

I hesitated about getting into a drosky* but once in I thought it charming. They are really very small low phaetons with a driver in front....[10]

In my despair about getting my trunk from the Custom House I went to our Consul General Pomertz and asked him what I should do. He rang the bell and sent for a man and he said the man would come at once and if any one could get it out of the Custom House, at once, that man could....I had $4 to pay but was only too glad to do it.

August 2. Today I have been to the Observatory of Pulkova. I started with my Commissioner who took 2 droskys, one for Willie and myself and one for himself and we went off at a rapid pace for we were late and the train might have left before we got there. As the Drosky driver started off I clung to the side of the little crazy carriage and to Willie. Willie begged me not to cling to him as he could scarcely keep his seat any way. So I suddenly remembered that every drosky driver wore a red belt and I caught at the belt of my driver and clung to him frantically....at Pulkova took a carriage and driver to the Observatory. I had never had a Commissioner before and I suffered about as much as I expected. I was fleeced....

The Director of the Observatory is Otto Struve. His father, William Struve preceded him. Properly the Director is in German Herr von Struve, but the old Russian custom is still in use and the

---

*drosky *(also droshky)* — a low, open, four-wheeled Russian carriage with a long, narrow bench straddled by the passengers.

servants call him Wilhelmvitch, that is, the son of William. Mr. Struve received us courteously and an assistant was called to show us the instruments.

There was very little ceremony at dinner. We had the delicious wild strawberries of the country in great profusion and the talk, which is always the best of the dinner, was in German, Russian and English.

Madame Struve spoke German, Russian and French and complained that she could not speak English. She said she had spent 3 weeks with an English Lady and she must be very stupid not to be able to speak English.

I noticed in one of the rooms, which was not so very immense, there was a circular centre table, a small centre carpet and chairs around the table. I have been told that in "Society" in Russia the ladies sit in a circle, and the gentlemen walk around and talk consecutively with the ladies, kindly giving to each a share of their attention....

St. Petersburg. 1873, Aug. 3. We went to St. Isaac's Cathedral to see the ceremonies of the "name day" of the Empress. As I do not know her name nor the name of the day, I cannot give it....

Aug. 4, 1873. I went to the bank and was pleased to see my name on the list of "Foreigners" who had letters....

Aug. 5. It would have been a pity to leave St. Petersburg without seeing the Hermitage, a museum of paintings, sculptures and gems but which would have been worth seeing for the beauty of its Halls alone. Like everything in St. Petersburg it is immense and each room is immense....

We took Commissioner and open carriage later and drove around, as we were about to enter the Cathedral of St. Peter and St. Paul, we perceived our Guide was stopped by an officer with a tone of authority and he turned and told us the "Kaiser was coming and no one could enter." We asked how long it would be before he came in and were told it would be about 15 minutes, so we stopped....But I wondered if he touches his forehead to the floor as the poor beggar women do! Probably he did. I asked Willie if he wished he was the Czar of Russia and he said "Not for the world" would he be in that man's place....

Aug. 6. We left St. Petersburg at 1 p.m. and came in a small compartment car to Eydkuhnen in 23 hours, quite by ourselves, 1st class....

Aug. 10. We left Berlin at 12 having had the good fortune to make a very pleasant acquaintance. ...

It was a fearfully hot ride of 5 hours to Dresden and when I reached Dresden, tired and warm, I indulged too freely in ice water and had a sickish night. We were at the Belleview Hotel which stands upon the Elbe... I left Willie and went back to the Hotel and lay down, hesitating about going on.

We started off at 3 p.m. and I have been well ever since, but obliged to lie down for most of the way while Willie exclaimed at the beauty of the scenery....

We were near Starving! Spoiled by the Russian Buffets, we supposed that we should find the same in Southern Germany. We had a hearty breakfast in Dresden at 9 and left at 3 with no additional meal, were on the car 22 hours and could get bread only and that of a poor kind. Willie got one cup of coffee and I had two. Under such conditions I thought we must stop at Lindau for the night....

Aug. 12. Lucerne. We left Lindau by boat for Romanshorn, a passage of 2 hours, very pleasant but no more romantic than the Hudson river trips.... Then we took rail for Lucerne via Zug. We stopped at Zug an hour and reached Lucerne about 5 p.m. The Lake is beautiful and we enjoy Pilatus which lies against the sky fogged and craggy like an old castle....

Aug. 14. The clouds did not lift and we started for Thun by rail... We reached the beautiful village of Thun at 6 p.m.... and we now saw the snow capped mountains of the Jungfrau and Mont Eiger. At Thun we took an hour and drove to the Hotel and Pensions to find Mr. Kendall, and we soon found that he could not be found....

We prepared a telegram to the Bankers to ask for Mr. Kendall's address but when we gave it to the Landlord he advised us not to send it but to look in the Interlachen Bulletin and see if we could find the names in the Stranger's list.... We went to bed somewhat depressed. Willie had counted on meeting his parents at Thun and I could not but fear that we might be some days in finding them....

When I awoke in the morning and went to the door, I found the paper which the Landlord had promised and the names of our party were first, at the Victoria and then at Pension Beau Site. Our way was now plain. These Hotels were in Interlachen and to Interlachen we must go....

At Interlachen we took a boy and walked to Pension Beau Site and we were soon told that there was a party in the house, who waited for two such persons as we seemed to be and the girl rushed up to Mrs. Kendall and said "*Votre fils est arrivé.*" Mrs. Kendall says she never understood French so readily. They had been exceedingly anxious. It seems we had passed through every city a little before their letters had come, and we had missed them every where....

Aug. 15. I am rooming in a chalet and go some 500 feet to my meals at the Pension Beau Site....

Aug. 15. Phebe and I went to Giessbach Falls, by boat on the Brienz lake for about 1 1/2 hours, by foot up a gradual ascent for 15 minutes and then the Falls, a slender cascade coming out of the mountains at a great height and then gushing about down and down from point to point... We go into Switzerland without passport or custom House, we land in New York and what then?...

Aug. 18....I left the whole party this morning and started off alone. I reached Basil, for it is now Basil and not Basle, being more German than French, about 1 1/2 p.m. and came to the Hotel Trois Rois.... I have been homesick and lonesome in Basil and wish I was in America. A rainy day alone is no better in Switzerland than in Hyannis....

Aug. 21, 1873. Russia—again. Yesterday I made the long journey from Basil to Cologne, 8:45 a.m. to 10 p.m. When I started a German lady was in the compartment who had lived 5 years in St. Louis.... Well, as I found she was going to a German boarding school to get a daughter 12 years old, I told her about Vassar....

She left me at 8 1/2 p.m. and there got in 4 women, three young girls and their mother. I thought they must be Dutch, for their talk was not German. After a while I began to talk and found they all spoke some English. I told them I had been to St. Petersburg. They were immediately interested and told me they were Russians and asked me why I had gone to St. Petersburg.

I told them partly to see the city and partly to go to the Observatory. They asked why I wished to see the Observatory and I told them I had charge of one in America, that I was in a College for girls. They were at once all interest and everyone asked a question.

"Were boys and girls together? Were the Professors men and women together? Did girls study both Classics and sciences?" And then to my surprise, "Do women take any part in the Government of the United States." I asked in return "Why do you ask such a question" and said "I am a Woman's Rights woman, are you?" and the reply was "Yes, all of us and most of the Russian women." "We are from Moscow." "Have you a College for girls there?" "No, we are always going to have one," said one with a sigh....

As I left them I begged them to study by themselves and so hold up a lesson for women. They said, "The Russians have not the energy of the Americans" and I reminded them that they had already three languages at their command and one said, "Yes, but when one speaks so many languages it usually happens that he knows very little of any of them."

Mitchell included almost nothing in her diary about the remainder of her trip back to England. In London, she visited the esteemed suffragette Frances Power Cobbe.[11]

Miss Cobbe. It was the 26th August and I had no hope that Miss Cobbe could be at her town residence but I felt bound to deliver Mrs. Howe's letter and I wished to give her a Vassar pamphlet, so I took a cab and drove.... She looked just as I expected but even larger, but then her head is magnificent because so large. She was very cordial at once and told me that Miss Davies had told her I was in London.... I had heard that she was not a Woman's Rights woman and she said, "Who could have told you that? I am remarkably so, I write suffrage articles continually, I sign petitions, etc."...

Westminster Abbey. I suspected that the shriveled guide who was taking us around was the same whom I knew 15 years since and so I asked him how long he had been in the business and he said 18 years. Then I asked him to show me where Sir John Herschel was buried. He showed me the spot and I copied the inscription. As you stand looking at the monument to Newton, the tomb of Sir John Herschel is a little on the left. Herschel has only a plain grey (probably slate) slab on the floor of just the color of Newton's, which is just before his monument. I went to the tomb of Dickens and of Macauley....

Steamer *Castalia*. Sept. 12. We are on the 13th day of our passage and only today am I able to write. The passage has not been bad but the pitchy motion which the head winds gave is very sickening and I was scarcely able to move for 7 days. Certainly for 3 days I was violently sick if I moved. And the worst sickness was the giddiness of the 8th and 9th days when if I moved, I was faint, or, my sight failed and things dimmed for a few minutes.

I did not walk across the deck for 10 days, although I crawled up nearly every day. One great cause was the crowded condition of the ship. We had 93 cabin passengers and over 100 steerage. As the dinner table must be set a second time, at every meal, we have little use of the cabin, the small ladies cabin below deck has been made up for sleepers and that on deck is occupied by the sick....

Following her eventful three-month trip to England and Russia, Mitchell returned to Vassar College and resumed her life as a resident faculty member and astronomer. In the years ahead, her activities would enter a wider stage as she played a key role in the establishment of the Association for the Advancement of Women.

CHAPTER 10

VASSAR COLLEGE, 1873 to 1880

Great is the self-denial of those who follow science.
They who look through telescopes at the time of a
total eclipse are martyrs; they severely deny themselves.

𝒮EVERAL MEMBERS of the early Vassar community wrote moving reminiscences about what it had been like to know Mitchell in her prime. From the available archives, we have chosen two illuminating descriptions of "Miss Mitchell" as representative samples. One presents a student's view, the other that of a colleague. Their comments are notably typical of the numerous reflections about the extraordinary woman from Nantucket. They give as instructive a view as we have of the working Maria Mitchell. The student, Helen Dawes Brown,[1] arrived at Vassar in 1875 with a personal recommendation from Ralph Waldo Emerson.

Concord

14 September [1875]

My dear Miss Mitchell,

Will you allow me to introduce to you a young townswoman of mine, Miss Helen D. Brown, who bravely designs to present herself for examination for admission to Vassar College. She belongs to a worthy family here and perhaps has been led by her acquaintance with Miss Folsom [Ellen M. Folsom, Class of 1871] to a strong wish to share the benefits of your university. Her own record at our High School, is I understand, of the best. May I ask for my young friend such counsel and such recommendation as you shall find her to deserve.

I could heartily wish that when you come to Massachusetts, I might have the honor and the pleasure of a visit from you in my house. Our little town has grown larger lately. Alas, it has not one telescope in it.

I think if you came hither for a few days we should rush to add one to our Library.

With great regards, yours

R. W. Emerson[2]

Twelve years after her graduation, Helen Brown gave a speech to assembled New York Vassar alumnae, recalling with undiminished admiration her fond memories of being a student of Maria Mitchell.

Think what it was to know her in those days of our girlhood! Do you remember the first visit paid to her in her observatory parlor? That room with its mysterious astronomical instruments and its bright flowers; with its book cases filled with plain, stern volumes; the bust of Mary Somerville by the window, the vines swaying behind it; and across the room the picture of Humboldt in his study. It was a room that to a sensitive girl conveyed a new conception of severe scholarship, that gave her a fresh and inspiring glimpse of the possible attainments of women; and yet it was a room with its flowers and sunshine and warm colors that was thoroughly human and friendly.

Perhaps we were allowed a sight of that quaint little old world garden, where the earliest roses and the latest chrysanthemums grew. Every spot had character, and subtly expressed its mistress.

There was a distinction about her and her surroundings that was felt by the most inexperienced of us. For the first time, possibly, we came under the spell of fame, and were all alive to the romance of it.

Reverent and fascinated, we approached near to illustrious people; for in our acquaintance with Miss Mitchell we completed a circuit. We established communication with the Herschels, with Humboldt, with Hawthorne, and Emerson, with men and women whose names were names to conjure with. Her talk was delightful, rich in reminiscence and racy anecdote. She knew people and she knew books; for she was of a liberal and genial culture. She had not only her favorite mathematicians, but her favorite poets. In her early Nantucket days, she was "tumbled into a spacious closet of good old English reading."

Alas that on those Sunday night visits there was not a Boswell among us to preserve some fragments of her sparkling talk! I wonder as the door closed after a party of girls, I wonder if a desire for the great world ever seized her.

In many respects, the conditions of her life at the college were ideal, but there must have been moments when she felt its limitations. To students the friendship with Miss Mitchell was simply a part of their liberal education. How many girls of fluttering and uncertain aims found method and meaning in their lives when they saw her day by day? They went out of her class room alive with energy and purpose. They often left her stimulated and delighted by the humor which was her invaluable ally in her teaching.

A chance meeting with Miss Mitchell, on the observatory walk, or on the first north corridor, gave one always an electric shock. At the slightest contact, a spark flashed.

She was not always a soft-spoken woman: truthfulness and humor such as hers have their temptations. But that is not what one remembers longest of Miss Mitchell. It is rather that beautiful smile that broke with a soft light over her rugged face, with a look of perfect kindness, that is to me my lasting memory of her. Many a girl discovered a tenderness in her that was not only womanly, it was motherly.

We cannot deny that she had her partialities. If a girl had poverty to recommend her, she stirred a chivalrous interest in Miss Mitchell. If a girl was ambitious, if she hitch her wagon to a star, why, naturally our astronomer took her to her heart. .... [3]

Frances A. Wood, a woman who first came to the college as a teacher and was later appointed librarian in 1880, fondly recalled those early years at Vassar and her association with Maria Mitchell.

...How one wanted to peep in that notebook of hers, usually carried in her pocket. An abstruse calculation jotted hastily down on one page, side by side with the latest anecdote or joke, a fact in regard to woman's education, an intimate personal reflection, what a mine of riches it contained!

"If thee has any secrets, thee mustn't tell them to Maria. She never could keep one," said dear old Mr. Mitchell, playfully. We understood

what he meant. While she would not reveal special confidence reposed in her, or give out in advance any college matter of importance, she simply was unable to bind herself to the petty and the trivial, and as a friend stated, "thought and word with her came pretty close together."

However interested you might have been in woman suffrage and all the other subjects concerning the "cause," you felt that in comparison with this grand woman you hardly knew the alphabet. She judged everything from the standpoint, "How is this going to affect women?"

I remember her indignation at being overlooked with the other two women of the Faculty by President Raymond in his demand for a list of what the members had published. "We may not have done so much as some of the men, but we all have done something." It took a good deal of apology on his part to soothe her wounded feeling and restore her natural good humor.

Every woman speaker of note in that day, Julia Ward Howe, Anna Dickinson, Mary Livermore, Elizabeth Cady Stanton, Ednah Cheney, were personal friends of Miss Mitchell, and at various times her guests at the observatory. Sometimes one would be invited to speak before the whole college, as when Mrs. Howe recited her "Battle Hymn of the Republic" and Mrs. Livermore told the story of her war experiences in a hospital. But the observatory was chiefly the place of meeting, with spirited talk and free discussion. What delightful evenings were there when a favored few were asked to meet distinguished guests! What personal anecdote and reminiscence! And what good coffee at the end!

She avoided irritating discussion and heated argument.... The earliest reports of departments were read in detail at Board meetings, and Miss Mitchell had a satisfaction that her labor in making out statistics had not been wasted, seeming, then, to count in significance and importance. In later years, this proceeding was no longer practicable.

Entering the President's office one morning she inquired a little aggressively, "Into the oblivion of whose hands do I consign this paper?" "Mine," came the meek reply, disarming her completely....

She appreciated gifts of flowers, and trifles that she could share, but once refused a lovely vase to stand on her study table, "I should have to dust it." Hearing her speak of wishing to see a volume of essays by John Weiss, the book was purchased and carried over to her. Later she returned it with thanks, "I have read this with much enjoyment. Now take it home and keep it. I do not want to accumulate things, too much trouble when I come to break up."...

Her standards were merciless. "Middlemarch" was, in her opinion, an immoral book; "Dorothea had no business to have had even a feeling of interest in Ladislaw. What if it did go no further, you say? She was a married woman." That settled it. And yet, Miss Mitchell admired George Eliot and condoned her marriage with Lewes, as a woman too grand intellectually to be subject to the petty verdict of the world's opinion. She would not relish the "problem" novel of today, and the aggressive methods of the modern suffragette would receive scant toleration....

There were only four or five of us outside of the students who had Unitarian preferences, and we were considered on account of this, by our orthodox sisters, to be indeed very black sheep religiously. The club was very informal, meeting every Sunday evening for supper at the observatory, or in the room of a member, entertaining in this way any guest visiting the college that Miss Mitchell considered in sympathy enough to invite. The aim was serious, excluding all gossip and light talk and while there was no straining after "high thinking," it was certain we had frequent hint of this in Miss Mitchell's independent, stimulating opinions, and from the friends who came as guests, bringing their best thoughts with them. ... She had a deeply religious nature; had no sympathy with free thinking, so called, or scientific speculations, flippant and irreverent....

She shared a cottage one summer with Mrs. Frances Hodgson Burnett,[4] whom she much admired and liked, though no greater contrast can be imagined than existed between the two women in temperament and tastes. Some of Miss Mitchell's college girls paid her a visit there one day, and she got Mrs. Burnett's permission to introduce the students to her. They had a delightful call in her room, made beautiful with antique furniture, pictures, rugs, cushions, everything that could appeal to cultivated eyes and aesthetic sense. Returning with them to her own quarters across the hall from the author's suite, Miss Mitchell waved her hand to the room just left: "Girls, that is Paris, and this," ushering them into her rather bare parlor, "this is Cape Cod."...[5]

In the fall of 1873, students reported in the *Vassar Miscellany* on some noteworthy activities beyond the campus of their esteemed astronomy professor.

> *October 1873. This year, Prof. Mitchell will again furnish to the* Scientific American *a monthly statement of the times for the rising and setting of the planets and the appearance of other celestial phenomena which would interest the popular mind. The computations will be made, as heretofore, by students in her department.*[6]

> *October 1873. Prof. Mitchell recently spent two or three days in New York, attending the Woman's Congress, an association for the advancement of women, educationally, morally, and physically. Many able papers were read, among them, one by Miss Mitchell on "The Higher Education of Women."*[7]

As noted in chapter nine, Mitchell had written in her diary about being seasick on her trip to England in 1873. After returning home, she wrote a letter to her sister Sally, expressing in more detail just how uncomfortable the trip really was for her. Sally herself was often in poor health, and this letter from Maria appears to have been written in response to a particular illness Sally was suffering at the time.

[No date given]

My dear Sally,

I went through all thy experiences, bodily, after I had been sea-sick for seven days. I could not see, if I moved quickly and I could not walk across the deck, even when it was still weather.

One day another passenger told me to notice the clouds. I had just crawled upon the deck. I said, "If you will wait until my sight comes back, I will look," and in a few minutes I could see. Of course it frightened me and I thought I had softening of the brain. There was a lady physician on board and I asked her what it meant, and she said it was nothing but weakness from <u>starvation</u>. I did not keep more than one fig down, for the whole seven days.

Now the <u>moral</u> of all this is—eat strengthening food and let beach plums alone. I think I have always been more careful of my diet than thee has. I do not now eat anything but bread and butter at tea time. I should never touch a beach plum after morning.

I was strongly tempted when I went to Europe to invite thee to go along, but it would not have done. The screw steamers are much worse than the side wheels. They bump you about terribly. We had no storm at all, either way, but I think I sat down six times one morning, when I was dressing, because I was thrown down. And one night a small trunk which I had in my state room and which I could not lift, went jumping about the state room quite briskly. Almost all the steamers now are stern wheel and not side wheel. They are safer, and I did not have a minute of fright about the steamer, but I was frightened about my excessive weakness.

M. M.

Do not let Anna Pitman suppose that her present is silver. It is probably tin; but it looked pretty to me, and so I bought it. If I am well and rich when her day comes, I will do something better for her.[8]

In a revealing letter to her close friend Elizabeth O. Abbott, Mitchell recalled some of the events of her trip abroad and the current events at the college.

Oct. 3. [1873]

My dear E. O.,

You don't mind shape of paper do you? "Not a bit," you say. All right then, if I go to the College for note paper this letter will never be written.

I did go to St. Petersburg and I did see Miss Cobbe.... Miss Cobbe entered, laughing at the dog's manners and saying at once that she ... was very glad to see me. Now don't ever tell it, but I, even I— gushed! I don't mean that I went upon my knees and put my arms around her, but I did tell her how glad I was that she lived, how much good her books had done me, etc., etc., until I became self-conscious and perceived what I was doing....

Now for college. The telegraph is in the college and is ordered for the Observatory but not yet in. I suppose I shall have to push. The collimators* were referred to the Ex. Com. and I know I must push in that quarter. But the spirit is good and I am well heated. The Observatory is all painted inside and was in perfect order when I arrived—schoolroom floor is mended and painted. Class is large, 8 advanced and 19 beginning with two more expected.

---

*Collimators are small telescopes that used to adjust the transit circle to make it more accurate.

In an effort to make it unreadable, a back page of this letter to Elizabeth Abbott had later been pasted over with a blank sheet; but the words
can be clearly read by looking through the paper at a strong light. This
censored part of the letter is nothing more than typical faculty gossip.
Mitchell discusses the candidates for the College Physician position soon
to be vacated by Dr. Avery.

> ...Miss T.,[9] Dr. Avery and I all prefer Dr. Tyng to any others whom
> we have seen.... We have had a Dr. Stinson, a woman of about my
> age, 6 ft. high, with a mass of elegant gray hair and sweet face, said to
> be very radical. Her age is considered a great objection. (Privately, I
> think the president is afraid of her radicalism and Miss Terry, I think,
> is afraid of her in some way....) I think that we are all too critical
> about the incoming doctor. We forget that at first sight no one of us
> was exactly what was desired....
>
> M.M.[10]

Despite her preference voiced in this letter, Dr. Tyng was not ulti-
mately the college's choice for their new physician. Instead, Dr. Helen
W. Webster, M.D. replaced Dr. Avery in 1874.

Mitchell's diary includes a brief note about "small grievances"—"an
interview with L. P., a bad cold, mouse in room, servant girl ill." But at
this point in the diary book, seven pages are missing—removed by
Maria's sister, Phebe. She justifies this action by writing: "These pages
were marked PRIVATE and pinned together. The interest of the writer
has been respected and for that reason they have been removed."

> Vassar, Oct. 28, '73
>
> My dear Lizzie,
>
> As you suppose I have been exceedingly busy. I lost a few days
> going to see my brother Henry married[11] and a few lately, going to
> the Woman's Congress, etc. My class is large and I have my hands
> full. I have had to push to have the telegraph brought into the obser-
> vatory and to have some other improvements and it all takes up time.
> I had a very long passage home and was sick 7 days and well 7....
> Miss Wood is well but very sad.

I have at the Observatory, Ella Arnold ['79] and Ella Gardner ['77] of Nantucket, both good girls....My advanced class Cushing, Cutter, Stowe, Arnold, Reed, Smiley, Fisher, Bennett[12]—no stupid girl among them, three of them Unitarians, and there is a comfort in that. All of them come to the Observatory on Sunday evenings occasionally, but the Sunday evenings were an Institution of Father and the old glory will not come back.

Miss Wood, Miss Green, Miss Avery and I meet at tea time on Sundays and read something that is Liberal and then we separate. We enjoy it very much but even that gathering has lost already Miss Abbott and must soon lose Dr. Avery. Miss [E.O.] Abbott is teaching in a school in Providence. Sarah Glazier has gone West and Mary Whitney has her place. Sarah has not given up the idea of the Wellesley school however....

Your old maid Aunt,

M. M.[13]

[postcard. No addressee]

Nov. 7.

The telegraph wire is in the Observatory; the bust of Mrs. S[omerville] has reached New York; the order for the collimators is in my pocket; and Col. Higginson lectured here last night. The earth moves in its orbit.

M. M.[14]

The bust of Mary Somerville became one of Mitchell's most prized possessions and occupied a place of honor on her desk at all times.

Observatory – Dec. 5, 1873

President Raymond,

A plaster cast of the head of Mary Somerville by the sculptor Moe Donald, has been received as a donation to the Observatory. It is not only a beautiful ornament in itself, but it has the additional value of being the gift of another remarkable woman Frances Power Cobbe of London. I have supposed that some other notice should be taken of it, beside the unofficial letter which I shall write to Miss Cobbe.

Maria Mitchell[15]

MARIA MITCHELL'S ROOM ON THE SECOND FLOOR OF THE ORIGINAL VASSAR OBSERVATORY. For most of her twenty-two years at Vassar, this room was Maria Mitchell's residence. Because she entertained here and the students needed to use the clocks in the room, her privacy must have been minimal. Originally, she slept in this room, perhaps on the cot to the right.

Detail at right: Prominently displayed on her desk is one of Maria's most prized possessions: a bust of Mary Somerville, the famed self-taught scientist whom Maria called "the most learned woman in all Europe." Mitchell enjoyed a memorable visit with Somerville in Italy in 1858. On each side of the bust are photographs of the sun taken during Maria's observations at Vassar. The clock to the left of the central window and the timing mechanism to the right still sit in the positions shown in this photograph.

Maria Mitchell

Despite the fact that Mitchell had agreed to present various "Popular Astronomy" lectures at Vassar, she was still resisting teaching a general course. She also expressed to President Raymond her ongoing reservations about giving grades.

> Vassar College [1873]
> My dear President,
> Your note of Dec 8th touching Mrs Somerville &c is just received! I keep a "Vanity Book" for my complimentary letters and it shall certainly go into that and as several of my little students are intending to write my Biography, it will doubtless some time come into print!
> But I confess to a small drawback! Whenever you are uncommonly pleasant and agreeable I suspect there's a little pill behind the coating and I haven't a doubt, by tomorrow, I shall have a hint about "Sophomore Lectures" or the "Marks in the permanent Record" or something else that I do not fancy. So I take care not to be over grateful.
> M.M.[16]

Mitchell was increasingly involved in various women's organizations. In January 1874 the *Vassar Miscellany* noted:

> *During Prof. Mitchell's recent visit to Boston, a reception was given her by the New England Woman's Club, of which she is a member.*[17]

During that same month, the Sorosis Club unanimously elected her "Orator of the Day" for their sixth Anniversary, scheduled for Monday, March 16, 1874.[18] When informing Mitchell of the honor, the club's secretary, A. C. Fletcher, added a personal note: "The Society is happy to know one who so nobly represents attainment in Woman." Nonetheless, Mitchell notified Fletcher that she was unable to accept the "Orator" honor.

In the early days of her fame, Maria Mitchell had found it "amusing to find oneself lionized." Now, more than two decades later, she again found amusement in how her fame affected people around her.

> 1874, March 12. Charles Kingsley[19] lectured on Greek drama. He gave us a very pleasing view of the Athenian theatre, with Socrates in the audience, of the seriousness and the earnestness of the lessons of the plays. He read (very badly) from some of them. ... Last night at dinner he was next to me and barely noticed me, when I attempted to

talk to him. Today he called and it seems he couldn't do me too much honor. Someone had told him who I was. He was so agreeable! He knew the same people whom I knew! He was fond of Miss Cobbe, he liked Theodore Parker, he had known Dr. Whewell intimately, he was also intimate with Prof. Sedgwick.

He looked over my photograph book and was delighted at that of the Princess of Wales. When I said "You know her I suppose" he said "She is my mistress!" and he showed me a bent sixpence, which she dropped and he picked up and wore attached to his watch chain as a "love token."

I can't say that I was quite pleased with his instantaneous interest in me when he knew who I was! It does seem a little snobbish, even if it's Kingsley. Then it was clear that vice in princely halls was quite different from what it was in common life....[20]

One letter to Mitchell in 1874 came from Susan B. Anthony. It is the only letter in the Maria Mitchell collection from this famed leader in the movement for women's suffrage.

Whether Mitchell attended any of the meetings noted in Anthony's letter is not clear. Although clearly sympathetic to women's suffrage, Maria's role as president of the Association for the Advancement of Women was consuming much of her time at this point.

> *National Woman Suffrage Association*
> *New York, May 18th, 1874*
> *Dear Miss Mitchell,*
>
> *I met Miss Sallie Holly and Dr. Miller an hour ago. She told me of your recent call there and wish that you were able to attend our meetings the 14th and 15th—I at once take the liberty to address you and solicit your presence to at least one of the Friday sessions—and a word from you—thus giving to the Cause of Woman Suffrage the weight of your name and influence—*
>
> *I hope you can comply with our most earnest wish—but if you cannot thus aid, will you not give me a letter that I can read at our meeting. If you believe in the ballot for woman, I want the whole world to know it.*
>
> *With most profound respect,*
> *Susan B. Anthony.*[21]

Maria Mitchell

Although there is no record in the archives of Maria's response to Anthony's specific requests in the May 1874 letter, Mitchell's diary records show that she attended a suffrage meeting in March of the following year. And, as president of the Association for the Advancement of Women, she sought to promote the overall causes of women.

Jan. 26. [1875]

My dear Lizzie [Williams Champney, '69],

I put your letter down and write at once in fear that I may not write at all, if I wait for suitable time and paper....I wish I could, to tell you how much we are working, like all of you in Europe, feeling how little we accomplish but enjoying the effort. If I were rich today I would found a college and every good girl who has been with me at Vassar should come in and found her Department and model a school of her own. You should have yours and Mary Whitney hers and Kate Lupton hers, and as for Miss Abbott, I think she would have to be guardian angel.

But I meant to tell you of other kind of work. Do you know that we have a large body of women, some 400, who come together as "Association for the Advancement of Women." I am president for this year and shall preside next Oct.

Shall you be back? Could you prepare a short essay, to be used or not, as I may think proper, on study in Art, with practical suggestions? I am not the Com. on papers and it might get crowded out, but I want such as you would write in order to crowd out (if necessary) weak papers which may be offered. Ellen Swallow furnished one for last year's, a good one.

I may not be able to write to Mary, but I wish you would send this note to her and ask her to write a short essay for Science, if she can. You perceive that both of you would be high-toned and scholarly — and of course, among 400 women, a great many are Temperance people or Missionary women, very good in their way, but we have enough of them.

We want practical suggestions for women's work. I can get Miss Swasey to read for you, if you are not on hand. But I hope you will be back.

Class coming in!

M. M.[22]

CONTROVERSIES ABOUT WOMEN'S EDUCATION were never far from Maria's experience during this era. One of her letters was in pointed rebuttal of Edward Clarke's *Sex in Education* (1873), a polemic against the education of women.

To prove his point, Clarke had cited supposed instances of how education had ruined the health of several Vassar students. In her response, reformer Julia Ward Howe edited a series of essays against Clarke's view, published in 1874 as *Sex in Education: a Reply*. Mitchell's letter to President Raymond about the issue was written while she was away from the college, probably during the Christmas break of 1873.

123 Inman St.

Cambridgeport, Mass.

My dear President,

No sooner am I in Boston than I have to begin the battles for the College!

Dr. Derby, prominent physician in the city, asked me about the number of students who graduate before nineteen—about the number who are hurt by rooming on the 4th floor—&c, &c with medical details of his patients from Vassar, not particularly pleasant to hear.

I combated the implied fault-finding at the physical training at Vassar until I was pretty well tired, and coming out of the Office met at once a Reporter, Miss Joy, who asked me if she would come up to Vassar with a view to writing a letter for the *Boston Post*. I asked her to come as my guest, when the holidays were over.

Upon a second thought, I have remembered that it might not be convenient at that time to Miss Terry [the Lady Principal]—or that you might prefer some other time—in which case will you or she or Miss Morse, let me know.

But it does seem to me desirable that whether we are right or wrong at Vassar, those who will write about us should know what Vassar is. I know Miss Joy only as a woman well received at the Boston Woman's Club and as a clever, but somewhat gushing Reporter.

Dr. Derby tells me that Dr. Clarke has a list of the names of those who have graduated before nineteen years old. Is not Miss Swift the only case? Could not statistics on that particular point be gathered and printed?

Maria Mitchell.[23]

> *[Added note on letter in President Raymond's hand]*
>
> *If this needs answering, will Miss Terry please answer. I have no choice as to the time of Miss Joy's coming—and no time now to look up the age of our graduates. Perhaps Dr. Avery knows. J.H.R.*

The following letter from Massachusetts clergyman and author and Edward Everett Hale[24] appears to have been written during the same controversy.

> *March 1, [c. 1874]*
> *Roxbury*
> *My dear Miss Mitchell*
> *…The article which you take exceptions to was written by one of the most skillful and learned of American physicians. I sent the book to him because I knew him to be ever chivalrous in his dignified respect for women.*
>
> *You have read hastily if you have thought he said that teachers were "monstrosities." He says what I am afraid you would say much more bitterly than he, that the one-sided <u>education</u> of many women is a monstrosity. I should say that this was true of anything one-sided.*
>
> *The questions which relate to the education and work of women has [sic] been so long conducted in a Laura Matilda way as if they are only matters of sentiment, that Dr. Clarke's book seems to have excited unmercifully surprise. I am sure that you do not share that surprise. I am sure that you believe that a mention of sex must be discussed as a question of sex.*
>
> *I have it in my power to say that questions of sex shall not be discussed in my magazine. Thirty years ago I probably should have said so. It is not I or people who think as I do, who have brought these prominently forward into general conversation and argument. Now that they are so brought forward I think it would be absurd for old and new to decline to recognize them.*

> *It would be a very great pleasure to us if you would write us an article giving your view of the matter—especially if you chose to treat it from the practical side—or the point of observation of a teacher.*
>
> *I had the pleasure of voting for a pupil of yours last week to occupy a place in the Roxbury Latin School. I think you will remember Miss Meade, as she seemed to be very fond of you. I hope she may prove to be as good a Latinist as mathematician.*
>
> *Edward E. Hale[25]*

Privately, Mitchell may have worried about the effect on her students of a rigorous academic life, but not because she doubted their ability. She later recorded:

> I have seven advanced students, and today, when I looked around to see who should be called to help look out for meteors, I could consider only one of them not already overworked, and she was the post-graduate, who took no honors, and never hurried, and has always been an excellent student....
>
> We are sending home some girls already [November 14], and ___ is among them. I am somewhat alarmed at the dropping down, but ___ does an enormous amount of work, belongs to every club, and writes for every club and for the 'Vassar Miscellany,' etc.; of course she has the headache most of the time.
>
> Sometimes I am distressed for fear Dr. Clarke is not so far wrong; but I do not think it is the study, it is the morbid conscientiousness of the girls who think they must work every minute.[26]

> 1875, March 7. Went to a picnic for Women Suffrage at a beautiful Grove at Medfield. It was a gathering of simple country folk, a club of 75 persons from Needham, whose President, a Mrs. Le Croix, seemed to be vigorous and good spirited.
>
> The main purpose of the meeting was to try to affect public sentiment to such an extent as to lead to the defeat of a Mr. Ide, who, when the subject of Woman Suffrage was before the Legislature, said that the women had all they wanted now; that they could get anything with "their eyes as bright as the buttons upon an angel's coat...."[27]

Maria Mitchell

Newport, R. I.
May 22, 1875
Dear M. M.,

Here is my circular for the Congress as well as I can make it out. Please look it over very carefully with anything that seems amiss, even if only a little so. Note besides that I have not said, at bottom of p.4 to whom papers shall be sent.

It did not seem to answer very well to have them write to Alice Skelton last year, at least, I have thought that more might have been sent if we had given the names and addresses of our whole Committee on topics, etc. I have also left the call unsigned because uncertain as to the order of the names who should be appended....

Can't write more just now,

Yrs affect,

J. W. H.

[Julia Ward Howe]

I shall be in Boston most of this week, until after June 2nd, please address Newport.[28]

1875, June 20.

A meeting of the Officers of Congress was called at the house of Mrs. Hanaford, 5 Summit Ave, Jersey City. The weather was intensely cold. I went to New York on the 19th and stopped with my friend Mrs. Clapp, 100 W. 54 St....

It was a question who should preside. Mrs. Hanaford thought the Chairman of the Executive Committee should and I had been told that I should, etc. The question was settled by the non-arrival of Chairman of Ex. Com. I called them to order at an hour after the time appointed. Of course I made many blunders, as I had never presided before, but I continued for 4 hours. We did a few good things....

The most serious question in my mind was the looseness in regard to membership. We had previously voted in Ex. Session that no person could enter as a member, unless endorsed by some of the other members and then accepted by the Board. It seems that at Chicago, [name crossed out] had been careless of this and had called upon persons present to form the Society, by signing the constitution and

paying $2 and it is feared that we have, in consequence some unde-
sirable members. This I feel to be a very important thing and the preceding year [name crossed out] had taken the most conservative
ground.

Now, as a member pays $2 and as all can come in and listen, the
question is, who is entitled to read a paper and who is entitled to a
place in the debate, and if all are, for what does a member pay $2? If
we publish proceedings the book comes in as a return for the $2, but
we do not, perhaps publish at all. I spoke for a tight rule in this
respect, and begged for high-toned character in our papers, and for a
very very high toned morality in our membership. I was amused to
find myself talked of as so "decidedly conservative...."[29]

Aug. 29, 1875. Went with Miss Shelden to Baptist Church and
heard Rev. Mr. Fonce.... The Lesson was wholly without logic... No
man or woman went out cheered or completed or stimulated. On the
whole, it is strange that people who go to church are no worse than
they are....

In 1875, the Association for the Advancement of Women met in
Syracuse, New York, with Mitchell serving as President and presiding
officer.

On the 11th Oct. I went to Lyceum faint-hearted enough. The
Local Committee told us that our audience would be very small and
would seem lost in the great opera House. To our surprise, 40 members answered to the first roll call and at the last balloting 60 votes
were cast. At the first public meeting about 700 were present, at the
last about 1700.

I was amazed to find that they considered me a good Presiding
Officer. I made my little speech boldly and fearlessly. I gave the four
days wholly up to the affair and went into no other house than the
two, the Hotel and the Opera House....

Now, here is a small problem. Dr. R[aymond] declares that my
silent prayer was just the right thing, yet he is pushing (so I am told)
prayer meetings in the college with all his might. Today I am especially cross, because I find our beautiful reading room is to be given
up to prayer meetings, when we have a Chapel! [Unfortunately, five
pages have been deleted from Mitchell's diary at this point.]

Maria Mitchell

VASSAR ASTRONOMY STUDENTS IN THE OBSERVATORY'S DOWN-
STAIRS CLASSROOM. These members of the Class of 1878 are, *from
left to right:* Jessie Davis, Ella McCaleb, Martha Hillard, Harriot Stanton and Mary Abbott. The "Dolland" telescope is in the window.

...[Trustees] have passed a vote that "Wellesley College shall be Collegiate in its Course of Study but Seminary in its Government." It is certainly a bad feature that the Trustees openly endorse such a method, but in reality, it is not much different from our own method. The Trustees compel the attendance on Bible classes at Vassar, they exceed that at Wellesley by compelling attendance on prayer meetings.

Miss Storke was evidently troubled by a question which disturbed me. How much have I a right to influence students to petition for changes, in the College discipline. I really and truly believe that the girls here submit too much to rule, that they should combine and protest against some of the petty laws, fitted only to the needs of children....

Oct. 25, 1875....I have scarcely got over the tire of the congress[30] yet, although it is a week since I returned, I feel as if a great burden was lifted from my soul....

It was a grand affair, and babies came in arms. School-boys stood close to the platform and school-girls came, books in hand. The hall was a beautiful opera-house, and could hold at least one thousand seven hundred. It was packed and jammed, and rough men stood in the aisles.

When I had to speak to announce a paper I stood very still until they became quiet. Once, as I stood in that way, a man at the extreme rear, before I had spoken a word, shouted out, 'Louder!' We all burst into a laugh. Then, of course, I had to make them quiet again. I lifted the little mallet, but I did not strike it, and they all became still. I was surprised at the good breeding of such a crowd.

In the evening about half was made up of men. I could not have believed that such a crowd would keep still when I asked them to. They say I did well. Think of my developing as a president of a social science society in my old age![31]

1875, Nov. 2. In College. When I came back everything struck me as pleasant, a room had been built for my domestic comfort.

In a piece shedding light on Maria's reference to "domestic comfort," the Vassar student newspaper reported:

> *During the summer the coal bin has been made into a bedroom for Professor Mitchell who has been sleeping in a box of a room. A stone pier rises at the north end and this is surrounded by a mantelpiece.*[32]

Her new room not only made news in the college paper. It also elicited a poem from her friend and former student, Elizabeth O. Abbott (Class of 1873), which began:

> *Beautiful Venus, pride of the morning,*
> *Tell it to all little stars who have fled*
> *That in a sweet chamber that needs no adorning*
> *Miss Mitchell sleeps in a bed....* [33]

The following "remonstration" after an alumnae meeting in New York shows that Mitchell had a keen eye for details—and a strong penchant toward frugality.

Obs. Vassar College, Jan. 5, 1876

My dear Miss Knowles

[probably Cornelia Knowles, Class of '73]

You are likely to be active, I am told, at the meeting of the Vassar graduates to be held in New York. May I say a few words to you upon the plebeian subject of economy?

At the meeting in Boston, which was on the whole very pleasant and encouraging, I was surprised to find that what was called a "lunch" was not only a full meal, but a very expensive one. I consoled myself by recollecting that when I was present at one more elaborate, given by Sorosis, the cost was only one dollar each, and I hoped this might be less. I learn that the charge was two dollars each. We were twenty-six persons. You will see what the amount is.

If I had known it at the time, I should have remonstrated on the spot.

On the day following the meeting, I went to a dinner given for me at the room of the Woman's Club, Mrs. Howe presiding. It was a company of about the same number. When lunch time came, the ladies themselves handed around a cup of coffee, sandwiches and cake—not a servant was in sight—not a servant was in the house. And yet in that company were not only the finest intellectual persons in Boston, but some of the wealth; they preferred to spend their money on better objects than those of the table. I am told that the luncheon at the Club cost 25 cts. each.

I have no doubt there are parlors in New York which would gladly open for your gathering, and save you the cost of a room in which to meet—indeed I should think it likely that rooms and a simple lunch might be offered by some student I hope you are not already committed to any plan.

When I go to New York (as I have frequently done) to meet Committees of some dozen ladies, I go to a boarding house, (generally Mrs. Miller's on 26th St.) I ask for a large room, and receive my Committee. If the meeting is protracted, and I fear they need a lunch, I inform them that lunch can be had in the house, and they call for what they wish; I do not believe anyone spends a whole dollar on her repast.

If you have a dinner, such as we had in Boston, with flowers at every plate, colored waiters and printed bills of fare, I fear it may get into the papers, and leave anything but a favorable impression on the minds of sensible people.

I hope you will not be desirous of doing anything which shall seem foolishly sensational, and I hope my remarks will seem to you a timely, as well as a kindly warning.

Yours truly,

Maria Mitchell.[34]

Jan. 8, 1876 At the meeting of the graduates at the Deacon House the speeches that were made were mainly those of Dr. R[aymond] and Prof. B.[35] I am sorry now, that I did not at least say that the College is what it is, mainly because the early students pushed up the course to a collegiate standard. At the meeting of graduates in New York, Miss Abbott said that what we wanted was to keep preparatories out, to have single rooms, to have better instruction in the departments, to endow professorships.

It is evident that the graduates feel much more disposed to lift the college than to help poor girls to come into it. I feel with them. But I also think that money can be raised for poor girls, while it cannot be raised for the college.

It has become a serious question with me whether it is not my duty to beg money for the observatory while what I really long for is a quiet life of scientific speculation. I want to sit down and study on the observations made by myself and others.[36]

The next diary entry bears further notice that Mitchell might need to start fund-raising for the observatory. As subsequent diary entries show, the fund-raising would occupy a growing amount of Maria's time.

Jan. 25, 1876. I have kept myself so free from college affairs, that, at this date, so far as I know, not a ripple disturbs the tranquillity of college life. All is smooth and serene. It has become a serious question with me whether it is not my duty to beg money for the Observatory.

March 8, 1876. It is said that we have had and are having a "revival" here. I know only what I hear from the students. When I heard that a little girl, one of the preparatories, had stood up in a large meeting and confessed that she had come to Jesus, or something like it, who was the child of a Quaker Father, I sent for her, and advised her before she took another step to write to her Mother and get her permission. She promised to do it.

I have been told that 45 prayers were made at one meeting. It seems to me that to sit still awhile, would be becoming. The little girl, whom I interviewed was in a state of exaltation and felt that she must show her light. I suggested that she should live quietly for a year and then if she desired it, begin her public religious duties.

I was careful not to interfere with her religious teachings but when she told me that the person leading the prayer meeting called upon those who felt that they had received new light to rise, I could not refrain from saying that I thought it was very unwise. I found her religious adviser had been another girl, a little older than herself, who she said "was so wise and knew so much."

On the 4th I went to New York and had an interview with Dr. MacDonald in relation to aid for the College. I think he means to do something and wisely manipulated, may do it wisely. He seems to me honest, impulsive [word crossed out by Phebe]. I was glad to see that he is a temperance man and a suffragist.

A letter from Maria Mitchell discussing her family and her health was probably written shortly after the funeral of her sister Sally Barney, who died on March 25, 1876.

I came back to the College meaning to have Sunday teas every Sunday. But I have had pharyngitis, (the Doctor says) which means that I've had a sore throat and a buzz in my ears and have been wretchedly dispirited. Mrs. Kendall [Phebe] says that "Julia Ward Howe forgets her body — what a pity Maria can't!"

My brother-in-law, Matthew [Sally's husband] has been here and I said, "To think that Sally had 60 years of feebleness and I had 60 years of health — how can I be grateful for both?"

And he says, "Yes, but there are compensations — she was sweet and lovely."

So you see what Job's comforters one's family can be![37]

As colleague Frances Wood later observed, Maria's personal friends seemed to have included "every woman speaker of note in that day." Often, her visiting friends would meet at the observatory for lively discussions, joined by "a favored few" whom Maria would invite from the campus to meet her special guests.

Mitchell routinely took visitors on tours of the observatory, but some of these visitors were anything but routine.

June 18, 1876. I had imagined the Emperor of Brazil [Dom Pedro II] to be a dark swarthy tall man of 45 years; that he would not really have a crown upon his head, but that I should feel it was somewhere around, hand-like, and that I should know I was in Royal presence. But he turns out to be a large old man, say 65, broad-headed and broad shouldered, with a big white beard and a very pleasant, even chatty manner.

We had decided that we must not offer to shake hands, but wait for him. We did not have to wait long; he offered his hand at once. I asked him to see the rooms, knowing that his time was very short.

As he entered the Dome, he turned to ask who the photographs of Father and Mother were. Once in the Dome, he seemed to feel at home. To my astonishment he asked me if Alvan Clark made the glass of the Equatorial. As he stepped into the meridian room and saw the instrument he said "Collimators." I remarked, "You have been in observatories before," and he said, "Oh yes, Cambridge and Washington."

He seemed much more interested in the observatory than I could possibly expect....I promised to send him some [periodicals]. If it was merely to please me it was taking a great deal of pains.

I did not see the Empress. She was somewhat feeble and remained in the museum, those that saw her were much pleased with her.

Maria Mitchell

Shortly after her gratifying visit with the Emperor of Brazil, Mitchell headed to New England for her summer break. In early August, she headed back from Boston by boat to the Vassar campus. Her immediate mission at the Observatory was to get a very accurate time determination so that she could determine the exact instant when the moon passed in front of Saturn.

> Aug. 20, 1876. On Aug. 4, I went to New York by boat. Went up the Hudson Aug. 5 in the extreme heat and reached the College at 1 [p.]m. I went to work at once, to get the chronometer time and worked until 6 1/2 p.m. I had no gas and could work only by day light. On the 6th I tried again for stars at night, having computed Zenith stars all day. At 10 p.m. on the 6th I began to observe and worked until 11 1/2 or midnight. On the 7th I copied observations and computed some. On the 8th I came back to Boston. I felt that I had done 4 days of hard work. I was abundantly paid, by the view which I had of the occultation* of Saturn by the moon.

Maria Mitchell must also have felt "abundantly paid" for the sacrifices she made for her students when she received notice of honors like this one from the Champney family.

> *Deerfield, Mass*
> *Sept. 18, 1876*
> *Dear Miss Mitchell,*
> *A fat little daughter born to us this morning we desire to announce to the world as Maria Mitchell Champney. My wife, your former pupil Lizzie J. Williams[38] is very anxious that you should allow us to christen our little girl thus; our first child, a boy, I named for my art teacher Edouard Frere. It is Lizzie's "Choose" today and I write in her name, adding whatever weight I may to her desire....*
>
> *Not only have I this request to make, but Lizzie still further to show her love for you desired me to ask your permission to allow a little child's book which she has written this summer and which is to be published for the Holiday season in Boston under the title of "In the Sky Garden" be dedicated to you as her beloved instructor and friend....*
> *J. W. Champney[39]*

---

*An occultation occurs when the moon passes in front of a star or planet.

The Fourth Congress of the Association for the Advancement of Women (A.A.W.) was held at St. George's Hall, Philadelphia, October 4–6, 1876. Maria's friend Julia Ward Howe was now serving with Mitchell as an executive of the Association. In the paper she presented at the Congress, "The Need of Women in Science," Mitchell ponders:

Does anyone suppose that any woman in all the ages has had a fair chance to show what she could do in science? ... The laws of nature are not discovered by accidents; theories do not come by chance, even to the greatest minds; they are not born of the hurry and worry of daily toil; they are diligently sought, they are patiently waited for, they are received with cautious reserve, they are accepted with reverence and awe. And until able women have given their lives to investigation, it is idle to discuss the question of their capacity for original work.[40]

Nov. 15, 1876. Congress. The Woman's Congress met in Philadelphia. The papers were numerous and excellent. Mrs. Howe's on Paternity the most successful. Grace Anne Lewis, ABB [Antoinette Brown Blackwell], Mrs. Diaz [Abby Morton Diaz], Mrs. Perus and others had very good papers. The newspaper treated us very well. The institutions opened their doors to us, the Centennial gave us a reception.

But—we didn't have a good time!

1st. The Hall was a very bad one to speak in, almost no one could be heard.

2nd. The Women's Committee of Philadelphia led by Mrs. Bartol, attempted to control us. They sent a note saying, "We protest against the subject of 'Woman Suffrage' being introduced." The note did not come before us, as a body, but was handed to me in private. I did not hesitate to say at once that we were not to be controlled in that way, by any Local Committee. That they might take away the Hall but I would hire another even if it cost me $1000.

It turned out, that there had been no "meeting" of the Committee but that three women had got frightened and had written this note, as the "Committee." The result was that a suffrage paper was presented and Lucy Stone and M.A.L. [Mary Livermore] spoke.

3rd. When the new officers were to be elected and I read "For President, Julia Ward Howe" some one in a loud tone said, "I nominate

Frances Willard" and another said "I nominate Mrs. Thomas," another said "I nominate ——," and it was really a "mob." They claimed that they had not organized but I noticed they sat together and Mrs. Molsen was their champion. She said, "She objected to Mrs. Howe, because the West should be represented, if the Society was to be National, it should not be sectional." Decidedly the opposition was to New England.

...I am told that they charge me with carrying things with a high hand which is doubtless true. I saw that I must either go under the feet of a mob, or stand firm and control by sheer force. I lost my good opinion of P.A.H. completely. I was tried by the childish impulsiveness of M.A.L. But for Abby May who saw my difficulties and stood by me, I should have shown a shakiness. Mrs. Howe will have a hard time next year. If she goes to Europe I shall try to have Abby May preside....It is all very uphill work, mainly because women have so little money, or control it so little when they have it.⁴¹

March 13. 1877. We are hoping that the election of [Rutherford B.] Hayes may be beneficial to the College, to the country, and to women, not that I would put them in that order. Really I should put "women" first.

I have heard that Hayes is a suffragist, I doubt it much. I have heard that Dean Academy is to become a college, I cannot find what that means but am afraid it is as little true as that Hayes is a Suffragist. Neither is very important. However much Hayes is a Suffragist, he can do nothing, however much Dean Academy may try to be a college, it can't be, unless it has an enormous amount of money.

Mary Livermore lectured at the college in 1877. Evidently Mitchell did not like how President Raymond introduced her; this straightforward rebuttal was one of the few strong reactions in writing that he made to Mitchell's criticisms.

> *Pres. Off. Monday A. M. [1877]*
> *My dear M. M.,*
> *I made no "apology" for Mrs. Livermore—the idea is absurd. Knowing that many thought of Mrs. L. as an advocate for woman's suffrage, and, fearing that prejudice might keep some away, I, for their sake,*

not for hers, told them she was not here to advocate any special views,
but, being here, had consented in my invitation to talk to them. And I
made as strong an expression of my personal confidence in her, and of the
public estimate of her talents and worth, as I knew how to. — I wish too,
that you could be present when I make remarks in chapel. Your personal
criticisms are always welcome, but I don't like to chase echoes — to cor-
rect reports at second hand.

> *J. H. R.*[42]

In her ongoing and often amiable correspondence with Raymond,
many of Mitchell's "criticisms" were far too lighthearted to merit so
serious a response.

My dear President [Raymond],

I have worked away with a will, to find some fault with your capital discourse and have found it! You didn't do justice to the butterfly!
The pretty little fellow furnishes me with the webs for what are called
"spider lines" in my telescopes. He methodizes his activity before he's
born, and helps the astronomer measure the distances to the stars.

Yours, with my thanks for all the rest of your discourse.

M Mitchell[43]

During the spring of 1877 Emma Brigham sculpted a bust of
Maria Mitchell. The *Vassar Miscellany* offered the following colorful
report:

April 1877. The Observatory, that abode of science, hitherto sacred
to the stars, opened its doors to Art, shortly after Christmas vacation,
and converted itself for a few days into a sculptor's studio with Miss
Emma Brigham as the artist. Prof. Mitchell was the subject. The work
of modeling progressed rapidly, and those of us who were favored with a
glimpse into the studio, saw the dark clay fast taking on a wonderful life-
like aspect.

Even in the incomplete state in which we beheld it, the face wore a
strikingly natural expression, giving ample promise of the success that
has characterized Miss Brigham's former work. The first cast of the
model is to be completed in June.[44]

The final bronze bust was eventually completed by Emma Brigham, and is now mounted in a niche above the entrance to the original Vassar Observatory, a gift of the Class of 1877.

> *June 25, 1877*
> *Vassar College*
> *President Raymond,*
> *In behalf of the Senior Astronomy Class of 1877 I am authorized to offer for the acceptance of the College a bust of Professor Maria Mitchell, modeled by Miss Brigham.*
> *Will you have the kindness to communicate the offer to the board of Trustees?*
> *C[ora] Harrison.*[45]

> *Mansion House*
> *Jan. 21, 1878*
> *My dear Prof. Mitchell,*
> *You doubtless have been expecting to hear from me and have been anxious, I trust, to know what progress the bust has made during this interval of silence. I am happy to say that the latest criticism was passed upon it by Charles P__, a few weeks ago, when I was so highly favored as to receive a visit from him. He considers it the finest bust I have done, superior to Dr. Neale's, the favorable notices of which you may have seen in the Boston papers. He thinks the pose is fine but the alterations he suggested in the drapery and hair were so fundamental that I have had to remodel both. He knows by his own experience the difficulties of working without a sitter and ... thinks I have succeeded wonderfully with the likeness but advises me to ask you for another sitting before I have the bust cast. ...*
> *When may I hope to see you? Will the commencement of the new semester in February be a convenient time for you to come? Of course I shall be glad to have you sooner if possible, and thankful to have you at any time. ...*
> *Emma T. Brigham*[46]

Her work on A.A.W.'s "Congress" continued to occupy much of Mitchell's time. For help in arranging a private meeting room in Washington, D.C., she called on her old friend Joseph Henry of the Smithsonian Institution.

25 Oct. 1877
Vassar College
Prof. Henry
Dear Sir,
I have a favor to ask of you. You may have heard of a body of Women known as a "Congress" which meets once a year, in one or the other of the large cities, to discuss questions of Social Science— Education—Temperance, etc. I am one of the officers and have been for years.

The officers hold intermediate meetings, one is to be held in April and held in Washington. The officers generally are a group of some dozen persons, some of the best women in the country. Now I do not fancy accepting the invitations which may come to us, to hold our meeting in some private house. Is there a small room in the Smithsonian, in which we could meet, and can you offer the room to us? Our meeting will be for a few hours only, and in private. Even, for so small a meeting, it would help us in the eyes of many who do not investigate if we were under the roof of a building devoted to the diffusion of knowledge.

Pardon me, if it seems an unreasonable request.
Maria Mitchell[47]

April, 1878. I called on Prof. Henry at the Smithsonian Institute. He must be in his 80th year. He has been ill and seems feeble but is still the majestic old man, unbent in figure and undimmed in eye. I always remember when I see him, the speech of Miss Dix, "He is the true-est man that ever lived."

He went to a desk and looking into the drawer pulled out an old copy of Gregory's *Astronomy* and said, "That book changed my whole life, I read it when I was 16 years old. I had read only works of the imagination and at 16, being ill and in bed, that book was near me. I read it and determined to study science."[48]

April 1878. The conference of Woman's Congress officers met in Washington. Because we had one member in Washington we were invited to meet in that place. I went on at a great expense of time, money and strength....

We were in session at least nine hours. I think that more than half of that was used by Mrs. Spencer and Mrs. Sayles. The only motion which I carried through was that to pay the Secretary $200....

May, 1878. Mrs. Wolcott and Miss Eastman made me a visit on their way home. Miss Eastman read a paper on the Immortality of the Soul on Sunday to the Teachers. They came to the Observatory, there being a large representation. The paper was very able.

I started a discussion as soon as Miss Eastman was through and I was at once followed by Miss Morgan, one of our Latin teachers. I had not known Miss Morgan before and was much pleased with her ability and good humor. She pushed Miss Eastman pretty firmly to answer to the questions she put and Miss Eastman answered good-naturedly.

On the whole I thought Miss Eastman had an able opponent. Miss Wiley spoke a little and Dr. Webster spoke several times. It was a very enjoyable debate and I was glad that for once, the Teachers mixed up with people who hold very radical views.

One of the student projects initiated in the Observatory by Maria Mitchell was photographing the sun on every clear day. These photographs could be used to study sunspots and their changes. They also photographed a transit of Mercury and the rare event of a transit of Venus several years later. Some of these photographs can still be seen in the college archives.

May 6, 1878 Between the clouds, Miss Spalding obtained 7 photographs of Mercury on the Sun. It is a comfort to me to be able to plan and do a new kind of work. The large telescope worked better than usual, Clark having just been to the Observatory.

A May 1878 blurb in the *Vassar Miscellany* announced an upcoming summer event:

> *May 1878. Prof. Mitchell will be in Denver in July, to observe the eclipse. She will be joined by Miss Harrison of '76 and Miss Culbertson of '77.*[49]

In the eclipse of this year the dark shadow...with its limitation of 116 miles lay across the country from Montana territory, through Colorado...and entered the Gulf of Mexico between Galveston and New Orleans. This was the region of total eclipse. Outside of this would be a partial eclipse all over the country.

Courtesy of Special Collections, Vassar College Libraries

COLORADO EXPEDITION, OBSERVING TOTAL SOLAR ECLIPSE OF 1878.
Leading the way in providing opportunities for students to be directly involved in their studies, Maria Mitchell is shown here *(seated at far left)* with her Vassar students near Denver on July 29, 1878. They were serving as official observers of the total solar eclipse of that day.

Maria Mitchell

Looking along this dark strip on the map, each astronomer selected his bit of darkness, on which to locate the light of his science....My party chose Denver....

We started from Boston, a party of two, at Cincinnati a third joined us; at Kansas City we came upon a fourth who was ready to fall into our ranks, and at Denver two more awaited us; so we were a party of six—all good women and true....

One of our party, a young lady from California, was placed at the chronometer. She was to count aloud the seconds, to which three others were to listen. Two others, a young woman from Missouri, who bro't with her a fine telescope and another from Ohio, beside myself stood at the three telescopes. A fourth, from Illinois, was stationed to watch general effects and one special artist [perhaps her sister, Phebe M. Kendall] , pencil in hand, to sketch views....absolute silence was imposed upon the whole party a few minutes before each phenomenon.

How still it was....It was now quiet work. Each observer at the telescopes gave a furtive glance at the unsunlike sun, moved the dark eye pieces from the instrument, replaced it by a more powerful white glass and prepared to see all that could be seen in 2m[inutes] 40s[econds]. They must note the shape of the corona, its color, its seeming substance and they must look all around the sun for the 'interior planet'....

Happily some one broke through all rules of order and shouted out "The shadow, the shadow" and, looking toward the southeast we saw the black band of shadow moving from us over the plain and toward the Indian territory. It was not the flitting of the cloud shadow over hill and dale, it was a picture which the sun threw at our feet of the dignified march of the moon in its orbit. And now we looked around. What a strange orange light there was in the north and east. What a spectral hue to the whole landscape. Was it really the same old earth and not another planet!

Great is the self-denial of those who follow science. They who look through telescopes at the time of a total eclipse are martyrs; they severely deny themselves. The persons who can say that they have seen a total eclipse of the sun are those who rely upon their eyes....

We saw the giant shadow as it left us and passed over the lands of the untutored Indian; they saw it as it approached from the distant west as it fell upon the peaks of the mountain tops, and, in the impressive stillness, moved directly from our camping ground. The savage to whom it is the frown of the Great Spirit is awestruck and alarmed; the scholar to whom it is a token of the inviolability of law, is serious and reverent.[50]

SHORTLY BEFORE THE DEATH of President Raymond in 1878, Maria wrote a melancholy letter to her Vassar colleague, Frances Wood. Mitchell clearly felt that the very survival of the college was in doubt without Raymond at the helm. Fortunately, history shows that her fears were unwarranted.

V. C. Aug. 12 [1878]
My dear Miss Wood,
A hard future is before poor Vassar. The Pres't is failing and there is no hope.
Let us work together bravely for the sake of women, and try to carry the college over its stormy seas. I know of no plan, but for one year we are all pledged and must do our duty. I shall stay until all is over and then go to Lynn.
M. M.[51]

Aug. 20, 1878. Dr. Raymond is dead. I cannot quite take it in. I have never known the College without him and it will make all things different.
Personally I have always been fond of him, he was very enjoyable socially and intellectually. Officially, he was in his relations to the students, perfect. He was cautious to a fault and has probably been very wise in his administration of college affairs. He was broad in his religious views. He was <u>not</u> broad in his ideas of women and was <u>made</u> to broaden the education of women by the women around him. He was not broad toward women at all. He never really recognized the equality of the women in the Faculty.
He was timid by nature and if a man made a motion, it reached him as a woman could not. For he feared the men and he trusted the women. One of his last measures was to try to get women into the

Trustee Board. I think he saw the justice of the measure, and when he saw that a thing was just, he did it.

His great weakness was his attempt at policy. It was less and less striking as he grew stronger in place, but as I look back, I plainly see that he has been timid about my position, and the wisdom of keeping me at Vassar.

No one of us knows whether he liked us or not, he was pleasant to all and as a general thing non-committal. He was almost always courteous. He dreaded a fight, but when he went into a fight, he fought like a tiger and did a war of extermination.

He was of science wholly ignorant and he took no interest in it. When he asked me once to give some "shows" to a class he did not ask it for the sake of broadening the intelligence of the girls, but for the sake of the effect it would have on the Trustees.

I consented at his request to give Lectures to the Sophomores, he did not himself desire it, but the Trustees did. He almost never asserted anything. He would say to the students in his sermon "I do not say that I believe this, I say it is what the Bible teaches."

I shall miss him exceedingly. I mourn for him, and it seems to me that my position will be more uncomfortable than before. [Two lines have been crossed out by Phebe, and four pages cut out.][52]

Despite her profound grief over the loss of President Raymond, Mitchell kept up her usual activities, including lectures outside the campus. The *Miscellany* reported in late 1878 that she had "delivered a lecture on the July 29 solar eclipse before the Sorosis Club in October and again in Poughkeepsie on November 20." In February 1879, the college newspaper offered this story:

> *Dr. R. H. McDonald, of San Francisco, has recently presented to the Observatory funds for the purchase of a small telescope. It is to be furnished by Alvan Clark & Sons of Cambridgeport, and is to have an object glass measuring three inches.*

A month later Mitchell was back in the *Miscellany* news:

> *Under the auspices of Professor Mitchell there has been formed in Poughkeepsie the Association for the Advancement of Women. A series of lectures is now being given in the rooms of the Y.M.C.A.*

After five months without a college president, Mitchell expressed her deep concern about the delay in appointing a successor to Raymond. On January 23, she wrote:

As I watch the College I am alarmed in fear of the taking hold of affairs by the Executive Committee for its seems to me to be too long a time during which the new President does not take hold.

Eleven days later, she again expressed how unsettled she was about the direction of Vassar's Executive Committee. Maria's diary entry for February 3 questions: "The Ex Com. of the College have invited [name crossed out by Phebe] to sit with them. Why is he so valuable?"

Eventually, the trustees appointed Samuel L. Caldwell as the new president of Vassar College. One of the trustees apparently viewed this as an opportune time to question Maria Mitchell's desirability at Vassar.

Nathan Bishop, a Vassar trustee from 1861 to 1881, immediately wrote a letter to the new president, voicing his grave reservations about two faculty members—Truman Backus[53] and Maria Mitchell. Bishop, whose early support of women professors was noted earlier, protested the presence of Mitchell because of her Unitarian beliefs.

Private

New York, March 1st, 1879

My dear Dr. Caldwell;

These two articles express a somewhat general impression in regard to one or two Professors in Vassar College. I have been informed, on the best authority, that the writer of the short article is a Baptist clergyman, a graduate of a respectable college, and also of Dr. Broadus' Theo'l Seminary, and is ranked among the first class of Baptist Ministers in Mo. The other article was written by Rev. Dr. S. Irenius Prince, the editor-in-chief the N.Y. Observer. He told me that complaints—written and verbal—made to him by the parents of students in Vassar College led him to write what appeared in the Observer this week. He said he made the article general in its application in order that no one College would be injured more than another.

I told him that you entered into the inheritance of Professors which Dr. Raymond left in office, and you could not recommend any changes till the next annual election.

> Dr. Prince has considerable testimony against Prof. Mitchell, and
> not a little against Backus. I am extremely sorry to learn that Prof.
> Backus has manifested so bold "Skeptical" views that a committee of
> Trustees waited on him before you were elected. I was aware that Miss
> Mitchell was a "Rank Theodore Parker Unitarian" when she was
> elected. I believe she has kept away from Vassar five times as many stu-
> dents as her influence has drawn to it.
>
> Nathan Bishop[54]

Professors Backus and Mitchell survived this trustee's pointed effort
to have them removed from the Vassar faculty, serving at the college
longer than Bishop.

MARIA MITCHELL WAS PRIVILEGED to know a great many of the
members of the famed Concord school, among them Ralph Waldo
Emerson, John Greenleaf Whittier, Bronson Alcott, and Elizabeth
Peabody. In the summer of 1879 she attended one of their meetings
and wrote her account in her diary.

> August 1879. To establish a school of Philosophy in Concord had
> been the dream of Alcott's life and there he sat as I entered the
> vestry of a church on one of the hottest days in August. He looks
> full as young as he did 20 years ago, when he gave a Conversation in
> Lynn.
>
> Elizabeth Peabody came into the room and walked up to the seat of
> the rulers, her white hair streamed over her shoulders in wild care-
> lessness and she was as careless as ever about her whole attire. She is
> poor, old and very homely and it was beautiful to see the attention
> shown to her by Mrs. Sanborn and Mr. Alcott.
>
> She took her seat among the leaders. Emerson entered, pale, thin,
> almost ethereal in visage, followed by his daughter Ellen, who sat
> beside him and watched every word that he uttered.
>
> On the whole Emerson was the same man. He stumbled over any
> quotation as he always did, but the thoughts were such as only
> Emerson could have thought, and the sentences had the Emerson
> pithiness. He made his frequent sentences very emphatic. It was

impossible to see any thread of connection but it always was. The sentences made the charm. The subject was "memory."...

I had a great deal of talk with Miss Whitney of Smith College. She says that the girls will probably demand a Commencement Day. She thinks that President Sayle objects because he does not wish to see women on the platform. He is much interested in getting up an Art Collection when they need everything else. Mr. Eliot was invited by the Senior Class and not by the college. He knew nothing of the college but took its catalogue and read up.

Miss Capen who teaches Chemistry is a very superior woman and she sat and heard Eliot congratulate the college upon having only men professors, while a very young man sat there as Professor. He should have felt humiliated when he must have known his inferiority. Of course Eliot knew nothing about the state of things. The senior class divided about even in approval or disapproval of Eliot.

Miss Whitney says Smith has a great many special students. I asked her if they had students who knew no Latin and she said, "Oh, yes." I asked her if there were careful examinations before they were passed from class to class and she said, "Oh no. We are hardly systematized yet enough for that."[55]

That same summer Mitchell traveled to Saratoga, New York to attend a meeting of the American Association for the Advancement of Science.

August 27, 1879. The Scientific Association assembled at about 10 a.m. A prayer was made by Rev. Peter Stryker, closing with the Lord's Prayer. The gathering was 100 perhaps and was marked by entire independence of manner. Some of the gentlemen and one lady rose during prayer, half a dozen bent their heads, but mainly the congregation, except that it was silent, remained in the condition in which the first words found them....

A paper by a very young man, Michelson[56] was much lauded by Prof. Peirce, Newcomb and others. Prof. Peirce, now over 70, was much the same as ever....

Prof. Peirce's paper was on the Heat of the Sun. He considered the sun fed not by impact of meteors, but by the compression of meteors. I did not think it very sound.[57] A compression involves the effect of

Maria Mitchell

PROFESSOR MITCHELL'S STUDENTS USING THE MERIDIAN CIRCLE IN THE OBSERVATORY. These Class of 1878 students are *(from left to right)*: Harriot Stanton, Mary Abbott *(looking through the telescope)*, Ella McCaleb *(behind the telescope)*, Jessie Davis and Martha Hillard.

gravity (it seems to me) and the meteors are really too small to amount to so much. Then they are very irregularly scattered through space and the sun's heat is so far as we know, very steady and uniform, all over the surface....

I wanted to nominate some woman on some of the Committees of the Association but my friends assured me that I should do more harm than good.

Mrs. Howe has written a poem for the party again.[58]

The following note from Mitchell was written one afternoon just prior to a class. Though the note is undated, we can safely assume that Maria had been at Vassar for quite some time—freely expressing herself in a breezy, but to the point, complaint to Ann Eliza Morse, the president's longtime assistant.

> 2 3/4 P. M. (class just coming in)
>
> My dear Miss Morse,
>
> It's very fortunate for you that I am not standing near an open window with my arms around you!
>
> As it was definitely settled that you, and not I, have the care of the blackboard so comfortably arranged for Prof. G[oodwin],[59] I dismissed the whole subject from my mind, and now, as I want to sweep through the curve of an elegant ellipse—I look up and behold, no blackboard! The parabola that you should describe if I could reach you! Its asymptote should tote you in a way you wouldn't forget!
>
> Yours breezily,
>
> M. M.

Another undated correspondence in the archives provides a revealing glimpse into the very warm friendship between Maria Mitchell and Julia Ward Howe.

> *Jan. 25th*
>
> *Dear M. M.,*
>
> *I write in great haste to say that a certain publisher of good repute has offered me a sum of money for your life!!! i.e., for a biographical sketch[60] of you some 8000 words in length, to be ready by March 1st. Now shall I get true material for it, if you are willing that I should do the deed?*

I will return to Boston on Saturday or Sunday night, so as to be here on Monday 29th. Now, I could come up to Vassar to confer with you on Saturday by morning train, if I could get away that night, or Sunday night, so as to arrive in Boston on Monday.

Won't you please, on rec't of this ascertain the facts and telegraph me to the above address? I shall not be able to answer any telegram today, as I am going into the country for 24 hours. But I shall get your telegram easily tomorrow, and will then make my plans and let you know of them.

Yours in great haste and regard,

Julia W. Howe[61]

Scattered throughout Mitchell's journals are ideas for talks and articles, written as they occurred to her. It is often not clear if and when they were eventually aired publicly, but she does list dates for some of them.

As most lecturers would do, Mitchell presented some of her talks several times. Some of her lecture themes are collected here from the diaries of this period.[62]

I am but a woman.

For women, there are undoubtedly great difficulties in the path but so much the more to overcome. First, no woman should say "I am but a woman." But a woman! What more can you ask to be. Born a woman, born with the average brain of humanity, born with more than the average heart, if you are mortal, what higher destiny could you have. No matter where you are or what you are, you are a power. Your influence is incalculable, personal influence is always underrated by the person. We are all centres of spheres, we see the portion of the sphere above us and we see how little we affect it, we forget the part of the sphere around and beneath us. It extends just as far every way.

Society expects that women should be elegant, artistic, pleasing, especially not profound or solid. You will find this as soon as you are out of college.

Another common saying: "It isn't the way."

<u>Who</u> settles the way? Is there one so forgetful of the Sovereignty bestowed on her by God, that she accepts a leader—one who shall carry captive her mind. Especially do not accept society as a leader, so not accept custom as a leader, for you there is no way, except the way

you make for yourselves. "Through brush, through brier," let it be your way and let that be God's way.

There is this great danger in student life. Now we rest all upon what Socrates said or what Copernicus taught. How can we dispute established authority that has come down to us all established for ages? We must at least question it. We cannot accept anything as granted, beyond the first mathematical formulae. Question everything else.

"The world is round and like a ball, seems swinging in the air" [From Peter Parley's *Primary Geography*]. No such thing! The world is not round, and it doesn't swing, and it doesn't seem to swing.

One of the unfavorable results of the attempt to popularize science is this—the reader of popular scientific books is very likely to think that he understands the Science itself, when he merely understands what some writer says about science....

I tell, with all the school masters and all the teachers and all the books, the ignorance of the unscientific world is enormous. They are ignorant both ways, they underrate the scientific people and they overrate them....

When crossing the Atlantic an Irish woman came to me and asked me if I told fortunes and when I replied in the negative she asked me if I was not an Astronomer. I admitted that I made efforts in that direction. She then asked me what I could tell, if not fortunes. I told her I could date when the moon would rise, when the sun would rise and she said "Oh" in a tone which plainly said "Is that all!"

CHAPTER 11

VASSAR COLLEGE: 1880 to 1888

In February, 1831, I counted seconds
for father...In 1885, fifty-four years later,
I counted seconds for a class of students at Vassar.

HE NEW DECADE found Maria Mitchell continuing her work for women's education in a wide variety of ways. In October 1880 she read a paper to the Congress of the Association for the Advancement of Women held in Boston. Her paper, later published in an anthology entitled *Women and the Higher Education,* was entitled, "Whom shall we help to collegiate education?"[1]

Her answers to that question would undoubtedly shock most people today, demonstrating how dramatically our ideas have changed over the past century. She says:

> Do not attempt to put the daughters of the very poor through a college course. It is barely possible that a rare genius may be found even among the unworthy poor, but the chance is so small that we shall waste time in looking for it.

Mitchell's second point reflects her ongoing conviction that she enjoyed better health working in the open air.

> Do not aid the sickly girl to enter college....I should dissuade the delicate girl from the attempt to take a regular college course. Let her study in the open air!

Finally, she argued against the system of prizes in the colleges.

Do not aid by founding prizes. You then add an artificial struggle
to that which is healthy and invigorating.

It should be noted that much of her talk on "Collegiate Education"
is quite representative of current educational ideas. Calling teachers
"the noble army of martyrs," she says, "The work of a teacher should be
such as does not kill." She also expresses her oft-repeated concern that
teachers are required to teach too many students.

We should increase the number of teachers by lessening the number of students to each, and diminish the number by retiring the old
and worn out....Our colleges are too expensive for the class which
most needs them. We ought to reach the large middle class. We do
not.

Mitchell finishes her presentation with a broad appeal for aid: "What
our colleges need is endowment."

This call for endowment, echoed by colleges throughout the ensuing
years, would motivate Maria to begin a fund-raising effort to obtain
money for the observatory.

In subsequent years, Mitchell offered her talk on collegiate education several more times prior to its publication in the aforementioned
book. In early 1880, she recorded in her diary the response to her initial presentations in the Boston area.

Jan. 1880.[2] I read a paper in Boston, Dec. 27, to the University Association. The points I attempted to show were: that we attempt too
many studies for thoroughness; that the whole system of prizes and
marks is immoral; that the great need of colleges is money and that it
is the cause of these; that we have not money because our people do
not believe in the education of women.

I read this paper in Boston, in Lynn and in Cambridge. It was dis-
cussed ably in all the places. Most so in Boston, as Miss Eastman,
Mary Sufford Blake and a Mrs. Knox were present. Also, the principal of the Normal School at Framingham.

In Boston most of the discussion turned upon the "marks." Miss
Eastman seemed to be surprised that "marks" were still in use. She
said, "Stop them at once."

Maria Mitchell

Dr. Blake thought I was wrong in not desiring "aid" for students. She said she saw so much suffering from girls who wanted an education and could not afford it. (I had advocated giv[ing] small aid and loans.) Mrs. Knox agreed with me.

Mrs. Talbot said in regard to the <u>diminished</u> call for collegiate education that at one time 1/2500 of the boys were educated, now only 1/4500. Mrs. Wolcot said that because as Colleges raised their standard, fewer applied for admission.

In Lynn, Dr. Flanders took the same ground that Dr. Blake did and urged "plenty of aid." I contended that girls who lived at home on bread and water should not go to college, the family at home needed their labor. The debate in Lynn turned upon the same points, the "marks" and the aid. The debate in Cambridge was largely conducted by college trained young women and one of them advocated the "marks."

I learned in the course of these meetings several things. I found some of our graduates were crying out "not too much aid to any one student." I learned that a good many of them were in "studies by correspondence" schemes and one of them has even 20 students in astronomy and mathematics.

I attended a meeting of the Woman's Club and heard John Fisk read a paper, on Aryan Folk-lore. Also I attended a moral reform association meeting and heard Miss Tolman … read a paper on "Woman, a Poet." Both papers were good, in both cases the discussion was feeble compared with that on questions of education.…

I hear that Mrs. Howe has returned fresher and brighter than ever. She had a bad cold and I felt how much I valued her when I perceived that it alarmed me.

Concord, Jan. 27, 1880

Miss Maria Mitchell

At the Annual Meeting of the American Social Science Association held in this city on Jan. 14th you were elected to the office of Vice President.

F. B. Sanborn[3]

1880, Feb. 16. I sent a note to Mr. Swan this morning to ask about the power that I may have to vote for school officers and to ask where I must register, what tax I must pay, etc. I also suggested to Dr.

Webster to write to another of our Trustees. They may rule us out as citizens but we have lived for years within the precincts of some town.

It is possible that we must hold real estate in the town, but I know that my Father voted although he did not even pay a poll tax. He and Nathaniel Barney voted together; it was the last vote that they cast; Father was 75 and Mr. Barney 74 and the crowd at Bull's Head where the voting house was, opened to permit the two old men through.

The two old men voted on opposite sides when they were 21 and 22. They died nearly together, Father died in April and Mr. Barney in August of the same year. I felt a gleam of joy when Mr. Barney died at the idea that he would meet Father.

1880, Feb. 17. Mr. Swan replied referring me to a neighbor, who, I find knows no more about [voting] than I do. ...

1880, Feb. 19. The Po'keepsie paper (Eagle) argues that the "fair" of Po'keepsie cannot vote. ...

The founding of a new women's college, Bryn Mawr, evoked questions from Maria Mitchell about the organization of the college, the role of women on the faculty and on the board of trustees, and the place of astronomy on campus. She received the following response from one of the trustees appointed to help establish Bryn Mawr.

> *Philadelphia*
> *2 mos, 25, 1880*
> *Maria Mitchell*
> *Respected friend,*
> *My friend James Taylor of Burlingham, N. J. has given me thy letter of 21st to reply to. The College for women founded by his brother, the late Joseph W. Taylor, will be located at Bryn Mawr, Penna, about 10 miles from the city of Philad[elphia]. The founder had bought the land, and commenced to build before his death. In his will, he appointed a Board of 13 Trustees who are all men.*
>
> *The location of the College is within a mile or two of Haverford College, where young men are educated, and which was founded nearly 50 years ago and belongs to the Society of Friends. At this College there is a very fine Astronomical Observatory, which Prof. Sharpless would be very glad to show thee, if thou art ever in the neighbourhood.*

Maria Mitchell

> *While there are no women on the Board of Trustees of the College for Women, yet the Founder in his will encourages the Trustees to make the cooperation and counsel of a few wise women to aid in the work.*
>
> *I should think it likely that the Trustees in selecting officers of Instruction and Government would select those best fitted whether men or women, probably giving the preference to women, other things being equal. I merely give my own opinion about this and do not venture to speak for the Trustees. They have not formally considered this subject yet.*
>
> *No plans have yet been arranged. It is hardly likely that the college will be opened for 3 or 4 years yet.*
>
> *If any suggestions occur to thee in connection with the organization of the College they would be very gratefully received by*
>
> *Thy friend truly,*
> *James Whitall[4]*

In the spring of 1880, the *Vassar Miscellany* reported that "Mitchell's astronomical work proceeded apace," noting:

> *[Mitchell] has been taking a series of observations on sun spots. For over a year none have been visible, but from February 6 to 10 and 24 to 27 several groups appeared which she photographed. Professor Mitchell considers that during the past year we have witnessed the minimum of these spots.[5]*

During the college's spring vacation, Professor Mitchell was in Boston for a reception in her honor at the Woman's Club. She also made stops in Cambridge and Newburyport, provoking this personal critique of the teaching she witnessed there.

> 1880, April. I went into what is called the Harvard Annex. Prof. Byerley was teaching a class of 3 persons, Miss Ranlet, Miss Longfellow and Miss Harrison. The poet's daughter was handsome. The poet's daughter was not a mathematician. Prof. Byerley was teaching "Conics." He was Lecturing. He put [a] simple equation up on the board....
>
> Why should Byerley or anyone lecture that which is in a book? All this was to be found in the book.[6] He gave some problems, very simple. I noticed that Miss Harrison did them readily. But if the

VASSAR ASTRONOMY CLASS WITH MARIA MITCHELL. Posed in front of the observatory, the students shown here are all members of the Class of 1878. The small telescope on the table to the right was called "The Dolland" and was used by Mitchell on Nantucket when she discovered her comet. The students *(from left to right)* are: Ella McCaleb, Martha Hillard, Jessie Davis, Harriot Stanton (daughter of Elizabeth Cady Stanton), and Mary Abbott. The woman on the left is not identified. *Below:* A portion of Mitchell's notes about her astronomy curriculum.

[handwritten note in Maria Mitchell's hand]

Maria Mitchell

Harvard Professors give only such instruction as this, young women could unite in classes and be taught by Miss Harrison just as well as by Byerley. We turn out from our Women's Colleges every year some 50 young women who could do as well as this.

The Lecturer in Physics has no apparatus, nor has he of Chemistry so that the Boys at Harvard have very much greater advantages than the Girls of the Annex.

I went for a second visit to the Boston University and heard a class in German. The same thing was to be noticed as on my first visit. That the boys looked like young men from the farm and the mechanics shop and the girls looking as if coming from refined homes.

The City Clerk of Newburyport told Mrs. Spalding that he had no book for the names of women but he would turn the book for men upside down and let them write their names and then he would put the proper heading to the list of names. Mrs. S. was afraid he would put the word "geese."…

As a member of the visiting committee for Boston University, Mitchell expressed some of her ideas on education to a Dr. Twombly.

All colleges attempt to crowd too much study into too little time and so encourage cram[ming]. All colleges introduce a little bit of too many studies, and encourage superficiality. All colleges hold up Commencement prizes and honors in a way that leads to unhealthy competition. All colleges run too much uniformity and routine and too little recognize individuality. (In short, all colleges are poor.)

I am steadily leaning more and more to the introduction of manual labor into the schools. Let a girl work for pay. It is objected (always) that if all girls went into labor, while at college, there would be no loss of caste, it is because a part of them must and the other part may not. I train a certain class of my students to earn money. Rich or poor, I try to have them know the sweetness of hired labor.

But the girl who cannot face the stern possibilities of accounting with the Irish born for the sake of an Education, is scarcely made of the material for a sound scholar. I dare not say, "Go into Debt." There are very few young women who would not lie awake o'night if the pressure of debt were upon them.[7]

May 30 1880

V.C.

My dear Dr. Lossing,

Don't you think that the Trustees of Vassar College, if called together just after Mrs. Livermore's speech,[8] would have elected her a member of their Board, by acclamation? And if it could have been done then, with enthusiasm, could it not be done in June, with moderation?

And are not you just the person to bring it forward?

Maria Mitchell[9]

During the summer of 1880, Mitchell's vacation travels in New England included "running around" to see family members, as well as a return visit to Concord to participate in the celebrated meetings there.

July 12, 1880. The School of Philosophy at Concord has built a shanty for its meetings, but it is a shanty to be proud of for it is exactly adapted to its needs....

The rain began to come down soon after we entered and my philosophy was not sufficient to keep me from the knowledge that I had no rubbers and no umbrella. I remembered too that it was but a narrow foot path through the wet grass to the omnibus....

But I listened to Prof. Harris and enjoyed the first hour, the second hour was a written account of what he said in the first hour and was wearisome. He must have talked and read two hours....

Aug. 19 [1880?] Lynn

My dear Mrs. Raymond,

... I have kept my trunk in Lynn, but have run around generally— to the summer school of philosophy at Concord and to Mt. Desert and to Cambridge and to Boston of course—not yet to Nantucket. I am boarding nearer to Mrs. Dame [Mitchell's younger sister, Kate] than usual—a little way behind the Paiges house and nearer to Broad St. and Green where Mrs. Dame is. I had imagined that a woman of 47 years could not successfully nurse a baby and that I must help her but she is wonderfully well and as she has 5 girls to help her, is not worn out. She will, in 6 weeks, begin to feed the baby and gradually to wean him....

Mrs. Macy and Fanny are at Nantucket and both write that Mrs. Macy is entirely well, hence I conclude that she is not ill and will in time be well. On any other subject I should believe them exactly, and probably they think they are telling the truth. All my brother Henry and family, my brother Frank's family and Forster (not Frank), expect to be together at Nant[ucket] tomorrow—I do not go on yet, if at all....

Maria Mitchell[10]

1880, Aug. 28 (Science Association) It was pleasant to have the Nautical Almanac computers of 20 years ago, gather around me today. Mr. Sprague of Malden; Mr. Kerr of N. Garden; Mr. van Vleck of Wesleyan College, Middleboro', Conn.; Prof. Newcomb, Prof. Hedmet, Prof. Ferret were at the meeting.

In October 1880, the *Vassar Miscellany* reported that the senior astronomy class was furnishing an astronomical column for the *Scientific American*. Just three months later, however, the *Miscellany* noted that the seniors would no longer make this contribution. That development may have been related to this December report: "Professor Mitchell is absent from the college, on account of her health. Miss Whitney is temporarily filling Prof. Mitchell's place."[11]

Mitchell was gone from Vassar for about two months in 1880; and upon her return to campus, she did not take up her diary again for another two months. Mary Whitney, one of Mitchell's first students, was an able replacement in whom Mitchell put great trust. When Mitchell retired, Whitney became her replacement.

1881. [Feb. 25] I was ill and at home in Cambridge and Nantucket from Nov. 1 to Jan. 3, 1881. I had an attack of pharyngitis, accompanied by noise in my ears. Also a slight attack of malaria. I think I was hurt by quinine, although I took only 6 grains a day, but it was continued for two months. At this date, Feb. 25, I consider myself well, but at times my ears trouble me.[12]

1881, Feb. 26. Miss Whitney read Frances Power Cobbe's "Lectures to Women" aloud to me. In the main they are excellent. I agree almost at every point. What she says about the duty of women in veracity, in cultivating both physical and moral courage, etc., in demanding not "favor but justice"...

The advice to women to be cheerful and to try to promote cheer around them is excellent. I wish I had thought about that earlier in my life and practiced upon it. I believe I tried to keep Mother cheery, but at that time I cared for no other person's cheer....As it is, I am more cheerful because I have read the book, Miss Whitney is invaluable to me.

Two postcards came to Mitchell from her young niece, Polly, at this time. They were probably written to help cheer up a sick aunt. Polly was Henry's only child.

> *Feb. 2, 1881*
>
> *Dear Aunt*
>
> *Maria Emily and Daisy have the measles. Nate has had them. Mamma thinks I may have them. I have a coast in my yard. I coast a good deal. I hope you will go to Nantucket next summer and go in bathing with me. Mamma and I send love. I have a desk. I am writing on it.*
>
> *Your niece,*
>
> *Polly*

> *March 7, 1881*
>
> *My dear Aunt Maria,*
>
> *I thank you for your nice letter. Mamma knew it was a kitty right off. I had 27 Valentines. Kitty Dame has a party today, I can't go to it, it is too far for me to go to Lynn. I wish I could see the black kitty. Sarah will be a big cat when I see her.*
>
> *Papa is going to build a house at Nantucket if Mr. Gibbs don't ask too much.*
>
> *Love from Polly[13]*

1881, Mch. 19. On Mch. 17, Mr. Head, a gentleman whom I knew 22 years ago in Rome, Italy, called to see me. I never before saw so happy a man. He said "he had had a good time." He was 49 years old, had a wife and 3 daughters and money. It was touching to find how much Miss Shepard and I had been to him in Rome. He was alone and lonely and he was allowed to escort us around. He went with us to some ruins outside of Rome (2 miles) and in London he had escorted me to hear Charles Keene and Charles Dickens. ...

Mch. 27. Dr. Lyman Abbott preached. I was surprised to find how liberal Congregational preaching had become, for he said he "hoped and expected to see women at the bar and in the pulpit" altho' he believed they would always be exceptional cases....

I have another letter from Mrs. Levitt of Brooklyn, her mind seems to be exercised on the subject of the "social evil" and she knows a woman who for 20 years has received "lost women." Gertie Merch asked her Father "was there ever a lost man?"

1881, Mch. 28. This morning I perceived that the juniors who came in early, were looking at patterns and supposing they were gingham or calico, I asked to see them; they were white satins! I said "who is going to wear white satin?" They replied that they were and it was not expensive. But the real reply was "We have not the control. Our Fathers will get us new dresses but will not give us money."

I asked them if they could not do missionary work with the Fathers. Miss Coleman said that she never asked her Father for money, but she asked for a new dress and she always had one when she asked.

All admitted one thing, that they did not have money. They claimed that white satin was cheap because it was kept so long and worn only on state occasions. The worst of it is we cannot reach it. It seems to be none of our business. And we claim that we put home influences around these girls. ...

Prof. Nunn (Miss) of Wellesley called. She is bright and talky, but I was tired and could not enjoy her. She seems a little spiteful toward Harvard and does not want the "Annex" to succeed. It seems to me wrong not to wish the success of all Educational Institutions. But Miss Nunn must be doing good work at Wellesley.

1881 Apr. 2. Willie came up and spent a day. It makes me lonesome to know that he is going to Europe in May, to stay a year. It does seem as if he and his parents should not be separated.[14]

This evening I have been to a party at the gymnasium given by Freshmen to Seniors....Returning through the College, I found another gay party in Room G. It was the Preparators who were dancing a Virginia Reel in masquerade. The masks were veils but the disguise was complete. On the whole the gaiety of the college is well kept up, even in Lent. The President and his wife and guest were at Society Hall.

1881, Apr. 20. I have spent eleven days at New York and have enjoyed it very much. I met a good many interesting people at Miller's Hotel...

Dr. E. P. Miller's

37, 39, 41 West 26th Street,

New York, Ap. 16. [1881][15]

My dear Matthew [Barney, brother-in-law],

I am glad that you are getting along decently well. I am very much better than I was and begin to enjoy life again. Lydia Dame is with me for a few days. Anne you probably see; she left Thursday. I enjoyed her visit very much.

Yesterday (Good Friday) the city was packed and crammed and I suppose it will be on Sunday. I am glad you are at the Swan's, as I want to know what kind of place it is. I want a place to stop at, in Boston, that is not very expensive. It is better to have a certain place and to keep going to it; they take care of you!...

Tomorrow (Sunday) Lydia expects to go to Trinity; probably she will have to stand. After Easter has passed, I mean to buy Easter Eggs. I suspect they will be cheap. The streets are exceedingly pretty; some of the Easter cards are very pretty and the roses are beautiful. You pass thousands of them on Broadway.

Love to L_,

M. M.[16]

1881, May 2. "Founder's Day"[17] was remarkably successful. Mr. Collyer gave us a sermon he had preached in his own church, on George Eliot as Marian Evans....It seemed to me that he deprecated her marriage with Mr. Cross more than he did her relation to Lewes. Of course I do not know what the latter was; it may have been wholly a literary tie, if so, why did she not marry Mr. Cross before the death of Lewes. I see nothing to mourn over in the marriage with Mr. Cross. She had as good a right to marry as a man of 60 years has and no one mourns over that; the friends rush to congratulate him and consider it eminently proper.

1881, May 6. Yesterday we went to town to see the opening of the Vassar Brothers Home for old men. I looked at Matthew Vassar [the founder's nephew] with admiration. It is a good deal to be successful in getting money, to give it away by tens of thousands is more! And to see a man upwards of 70 stand up in a crowd and say exactly the right thing and sit down before the audience was tired, is not usual....

1881, May 7. An illness spoken of on page 60 [of her diary], I believe is now over [see February 25, 1881 entry in this volume for reference to two-month illness]. I have kept a record of my health changes to show myself that there was real improvement. The daily accounts are to be destroyed today. It is not my wish to preserve a record of my discomforts.

I suffered from the pharyngitis for at least 6 months. It was far worse to me than were the fever turns. The fever turns were for a little while and over, the buzz in my ear or ears was day in and day out. My nerves were badly affected. It was as if someone whispered to me and all confused noises were by me, imputed to my ears.

But for my starting early to the sea side and to be with my family, I think it would have continued much longer. Annie was invaluable, she took me to Nantucket and devoted herself to me. She fed me on the best. It makes me laugh to think how wanting in tact I was. I actually ridiculed her servant which nearly broke Annie's heart. But, sick and feverish as I was, the woman's talk was wearisome. I soon learned to like the servant who ministered so kindly to my wants.

I was ill about six months. I was under physicians care for about 3 months. I was never in bed in day but there were 3 days at Nantucket when I did not go out on account of storm.

I think I gave up to my illness too much. I could have studied more and worked more. What does a mother with a family do, when she has such an attack. She suffers of course.

Mrs. Shaw, the sewing woman, was ill at the same time and her three children also, with malarial fever. The stewardess of one of the river boats had a similar illness. The stewardess lost 38 pounds of flesh, I must have lost 25 or 30 pounds. I have weighed 160 and now it is 131 but I may have lost some before this illness. Today, altho' I am hoarse, I am not uncomfortable at all.

1881. May 13.... Today I hear of the death of a lovely student whom I had in my class last year, Miss [Harriet Livonia] Cady, '81. I remember how much I counted upon her, as a student; she was a very superior girl. Since I was ill in November I have lost the following friends, not all intimate friends, but all valued by me. (Of my own age or about that) Mr. Coffin, Eliz. Churchill, Eliz Arthur, Jas. J. Fields, Mr. Boardman; Of young people: Alice Barnard, Miss Cady, Emma Brigham (sculptor). It is more than one a month. Emma Brigham's was the least expected. [She had sculpted the bust of Mitchell.]...

1881, May 30. 4 p.m. I have been very well, all day. I think I never felt better. My cold is nearly over and I have no nervous depression. If I am to get really well, may I be enabled to work for others and not for myself.

1881 June 5. We have written what we call our Dome poetry. Some nice poems have come in to us. I think the Vassar girls, in the main, are magnificent; they are so all alive. Miss Whitney is reading "Anne" to me, evenings.

I worked an hour and a half in the meridian room last evening and really enjoyed it. The Dames (Maria and May) expect to come on Monday night. If it is fine I mean to go down to meet them. It is squally enough now.

1881, June 6....I have been clearing up drawers. A sad business when it comes to burning letters or not burning, of those who have passed away....

1881. June 9. The Dames are here and I enjoy them as much as I ever did. I enjoyed the going down to New York to meet them.

1881. Sunday, June 12. The eclipse at one o'clock this morning was beautiful. It had rained for a week and cleared off last evening. ... I got out a little before 1 a.m. and went to bed at 2 [a.m.]. Roses are plenty.

1881, June 18. The Dome party today was 62 in number. It was breakfast and we opened the Dome, seated 40 in the Dome and 20 in the meridian room....I had the handsomest bouquet that I ever had in my life. I paid $34 for the Dinners, $7 were returned to me, so it was $27.

1881. July 5. I left Vassar June 24 on the stern-wheel steamer *Galatia* from N.Y. to Providence. I looked out of my stateroom window and saw a strange looking body in the Northern sky. My heart sank. I knew instantly that it was a comet[18] and that I must return to the College. Calling the young people around me and pointing it out to

Maria Mitchell

them, I had their assurances that it was a comet and nothing but a comet. We went to bed about nine and I rose about 6 a.m. As soon as I could get my nieces started for Providence, I started for Stonington as the most easy of the ways of getting to New York, as I should avoid Point Judith. I went to the boat at the Stonington wharf about noon and remained on board until morning. There were few passengers, it was very quiet and I slept well. Arriving in N.Y. I took cars at 9 a.m. for Po'keepsie and reached the college at dinner time [noon]. I was so well that I went to work the same evening.

Same Evening. June 26, 1881. As I could not tell at what time the comet would pass the meridian I stationed myself at the telescope in the meridian room by 10 p.m. and watched for the comet to cross the meridian. As it approached the meridian I saw that it would go behind a scraggy apple tree. I sent for the watchman Mr. Crumb to come with a saw and cut off the upper limbs. He came with an axe and chopped away vigorously, but as one limb and another fell and I said "I need more cut away" he said "I think I must cut down the whole tree" and I said "cut it down." I felt the barbarism of it but I felt most that a bird might have a nest in it.

I found when I went to breakfast next morning that the story preceded me and I was called "George Washington." But for all this I got almost no observation. The fog came up and I had scarcely anything better than estimation. I saw the comet blaze out just on the edge of the field and I read its declination only.

...I worked five nights, one (which was rainy) I slept through. My way was to go to bed at 8 p.m., sleep two hours, and get up before 11 p.m. and stay up about one hour and a half. I then slept immediately. Between June 12th and July 2nd I was up at midnight 6 times. i.e. in 20 nights I was up 6 times. I slept some in the day time.

I left Poughkeepsie to return to Boston just as the news came of the firing on President Garfield. In half an hour we got the news that he was not "shot dead" and we were hopeful. (Even now, July 7, he is not out of danger, but every one gains courage.)[19] The sea air was delicious to me. They call it warm in Lynn, I feel only the bracing effect of the sea....

1881, July 10th. Lynn. I have been in this place almost a week.

July 14. I do not believe in raising a large sum for the President. He has been unfortunate but he cannot be cured by money and it may not be good for him to be rich. I am afraid he will not like to offend

THE "OLD APPLE TREE" DIARY ENTRY. In the summer of 1881, Mitchell recorded her attempts to observe the "The Great Comet" of that year, involving numerous observations past midnight. One particular problem she encountered was that the comet was low in the sky and the view was obscured by a "scraggy apple tree." To depict the scenario in her diary, Maria drew this sketch and added amusing details as Mr. Crumb, the night watchman, chopped down the tree to clear the way. *(See June 26, 1881 diary entry on opposite page.)*

those who have raised 1/4 of a million for him. And, I fear, if he lives he will have ups and downs of popularity as Grant had. Grant went into the Office almost by acclamation; in eight years it was "anything to beat Grant;" in four more there was danger that he would go in again.

1881. July 24. Is it possible that the two comets in the north are divisions of one large one?[20]

1881. July 29. Taking up a number of the *New York Tribune*, I find a statement that Mrs. Ray, L. P. [Lady Principal] of Vassar has resigned.[21] It is all news to me. She certainly had no intent of resigning when I left the College [for the summer]. On the whole, I am sorry.

The place [position of lady principal] is an absurdity in itself. It must be occupied: first by a society woman, a boarding house keeper, an orator, (make speeches) a motherly woman, an intellectual woman, etc. etc. No such person exists and if such did exist, she would not accept such a position. She is the "excusing officer" and she does all the disagreeables.

The very constitution of the college makes the President popular. He does the agreeable, she does the petty, the obnoxious and restraining. Miss Lyman took the control and was fairly dealt with by the President. In the 16 years the office of L.P. has steadily declined; it is now simply as far as I understand it the exponent of the President or of the Faculty or of both combined. It is said that when Mrs. Ray had said "no" to a girl, she can go to the President and he will say "yes." It is also said that when Mrs. Ray has said "no" to a girl, she has been known to say, "I will go to the Doctor and get her to say 'yes' on health grounds."

I cannot give even a guess as to what will be done! I suspect Matthew Vassar [the founder's nephew] to be behind it all! The college is running down in numbers. He is Treasurer. Mrs. Ray is unpopular. I think if I had the control I would have no Lady Principal but split the college into families. Why not 8 corridors and 8 families as well as 8 departments of study.

1881. July 31. I am 63 tomorrow. I cannot see that I am in the least ill, nor have I been for the whole of July. I hope I may use my strength for good and if I return to Vassar work conscientiously for the good of women.

1881. Aug. 3. Dr. Caldwell writes, "The L.P. of Vassar and the Dr. have resigned. Their resignations have been accepted."[22] It may be for the best but I doubt it. The Dr. has been very unwise in talking freely with the girls. The Lady Principal lacks tact. Can it be a congruence of two Comets? The comets are convenient scape-graces!

1881. Aug. 5. In thinking of returning to Vassar I mean to be careful. Not to do too much work; but to do it slowly and in a better way. Photograph sun spots, when they are large only. Observe for time twice a week. Take two stars always and four if I can. Read level always. Observe Saturn for one hour a night. Take over to the Observatory one pupil at a time. Keep meteorological journal. Lecture to Juniors once a week as in former years. Do no work with the telescope below +5. Do no work when I am ill. Direct my mind from myself. Encourage students (the advanced) to sweep for comets. Divide up the sky into quarters and appoint times.

1881. August 11. Matthew Vassar [the founder's nephew] is dead! I am sorry. I have met him at least once a day for 16 years and I never saw him cross or ill-natured. It is a good deal to be able to say as much as this of any man.[23]

The first question for the college is, has he left the Institution [Vassar College] any money. I am afraid not. He is called a millionaire. I do not expect that he has more than 1/4 million. I hope his accounts will be found to be straight. If all is right and safe, he may be more of a man than I thought for.

In his will, Matthew Vassar left a sizable amount of money to the college. One of the bequests established several professorial chairs. This bequest stirred up a great deal of controversy because he specified that these chairs could not be held by women.

Sometime after Vassar's death, Maria wrote a letter to Ann Eliza Morse, cousin of Cornelia M. Raymond, Vassar Class of 1881.

The new Doctor [Mary E. Allen. M.D.][24] fits in very nicely. She is a little like Dr. Avery in her nicety and like Miss Powell in being pleasant. In short, all moves smoothly. We have had 298 students and shall probably be able to touch 300 before June.

We still debate about Mr. Vassar's $80,000 with its restriction; Miss Goodsell [the lady principal] and Prof. Braislin on one side, Dr. Allen and I on the other and Dr. Lossing with us. New York alumnae disapproved but took no action; Boston alumnae disapproved and recorded their disapproval and sent a copy to Trustees. (I think they did not send a copy to Trustees—but decided to bring it up at a general meeting.) Poor Mr. Vassar! I pity him that he could leave no more generous-spirited legacy; but he wasn't born to be generous. We wonder if John[25] will do the same!...

M.M.[26]

On June 12, 1883—nearly two years after the death of the founder's nephew—Dr. Benson Lossing offered a resolution to the board of trustees that Vassar's restrictive bequest be declined. His resolution was voted down, fourteen to two.

1881. Aug. 16. I have spent a day pleasantly at Seabrook, an old farmhouse where Sally went about 45 years ago. For a simple country place it is charming. We were 2 miles from the village. 6 p.m. I have been very well in every respect all day.

1881. Aug. 20. In looking over the science statistics[27] (which I enjoy exceedingly), I find that Syracuse is the banner town. Indianapolis good and I think Rochester stands high. Given one wide awake woman in a town and you can rouse the whole. But how slowly women work science!

After her summer in New England, Maria Mitchell returned to Poughkeepsie for another semester of teaching astronomy on the Vassar campus.

1881 Sept. 6, 2:30 p.m. The air is so smoky and it is so dark that I cannot see to write. We suppose there are fires and it is the smoke from the burning bushes. (This was the yellow day.) I could not see well enough to read the newspaper, 4 feet from the window, at noon day with my glasses on. The saffron hue which was very depressing diminished about 5 p.m. This peculiar hue, gave the grass a blue-green appearance; and the flowers lost their clear colors and were mixed.[28]

1881 Sept. 11. If I am measurably well next summer, go to a watery place, hire a man (or a woman) and put up my own telescope and have the man to give shows.

Sept. 23. The new Doctor [Mary Allen] is a sweet looking Quaker woman. My only fear is, that she will be too mild.

Sept. 24, 1881. Mr. I. [van Ingen] says that he knows of no reason that required the resignation of L. P. He was pretty severe on the Chief [President Caldwell] for his "inert" policy but agrees with me to sustain in all that can be done.

He reminds me by telling me that Dr. Raymond objected to someone as a teacher, because "too far west of the Mississippi." Mr. I. thinks that not a person on the Board of Trustees would approve of the clause in Mr. Vassar's will which objected to women as occupants of chairs.

Sept. 26. There are college prayers in the Chapel. Dr. Caldwell has gone off and it is said three of the gentlemen Professors will take part in the Chapel exercise. I do not find that the women have been asked to cooperate.

Sept. 30. Our new Doctor says she has known Professors who are appointed by the Corporation of a Medical College to Lecture to the women, who have complied with the requirements but who have lectured with their backs turned to the women! Moral, some women are too saintly to live!

Oct. 3rd, 1881. I lectured to junior class this morning, received seniors at noon, and went to Faculty. It is now 5 p.m. I think that I never felt better in Health. I hope to work this evening. I found a Miss Mitchell had entered the college, and I went to see her.

Nov. 4. Yesterday I went to town and ran around a good deal....

Today, I am uncommonly well and I was at once when I had some tea....I am really enjoying life of late, I have felt so well. (I hope I may be kept in the right path, for my remaining years). We have had 2 1/2 inches of rain in two weeks.

Nov. 13. I observed in the meridian room last night; working with telescopes always cheers me. Today is fine and I am feeling uncommonly well. I am hoping that the cramping of my hands means nothing, but it is new to me. I did not go to Chapel today, but worked on a lesson. I have Prof. Peirce's "Ideality" book. How full of faith many great men are! I have read two of these essays with great satisfaction.

Dec. 9. The events of the past month are a journey to Philadelphia, a stay in that city of three days, the celebration of the anniversary of the Philalethian Society, the visit to me of Abby Hutchinson Patton and the painting of Katy by Fanny Macy. In Philadelphia the New Century Club gave me a Reception. It is a club of men and women; the reception was very informal, about 30 persons were present. Of these about half I had known before. The custodian was a Nantucket woman, and about four others. I was glad to meet Prof. Lesley whom I had met 30 years before at Prof. Hall's in Albany. The club carries on some missionary work in the shape of classes. I saw a group of adult women who were learning to write. They were apparently the better class of servant women. Martha Earle, the sister of my old friend Linnie Earle, was Pres't of the club. The rooms were cheerful and tasteful and the refreshments very simple as they are in Boston....

The portrait of Kate by Fanny strikes me as good. Van Ingen says the forehead, and side of face and chin are good painting, left side of face he says cannot be true to life; the shades are too dark. He thinks it decidedly bad on that side. He says it looks "Dutchy" all through. He says she must paint what she sees and he cannot believe that she could have seen that molasses color, that it does not look like flesh, while the forehead and chin do. He said "the forehead, right side of face and chin are good painting and so is the hair."

I worked on Saturn last evening. It was the 15th evening on Saturn. I mean at some time to collect the "peculiarities" of Saturn and to publish them on a sheet of paper and scatter them around....I find one record in Dawes of a star seen between ball and ring.

A rather unique honor came to Mitchell during the Christmas break of 1881. The *Vassar Miscellany* reported:

> *During the holidays a reception was given to Prof. Mitchell by the New England Woman's Club in Boston. At the close of the evening it was voted to hold such a reception yearly, some time between Christmas and New Year's, the day to be called "Maria Mitchell's Day."*

1882 Jan. 4. During the Holidays I heard "Patience" once, went to a Reception given to me by the Woman's club, and went to the meeting of the Boston Alumnae. I spoke at both the last meetings....I asked Mrs. Cheney and Mrs. Howe separately, if, in their opinion Vassar should refuse the money offered by Mr. Vassar, coupled as it is with the condition that no woman shall be appointed to those Professorships which he endows.

Mrs. Cheney said unhesitatingly "It is always good policy to stand by principle. I should say 'refuse the money.'" Mrs. Howe said: "1. If the money pays good gentlemen professors, it is still used for the benefit of women. 2. It does give a fling at women. 3. You need the money." She said she could not decide at once.

At the Alumnae meeting I was very much pleased with remarks of Miss Hawes of Boston. They propose to form an Association of Graduates from the Colleges open to Women. I suggested to them the graduates of Oberlin and Antioch. They seemed to have forgotten them.

Jan. 12, 1882. There is a strange sentence in the last paragraph of Dr. Jacobi's article on the study of Medicine by women, to the effect that it would be better for the husband always to be superior to the wife. Why? And if so, does not it condemn the ablest women to a single life?

Jan. 22, 1882. Agnes Cuttere says, "Call on me when you will for money for the observatory. Maria Dickinson (Mrs. McGrew) says she wishes that Fanny would paint me for her.

Feb. 5, 1882. We have had two heavy snow storms since Feb. came in. We have twice been unable to get out of the Observatory without help. The first time 6 men, two horses and a girl came to our rescue; today four men and two horses and the girl came.

Phebe's picture, painted by Fanny came; it is far the most pleasing she has done.

1882 Feb. 14....I have a new servant girl. I was obliged to show her how to help me in the dome. I turned down the large telescope, Miss Whitney placed the step ladder near and I said "Go up the steps and put on the hood." (I meant to cover the object glass). She took the hood, put it upon her own head and stood before me. As she stood before me I was dazed. I could not think what she meant and it was some minutes before I could believe that she really thought I meant for her to put it upon her own head.

Mar. 7, 1882. I had a few minutes of seeming to be deaf, in class. It would not trouble me, if it had not set my heart to beating and my fingers, for perhaps a minute, felt bad. I put my hands into warm water and it was immediately over. This is the only illness I have had of 5 minutes duration in 4 months. I had eaten some very peppery hash! This is just a year since a similar ill turn a year ago.

Mch. 10. 10 a.m. I get up well and feel very well. No ear trouble at all. Weather good. I am disturbed at letters from Lydia and from Kate.

Sunday Mch 12. I have been very well although it is a very rainy day....A cheery note came from Lydia Dame [Mitchell's niece] yesterday. I have written all the letters I owe to any one; I have paid all my debts.

1882. Mch 13. 3 p.m. I start for Faculty. As I sit, I feel as well as I ever did in my life; I go to Faculty and we probably shall elect what are called the "honor" girls. I dread the struggle that is pretty certain to come....The whole system is demoralizing and foolish. Girls study for "prizes" and not for learning when "honors" are at the end. The unscholarly motive is wearing. If they studied for sound learning, the cheer which would come with every day's gain would be health preserving.

Mch 14. I was never in better health in my life, so far as I can feel. Faculty adjourned until 3 1/2 today. I hope we may be amicable. [later] Faculty lacked two hours but was very pleasant.

1882, Mch 20. I had five teeth taken out yesterday. I never felt better than I do today. I stay away from Faculty because I can't talk plainly.

Mch. 24. Spite of my toothless gums I lectured to Sophomores last night and kept their attention.

Apr. 1. At Miller's, New York. I met Mrs. Ray, as I entered the house. She spent 2 hours with me. She blames Dr. C[aldwell] very much. She says she can forgive Dr. W[ebster] but not Dr. C. She was handsomer than ever....There is a rumor that a Vassar girl has inherited $100,000! I do not believe it....My health is excellent, with the exception of five minutes, it has been for 5 months.

April 6, 1882. Last night I went to Champney's to a Reception....
My little namesake is lovely. [Lizzie J. Williams Champney, '69, had
named her first child after Maria Mitchell; see September 18, 1876
letter on page 242.]...The weather is dismal in the extreme. Lydia
Dame [niece of Mitchell] arrived this morning. Miss [Rose] Herschel[29]
called yesterday. She is very pleasing. She will probably go back to
Vassar when I go....

Ap. 26. Miss Herschel came to the College on the 11th and stayed 3
days. She is one of the little girls whom I saw 29 years since, playing
on the lawn at Sir John Herschel's place, Collingwood. She showed
herself to be a pleasant well-fitting in person, more cosmopolitan
than one would then have supposed an English girl could become. ...
Fanny is painting my portrait. I have given her 8 sittings. It is amus-
ingly good.

Ap. 30. I am very well, but age tells on me. My feet are lame if I
wear old shoes, my new teeth make my gums sore. It is useless to
try to console myself with the recollection that when I was young
new shoes harassed me and old teeth kept me awake; the pains of
youth are easily forgotten and quickly remedied; those of age cling
to you and must be borne. I am thankful to have nothing worse of
physical ills.

Emerson's death is a grief to me. He would have done no more for
the world, but it was good to see him and rarely to hear his voice.
One could wish to have lived his life. I have rarely felt this; but I did
when young, for Dr. Bowditch, later for Mrs. Somerville and now
for Emerson. To Emerson's daughter and wife the loss must be
incalculable.

May 20, 1882. Vassar is getting pretty. I gathered lilies of the valley
this morning. The young robins are out in a tree close by us, and the
phoebe has built, as usual, under the front steps. I am rushing dome
poetry, but so far show no alarming symptoms of brilliancy.[30]

July 29. I think I must subscribe for the *Scientific Monthly,* narrow as
it is. I need to know what it has to say on Science and I find the number I happen to have on hand very readable....

Aug. 3. The news comes of the death of Uncle Peleg [William Mitchell's brother] and also of the dangerous illness of Prof. Braislin's mother. ...

Aug. 23, 1882. Plan to work through the autumn with meridian Inst[rument] on account of the Transit of Venus. Do not begin on Saturn until after frost.

1882 We visited Whittier Aug. 22, 1882. We found him at lunch, but he soon came into the sitting room. He was very chatty and seemed very glad to see us. ...

In October 1882, the *Vassar Miscellany* conveyed the news that Mitchell "had the title of LL.D. conferred upon her by Hanover College at its last Commencement."[31] Mitchell did not mention this exceptional honor in her diary.

Oct. 1882. In the period of 15 months between June 1881 and Oct. 1882, four comets became visible to the naked eye. Undoubtedly the earth passed through a cometary region. Of these, the comet of June 1881 was first seen by us in the north before twilight was over and the magnificent one of 1882 rose in the early mornings of October.[32] As observers become more numerous, more and more comets will be found, but this is the only case known to me of 4 large comets in so short a period of time. ...

It seems strange that a comet should be an object of terror. The beauty of this comet and that of 1861 and of 1881 and the general prosperous condition of the world affairs should do something to destroy this unfortunate prestige. So far, in the records of history we have no knowledge of harm coming from these startling visits and in the doctrine of probabilities it is an even chance that good and not evil may accrue from novel changes. Prof. Renee declared that the chance was more than even for the close approach of a comet to the sun or to the earth to be beneficial. ...[33]

In December 1882, the *Miscellany* reported:

> The transit of Venus[34] on December 6, the principal astronomical event of the year, was observed by Prof. Mitchell with considerable success. The weather during the morning was unfavorable, and there seemed little prospect of obtaining any satisfactory views.

TRANSIT OF VENUS. This Vassar Observatory photograph from December 6, 1882 displays an observation of the planet Venus, silhouetted against the sun. Venus is the large circular shadow in the sun's upper portion. The image is the result of the hand-poured emulsion which Maria Mitchell used with her Vassar students to record the sky. It is one of the photographs uncovered in 1959 by Professor Henry Albers, preserved for nearly a century in the original Vassar Observatory. Each glass plate was enclosed in a paper sleeve which included specific information about the observation *(below)*.

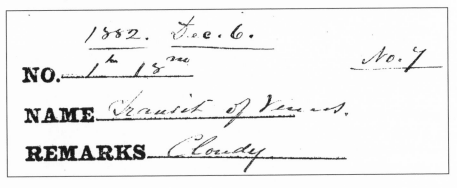

The first contacts, external and internal, were not seen; but a few minutes after the latter, a break in the clouds reveal the black disk of the planet just within the sun's limb. At half past eleven the sky was comparatively clear. The second internal contact and the last external were observed under favorable conditions.

Miss Gardner, resident graduate, assisted Prof. Mitchell in the contact observations. The haziness of Venus' outline, caused, as is supposed, by the planet's atmosphere, was noted, also an irregularity on its dark surface in the form of a whitish spot near the center.

Prof. Mitchell made continuous observations during the transit with the view of detecting a satellite, but no sign of one presented itself. During midday nine photographs were taken by Miss Whitney, assisted by members of the Junior astronomy class.

December 1882. Miss Whitney addressed T. and M. Nov. 19, on the Place of Science in the Education of Woman. The paper was originally written for the Woman's Congress, and gives a thoughtful, thoroughly womanly view of a most interesting question.

Mch. 1883. The students are trying to modify commencement so that it shall not be a "prize" effort; i.e. they desire to have no commencement or, to call in the Alumnae to make speeches.

By a unanimous vote they asked the Faculty to make a change. Prof. B, Prof. H. and I were the Committee....I asked permission to state my views plainly. The Faculty was with me. We voted to send this resolution to the students: "The appointments at Com[mencement] are made with reference to scholarship, character and literary ability."

The students feel themselves snubbed and are holding stormy meetings. Nothing will come of it....

May 4, 1883....I have been asked to lecture in Pittsfield late in the summer and in Po'keepsie (to Science Association) in September. I take Saturn for the latter and probably the Herschels for the former. I have also been asked to teach Miss Bidwell of Mt. Holyoke how to adjust a transit instrument. I have written that it will be better for me to go to South Hadley and that I do not like to work in July or August. It looks as if I could get light employment if I gave up Vassar.

June 21, 1883. I set out on the Mary Power on June 18th for Boston, got to N.Y. at 11 a.m. and went on board of the boat at once. I disliked my stateroom and decided to go by land as it stormed. I left N.Y. at 10:30 and worried half-sleeping through a hot night. I reached Kendall's just as they were at breakfast. How glad I was to find them all well, and the same at the Dame's and Barney's the next day.

Today, I have been at the Bond's to look at chronometers. I want one at $200 which has been tested and is only about 6 years old. Its rate is remarkably steady even when at sea. Also, I bo't a mantle, a head dress and a fancy pink shawl....

1883, July. I heard Mr. Adams at the Universalist Church....I was most surprised at his fear of Tyndall, Huxley and Spencer. Can the study of _truth_ do harm? Does not every true scientist seek only to know the truth? And in our deep ignorance of what is truth, shall we dread the searching after it?

I hold the simple student of nature in holy reverence and while there live sensualists and despots and men who are wholly self seeking, I cannot bear to have these sincere workers held up in the least degree to reproach. And let us have _truth_ even if the truth be the awful denial of the good God. We must face the light and not bury our heads in the Earth. I am hopeful that scientific investigation pushed on and on, will reveal new ways in which God works and bring to us deeper revelations of the wholly unknown. The Physical and the spiritual seem to be at present separated by an impassable gulf, but at any second, that gulf may be overleapt, possibly a new revelation may come.

July 7....As yet I see no articles in the new journal called "Science" written by women....

1883, July 31. I have had two or three rich days. On Friday last, I went to Ashland (Holdernness) to the Asquam House. I had been asked by Mrs. Dr. Talbot, to join her party....May [Dame] and I arrived at tea time, Friday night, we remained 2 1/2 days....

Aug. 3, 1883. Polly's birthday. Aug. 5. It is two weeks today since I had a bad fall. I never felt better in my life.

Maria Mitchell

Lynn, Mass.

[Aug. 10, 1883]

My dear Mrs. Raymond,

...I am having a very good summer; doing nothing. I took May Dame down to the White Mt. region, for ten days; we spent two at the Twin Mt. House, five at Bethlehem, and three at the Asquam House in Holderness....

[John Greenleaf] Whittier is lovely! He is seventy-six years old, and his friends say he fails neither outwardly nor inwardly. When I came away, he came out to the wagon and said "When thee sees the 400 Vassar girls, give them all the love of an old bachelor." What a pity that the 400 girls cannot see him!...

All the Dames are at home. Lydia returns to Washington in September and her pay is raised to $1200. As yet, Maria has no chance that suits her. Except for the fear that she may be restless herself, the parents would be glad for her to have none....

I try not to look far ahead. The changes at Vassar are very trying; I shall feel your loss extremely. It makes me still more, the oldest. I find the society of those of my own age very pleasant and soothing. I met Prof. Shackford of Cornell a few days since; I attended his church in my Lynn days: he is sixty nine years old and says he shall feel that he must retire at seventy; he has been twelve years at Cornell and looks younger than when he went. He needs Dr. Lossing to tell him that if he is well, age counts for nothing—or Dr. Magoon who claims that he grows young every year....

Yours,

Maria Mitchell[35]

The continuance of scientific study, seems to be on the increase. Women do not so much take up science for the amusement of a lonely learning. That there is serious study of science from a love of it which looks for no reward and seeks no recognition there can be no doubt. Boys collect insects and birds but could they not be studied alive without the wanton killing?...[36]

Dec. 12, 1883. I took the 12 advanced students into the Dome to show them Saturn. Eleven saw it before the clouds came up.[37]

Jan. 9, 1884. Mr. [Matthew] Arnold has been to the college and has given his lecture on Emerson. The audience was made up of three hundred students, and three hundred guests from town. Never was a man listened to with so much attention.

Whether he is right in his judgment or not, he held his audience by his manly way, his kindly dissection, and his graceful English. Socially, he charmed us all. He chatted with everyone, he smiled on all. He said he was sorry to leave the college and that he felt he must come to America again.

We have not had such an awakening for years. It was like a new volume of old English poetry.[38]

March 31, 1885

My dear Matthew [Barney]

It is very long that I have not heard from Nantucket. I wish you would write. I don't like Nantucket, but I do like the people....

Our March has been terrific. The ther[mometer] has been about zero, every morning but one, for a week. I do not go out to breakfast. If you are in NY I hope you will run up to Vassar. I expect Anne in April. I shall probably be away Ap. 1 to 3rd as we have holidays.

M. M.[39]

WHEN SHE WAS TWELVE YEARS OLD, Maria Mitchell had helped her father in his observations of an eclipse of the sun visible from Nantucket; more than a half century later, she was doing the same thing for her students.

Eclipses repeat in a pattern of approximately eighteen years called the "Saros," which has been known since antiquity. Fifty-four years represents three of these intervals, so Maria could truly say, "it was the same eclipse."

March 16, 1885. In February, 1831, I counted seconds[40] for father, who observed the annular eclipse at Nantucket. I was twelve and a half years old. In 1885, fifty-four years later, I counted seconds for a class of students at Vassar; it was the same eclipse, but the sun was only about half-covered. Both days were perfectly clear and cold.[41]

Maria Mitchell

After seven years of service as Vassar's president, Samuel Caldwell resigned his post. He wrote a personal letter to Mitchell, thanking her for her friendship during those years.

> *June 12, 1885.*
>
> *My dear Miss Mitchell,*
>
> *Your friendship has been a long time of sunshine through seven years. And now that we go away we hope to carry it with us to the end of the chapter.*
>
> *It is the one hard thing in our going that we leave friends with whom our daily life is so united. Otherwise there is relief and the anticipation of a tent pitched by more quiet waters, where we shall hope and be glad to welcome you.*
>
> *Mrs. Caldwell joins me in a hearty good bye.*
>
> *Samuel L. Caldwell[42]*

Mitchell's diary shows clear evidence that her teaching was up-to-date with this brief entry: "Sept. 28. I lectured on variable stars and the bright star★ seen in Andromeda's nebula."[43]

Early in 1886 Maria Mitchell started a fund-raising effort for the Vassar Observatory with the hope that enough money might be raised to keep its programs going at a level acceptable to her. The ultimate result of this effort was the establishment of the Maria Mitchell Chair of Astronomy, shortly after her death.

> *Jan. 12, 1886*
>
> *Prof. Maria Mitchell*
>
> *The Boston Association of Vassar Alumnae feels deeply the need of an endowment for the astronomical department at Vassar College and having heard that you were willing to try to raise the amount necessary for such an endowment, they offer you the sum of five hundred*

★This star in the Andromeda galaxy (M31) is now well known as the Supernova of 1885. Her statement in 1885 serves to show that Maria Mitchell was very up-to-date in her teaching of astronomy. Today, carrying on in the tradition of Professor Mitchell, one of the research projects carried on at the new Vassar Class of 1951 Observatory is the search for similar supernovae in other galaxies.

dollars ($500) to cover any expenses which you may incur in travel-
ling. This sum will be paid to you as soon as you desire.

The Alumnae wish to express their appreciation of your readiness
to undertake this work and their pleasure in being able to cooperate
with you, however slightly.

Very sincerely yours,

Elisabeth M. Howe, Sec'y[44]

Pittsburgh, Pa.

Mar. 17, 1886

Dear Miss Mitchell

Your note forwarded by my daughter Mrs. Thompson duly reached
me. She had been conferring with me relative to an effort of the Alum-
nae to raise a fund of $10,000 to strengthen the maintenance of your
observatory at Vassar and I understood that some twelve hundred dollars
were needed to complete that sum. I have therefore ventured to assume
that it would be the same in the end for me to subscribe to the 10,000
fund as to send the sum I devote to that end directly to yourself.

I have given my daughter five hundred dollars to be applied in this
way of which she will also advise you. It gives me great pleasure in this
contribution to give some expression to my high respect and regard for
yourself as the motive inclining me to the gift. I only regret it is so small
owing to my already considerable appropriations to similar object.

W. Thaw[45]

Danvers, Mass

3rd Mo 31, 1886

My dear Friend

I hear thou art raising funds for the Vassar Observatory. I enclose
check for $25 just to show my good will as I am unable to make a sub-
scription in accordance with my wishes.

Hoping that thy efforts will be successful, I am thy sincere friend,

John G. Whittier[46]

Though significant contributions and encouraging support came
from far and wide, Mitchell's efforts were not always successful. As she
records in her diary on February 5, 1886: "I asked Miss Farwell for
$1000. I expect to get $100. [Added later] I got nothing."[47]

Maria Mitchell

Boston Sept. 30, 1886
Received of Maria Mitchell two thousand two hundred and twenty
five dollars ($2225.00) payable on demand, in trust for the Observatory
of Vassar College, said funds being deposited in my name in the New
England Trust Company Boston.
  Sarah L. Day ['78][48]

Professor Mitchell's thoroughly developed ideas about the ideal observatory for teaching—and what one ought to teach in a college astronomy curriculum—are spelled out nicely in the following letter. Her detailed ideas and specific guidance for Mr. Cunningham are based on Mitchell's vast experience of many years of teaching at Vassar College.

My dear Mr. Cunningham,

I reply to your questions concerning the observatory which you propose to establish.

And first, let me congratulate you that you begin small. A large telescope is a great luxury but it is an enormous expense and not at all necessary for teaching. If you work to determine the places of small stars, to settle with extreme accuracy minute changes of position, a large instrument is necessary.

I would begin with teaching them to use their eyes. The eyes are the best telescopes and watching the heavenly bodies is a good use to which to put them. Dr. Derby of Boston says that Sea Captains and astronomers keep their eyes "because they look at the offing."

I do not teach the constellations, partly because I do not know many of them,* partly because they can learn them, if they wish, without a teacher. But I would have them watch for changes and motions, for meteors.

For instruction, small instruments, mainly portable ones, are preferable. My beginning class uses only a small portable equatorial costing $200, presented by Dr. MacDonald of San Francisco. It stands outdoors from 6 a.m. to 9 p.m. The girls are encouraged to use it.

---

*This statement is very hard to believe. Maria Mitchell surely had an intimate knowledge of the sky from her years of using telescopes. In some of her lectures she clearly demonstrated that she knew the constellations intimately. It seems more likely that she did not want to teach constellations because of her position that "astronomy is not star gazing."

Courtesy of Special Collections, Vassar College Libraries

MARIA MITCHELL WITH STUDENTS IN THE VASSAR OBSERVATORY. Mitchell's room opened directly into the dome of the Observatory. The telescope is visible in the rear of the photograph; the door to the left leads to the front porch of the observatory. The students *(clockwise from left)* are Jane E. Ricker, Lucy Davis, Mary Ricker, Elizabeth Deming, Anna Wheeler, Lavinia Gould. As all are Vassar students from the class of 1885, they may have been Mitchell's senior astronomy majors. *(See page 227 for view of room in the opposite direction.)*

They are expected to determine the rotation of the sun on axis by watching the spots. The same for the planet Jupiter. They determine revolution of Titan (of Saturn) by watching its motions.[49] The retrograde and direct motion of the planet among the stars, the point of the sun with reference to its setting in winter and summer, the phases of Venus.

All their book learning in astronomy should be mathematical. The astronomy which is not mathematical is what is so ludicrously called "geography of the heavens" is not astronomy at all.

My senior class, generally very small, say six, is received as a class, but in practical astronomy each girl is taught separately. I believe in small classes.

I instruct them separately first, in the use of meridian instrument and next in that of the equatorial. They obtain the time for the college by meridian passages of stars. They use the equatorial just as far as they can do with very insufficient mechanism. We work wholly on planets and they are taught to find a planet at any hour of the day, to make drawings of what they see and to determine positions of planets and satellites. I should add to this the angles of distance and direction of double stars if my mechanism would warrant the effort.

With the clock and chronograph they determine differences of R.A. of objects, by the electric mode of recording. They make sometimes very accurate drawings and they learn to know the satellites of Saturn, Titan, Rhea, etc. by their different physiognomy as they would persons. They have sometimes measured diameters.

If you add to your observatory a meridian instrument I should advise a small one. Size is not so important as people generally suppose. Nicety and accuracy are what is needed in all scientific work. Startling effects by large telescopes and high powers are too suggestive of sensational advertisements.[50]

Following the 1885 resignation of Samuel L. Caldwell as president, the Vassar trustees appointed J. Ryland Kendrick as acting president for one year. Later they chose James M. Taylor, D.D., as president. He served until 1915 and became a close friend of Mitchell's.

1886, Ap. 6. Our Board of Trustees met yesterday and elected Jas. M. Taylor as President. The number present was 19, and 18 voted for him.

At night a Committee from the Board called the Faculty together and asked them, if the preparatory school were abolished, if the Professors would voluntarily relinquish their salaries in part. Every member of the faculty declined to encourage such an arrangement. It was mentioned that it could not be expected, that those who had large families could not be expected to do it. The idea was advanced that our whole salaries would not make up the difference.

I was very cautious but I mentioned that some years the half of my salary had gone back into the College. Dr. [Ezekiel] Robinson[51] seemed to be astonished at the board we women paid....I mentioned that altho' we had not families, in the ordinary meaning of the word. every one of us had dependencies and I aired a remark which I have often made that "the man who asked salary on account of his family, did not ask pay for his services but charity for his children."

At this point in her diary Mitchell put together a long list of persons she had called on, or written, in her attempt to raise money for the Observatory. Her fund-raising efforts consumed a great deal of her time, as the following letter attests.

Aug 22d 1886

My dear Mrs. Blackwell,

Can you not get up the science Report for Congress? I cannot go— cannot get it up. I have given myself over to Mammon—i.e. am begging for the Obs. of Vassar and am pulling wires. I have taken about $2700 add a zero and I will have done with such work forever.

But I've had a good time, seen lots of nice people whom it would have been a pity not to know and am ready to ask, "where are the vulgar rich?" for my rich are as elegant and as courteous as can be found in the old Sir Charles Granderson novels!

So, help me out of my Report—there's a good girl!

Maria Mitchell[52]

August 1, 1886. I had been told to call on Mary Shannon at Bar Harbor, but I had no letter. I imagined a decrepit old woman of 80. I found a lovely cottage called "Ledge Lawn," i. e., a cottage surrounded by rocks, the rocks fringed with flowers and level enough for good footing and for easy clambering walks....Just as I was about to enter, there stepped forward an elderly woman in a broad hat with a lovely face overhung with heavy grey curls.

I asked for Miss Shannon and she said "There are two." I said "Mary Shannon" and she said "There are two." But I knew I had the right one. It seems they are called Mary and Little Mary, one aunt to the other. I entered and announced myself. Miss Shannon had met me before. ...

And now began a series of kindnesses and in 48 hours I had received so many attentions that I tried to think if there was anything left that I could desire. They offered horses, flowers, drives, walks, lunches, visitors, Indian baskets and $100 in cash for the Observatory. They must have been in great need of recipients!

Aug. 26, 1886. ... It wears upon me when I hear women say, "Men are no longer so ready to give up a seat in the cars, since the woman's agitation arose." I wish to ask if the agitation arose only recently? Also, is such a statement true? If true, is it of any consequence? Also one grain of <u>right</u> fair dealing is worth more than a <u>bushel</u> of courtesy. ...

Nov. 24, 1886. I had always heard of Geo. W. Childs but I scarcely knew in what way. I went to the Librarian and I asked "who is Geo. W. Childs?" She replied "The publisher of the Philadelphia Ledger." I took up a newspaper which said "Mrs. Geo. W. Childs is a daughter of Mrs. Bouvier." Mrs. Bouvier is the author of a book on astronomy. I asked the head of the book department at Wanamakers for a letter of introduction to Geo. W. Childs. He gave me a very proper short note.

Entering the office I asked if I could see Mr. Childs. ... In a few minutes Mr. Childs came into the room in which I sat, shook hands and asked me into an inner office.

I told him in few words that the Vassar Alumnae having raised $10,000 to endow the Observatory had asked me to add to it. I said "I come to you to get all the money you can give and suggestions to me."

Almost instantly he said "I will give you $500." It was done! I had planned to flatter, to persuade, to cajole, as much as I could sincerely, and it needed no flattery, no cajolery, no persuasion. The only tolerably pretty speech I had made was this. "Thirty years since I went to England; The first astronomer I met said to me: There is a lady astronomer in America named Bouvier, I have her book."

I had touched the right chord. Mr. Childs revered the name of his mother-in-law. It was the beginning of much talk....His own mother in-law had been a remarkable woman. He added, "I have several women on my paper as Editors they receive salaries of between 2 and 3000 dollars. Gents sometimes meet me and say 'What man wrote that excellent article yesterday?' and I reply 'A woman.'"...

Jan 26 1887.

My dear Mrs. Raymond,

...We are trying to improve our curriculum of study! The course of study, over which some of us have worked a score of years! Miss Abby F. Goodsell [lady principal], Miss [Priscilla H.]Braislin [professor of mathematics], Prof. [William B.] Dwight [professor of natural history] and myself, with Dr. [Lucy M.] Hall stand by the old way, the newer members try to require studies. We suspect Dr. [Ezekiel] Robinson to be behind the effort! Good fellow as he undoubtedly is, we prefer our own way! So, we have long Faculty meetings as we did in the early days....

My own family is only comfortably well. My brothers, Frank and Forster, seem less vigorous than usual, altho not really ill. [Both brothers outlived Maria; Andrew had died in 1871 at the age of fifty-seven.] The sisters seem to bear increasing age better than the brothers. I mean to try to go to the New York alumnae meeting this week and may meet some of the old graduates....

Maria Mitchell[53]

Feb. 10, 1887. When I came to Vassar I regretted that Mr. Vassar did not give full scholarships. By degrees I learned to think his plan of half scholarships better and today I am ready to say "give no scholarships at all." I find a helping hand lifts the girl as crutches do, she learns to like the help which is not self help. I have the aid of poor scholars and it is poor aid. If a girl has the public school and she wants to learn enough, she will learn. It is hard but she was born to hardness. She cannot dodge it. Labor is her inheritance....

July 12, 1887. I have just returned from Nantucket. I called on every first cousin I had on Nantucket and many others. I have a list made by Mary. I received more than 38 callers...

Maria Mitchell

July 16, 1887. I went to the Unitarian church at Nantucket. Some 20 years ago I went to church late and went far forward to my seat. I was one of 600 persons and I felt the embarrassment of being late. When I went into church now I made the 66th person. I sat far back and I think no one turned his head. Seen from behind I knew only Mrs. Catharine Starbuck and Maria Owen. When they came to me, after church, I found that I knew nearly all, but in 20 years the young men had become middle aged, and the old men had gone. I never saw 65 better dressed and better deported people but it was lonesome. The best looking man was Capt. Baxter.

The students used to say that my way of teaching was that of the man who said to his son "There are the letters of the English language, go into that corner and learn them." It is not exactly my way but I do think as a general rule, teachers talk too much, do let them occasionally listen! A book is a good institution! To read a book! To think it over and to write out notes is a useful exercise. A book which will not repay some hard thought is not worth publishing.

The fashion of lecturing is becoming a rage and a fashion. The teacher shows off herself. She does not enough try to develop her pupil. The greatest object in education is to give you a right habit of study. Especially the teacher should not show off herself. For once let her forget herself.

July, 1887. I went to Newport to attend a suffrage meeting for women. The speakers were Julia Ward Howe, Lucy Stone, the Sec'y (whose name I forget) and Mr. Chase, member of the U. S. Senate....

Aug. 31, 1887. Resolved: To work for the good of the whole college.

Sept. 23, 1887. Miss Goodsell says that altho' I am to have what I choose for my meals, it is not to become the table rule. She says when I eat one egg, Prof. [Manuel J.] Drennan orders one and Prof. [Charles J.] Hinkel eats two in addition to a large piece of steak....

In the case of the telescope the clamping is improved. The electric light is a gain but the <u>reading</u> of the <u>circles</u> is difficult and I must have a chair, or more assistance than I now have....

Columbia College
President's Room, Nov. 9, 1887
My Dear Miss Mitchell,
    Some time in October I had the honor to transmit to you by post,
a diploma attesting the action of the trustees of Columbia College in

conferring upon you at the Centennial Celebration in April last, the honorary degree of Doctor of Laws.[54]

As I wish to make my final report on the subject to the trustees, I should be glad to be assured that the diploma has reached its destination. If not, it will give me pleasure to furnish another copy.

F. A. P. Barnard[55]

Nov. 11, 1887. Today when I feel well it seems to me that I may, when I retire, lecture some. Every year I decline one or two invitations to lecture. The Herschels make one very long Lecture; the St. Petersburg another; Saturn a grave one, Jupiter a grave one. The visit to Cambridge, England.

Just now, my electric light does not work which troubles me much.

Anne, Phebe and I all went to the A.A.W. meeting in New York. I heard two good papers, one by Anna Garlen Spenser and one by Mary Wright Sewell.

Dec. 21, 1887. I have worked a long time on three formulae, page 88 of Loomis' Algebra, the easiest Algebra, I ever knew. Continually I mistook figures. Possibly my glasses are too weak. I have at length done it and am thankful to know that I may yet work.*

It is painful to know that my old assistant has procured work. Is it wrong in me to be pained? Why should she not be as willing to work for me as for a man?

Within two weeks of writing this journal entry, Mitchell resigned her professorship because of ill health. She left the college shortly thereafter and never returned to the campus where she had served for twenty-two years.

---

*Near this entry in Maria's diary are two pages containing algebra problems worked out. If these are the problems to which the diary refers, then she solved one of them correctly, albeit by a rather complicated method; but in doing the second problem, she forgot one of the terms and came up with a very complicated (and wrong) answer. Her December 21, 1887 comment indicates that she may have erroneously thought her solution was correct.

Maria Mitchell

Courtesy of Special Collections, Vassar College Libraries

MARIA MITCHELL, 1887. Despite her failing health in 1887, Maria Mitchell was still actively involved in teaching, fund-raising, and attending suffrage meetings. She also received an honorary LL.D. degree from Columbia University that year. In light of the frequent invitations she was receiving to lecture across the country, Professor Mitchell was contemplating a lecture tour after her retirement from Vassar.

CHAPTER 12

THE FINAL YEARS

I am studying Greek! It will take 30 years,
but I may find chances for it, in the other world.

 EARLY SEVENTY YEARS OLD when she resigned from Vassar in early 1888, Maria Mitchell immediately moved back to Lynn, Massachusetts. Her deteriorating health had finally forced her to accept the fact that she could no longer carry out her duties as professor of astronomy. The exact nature of her health problem is not known, but her diary clearly shows that she had been concerned about her health for a long time.

For many years, Mitchell had maintained a rigorous schedule of teaching, lecturing, and traveling—as well as keeping up observing sessions in a cold observatory dome. By 1888, she acknowledged: "my more than half century of work has worn and tired me."

At the time of her resignation, Maria Mitchell had been teaching at Vassar for twenty-two years and earning her own living for more than fifty years. Her letter of resignation no longer exists, but we do have the letter she wrote to President Taylor explaining her action. We learn that she was very reluctant to resign, but that her "physicians advise rest." The trustees deferred action on her resignation until the spring, when they named her professor emeritus.

She moved to Lynn to be near her relatives, including her three sisters; Kate was in Lynn, Anne in Boston, and Phebe in Cambridge. Maria soon initiated the construction of a small observatory in Kate's backyard—with the hope that she could continue her astronomical research.

Her new Lynn observatory undoubtedly served more as a morale booster than anything else; there is no indication that Mitchell used its new telescope with any regularity. With her health steadily deteriorating, the retired professor would only dwell in Lynn for eighteen months. She died on June 28, 1889, just a month short of her seventy-first birthday.

IN A JANUARY 1888 letter to President Taylor, Mitchell had indicated her hope to finish the academic year at Vassar before retiring. But the normally resolute professor was unable to fulfill this desire. In her succinct and gracious explanation of her rushed resignation, she offered the president suggestions for her replacement, as well as best wishes for the college.

Maria also wrote to Mary Whitney, alerting her of her mentor's recommendation that Whitney be Mitchell's successor. President Taylor's reply to his esteemed professor indicates that she had talked with Taylor earlier about resigning, even though the immediacy of her action was unexpected. By not accepting her resignation immediately, he gives Mitchell time to settle her affairs; moreover, as the trustees placed her on a leave of absence, she could continue receiving her salary.

Jan. 8, 1888
President Taylor
Dear Sir,
You are probably somewhat prepared for the announcement of my resignation of the Professorship at Vassar. I had much hoped to continue until June, but my more than half century of work has worn and tired me; my physicians advise rest.

I wish to suggest to you to call Miss Whitney, whom you know, to fill the vacancy—she is able both as scholar and as Teacher and has always been a good friend of the college. May I suggest to you, some consideration for Miss Palmer,[1] if possible; she is remarkably faithful and conscientious.

Courtesy of Special Collections, Vassar College Libraries

BUST OF MARIA MITCHELL. Sculpted by Emma Brigham, this bronze bust was a gift of the Vassar Class of 1877. Now mounted in a niche above the entrance to the original Vassar Observatory, the bust was the topic of an article in the April 1877 issue of the *Vassar Miscellany:* "The Observatory, that abode of science, hitherto sacred to the stars, opened its doors to Art, shortly after Christmas vacation, and converted itself for a few days into a sculptor's studio with Miss Emma Brigham as the artist. Prof. Mitchell was the subject. The work of modeling progressed rapidly, and those of us who were favored with a glimpse into the studio, saw the dark clay fast taking on a wonderful life-like aspect."

I send best wishes for the growth of the college with the expression of my belief that it will be a power for good in coming years.

Sincerely yours,

Maria Mitchell[2]

She left the college almost immediately after this letter to the Vassar president, as evidenced by a subsequent letter she wrote from Lynn, Massachusetts dated January 11, 1888. Mitchell also sent a postcard to Miss Whitney, addressed to 124 Dartmouth St., Boston. The card, postmarked in Lynn, told Whitney:

I have resigned at Vassar. I have commended you. I have also asked Dr. Taylor to do something for Miss Palmer. All awaits the meeting of the Com[mittee]. Dr. Taylor writes handsomely. Mrs. Macy[3] and Maria Dame[4] have gone on to superintend the packing. I am hunting up my own telescope.

MM [5]

Vassar College

Poughkeepsie, N. Y.

Presidents Office

Jan. 9, 1888

My dear Miss Mitchell,

Your letter embodying your resignation of the Professorship of Astronomy at Vassar College, reached me today. Had I been told yesterday that such an event was imminent I should not have believed it, but I had a hint this morning that you were really contemplating this step.

Of course I knew that you often thought of it, and I had begun to think that you would urge it in June, but it has come unexpectedly, undesired—and I would add unwelcomed, did I not think that your judgment is probably founded on recent experiences that have demanded your action with a view of gaining the rest needed to prolong your life and usefulness.

I do not send you a formal acceptance of your resignation; I merely acknowledge your letter. I shall submit it to the Executive Committee at the approaching meeting.

If my own wishes are realized your resignation will be laid on the table till the Board meets in June. I wish I might also give hope that your salary will be continued till then—but you know how closely our Beloved College sometimes trims to reach port safely. I shall favor, at that time, a proposition making you Professor Emeritus for life, offering you a home in the College, and the use of its Observatory, at any time you may desire to reside here.

And you may be sure that we shall be glad to do all we can to honor one whose faithful service, and whose honesty of heart and life, have been among the chief inspirations of Vassar College throughout its history. Of public reputation you have doubtless had enough, but I am sure you cannot have too much of the affection and esteem which we feel towards you who have had the privilege of working with you.

I will see what can be done for Miss Palmer. Unhappily our funds cannot be used for her.[6] She will finish the work of the Semester. What will then be done I cannot yet say. My own wish is to call Miss Whitney, as you suggest, but all must remain uncertain for the present.[7]

With every good wish for your future, believe me, with highest esteem and friendliest regard

Sincerely yours,

James M. Taylor[8]

Although President Taylor may have had some foreknowledge of Mitchell's intention to resign, other members of the college community were shocked at the news. In a letter to Mary Whitney, Abby Goodwin, associate professor of Latin, conveys the faculty reaction to the announcement.

January 11, 1888.

My dear Miss Whitney:

I have been waiting as usual for an opportunity to write you a letter but, as usual, life begins with a rush on our return and regardless of the fact that we have just been taking two hours to live one, we are called upon to live two in one. Is your mathematics equal to that? and now I can get in only an assurance of the safe arrival of me and "mirabile dictu," my trunk; an expression of gratitude and affection for your kindness and yourself; and an exclamation at the news which was broken to us almost as soon as it arrived, i.e. to Faculty meeting, of Prof. Mitchell's Resignation!!

It was so unlooked for here, a dead silence followed, and it did seem that no business could be done that day in spite of the fact that there was an accumulation. But we had to go on and now Mrs. Macy and Miss Dame are here packing up. It seems very trying to have everything rushed so but perhaps it is better for Prof. Mitchell as she will feel less harassed, though I wish it could have been otherwise—Action is yet to be taken by the Faculty as well as by the Com. but it was all too sudden Monday p.m.

Give my best love to your dear Mother and Sister and believe me (hoping to see you soon) affectionately yours—

Abby M. Goodwin

Many members of the college community wrote letters expressing their dismay at Professor Mitchell's resignation.

Jan. 11, 1888

Jas. M. Taylor, Pres. Vassar College

My Dear Sir—Word comes to me that Prof. Mitchell has resigned her official connection with the College. I trust I was misinformed. If however it is true I hope she may be induced to withdraw it, or that it may not be accepted. It would be very desirable in my judgment that her name be kept officially associated with the College on some terms during her life. I can scarcely overstate the importance I attach to this suggestion.

C. Swan[9]

The omission of her name from the list of Committees I have always regretted.[10]

Among those who expressed their personal appreciation for Mitchell were students whose lives were profoundly enhanced by her life at Vassar. Two anonymous letter fragments were quoted by Phebe Kendall.[11]

Jan. 10, 1888. You will consent, you must consent, to having your home here, and letting the work go on. It is not astronomy that is wanted and needed, it is Maria Mitchell.... The richest part of my life here is connected with you....I cannot picture Vassar without you. There's nothing to point to!

May 5, 1889. In all the great wonder of life, you have given me more of what I have wanted than any other creature ever gave me. I hoped I should amount to something for your sake.

Photograph courtesy of Special Collections, Vassar College Libraries; Frame added: courtesy of Auto F/X Corp.

MARIA MITCHELL. As the most illustrious of the original faculty members of Vassar College, Maria Mitchell had become an institution at the college by the 1880s. Upon hearing of her resignation, one student begged her beloved professor to stay at Vassar in her retirement. "It is not astronomy that is wanted and needed," the student wrote her, "it is Maria Mitchell.... The richest part of my life here is connected with you.... I cannot picture Vassar without you."

308 *Maria Mitchell*

Of the original eight professors at the college, only Henry van Ingen, professor of art, served longer than Mitchell. None of the others, who resigned for various reasons, had reached what today would be called "retirement age."

Faced with a unique situation, the trustees were quite generous to their retiring Professor of Astronomy. They continued Mitchell's salary through the end of the spring term, offered her continued residence on the campus, as well as an annuity. She chose to turn down both the annuity and residence; but she did accept the title of professor emeritus.

> *President's Office*
> *January 11, 1888*
> *Professor Maria Mitchell,*
>
> *At a meeting of the Executive Committee of the Board of Trustees of Vassar College held this day, I was authorized to transmit to you the following minute, which was adopted without dissent.*
>
> *"Whereas Professor Maria Mitchell has deemed that her declining health and a half century of service in the cause of Science—nearly twenty five years of which have been spent in this College, justly entitle her to offer her resignation, therefore*
>
> *Resolved, that the Committee fully recognize Professor Mitchell's eminent services to this College and her faithful adherence to its interests, and it is with extreme regret that we feel that the College must be deprived of her teaching.*
>
> *And further, Resolved,—That this Committee lay her resignation on the table for action of the whole Board of Trustees at the next June meeting, and that Professor Mitchell has leave of absence henceforward and that she be entitled to draw her usual salary up to the time of said meeting of the Board."*
>
> *I count it a privilege to be permitted to communicate this action to you, and beg leave to assure you that it was accompanied by the heartiest expressions of appreciation of your labors and by the most cordial good wishes for your well being.*
>
> *I am, dear Madam, with great respect, yours faithfully,*
> *James M. Taylor[12]*

Lynn January 15, 1888.

President Taylor,

Your official letter of Jan. 11th has just reached me. I am much pleased with your account of the action of the Executive Committee of Vassar College, and am gratified at your mention of the unanimity which prevailed.

Very sincerely, I am your friend and that of the College,

Maria Mitchell[13]

[Postmarked January 15, 1888, Lynn, Mass.]

Robert Taylor, Esq.[14]

Dear Sir,

Thanks for your note. Thanks to you for remembering your pledge.

I had hoped to reach June but the fatigue of the winter journey showed me that my strength was waning. I am at once recuperating, but shrink yet from the open skies. And I am feeling as I knew I must, the breaking of the Vassar ties. The college will start off with new vigor and will live and grow in its long centuries and continue to bless the world....[15]

Confidential. Jan. 17, 1888.

President Taylor.

A letter from Mr. Swan of Jan. 15th encloses one from you of Jan. 12th. From this I learn that there has been some talk of an "Emeritus" for me, and an "annuity."

I was pleased with the vote of salary through the remaining part of the year—I am pleased with the prospect of a new title in my old age—but when it comes to an annuity, I shall say "Don't!" My life has been one of careful economy, and with continued care I can live respectably and comfortably and perhaps do some work yet, in science....

Maria Mitchell[16]

At the end of January, Mitchell tabulated her financial position in her diary. She had saved carefully over the years and had become financially independent.

310

Maria Mitchell

When her will was probated after her death, the estate was valued at slightly over $22,000, which would be equivalent to about half a million dollars in the year 2001.

Jan 30 1888
$5236 AMM [Anne M. Macy]
3760 Owen [Dame]
2400 Mitchell
2350 Bonds
2880 Po[ughkeepsie] S. Bank
1000 NY S. Bank
1000 Suffolk
1150 5 Cent Bank
240 PMK
200 Notes
18554
2000 House
1000 Vassar till June [her Vassar salary]
309 Salem bank.

Throughout the spring, Mitchell's condition seemed little changed. Resting and making plans for the future, she arranged to have a small observatory constructed to set up her telescope.

Occasionally, the retired professor went out to visit nearby schools. She made plans to attend meetings of the suffrage association, and voiced her hope to return to Vassar at some time. In letters, she reported how homesick she was for Vassar.

In the little correspondence we have from this phase of her life, one can sense that Mitchell is not her old self; her mental and physical health is deteriorating. Mitchell's younger sister evaluated her condition in this letter to Mary Whitney.

> *March 21, 1888.*
> *My Dear Miss Whitney,*
> *Your letter, received yesterday, shall have a reply at once...I spent Saturday and Sunday in Lynn. M.M. seemed very bright and though with little strength yet enough to get out every day. William Kendall [Mitchell's nephew, an architect] has made her a pretty plan for a plain observatory, which business rather absorbs her mind we hope, making her forget her body, will have a good effect and prolong her life many years.*

I cannot say that she takes an interest in her surroundings yet is not depressed as much as she was. Her life is very tame for a well and active woman but, as she has relinquished both of those qualities she settles down content. She has never ceased to rejoice that she has left Vassar.

The grasshopper had long been a burden. I feel almost condemned in her presence my nature is so vivacious, but it is very uncertain how many of her younger brothers and sisters will go before her. Her characteristics are intensified except those which require mental exertion....

Anne Mitchell Macy[17]

March 22, 1888. Kate and I have been visiting the High School. At first we heard a class in Geometry, very well conducted, very well treated, only ordinary in its work....The teacher said "Miss Dame and Courteney were the best girls." I found he did not know who I was, a boy who was very handsome seemed to be a dolt.[18]

My "sweet Fanny Wood"[19]

As somebody said before me! How good of you to write to me twice, when I ran off so sensationally! The fact is, I couldn't come back to face it all!

Do come and spend a few days with me, in Spring or in Summer? I have two rooms if you call a hall room a room and not a closet the chief merit of which is they are six doors from Kate and her group. (Kate would so like to talk with you, of the experiences [of] the 15 year old girl.*)

I am at present as much worn with setting up my room and a half as I would be with college work. I want for the Spring days to set up my own little observatory, and play work perhaps a little longer. That is, I shall try to do some little work! I was only tired! But oh, so tired! I meant, anyway to leave in June, and I wanted to reach June...

I sleep so well now! My only fear, for the college, is the overwork of the Teachers! Mrs. Kendall, who is on the School Com. fears the same — the overwork of student and Teachers.

It's getting dark and I save my eyes — do write often. It was touching to me that Mrs. Holbrook wrote to me!

MM.   *The Methodists have got hold of her.[20]

312 *Maria Mitchell*

[Spring 1888]

My dear Mary [Raymond],

...My Obs[ervatory] is done, but the Telescope is not yet out of Clark's hands. I have kept up steady occupation, but am mostly out of doors, therefore, well.

I think I am in better health than if I had stayed at V. C. The only opportunities to Lecture which I have had, have no money temptation, there is too little pay. I should take a stupid boy, if one was round.

I am reading Todhunter and at last do it readily, but I made many mistakes, calling x for y and such like mistakes.

Also, I am studying Greek! It will take 30 years, but I may find chances for it, in the other world. Maria Dame is my Teacher. So far I know the whole alphabet! I have known 7 letters nearly as long as I have known a b c. Also, I have read "Little Lord Fauntleroy" and the "Daily Advertiser" and occasionally some scrap about John Guy Vassar.

I mean to go to Boston to the Suffrage Meetings this week if the waters are assuaged. The country is beautiful. I have many calls and many letters. Mrs. Shaw has written to ask about a Teacher and the Vassar girls write for recommendations.

Mrs. Dame is going to New York to see Lydia off—I am very glad for Miss Palmer—and also, for Miss Goodwin. I set plants, to day, at the Obs.

MM.[21]

May 29 [1888]

Lynn

My dear Mr. Lossing,

As the summer comes I think of Vassar and of your beautiful home and lovely family....

I have put up my small observatory and hope to work enough to keep my health, which is decidedly better than it was at Vassar. A note from Miss Whitney speaks in a lonesome way of Mr. Gibson but says dear Miss Holbrook is well. I hear also that Miss Goodwin goes abroad this summer. Indeed the summer plans of Vassar make me lonesome as I expect to remain where I am, with brothers and sisters around me.

[1888]

My dear Mary,

I hasten to assure you that I have read "Robert!" I have outgrown my old love of novels — 600 mortal pages are too much! I wonder if your mother could enjoy it! First the clothes and the skin are worthy of "Alonso and Melissa" the first novel I ever read! And why need we have not only Catharine but all the loves of her sisters and of Robert's friends!

I wouldn't read The Secret of Dean somebody — or two others that appeared at the same time! And yet Cabot's Life of Emerson was charming to me.... [22]

On June 12, 1888 the trustees officially accepted Mitchell's resignation. The tone of the resolution reveals the high regard the trustees now felt for the college's most illustrious professor.

Resolved: That it is with profound regret that the Board of Trustees of Vassar College feels constrained to accept the proffered resignation of the Chair of Astronomy in this Institution from Prof. Maria Mitchell, Philosophical Doctor, Litterarum Doctor, which she has filled with so much ability, dignity and honor to herself and profit to this Institution for almost twenty three years, by her professional ability the influence of her name abroad and her example among the students of the College as a noble model of true womanhood: and we desire to testify our sense of our obligations to her as a faithful and able instructor our personal regard and our earnest wish to perpetuate her connection with the College and its interests.

We therefore invite her to accept from the Board the position of Emeritus Professor of Astronomy in Vassar College, and the affectionate salutations of the members of this Board and with the assurance of their highest esteem and warmest friendship.

On motion of Trustee Swan it is, Resolved: that the action of the Executive Committee in continuing the salary of Prof. Mitchell to this date is hereby approved.

On motion of Trustee Swan it is, Resolved: that Professor Mitchell be hereby offered a residence in this College, and the use of the Observatory, whenever it may suit her convenience to occupy either, and that the Secretary transmit to her a copy of this resolution. [23]

Maria Mitchell

Thursday [June 1888]

President Taylor,

Your note is just received. Mr. Lossing and Fanny Swan had preceded you. The plan suits me exactly. I could not, according to my own ideas, have consented to receive money—honors I can take and the unanimity is very gratifying.

I think the fact that I hold the title may give me a chance to do some good to the College. I have rec'd unasked $90 this year which has been forwarded to the students (Miss Day, Treasurer).

Excuse my writing—it is one of the dark days.

Maria Mitchell[24]

Boston, Aug. 6, 1888

Dear Miss Mitchell,

... Your 70th birthday and mine are here. Let us congratulate each other and rejoice that we have had long and useful lives.

Always truly yours,

Lucy Stone[25]

Aug. 9, 1888. My birthday letters were from E. O. Abbott, Lucy Stone, Miss Storer, Elisa Worley, Miss Helen Storke, Dr. Avery, Robert Taylor, a card from Phebe's friend, a gentleman 77 years old.

I think I am weaned from Vassar and have entered on a little studying. Today Katy shakes off her invalid visitor and I hope will feel easier. Wm. Dame goes to his new house.

Aug. 10, 1888. I received papers from Dr. Avery—descriptions of Lick Observatory. The immense telescope can do some one thing well, but one only at a time, for instruction they are absurd. Every school should have a telescope—a small one—but the great dictionary getting up by the New York company would be as unsuitable for a school.

Aug. 11, 1888. I forgot entirely to look for meteors last night but I was in the Observatory until 8 1/2 and I looked out at 1 a.m. of the 11th and at 2 a.m. The Dames report a good many.[26]

Aug. 15, 1888. I read in the Century "A Browning Courtship." Excellent! The author is named "White."

Melrose, Aug. 20, 1888.

Dear Friend [Maria],

I hope the summer has been kind to you, and that you have had rest, and gained strength, during the not-very warm, bright days. I have intended to hunt you up, if you were in Lynn, every time we have taken a drive to Ocean Ave., or Nahant, all through the summer. But the grand-children, one or more always keep us company, in our drives, a vociferous and imperious little brood, and we always go elsewhere than was our intention, when they are at the helm.

I really hope, most earnestly, and affectionately, that you are rested, and well.

I am making up our "Afternoon Lecture course for Women," which I have run in Melrose, to the great enjoyment of about two hundred or more women, for the last six years. Women generally do the lecturing. I enclose the circular, giving information concerning our last course. I write now to inquire if you will not give one of the lectures in this next course, beginning Oct. 11....

I am allowed as compensation for the lecturer, only $15 and expenses. But if you can lecture for us, the money shall be paid you that you demand for the service. You can leave Boston at 2:30 p.m., and return at 5 p.m. Only I should hope you would stay to tea with me, and if possible stay the night, returning in the morning. That would be easier.

M. A. Livermore[27]

August 23, [1888]

My dear Mrs. Livermore,

I am better and apparently steadily improving. But I am pleased to be <u>asked</u> to lecture and shall <u>not</u> be pleased to accept your invitation.

Just as the Lick Observatory goes up, mine, the smallest in the world, peeps up, above the grass and among the morning glories — It is really intended as a health lift.

I am very glad to see your list of names. I ran a course of a similar kind once in Po'keepsie — I had 5 Lectures — and 5 good Lecturers and the whole cost was as small as is my observatory — I paid all the bills and no one complained — the sum total was $12! There wasn't a man asked to speak!

Maria Mitchell

But a better way is co-education.
Yours with love,
Maria Mitchell[28]

The last sentence of this letter is a revelation. After teaching at Vassar for twenty-two years, and becoming a leader in the women's education movement, Mitchell was stating a preference for coeducation—perhaps thinking that coeducation would indicate equality between the sexes. Eighty years later, Vassar did become coeducational, the first of the women's colleges to do so.

> Lynn, Aug. 29, 1888
> [Postcard addressed to brother-in-law Matthew Barney]
> On the day I was 70 [August 1] I went to a photographer and told him to make me young and handsome. I find that no one likes them, so I have ordered 3 only, one for Anne, one for Henry and one for you.
> Wiser, the photographer, may never do them, but if he does one shall be sent to you each.
> Also Mitchell will send a basket of peaches to Anne. Ask for some!
> M. M.[29]

President Taylor wrote a particularly kind letter to Mitchell during the fall term in 1888.

> *Vassar College Oct. 15, 1888*
> *My dear Miss Mitchell,*
> *My spirit is moved to send you a line of greeting tonight. Why? Not because I have <u>happened</u> to think of you, for we all often talk of you, and are not likely to forget our ownership in you.*
> *But it occurred to me at the close of this busy, driving, distracted day, that you were not so unlike the rest of us, great as you are, but that you would be pleased to be <u>told</u> <u>what</u> <u>you</u> <u>of</u> <u>course</u> <u>ought</u> <u>to</u> <u>know</u> <u>without</u> <u>telling</u>, that our hearts are with you and that though we keep somewhat still, so busy are we, that we do not let you drop out of the life here of which you were so long the central figure. Do not fear that we forget you. You have been too much to us for that.*

Courtesy of Special Collections, Vassar College Libraries

THE RETIRED MARIA MITCHELL OUTSIDE HER NEW OBSERVATORY. When Mitchell moved to Lynn, Massachusetts in 1888, she initiated the construction of a small observatory behind her sister Kate's house—hoping that she could continue her astronomical research.

Shortly after leaving Vassar, Mitchell received a gratifying letter from President Taylor in which he wrote, "...you may be sure that we shall be glad to do all we can to honor one whose faithful service, and whose honesty of heart and life, have been among the chief inspirations of Vassar College throughout its history. Of public reputation you have doubtless had enough, but I am sure you cannot have too much of the affection and esteem which we feel towards you who have had the privilege of working with you."

You will not forget that the doors here are wide open for you. Can't you visit us this year? It would give us great pleasure to have you. But I only meant to write a word of greeting, and will say no more.

J. M. Taylor

To Maria Mitchell, LL.D.[30]

Oct. 18 [1888]

President Taylor,

Some good impulse moved you to write to me! I have had almost nothing from the tired officers, since the college opened, and your letter was a godsend! I have been Vassar home-sick more than I expected altho' I knew it must come! I have improved in my general health and mean at some time to come and see you all. But not until I am over the homesickness!

I have put up my little observatory and send you a copy today. I hesitated about sending a photograph, for my collection is more than 2000 of card photographs and yours must have become a burden!

When I first came home I did a very meritorious thing. I told my legal heirs to remember to send you my picture of Humboldt which Bishop Hurst, I think, told us about, when I could no longer enjoy it.

And when a scrap of two lines (modest me!) appears in the *Woman's Journal* (about Vassar), remember that I know the Editor and that I am the highly distinguished author of those two lines!

Good health and good times to you all; the world is better while Vassar lives, because it is in it.

Love to all especially — (here I pause to decide which especially, certainly to dear little May to bright little Morgan and to brave Hunt — and to Mrs. Taylor — to the whole catalogue!)

M. M.[31]

[1888]

This was written and lying on my table, when yours came. It is for <u>you</u> only. The fact is, I am well every morning; I am ill at 3 P.M.

My dear Miss Wood,

You are very good <u>not</u> to notice me! My friends have been very considerate (<u>absent</u> ones), <u>present</u> friends declare that I am a perfect bore, as I talk of myself only.

There's not a question about my being much better than when I left the College. I have no fever that I know of. I have a steady and large appetite.

My weak point is that I do not sleep well. Having nothing to do I do not get tired and am not sleepy. I sleep not more than 6 to 8 hours in 24 and I take it at uncomfortable times—sometimes I get only 4.

I still hope to come back—but you may be sure that I can never work as I have worked and I look forward to "contract my firmament to the compass of a tent" (See Emerson for what Lois Anne calls "cheap classics") at no distant day, and rejoice that I can. I shall not come back until I feel sure that it is safe. If I am to develop nervous weaknesses, Vassar is the last place where I should be. My Doctor declares that I am not "sleepless" but that I want to sleep over much.

My mind has rested, since I sent Mary Whitney off. She is the most powerful rival that I could put in my place and I can only say "Good luck to her! May she surpass her Teacher and that by many times."

But I leave the future and try to live only one day at a time.

MM.[32]

[1888]

My dear Mrs. Raymond,

I thank you very much for your letter. I feel as Miss Morse says she did when I left—as if I had met a bereavement. I left because I tho't it was time and I have rejoiced at it every moment, but as I knew I should, I feel the dropping down of occupation. I am not really ill, but feeble and listless. I walk a good deal and have put up my small observatory, as I did nearly 30 years ago. I shall try to do some work. I seem to lack strength. I am writing up (for my younger sisters) our early family history[33] before the sicknesses and losses came, petty anecdotes of the many children.

All my sisters have been near me all winter. My obs. is in Mr. Dame's back yard. It is nearly done, and if I can make a few good observations it is all that I aim at.

My brothers are in Washington and in Chicago—none of them wholly well. I look for Henry and family today—they have done being young—the youngest is near sixty and Kate is 55.

Kate's oldest girl goes to Europe for the 3d time this summer and she is not thirty....There are three Dame girls and a Kendall boy, old enough to be married, but yet unengaged—all at good work but that is all — all good people and that is enough....Maria Dame came home for a year and has enjoyed it exceedingly. The 4th Dame expects to enter a college this autumn. The one boy is 8 years old.

You speak of failing memory. I was struck by the fact that you had improved in your penmanship! There was no illegible word!...

If you are in Boston this Summer, pray let me know. I can travel as far as Boston!

M. M.[34]

Jan. 1 [1889][35]

My dear Miss Morse,

It is long that I have heard nothing from you or the Raymonds. If you are well enough to write, do tell me where everybody is. Write a long gossiping letter — Tell me of every Raymond and of Mrs. Conant and great and small

How sad that Mrs. Merrick's life was so short[36] and I have felt Cora Harrisons ['76] loss very much — When I came to Lynn, I came to my own but I have felt the loss of all Vassar very much.

M. M.[37]

There are no diary entries or letters between this January 1 letter and Maria's death almost seven months later on June 28. We have few details about the deterioration in her health. Her death certificate cites "Brain Disease" as the cause. Only a few references to her health can be found and these do not shed much light on her illness.

Phebe Mitchell Kendall recalls that "a serious fall during her illness in Lynn, stopped forever her daily walks."[38] In a memorial minute published in the Vassar student newspaper, Mary Whitney said, "From the time of her withdrawal from the active duties of her department in January, 1888, her strength had gradually but steadily failed, and her death was preceded by two months of complete prostration."

Some years after the death of Mitchell, her sister Kate wrote to Mary Whitney. In the letter, Kate makes a brief, doleful allusion to Mitchell's final year:

> The Memoir of M. M. is in the hands of the publishers[39] but will not be ready for Christmas. Mary has enjoyed working on it with Mrs. Kendall the last two months. If I could only wipe out from my memory the last year of her life, I could enjoy it more....[40]

Immediately after Mitchell's death, members of the family wrote to President James Monroe Taylor to have him officiate at the funeral. Dr. Taylor was summering on Nantucket, where Maria's funeral was to be held.

> *June 28, 1889*
>
> *My Dear Dr. Taylor,*
>
> *It is the united desire of our family that you be present at the funeral ceremonies of our dear sister and officiate as friend and minister—Do not deny us in this, as I know it would be the wish of her heart.— We will inform you of the hour later, the day Sunday, and will provide means for your getting in. Please to answer at once if possible to.*
>
> *Anne Mitchell Macy*[41]

Dr. Taylor at once telegraphed the Macys: "Telegram complete surprise. Too late if funeral is in Lynn but otherwise will be there. Await letter." In a return telegram on June 29, Anne Mitchell Macy replied immediately: "Services at half past three o'clock, Sunday afternoon. Shall we send out a carriage or can you get one at Sconset [a small village on the island of Nantucket]."

Shortly after the funeral, Anne wrote him a heartfelt letter of appreciation.

> *Dear Dr. Taylor,*
>
> *Will you please send your bill for carriages and any other expense incumbered upon getting to town Sunday June 30th to Mrs. Alfred Macy, Nantucket, Mass.*
>
> *I cannot let the above business notice go to you without reiterating what we have said to you one and all, viz: the comfort that you gave us on the day of my sister's funeral will last always. If you had known her from her youth you could not have done greater justice.*
>
> *Do you remember that Miss Mitchell promised you the Humboldt picture! She often alluded to the fact during her illness and it is reserved for you. When we get to it, if before you leave for Vassar, shall it be sent to Nantucket or await the opening of the College? Hoping to see some of your household before you all take leave of the Island, I am,*
>
> *Anne Mitchell Macy*[42]

Maria Mitchell

123 Inman St.
Cambridgeport; Mass
Oct. 28, 1889.
Rev. J. M. Taylor, D. D.

Enclosed please find check for one thousand dollars ($1000) being the amount of the Legacy left to Vassar College by the Will of the late Maria Mitchell.

I don't know how much is proper to write in a business note, but I feel like saying that it is pleasant to us all to know that our sister will still be doing something to help along some Vassar girl. She rated Vassar girls very highly. I find mention in her papers of their high character and their conscientious work, and I am sure that her own ideal of a girl was very high.

I also want to take this occasion to thank you for the appreciative words spoken on the occasion of our sister's funeral which touched us all exceedingly. She held you in high esteem and it was pleasant to know that although you had never seen her at her very best you had still been able to see the very foundations of her character.

If you and Mrs. Taylor should ever be in Boston or vicinity I hope you will give us the opportunity to see us at our house.

With kind regards to Mrs. Taylor, in which Mr. Kendall joins, I am,

Phebe M. Kendall.[43]

In the fall, Taylor wrote out the words he had used at Maria Mitchell's funeral. His reflections reveal how well he knew his Vassar colleague—and how strong the friendship between them must have been.

At the request of members of the family of Maria Mitchell I write out the substance of what was said by me at the funeral service in Nantucket. I do so on the basis of notes I preserved and with the assistance of a report of a Memorial Service in the Chapel of Vassar College, held in November, at which the same address was substantially given. The address was not written out in full, and was given without notes, so that the writer can only vouch for the general accuracy of this report.

J. M. Taylor
Sept. 1890.

MARIA MITCHELL

IF THIS WERE THE FITTING OCCASION *to speak at length of the services Maria Mitchell has rendered to Science, of the distinguished merit she has gained and the honors she has worn, there are others who might speak more intelligently than I. And indeed, there are others of her associates and friends who have known her longer and who could bring a worthier tribute here, but none who could speak out of friendlier feeling concerning the woman, the teacher and the friend.*

You knew the woman; many of you knew her from her youth. It has amused us at times to hear her tell how in Nantucket they called her Maria whom we, and the world, knew as a renowned Professor of Astronomy. You knew the strong traits of character which distinguished her, her force and independence. All these were as marked in her later years, an independence, absolutely fearless, a love of truth whatever it might bring, the forceful traits of character which everywhere gained recognition and ranked her as a queen.

But this was only one side of her character. I have sometimes heard this independence dwelt upon as if it were the single remarkable trait she possessed and as if the striking speeches and acts to which it sometimes led, were alone characteristic of her. But no one who really knew Maria Mitchell dwelt most on these. There were great deeps of tenderness and love in the strong nature, a kindliness, a thoughtfulness of others, that beautified her strength and gave balance to her independence. One who has known her kindness to little children, who has watched her little evidences of thoughtful care for her associates and friends, who has seen her put aside her own long cherished nights that she might make the way of a new and untried officer easier, cannot forget the tenderer side of her character. She was a woman of remarkable strength, but she was a woman withal, with the characteristics most attractive in her kind.

If I were to select for comment the one most striking trait of her character, I should name her <u>genuineness</u>. There was no false note in Maria Mitchell's thinking or utterance. Doubt she might and she might linger in doubt, but false she could not be. Hers was a transparent character and her genuineness influenced her every word and deed. It was the keynote of her independence, it was the deep source of her strength,

Maria Mitchell

BORN AUG. 1.1818.
DIED JUNE 28. 1889

BURIAL SITE. Maria Mitchell died on June 28, 1889 and was buried in the Prospect Hill Cemetery on Nantucket Island. At her funeral, Vassar's President James Monroe Taylor said, "She has been an impressive figure in our time, and one whose influence lives." In the photograph above, the Loines Observatory of the Nantucket Maria Mitchell Association is visible behind Maria's grave. *Below:* Signatures of Mitchell family members as they appear on Maria Mitchell's probated will.

The undersigned, being all *of the* parties interested, having examined the foregoing account, request that the same may be allowed without further notice.

William M. Barney
Anne M. Macy.
Freda M. Kendall.
Henry Mitchell
Wm. F. Mitchell

Clifford Mitchell Administrator
of the estate of Francis M. Mitchell.
Eliza K. Dame.

COMMONWEALTH OF MASSACHUSETTS.

ESSEX, ss. *At a Probate Court held at* *Salem,* *in said county,*
on the *third* *Monday of* *October* *A. D. 18 .*

and <u>truth</u> must be <u>strong</u>, since God is truth. It was this perfect genuineness which gave her the strong hold she had on the admiration and affection of her students, it was this in her which attracted most we who loved her best. There were no concealments, what she said she meant, and what she thought she said. This princely trait of character she possessed in rare degree.

This genuineness explains also a marked feature of her religious experience. She would not use the language of faith often because it did not seem to her that she had clearly grasped the truths which came through faith.

It would be a grave error to infer from this that she was not a <u>religious</u> woman in a true sense. She was always a seeker for <u>truth</u>. She desired no semblance of the real thing: earnestly, honestly, she sought to fathom the mysteries of being and of destiny that press in on all, but she would not allow herself to say one word beyond what she felt she really <u>knew</u>.

I sometimes thought she did not give utterance to the hopes of her heart for fear she could not ground them entirely as facts. But she hungered for truth, this strong, brave woman was no trifler, she would <u>know</u> if she might, in any case she would <u>seek</u>; she fulfilled the exhortation of her friend Dr. Channing, "Worship God with what He most delights in, with aspiration for spiritual light and life."

Doubt, however, does not connote content, and hers was not a happy groping, sincere as the seeking was. But in later years I think she emphasized more the <u>hope</u> in her which would not, could not, die.

God's prophecy in us is of an eternal life, and in these latter months the shadow grew less, harbinger of a perfect light. "We shall know even also as we are known,"[44] surely that is true for every honest soul who yet seeks for the Eternal Light and Truth.

But it would be vain for me to try to tell just what it was in Miss Mitchell that attracted us who loved her. It was this combination of great strength and independency, of deep affection and tenderness breathed through and through with the sentiment of a perfectly genuine life, which has made for us one of the pilgrim shrines of life the study in the Observatory of Vassar College where we have known her <u>at home</u>, surrounded by the evidences of her honorable professional career. She has been an impressive figure in our time, and one whose influence lives.

Maria Mitchell

This leads me to say a few words of her work as a teacher. Her life became a strong influence in the lives of her devoted students. It was not that she impressed on them any peculiar views of hers; I have seen small evidence of that. But she wrought into their souls something of her own genuineness, her hatred of all shams—in college, in social life, her love of truth, her honest search after it. Many are those who will carry her impress as long as they live, who gained from her a new inspiration and who look back to that beautiful vine-covered Observatory as a birthplace of a new life in their souls.

I feel the inadequacy of all I can say, indeed, as I think of them, of the troops of young women now grown to matronly dignity, teachers, wives, mothers, women of society, who would bid me say more, while she in her simplicity of life and taste would have me say far less.

She closed her labors at Vassar a year and a half ago, but her connection with the college ceased only with her death. Only about a fortnight before her death I read to the Trustees of the College her name among those of the Faculty for the year to come, as Professor Emeritus of Astronomy.

I have spoken as a friend of the traits of Maria Mitchell's character which have most impressed me in the three years of my close personal acquaintance with her. But I cannot forget, as I close, that I am the spokesman of others, of Trustees, and Faculty and students of the College she served as faithfully and cherished as lovingly.

A cloud of witnesses gathers about me, a great company of those who have known and loved her and have felt the power of her character and life. From them all I bring to you, today, their sympathies and that which is always precious in such hours as these, their witness to the usefulness of the life of your own loved one, and to the love which they gave to her with you.[45]

Epilogue

$\mathcal{T}$HE REMARKABLE FRUITS of Maria Mitchell's pioneering work in the nineteenth century are clearly in evidence today. Her prominent role in helping break down the barriers for women in science has contributed to the slow but steady increase in the number of women engaged in scientific pursuits over the past century.[1]

At the time of her death in 1889, there were only a handful of women astronomers. By the turn of the century many women were employed in doing astronomical computations at the Harvard College Observatory. But on college campuses across the nation, the number of women employed as faculty members remained small.

Only with the renewed growth of the women's movement in the latter part of the twentieth century did women achieve their rightful place in the astronomical world. At the beginning of the twenty-first century, fully twenty-five percent of the members of the American Astronomical Society are women, filling a wide variety of roles— professors in educational institutions, directors of observatories, editors of journals, astronauts, and directors of astronomical programs. As Mitchell herself had demonstrated, women would contribute immeasurably to the field of astronomy, if only given the opportunity.

> Does anyone suppose that any woman in all the ages has
> had a fair chance to show what she could do in science?...
> The laws of nature are not discovered by accidents;
> theories do not come by chance, even to the greatest minds;
> they are not born of the hurry and worry of daily toil;
> they are diligently sought, they are patiently waited for,
> they are received with cautious reserve, they are accepted
> with reverence and awe. And until able women have
> given their lives to investigation, it is idle to discuss
> the question of their capacity for original work.
>
> – *Maria Mitchell, 1818-1889*

Maria Mitchell

Courtesy of Thurston Meloy

A LASTING LEGACY. The notable life of Maria Mitchell continues to be honored and celebrated in the twenty-first century, most especially on Nantucket Island and at Vassar College.

The birthplace of Maria Mitchell *(opposite page, top)* is shown as it appears today at One Vestal Street on Nantucket. Mitchell was born in a small room at the rear of the first floor of the large building on the right. Adjacent to the home, now maintained as a memorial by the Nantucket Maria Mitchell Association, are the Maria Mitchell Observatory and the Natural Science Museum.

The original Vassar Observatory *(opposite page, bottom)*, is now a National Historic Landmark. Maria Mitchell lived in the room opening off the balcony to the right; her father resided in the opposite wing. The large dome contained a 12-inch telescope. The transit instrument was in a wing extending from the rear of the building. At Maria Mitchell's funeral, President Taylor called her study in the Observatory "one of the pilgrim shrines of life ... where we have known her at home, surrounded by the evidences of her honorable professional career."

Today, the mission of Vassar's original Observatory is carried on in the Class of 1951 Observatory *(above)*. A modern facility completed in 1997, the new Observatory houses a 32-inch and a 20-inch telescope, both equipped with CCD cameras. In keeping with the legacy of Maria Mitchell, these facilities enable today's students to learn and apply the most modern astronomical techniques.

ACKNOWLEDGEMENTS

*A*N AUTHOR UNDERTAKING A PROJECT such as this owes a great deal to the many persons who offer assistance along the way. On Nantucket I received encouragement from Jane Merrill and Robert K. Noyes, past presidents of the Maria Mitchell Association, both of whom are regrettably now deceased. The librarians for the Association, Dr. Jane Stroup and Tanya Bresinsky, aided my search through Mitchell's papers; and Executive Director Kathryn K. Pochman has always been very helpful throughout the project.

At Vassar College, President Frances Fergusson provided me strong support, and Professor of History Dr. Benjamin Kohl urged the completion of this project, kindly translating from Italian the letter Mitchell received from Cardinal Antonelli granting her permission to visit the Vatican Observatory. Nancy MacKechnie, long-time Curator of Rare Books and Manuscripts at Vassar, assisted in the variety of ways that excellent librarians do.

Vassar historian Dr. Elizabeth Daniels has always been encouraging, offering helpful insights along the way. Dr. Debra M. Elmegreen provided an excellent foreword which skillfully introduces the book.

I have had financial support from the Office of the Dean of the College at Vassar, through a grant from the Mary Ridder Hartmann Fund arranged by Dean Nancy Dye and Assistant Dean Judith Hanna.

Ms. Cindy Buck edited an early version of this extensive work. In the final preparation of the book, Sally Guernsey and Irene Decker provided timely and invaluable assistance. My publisher and editor, Joseph (Trip) Sinnott reviewed the final manuscript in great detail, helped refine difficult passages, and added insightful comments.

Finally, I wish to thank my wife, Wilma, who read the entire manuscript with a skilled English teacher's eye. In addition, she accompanied me on numerous trips to archives and graciously accepted my long hours in front of a computer screen.

Of course, any mistakes present in this book are my responsibility alone.

SOURCES and ENDNOTES

*T*HERE ARE TWO MAIN SOURCES of archival material on Maria Mitchell: one on Nantucket and the other at Vassar College. On Nantucket, the Maria Mitchell Association maintains a library which holds the material that Mitchell herself collected. There are about seventy notebooks containing letters, diaries, speeches and classroom lectures as well as visiting cards, articles on astronomy, and other items that Mitchell had saved. This material was bequeathed to her sister Phebe and after Phebe's death in 1907 the papers were brought to the newly formed Association. Mitchell also willed her scientific library to her brother Henry and in 1903 he gave these books to the Association. This collection is the largest source of Maria Mitchell material anywhere. The American Philosophical Society has produced a microfilm edition of most of this material.

Contained in the Vassar College Special Collections are letters which Mitchell wrote to people within the college community. Here we find her annual reports, her letters demanding equality in salary, her concerns about the telescope and anything else connected with the college. Also among these Vassar archives are numerous letters she wrote to persons at the college with whom she was good friends.

There are other Maria Mitchell letters to be found in archival collections in many libraries. She was a prolific letter writer and corresponded with many important persons. Besides the two aforementioned sources, I am indebted to the following organizations for permission to quote from material in their collections: Harvard University Archives; the Houghton Library, Harvard University; Library of the Boston Athenaeum; the Caroline Dall papers of the Massachusetts Historical Society; the Smithsonian Institution Archives; Nantucket Historical

Association; Arthur and Elizabeth Schlesinger Library of the History of Women in America, Radcliffe Institute of Harvard University; the Rare and Manuscript Collections of Cornell University Archives; and the American Philosophical Society.

Few published books cite archival material directly. *Maria Mitchell: Life, Letters, and Journals,* compiled by Mitchell's sister, Phebe Mitchell Kendall, was published in 1896. It contains many reminiscences by Phebe about her famous sister and their life on Nantucket. She also gives extensive quotes from diaries that can still be seen at the Maria Mitchell Association, and a few diary entries whose originals can no longer be found. *Sweeper in the Sky* by Helen Wright has been the standard biography of Mitchell for almost sixty years but regrettably has some errors in dates and diary quotations.

Other books which give important information about the early days of Vassar College and Maria Mitchell are: Elizabeth Haight, *The Autobiography and Letters of Matthew Vassar,* 1916; Edward R. Linner, *Vassar: The Remarkable Growth of a Man and His College,* Elizabeth A. Daniels, ed., 1984, and Benson J. Lossing, *Vassar College and its Founder,* 1867. The early history of Nantucket is well documented in *The History of Nantucket* by Alexander Starbuck. For identification of comets I have used: *Comets, A Descriptive Catalog* by Gary W. Kronk, 1984.

NOTES

HUA — Harvard University Archives.

MHA — Massachusetts Historical Society.

MMA — Maria Mitchell Association. Nantucket, Massachusetts.

MMLL — Kendall, P.M., *Maria Mitchell: Life, Letters, and Journals.*

MMP — Maria Mitchell Papers. Maria Mitchell Association, Nantucket, Massachusetts. These papers are preserved in numbered volumes which are used as references.

NHA — Nantucket Historical Association, Nantucket, Massachusetts.

VCA — Vassar College Archives, Poughkeepsie, New York.

VCT — Minutes of the Vassar College Trustees.

VMisc — *Vassar Miscellany.* A student newspaper.

CHAPTER 1: EARLY YEARS ON NANTUCKET *(Pages 9–22)*

1. The ten Mitchell children were Andrew (b. 1814), Sally (1816), Maria (1818), Anne (1820), Francis Macy (1823), William Forster (1825), Phebe (1828), Henry (1830), Eliza (Henry's twin sister who died as a young child), and Eliza Katherine (Kate, 1833). *See also: Mitchell Family genealogy, p. ix.*

2. Alexander Starbuck, *The History of Nantucket*. (Boston: C. E. Goodspeed & Co., 1924).

3. William Mitchell, "Autobiography" (1868), vol. 1, MMP. This article is also available in *Historic Nantucket* (The Nantucket Historical Association: January 1983) 20.

4. Julia Ward Howe, "Maria Mitchell," *Our Famous Women* (Hartford: A. D. Worthington, 1884), 441.

5. Phebe Mitchell Kendall, *Maria Mitchell: Life, Letters, and Journals*. [MMLL] (Boston: Lee and Shepard, 1896), 9.

6. Henry Mitchell, "Biographical Notice of Maria Mitchell," *Proceedings of the American Academy of Arts and Sciences,* 25 (1890): 331.

7. Howe, "Maria Mitchell," 444.

8. William Mitchell, "Autobiography."

9. Charles James Folger (1818-84) was born on Nantucket just three months before Maria Mitchell. He was appointed secretary of the treasury by President Chester Arthur in 1881.

10. Howe, "Maria Mitchell," 441.

11. Kendall, MMLL, 7.

12. The complete set of verses is found in vol. 16 of MMP.

13. Maria Mitchell deeded her scientific library to her brother, Henry. Later Henry gave her books to the Nantucket Maria Mitchell Association. These books, with their annotations in Mitchell's hand, can still be seen in the library of the Association.

14. Nathaniel Bowditch, *The New American Practical Navigator; being an epitome of navigation.* (Salem: E. M. Blunt, 1802).

15. Henry Mitchell, "Biographical Notice," 333.

16. Ibid, 331.

17. Vol. 11 of MMP. A copy of this page can be found in Henry Mitchell, "Biographical Notice."

18. What Mitchell did was "count seconds." She watched the chronometer and counted out each second while her father looked through the telescope. In that way he always knew what time it was and did not have to take his eyes from the telescope while observing the eclipse. A skilled observer could record an event with an accuracy of about one-tenth of a second using this method.

19. *Nantucket Inquirer*, August 15, 1835.

20. *Nantucket Inquirer and Mirror*, vol. 55, 4, October 3, 1874. The author of the article is not identified further.

21. Howe, "Maria Mitchell," 441.

22. Polly was the only child of Henry and his second wife.

23. An orrery is a mechanical model which shows the relative position of the sun and planets.

24. A quotation from the poet Edward Young (1683-1765), *Night Thoughts*, Night IX, l. 771.

25. Anne Mitchell Macy, "An Astronomical Garret." *Wide Awake*, (May, 1888).

26. Kendall, MMLL, 1.

27. Pierre Simon, Marquis de LaPlace (1749-1827), French mathematician and astronomer, wrote the monumental *Mécanique Céleste*, one of the most important works in the history of celestial mechanics which was later translated by Nathaniel Bowditch. Karl Friedrich Gauss (1777-1855), was a German mathematician and astronomer. In *Theoria Motus Corporum Coelestium* (Theory of the Motions of Heavenly Bodies) he derived a new method for determining the orbit of a comet or asteroid.

28. Henry Mitchell, "Biographical Notice," 335.

29. Vol. 16 of MMP.

30. The youngest child, Kate, lived into her seventies. The other child referred to may have been Eliza, Henry's twin, who lived less than three years.

31. Kendall, MMLL, 16.

32. Vol. 55 of MMP.

33. *Minutes of the Nantucket Monthly Meeting of Women Friends*, August 31 and September 28, 1843. Nantucket Historical Association.

34. See pp. 322-326 of Chapter 12 for more extensive excerpts from President Taylor's funeral reflections.

35. Vol. 24 of MMP. From a lecture entitled "Endowments."

CHAPTER 2: MARIA'S COMET *(Pages 23–38)*

1. Kendall, MMLL, 19.

2. Vol. 7 of MMP. William Mitchell, diary.

3. Kendall, MMLL, 275. William Mitchell to William Cranch Bond (1790-1859), first director of Harvard College Observatory.

4. George Phillips Bond (1825-1865), son of William C. Bond and his successor as director of the Harvard College Observatory, to Maria Mitchell, October 30, 1847.

5. Vol. 2 of MMP.

6. William C. Bond, Diary. HUA V 630.4.

7. Comets had been discovered by women before, most notably by Caroline Herschel of England, who had several comet discoveries to her credit.

8. A. D. Bache to William Mitchell, October 18, 1847, vol. 2 of MMP.

9. Kendall, MMLL, 15.

10. Edward Everett (1794-1865). At this time he was President of Harvard College.

11. The rules and the correspondence appear as an appendix in MMLL. This appendix was later reprinted by the Maria Mitchell Association.

12. Heinrich C. Schumacher, (1780-1850), an astronomer who worked in Altona, was founder of the important journal *Astronomische Nachrichten*.

13 Edward Everett to William Mitchell, January 10, 1848. Vol. 18 of MMP.

14. William Mitchell to Edward Everett, January 15, 1848. Kendall, MMLL, 276.

15. Edward Everett to Heinrich Schumacher, January 15, 1848. Ibid., 277.

16. Edward Everett to William Mitchell, November 10, 1848. Vol. 18 of MMP.

17. Edward Everett to Maria Mitchell, March 29, 1849. Kendall, MMLL, 212.

18. Asa Gray (1810-1888), botanist, textbook author, and Harvard College professor.

19. *Proceedings of the American Academy of Arts and Sciences*. Vol. 2, 2.

20. William Mitchell to Asa Gray, June 30, 1848. Boston Athenaeum.

21. Charles Henry Davis (1807-1877), Superintendent of the Nautical Almanac and the Naval Observatory, to Maria Mitchell, August 10, 1849. Vol. 2 of MMP.

22. A. D. Bache to William Mitchell, August 22, 1849. Vol. 2 of MMP.

23. William Mitchell to A. D. Bache. Vol. 2 of MMP.

24. Maria Mitchell "The United States Coast Survey," *Christian Examiner*, 52 (1852): 77-96.

25. See Dorrit Hoffleit "Comets over Nantucket." In Celebration of the 75th Anniversary of the Maria Mitchell Observatory. Nantucket Maria Mitchell Association.

26. Comet 1849 II, discovered April 15, 1849 by Goujon in Paris.

27. William Mitchell diary, May 19, 1849. Vol. 7 of MMP.

28. This comet was probably Comet 1854 II (the Great Comet of 1854), which had been discovered on March 23 by Menciaux in England in the morning sky and reappeared in the evening sky on March 28.

29. Vol. 33 of MMP.

30. The 1851 painting of Mitchell by Mrs. Hermione Dassel is in the library of the Nantucket Maria Mitchell Association.

31. Maria Mitchell to Sally Mitchell Barney, June 29, [1851]. MMA, Neil Barney papers. The year has been determined from the reference to Kate's birthday. Sally's son, William Mitchell Barney, was born October 30, 1846. An earlier son of the same name had died before the age of three.

Maria Mitchell

CHAPTER 3: NANTUCKET DIARIES *(Pages 39–70)*

1. Kendall, MMLL, 15.

2. The diary entries from February 15, 1853 through March 2, 1854 are found in MMLL, 25.

3. Edward Brooks Hall, *Memoir of Mary L. Ware: Wife of Henry Ware, Jr.* (Boston: American Unitarian Association, 1880).

4. We now know that the different colors of the stars are due to their different temperatures. The redder stars are cooler. Astronomers today would characterize Rigel as blue-white, definitely not yellow.

5. Mitchell had obviously made some mistakes in her calculations for the *Nautical Almanac.* C. H. Davis had his headquarters in Cambridge.

6. Helen Wright, in *Sweeper in the Sky* (New York: Macmillan, 1950) 56, discusses a trip Mitchell took to Dutchess County in New York which may be the one mentioned in the diary. There is no diary record of such a trip.

7. Dorothea Lynde Dix (1802-1887), social reformer and philanthropist.

8. In spite of her low appraisal of her elocution ability, Mitchell became a very successful lecturer in the classroom and with large audiences.

9. The Atheneum was open Saturday evening, so she would have had to work that day.

10. Mitchell's ideas on the astronomy of Milton were published posthumously in *Poet Lore* 6, 312, 1894.

11. Any telescope, even in an observatory, is used at the same temperature as the outside air. Mitchell was working in the cold for hours, with no heat at all. Throughout her life she professed to love working in the outside air and to feel better for doing so.

12. Unless otherwise noted, all diary entries in the remainder of this chapter are found in vol. 16 of MMP.

13. The Rev. Henry Giles.

14. This is a reference to Sir David Brewster (1781-1868), a Scottish physicist credited with inventing the kaleidoscope and who published *More Worlds Than One* in 1854.

15. William Whewell (1795-1866), F.R.S., natural philosopher, master of Trinity College, and author of *Plurality of Worlds* (1853). Brewster was highly critical of Whewell's "antipluralist" viewpoint. When Maria Mitchell went abroad in 1857, she was a guest at Whewell's home.

16. Comet 1854 IV, discovered on September 11, 1854, by Klinkerfues.

17. At this time there was a regular ferry service from Nantucket to Hyannis by the side paddle wheeler "Massachusetts." The Old Colony railroad had been

extended to Hyannis in 1854, so Mitchell would have had a relatively simple time getting to Plymouth; see Alexander Starbuck *The History of Nantucket* (Rutland, Vt.: Charles E. Tuttle, 1969).

18. Monthly Notices of the Royal Astronomical Society.

19. Algol is a well known eclipsing variable star that undergoes an eclipse every 2.87 days. The light minimum lasts about 20 minutes. Evidently Mitchell was trying to observe the minimum but missed it by stopping her observations too soon.

20. Josiah Quincy (1772-1864), president of Harvard College, 1829-1845.

21. Matthew Hale Smith (1810-1879), Unitarian minister.

22. After going to Vassar College Mitchell became much sought after as a public lecturer. She lectured not only on astronomy but also about her European travels.

23. James Freeman Clarke (1810-88), Unitarian minister and author.

24. All astronomical calculations were made using logarithms which enabled the astronomer to replace a difficult multiplication by a simple addition. In the work that Mitchell was doing, it would not be uncommon to have several pages of logarithmic calculations to arrive at one answer.

25. These comments on travel books may explain why Mitchell never attempted to write a book about her extensive travels although she did give lectures on them.

26. Kendall, MMLL, 167.

27. Maria Mitchell to Alexander Starbuck, August 24, 1854, NHA.

28. "New planets" are now called asteroids, and thousands are known. They are quite different from comets.

29. Henry's twin Eliza, who died at age three in 1833.

30. Probably the wife of George Ripley, literary critic of the *New York Tribune*.

31. Kendall, MMLL, 22.

32. "Perturbations" are the effects of the planets on the motion of other bodies, usually a comet. Notice that Mitchell seems committed to going to Europe.

33. Kendall, MMLL, 167.

34. Sidney Smith (1771-1845), English clergyman.

35. Undoubtedly Comet 1855 IV which was discovered by Bruhns at Berlin.

36. Maria Mitchell to E. G. Kelley, October 20, [1856], Nantucket Atheneum.

CHAPTER 4: TRAVELS IN AMERICA *(Pages 71–84)*

1. Vol. 2 of MMP.

2. Vol. 38 of MMP.

3. Unless otherwise noted, all diary entries in the remainder of the chapter are from vol. 62 of MMP.

4. Wright, *Sweeper in the Sky,* 99.

5. Kendall, MMLL, 57.

6. Hyannis, on Cape Cod, is where Mitchell would have boarded the train after arriving by ferry from Nantucket.

7. Theodore Parker (1810-1860), Unitarian theologian and social reformer.

8. This reference to Niagara Falls evidently indicates that Mitchell visited the Falls on her way to Meadville, although there is no record of it.

CHAPTER 5: ENGLAND AND SCOTLAND *(Pages 85–108)*

1. Sir George Biddell Airy (1801-1892), Astronomer Royal for England, 1835 to 1881.

2. Vol. 59 of MMP. The drafts of these letters were given to the Maria Mitchell Association by Elizabeth L. Bond, daughter of George Bond.

3. The reformer Dorothea Lynde Dix, noted in Endnote 7 of Chapter 3.

4. Letter from Maria Mitchell to Dorothea Dix, bMS Am 1838 (466). By permission of the Houghton Library, Harvard University

5. Unless otherwise noted, all diary entries and letters in the remainder of the chapter are from vol. 69b of MMP. Letters written home from England are also found there.

6. Nathaniel Hawthorne (1804-1864) had been appointed Consul to Liverpool by Franklin Pierce.

7. James Martineau (1805-1900), Unitarian minister and theologian.

8. Admiral William Henry Smyth (1788-1865) had supported Mitchell in the attempt to get the gold medal for her discovery of a comet. He had written a book on double stars that Mitchell and her father often used in observing the stars on Nantucket.

9. Vol. 42 of MMP.

10. Ibid.

11. Ibid.

12. Extract from letter of Maria Mitchell to William Bond. Dated "1 Burlington Gardens, London. Received Sept. 17, 1857." HUA UAV 630.2.

13. This famous structure was moved in 1854, from Hyde Park to Sydenham where it housed numerous exhibits.

14. The library of the Royal Society is still in Burlington House. The Newton telescope that Mitchell saw here was the first reflecting telescope ever made, i.e. it uses a mirror instead of a lens to collect the light.

15. Robert Chambers (1802-1871), author and publisher.

16. Sir William Rowan Hamilton (1805-1865). The mathematical methods known as Quaternians are still among the most powerful means of analysis in mathematical physics.

17. The signatures of Maria Mitchell and Prudie Swift can still be seen in the visitors book.

18. Frederick Georg Wilhelm Struve (1793-1864), director of the Imperial Observatory at Pulkova in Russia just outside of St. Petersburg. One of the most influential astronomers of the nineteenth century.

19. Vol. 42 of MMP.

20. Struve at this time was working on a survey to determine the shape of the earth. Astronomical observations were used to determine the latitude of the station while the distance between two stations was determined by surveying methods. A comparison of the distance required to change your latitude by one degree gives an indication of the size and shape of the earth.

21. Sir Edward Sabine (1788-1883), F.R.S., president of Royal Society.

22. Rev. Baden Powell (1798-1860), F.R.S., geometer and philosopher, Savian Professor of Geometry at Oxford.

23. Dr. William Whewell, noted in Endnote 15 of Chapter 3, was best known for his book *History of the Inductive Sciences*. Whewell is also credited with inventing the word "scientist."

24. Adam Sedgwick (1785-1873), one of the most important geologists of the day.

25. Robert Willis (1800-1875). F.R.S., professor of natural and experimental science.

26. John Couch Adams (1817-1892) was the first person to predict the position of Neptune using mathematical calculations. See *The Discovery of Neptune* (1962) by Morton Grosser for a full discussion of this fascinating episode in the history of astronomy, including the Adams-Leverrier rivalry.

27. Vol. 38 of MMP.

28. The correspondence with Sir George Airy and Lady Airy is found in vol. 36 of MMP.

29. Nantucket Historical Association.

30. Vol. 42 of MMP.

31. Vol. 43 of MMP.

32. This most likely refers to Professor Joseph Peirce (1809-1880), American mathematician and astronomer on the faculty of Harvard College. He was later superintendent of the the U.S. Coast Survey.

33. Charles Babbage (1790-1871), F.R.S., made the first calculating machine.

34. Probably Dr. Neil Arnott (1788-1874), a Scottish physicist and experimental philosopher.

35. The aunt was Caroline Herschel (1750-1848), brother of William Herschel. Caroline Herschel assisted her brother in his astronomical research for many years by writing down his observations as he made them. She was an excellent observer herself and discovered several comets. The paper given to Mitchell was a page from a notebook on which she had recorded some of William Herschel's observations. This page can be found in vol. 38 of MMP.

CHAPTER 6: FRANCE AND ITALY *(Pages 109–128)*

1. Mary Somerville (1780-1872) and Maria Mitchell were kindred spirits in many ways. Both had a minimum of formal schooling which they overcame by learning Latin and mathematics on their own. Somerville's great contribution to science was her 700-page translation of Laplace's monumental *Mécanique Céleste,* with explanatory notes to the text. She also wrote a more popular *Connection of the Physical Sciences and Physical Geography.*

2. Unless otherwise indicated, all diary entries in this chapter are from vol. 69b of MMP.

3. There is no indication whether "we" referred to traveling companions or was used editorially although earlier she had written her father that she would not travel alone to the continent. Mitchell was usually very reticent about her traveling companions. In her diaries written in England she usually says "I" even though, as we know, Prudie was with her.

4. Francis Horner (1778-1817), British statesman and lawyer.

5. Lady Lyell was the wife of Sir Charles Lyell (1797-1875), British geologist.

6. Urbain Jean Joseph Leverrier (1811-77), mathematician and astronomer, director of the Paris Observatory. His computations led directly to the discovery of Neptune, although J. C. Adams, whom Mitchell had met at Cambridge, had done similar calculations at an earlier date.

7. Evariste Galois (1811-32), a brilliant French mathematician, was killed at a young age in a duel.

8. *The Heart of Hawthorne's Journals,* ed. Newton Arvin (Boston: Houghton Mifflin, 1929).

9. Julian Hawthorne recorded his remembrances of this trip in *Hawthorne and his Circle* (New York: Harper & Brothers, 1903, 249) and in *The Memoirs of Julian Hawthorne* (New York: The Macmillan Co. 1938)

10. Found only in Kendall, MMLL, 143.

11. Murray was the author of a standard guidebook used by tourists at the time.

12. Harriet Hosmer (1831-1908), American sculptor.

13. Translated from the Italian by Professor Benjamin G. Kohl, Andrew W. Mellon Professor of the Humanities, Vassar College.

14. Giacomo Antonelli (1806-76), Vatican cardinal and secretary of state to Pope Pius IX.

15. Vol. 70 of MMP.

16. Vol. 17 of MMP.

17. Nathaniel Hawthorne, *The Marble Faun*, Chapter V.

18. This stop is probably Hypogeum, an Etruscan cemetery.

19. Vol. 17 of MMP.

20. Ibid.

21. Johann Franz Encke, 1791-1865, German astronomer. Director of the Berlin Observatory.

22. Alexander von Humboldt (1769-1859), German naturalist and explorer.

23. Charles Kean (1811-68), famous English actor.

CHAPTER 7: FROM NANTUCKET TO VASSAR *(Pages 129-154)*

1. Kendall, MMLL, 167.

2. Alvan Clark (1832-87), the most important American telescope maker of the nineteenth century.

3. Howe, *Our Famous Women*, 455.

4. A reference to Comet 1858 VI, also known as Donati's Comet which Mitchell discovered independently in June. According to Gary W. Kronk, "the comet developed into one of the most impressive comets of the century during September." *Comets: A Descriptive Catalogue* (Hillside, N. J.: Enslow Publishers, 1984), 48.

5. Vol. 38 of MMP.

6. A reference to internal quarrels at Dudley Observatory, Albany, New York.

7. HUA UAV 630.2

8. Wright, *Sweeper in the Sky*, 126.

9. *Emerson's Magazine and Putnam's Monthly,* (Vol. V, 1857), 94.

10. HUA UAV 630.2

11. Vol. 59 of MMP.

12. Maria Mitchell, "Observations on Some of the Double Stars," *American Journal of Science and Arts*, 2nd ser. 36 (1863): 38.

13. Vol. 59 of MMP.

14. Maria Dame, Maria Mitchell's niece, was born May 3, 1861.

15. MMP.

16. Vol. 2 of MMP.

17. Ibid.

18. Smithsonian Institution Archives: Record Unit 26. Box 10, Folder 6.

19. William Mitchell Barney II , Mitchell's nephew, was born on Oct. 30, 1846.

20. Vol. 38 of MMP.

21. MMP. Henry Mitchell papers.

22. The early history of Vassar College can be found in Benson J. Lossing, *Vassar College and Its Founder* (New York, C. A. Alvord, 1867); Edward R. Linner, *Vassar: The remarkable growth of a man and his college,* Elizabeth A. Daniels, ed., (Poughkeepsie: Vassar College Publications Department, 1984); Elizabeth Hazelton Haight, ed., *The Autobiography and Letters of Matthew Vassar* (New York: Oxford University Press, 1916); James Monroe Taylor and Elizabeth Hazelton Haight, *Vassar* (New York: Oxford University Press, 1915).

23. As an example, the president of Harvard College, Charles Eliot, gave a speech at Smith College several years later in which he congratulated them for not having women on their faculty.

24. See Haight, *Autobiography and Letters of Matthew Vassar* or Linner, *Vassar* for further discussion of this and other issues during the early years of Vassar College.

25. Haight, Ibid, 144.

26. Although supportive of women as professors, Nathan Bishop was never happy with the appointment of Mitchell to the faculty. On March 1, 1879 he wrote to the president of Vassar: "I was aware that Miss Mitchell was a 'Rank Theodore Parker Unitarian' when she was elected. I believe she has kept away from Vassar five times as many students as her influence has drawn to it." VCA.

27. Vol. 2 of MMP.

28. This letter no longer exists. It would have been in regard a position for Joshua Kendall, Phebe's husband.

29. Item 185 of VCA. The letters of Mitchell are numbered in the Vassar College archive.

30. Benjamin Peirce (1809-1880), the American mathematician and astronomer noted previously in Endnote 32 of Chapter 5.

31. Alexis Caswell (1799-1877), president of Brown University.

32. VCA.

33. Vol. 2 of MMP.

34. Item 21 of VCA. Items from the Vassar College archives are referred to by their number in the Mitchell collection.

35. Haight, *Autobiography and Letters of Matthew Vassar*, 109.

36. Item 143 of VCA.

37. Vol. 2 of MMP.

38. Minutes of the Board of Trustees of Vassar College (VCT), Vassar College Library. All further quotations from the trustees are found in the same source.

39. Item 22 of VCA.

40. Item 23 of VCA.

41. Vol. 2 of MMP.

42. Ibid.

43. VCT

44. Vol. 2 of MMP.

45. Taylor, J. M. and Haight, Elizabeth, *Vassar*, 53. Taylor was president of the college while Mitchell was on the faculty, so his insights on her value to the college are especially germane.

CHAPTER 8: VASSAR COLLEGE, 1865 TO 1873 *(Pages 155-203)*

1. See Linner, *Vassar,* pp. 121-129.

2. MMP, Matthew Barney collection.

3. Vol. 34 of MMP.

4. Mitchell's view of Miss Lyman softened over the years as can be seen in a letter she wrote on November 23, 1870.

5. Kendall, MMLL, pp. 172-173.

6. Ibid, 177.

7. Caroline Healey Dall (1824-1912), early woman's rights advocate.

8. Mitchell, Maria. Letter to Caroline Dall, 9 December 1865. Caroline Wells Healey Dall Papers. MHS.

9. VCA

10. See diary entry for November 2, 1875.

11. Item 122 of VCA.

12. Item 126 of VCA.

13. Item 84 of VCA.

14. The year is indicated as uncertain in the VCA. If the letter by Raymond dated 1869 is a reply to this one, as seems likely because of its reference to having "read your paper through" and to the books Mitchell requested, then this letter should also be dated as 1869.

15. Charles Farrar was professor of natural science and Mitchell's immediate supervisor.

16. Item 83 of VCA.

17. Vol. 2 of MMP.

18. VCA

19. Ibid.

20. Ibid.

21. Ezra Cornell (1807-1874) founded Cornell University in 1865.

22. Cornell University archives.

23. Kendall, MMLL 241.

24. Benjamin Peirce was well known to Mitchell and he had written one of her recommendations.

25. Vol. 27 of MMP.

26. Linner, *Vassar*, 177.

27. In an entry in her diary dated August 11, 1881, Mitchell wrote: "Matthew Vassar is dead." This has erroneously been taken as a reference to the founder of the college. In fact, she was referring to the death of Matthew Vassar's nephew who shared his name.

28. Kendall, MMLL, 174.

29. Ibid, 176.

30. VCA

31. Ibid. Date "c. 1867" is indicated because Clare E. Glover graduated in 1868.

32. Mary Whitney would replace Mitchell in 1888 as the second professor of astronomy.

33. Ibid.

34. VCA

35. Ibid.

36. Vol. 38 of MMP.

37. Ibid.

38. Vol. 44 of MMP.

39. Vol. 41 of MMP.

40. Item 87 of VCA.

41. Proverbs 13:12.

42. VMisc.

43. Ibid.

44. Vol. 2 of MMP.

45. For an explanation of "counting seconds," see Endnote 18 in Chapter 1.

46. "Hours at Home" October 1869. p. 555. The women were Mary Whitney '68; Sarah L. Blatchley '68; Isabella Carter '68; Achsah M. Ely '68; Sarah M. Glazier '68; Helen L. Storke '68; Mary Reybold '68; Elizabeth Williams '69; Elizabeth R. Coffin '70; Laura (or Mary E.) Gay '69; Harriet M. Foote.

47. American Philosophical Society.

48. Smithsonian Institution Archives. Record Unit 26; Vol. 85, 539.

49. Vol. 2 of MMP.

50. Item 90 of VCA.

51. Probably Anne Maria Mitchell, born in 1847, the daughter of William Forster Mitchell.

52. Probably a reference to the death of Henry's first wife. He remarried in 1873 and Sally died in 1876 before his third marriage.

53. MMP, Henry Mitchell collection.

54. I am indebted to Beatrice Gormley for sharing this letter which is in her possession. She graciously granted me permission to reproduce the letter here.

55. VCA.

56. Vol. 34 of MMP. The year was added by someone at a later time.

57. A reference to the biblical passage in which Joshua commanded the sun and moon to stand still (Joshua 10:12-14).

58. Item 91 of VCA.

59. See reference to Dorothea Dix, Chapter 3, Endnote 7.

60. Houghton Library, Harvard University; bMS Am 1838 (466)

61. Item 165 of VCA.

62. Vol. 29 of MMP.

63. Vol. 68 of MMP. Probably Frances Elizabeth Willard (1839-98), later active in the temperance movement.

64. Emily Faithfull (1835-1895), English philanthropist who established a printing enterprise for women.

65. Vol. 68 of MMP.

66. Elizabeth Blackwell (1821-1900) was the first American woman to receive an M. D. degree.

67. Mary Putnam (Jacobi) (1842-1906) was also an early female physician.

68. Edward H. Magill (1825-1907), President of Swarthmore College, 1871-1890.

69. Ibid.

70. Item 182 of VCA.

71. Marie Agnesi (1718-99) was a pioneer woman mathematician.

72. Vol. 29 of MMP.

73. VMisc.

74. Vol. 38 of MMP.

75. Helen Marshall, Class of 1876. Letter to Margaret Harwood, October 6, 1934. Vol. 34 of MMP.

76. George MacDonald (1824-1905), Scottish novelist and poet.

77. Smithsonian Institution Archives. Record Unit 26. Vol. 134.

78. Vol. 68 of MMP.

79. Frederick Augustus Porter Barnard (1809-89) was president of Columbia College.

80. Vol. 68 of MMP.

81. Vol. 17 of MMP.

82. Minutes of Vassar College Trustees. All subsequent references to the trustees actions are from these same archives (VCT).

83. Item 89 of VCA.

84. VCA.

85. VMisc.

86. MMP, M. Barney file.

CHAPTER 9: EUROPEAN TRAVELS, 1873 *(Pages 204-217)*

1. Vol. 68 of MMP. In the notebook, her passport is followed by her visa for entering Russia.

2. Unless otherwise indicated, all diary entries reprinted in this chapter are found in vols. 48 and 49 of MM Papers.

3. In a letter to her sister Sally after she returned home, Maria gives further details of her ordeal with seasickness (see Chapter 10, page 223).

4. Mitchell had carried on an extensive correspondence with Mrs. Airy after her first European trip until Mrs. Airy became too ill to continue. Mrs. Airy died August 13, 1875.

5. Vol. 17 of MMP.

6. Vol. 48 of MMP.

7. Vol. 17 of MMP.

8. Vol. 48 of MMP.

9. Vol. 17 of MMP.

10. Vol. 48 of MMP.

11. Frances Power Cobbe (1822-1904), an early British suffragette and advocate of women's rights.

CHAPTER 10: VASSAR COLLEGE 1873 TO 1880 *(Pages 218-259)*

1. Helen Dawes Brown successfully graduated from Vassar College in 1878.

2. Vol. 68 of MMP.

3. Vol. 34 of MMP.

4. Frances Eliza Hodgson Burnett (1849-1924), American author (*Little Lord Fauntleroy*).

5. Francis A. Wood, "Earliest Years at Vassar," *Vassar Miscellany*, 38, (January 1909).

6. VMisc

7. Ibid.

8. MMP. Barney papers.

9. "Miss T." is most likely Harriet E. Terry, Vassar's Lady Principal from 1871 to 1877, who is mentioned later in the letter.

10. Vol. 34 of MMP.

11. Henry Mitchell married Margaret Hayward in 1873. His first wife had died several years before and Margaret would die in 1875.

12. Florence M. Cushing, Agnes E. Cutter, Lucretia A. Stow, Helen Arnold, Annie M Reed, Frances Fisher, Julia S. Bennett all graduated in 1873. Pamela Tarbell Smiley is listed as sp 71-74.

13. Vol. 34 of MMP.

14. Ibid.

15. Item 92 of VCA.

16. VCA

17. VMisc

18. Vol. 68 of MMP.

19. Charles Kingsley (1819-1875) was canon of Westminster at this time.

20. Vol. 50 of MMP.

21. Vol. 68 of MMP. 68

22. Vol. 38 of MMP. The year was written on the letter by E. R. C.

Maria Mitchell

23. VCA

24. Edward Everett Hale (1822-1909), American author and clergyman.

25. Vol. 2 of MMP.

26. Kendall, MMLL 194

27. Vol. 50 of MMP.

28. Vol. 59 of MMP.

29. Vol. 50 of MMP.

30. The annual meeting of the Association for the Advancement of Women, Syracuse, NY.

31. Kendall, MMLL 258.

32. VMisc

33. Vol. 34 of MMP.

34. Vol. 69 of MMP.

35. Probably Truman J. Backus, Professor of Rhetoric and English from 1867 to 1883.

36. Vol. 50 of MMP. All subsequent diary entries for 1876 to 1879 are in this same volume.

37. VCA

38. Elizabeth J. Williams Champney (1850-1922), a member of Vassar's class of 1869, became a prolific author of articles and books, including the popular "Three Vassar Girls" series. Maria Mitchell met her "lovely little namesake" when the girl was five years old. The Champney daughter eventually attended Vassar, missing by only a few years the opportunity to be taught by her mother's beloved astronomy professor.

39. Vol. 59 of MMP. The *Vassar Miscellany* noted the publication of "The Sky Garden" by Mrs. E. J. Williams Champney in January 1877.

40. Reprinted in *Papers Read at the Fourth Congress of Women* (Washington, D.C.: Todd Brothers, 1877).

41. Vol. 50 of MMP.

42. VCA

43. Ibid

44. VMisc

45. VCA

46. Vol. 59 of MMP.

47. Smithsonian Institution Archives. Record Unit 26. Vol. 168.

48. Vol. 50 of MMP.

49. VMisc

50. Kendall, MMLL 223.

51. VCA 145

52. Vol. 50 of MMP.

53. Truman J. Backus, A. M. was appointed Professor of Rhetoric and the English Language in 1867. He resigned in 1883.

54. VCA

55. Vol. 50 of MMP.

56. Albert A. Michelson had just completed his measurement of the velocity of light.

57. Mitchell was correct in her assessment of this theory which was soon shown to be impossible.

58. Vol. 50 of MMP.

59. Abby Moore Goodwin was Vassar's professor of Latin at the time.

60. This is probably a reference to the article that J. W. Howe wrote for *Our Famous Women* (A.D. Worthington & Co., 1884).

61. Vol. 2 of MMP.

62. Vol. 50 of MMP.

CHAPTER 11: VASSAR COLLEGE, 1880 TO 1888 *(Pages 260-300)*

1. Reprinted in *Women and the Higher Education,* edited by Anna C. Brackett. (New York: Harper, 1893).

2. Vol. 24 of MMP. All succeeding diary entries for 1880 and 1881 are found in this volume.

3. Vol. 59 of MMP.

4. Vol. 2 of MMP.

5. VMisc

6. Mitchell could not escape from her past. She had taught herself almost all of the higher mathematics she knew by reading directly from books without a teacher. Her self-education influenced many of her later ideas about education.

7. Vol. 24 of MMP.

8. Mrs. Mary Livermore spoke at the Founder's Day exercises in the chapel on April 30, 1880. She had previously spoken at the college in 1877.

9. Item 50 of VCA.

10. Item 104 of VCA. Mitchell's sister, Mrs. Dame, was born in 1833. In the letter she is referred to as being 47 years old, hence the year 1880 for the letter.

11. VMisc.

12. The subject of Mitchell's health arises more and more in her diary over the next few years. We do not know exactly what her medical problem was.

13. Vol. 59 of MMP.

14. William Mitchell Kendall graduated from Harvard College in 1876. He became a well-known architect and studied in Europe for several years. He died in 1941. See obituary, *New York Times*, August 9, 1941.

15. There are only two years possible for this letter. Easter fell on April 17 in 1870 and 1881.

16. Vol. 38 of MMP.

17. The college continues to celebrate Matthew Vassar with the annual "Founder's Day" near the end of the spring semester.

18. Comet 1881 III, "The Great Comet." It was discovered on May 22 from New South Wales. It was visible from the northern hemisphere by June 22, so Mitchell saw it soon after. The comet was very bright, and had a tail which extended over a wide area.

19. Garfield died of blood poisoning on September 19.

20. The two comets were 1881 III and 1881 IV, both visible near the north celestial pole. They were not the same comet.

21. Julia A. Ray was Lady Principal from 1878 to 1881. Abby F. Goodsell replaced her.

22. The lady principal was Julia A. Ray and the doctor was Helen W. Webster.

23. This diary entry has caused a good deal of confusion. As indicated in Endnote 27 of Chapter 8, it has often been taken to refer to Matthew Vassar, the founder of the college; it actually refers to his nephew, usually known as Matthew Vassar, Jr. The founder died on June 23, 1868, and the date of this diary entry is definitely August 11, 1881.

24. Mary E. Allen, M. D., Prof. of Physiology and Hygiene, 1881 to 1884.

25. John Guy Vassar, another nephew of the founder.

26. VCA 72.

27. Mitchell did a survey of women in science for the A.A.W. each year. She believed it was necessary to have these statistics so she could trace the advance of women in science.

28, Vol. 45 of MMP. Subsequent diary notes up to June 6, 1882 are in this volume.

29. Rose Herschel, whom Mitchell first met in England in 1857, was the daughter of Sir John Herschel. See entry for April 26.

30. Vol. 21 of MMP. Subsequent diary notes up to August 1883 are in this volume.

31. VMisc. Apparently the only record of this degree is found in the *Bulletin*, Hanover College, Hanover, Indiana, March 1, 1913; the Bulletin included an Alumni Record containing a "Roster of Persons on Whom the Corporation has

Conferred Honorary Degrees." In his "Biographical Sketch," her brother Henry gave 1854 as the year of this award which has unfortunately been perpetuated in other literature. I am indebted to President Russell Nichols of Hanover College for his assistance in answering this question.

32. From the dates given and the brightness of the comet, I infer the following diary entries refer to the "Great September Comet," or Comet 1882 II, first discovered in the southern hemisphere.

33. Vol. 33 of MMP.

34. VMisc.

35. Item 106 of VCA.

36. Vol. 21 of MMP.

37. Vol. 30 of MMP.

38. Kendall, MMLL 195.

39. Vol. 38 of MMP.

40. For an explanation of "counting seconds," see Endnote 18 of Chapter 1.

41. Vol. 21 of MMP.

42. Vol. 50 of MMP.

43. Vol. 30 of MMP.

44. Vol. 56 of MMP.

45. Ibid.

46. Ibid.

47. Vol. 37 of MMP.

48. Vol. 56 of MMP.

49. Titan is the largest satellite of Saturn. Students would watch its motion about Saturn and determine the period of this revolution.

50. Vol. 37 of MMP. All subsequent diary entries are from this source.

51. Rev. Ezekiel G. Robinson, D.D., LL.D. who was one of the original trustees.

52. Schlesinger Library, Harvard University.

53. Item 101 of VCA.

54. This diploma is now in the house on Vestal Street where Mitchell was born.

55. Vol. 59 of MMP.

CHAPTER 12: THE FINAL YEARS *(Pages 301-326)*

1. Margaretta Palmer, A. B., was a teacher at the college from 1888 to 1889.

2. Item 135 of VCA.

3. Mrs. Macy was Maria's sister Anne.

4. Her niece Maria Dame was the daughter of Maria's sister Kate.

5. Item 144 of VCA.

6. President Taylor's statement that "our [college] funds" could not be used for Miss Palmer carries the suggestion that some of Palmer's salary was paid directly by Mitchell to help her in the Observatory.

7. Mary W. Whitney was appointed professor of astronomy in June, 1888.

8. Vol. 2 of MMP.

9. C. Swan was one of the original college trustees.

10. Item 181 of VCA.

11. Kendall, MMLL, 263.

12. Vol. 2 of MMP.

13. Item 136 of VCA.

14. Robert E. Taylor was appointed a Trustee in 1885. His pledge was probably to the fund for the observatory.

15. Item 140 of VCA.

16. VCA 139.

17. VCA.

18. Vol. 37 of MMP. Unless otherwise indicated all diary entries are from this source.

19. Frances A. Wood had joined the college as a teacher in 1870 and was now college librarian.

20. Item 145 of VCA.

21. Item 51 of VCA.

22. VCA

23. VCT.

24. Item 91 of VCA.

25. Vol. 2 of MMP.

26. A reference to the Perseid meteor shower which occurs every year at about this time.

27. Vol. 2 of MMP.

28. Item 35 of VCA.

29. MMP. Henry Mitchell Papers.

30. Vol. 2 of MMP.

31. Item 92 of VCA.

32. Item 147 of VCA.

33. The location of this early family history, if it were ever completed, is not known.

34. Item 102 of VCA.

35, Although the year is not given on this letter, the content indicates it was written in 1889.

36. Priscilla H. Braislin came to the college as an instructor in mathematics in 1874 and was appointed professor in 1875. She resigned in 1887 and married Mr. Merrick; but she died within a year.

37. Item 68 of VCA.

38. Kendall, MMLL, 262.

39. The memoir was published in 1896 as *Maria Mitchell: Life, Letters, and Journals.* Compiled by Phebe Mitchell Kendall.

40. VCA.

41. Item 179 of VCA.

42. Item 177 of VCA.

43. Item 176 of VCA.

44. Cf. 1 Corinthians 13:12.

45. Vol. 2 of MMP.

EPILOGUE *(Page 327)*

1. See *Woman Scientists in America: Struggles and Strategies to 1940.* (Baltimore: Johns Hopkins University Press. 1982) by Margaret W. Rossiter for a more complete study of this topic. A series of articles on *Women in Astronomy* can be found in a special volume of *MERCURY: The Journal of the Astronomical Society of the Pacific,* (Vol. XXL, January/February 1992).

BIBLIOGRAPHY

Abbott, Frances M. "Three Decades of College Women." *Popular Science Monthly* 65 (1904): 350.

Airy, George B. *Autobiography*. Cambridge: Cambridge University Press, 1896.

Albertson, Alice Owen. "A Life and Its Sequel." *Vassar Quarterly* 3, (May 1923) 83.

Alumnae Directory Issue. *Bulletin of Vassar College* 55, no. 2 (1965).

Babbitt, Mary King. *Maria Mitchell as Her Students Knew Her*. Poughkeepsie, N.Y.: Enterprise Publishing, 1912.

Baker, Rachel, and Joanna Merlen. *America's First Woman Astronomer*. New York: J. Messner, 1960.

Batten, Alan H. *Lives of Wilhelm and Otto Struve* by D. Reidel. Boston: Dordrecht, 1988.

Belserene, Emilia Pisane. "Maria Mitchell: Nineteenth-Century Astronomer." *Astronomical Quarterly* 5 (1986): 133-50.

Bolton, Sarah Knowles. *Lives of Girls Who Became Famous*. New York: T. Crowell, 1886.

Brackett, Anna C. "Vassar Quarterly." *Harper's New Monthly* 52 (1876): 346.

——— *Women and the Higher Education*. New York, Harper. 1893.

Clarke, Edward Hammond. *Sex in Education*. Boston: Osgood & Co., 1873.

Dobson, Andrea K. and Bracher, Katherine. "A Historical Introduction to Women in Astronomy. "*MERCURY: The Journal of the Astronomical Society of the Pacific.* XXL, No. 1. 1992.

Drake, Thomas E. *The First Half Century of the Nantucket Maria Mitchell Association*. Nantucket: Nantucket Maria Mitchell Association, 1968.

Egermeier, Elsie E. *Girl's stories of great women*. Anderson, Ind., The Warner Press. 1930.

Everett, Edward. *Correspondence on Gold Medal*. Cambridge: Metcalf, 1849.

Furness, Caroline. "Maria Mitchell." *Dictionary of American Biography*, vol. 13. New York: Scribner's, 1934.

Gormley, Beatrice. *Maria Mitchell: The Soul of an astronomer*. Grand Rapids, Mich. W.B. Eerdmans, 1995.

Grosser, Morton. *The Discovery of Neptune*. Cambridge, Mass.: Harvard University Press, 1962.

Guillemin, Amedee. *Wonders of the moon*. New York, Scribner.

Haight, A. V. *General Catalogue of the Officers and Graduates of Vassar College: 1861-1890*. Poughkeepsie, N.Y.: 1890.

Haight, Elizabeth, ed. *The Autobiography and Letters of Matthew Vassar*. New York: Oxford University Press, 1916.

———— *The Life and Letters of J. M. Taylor*. New York: E. P. Dutton, 1919.

Hannaford, Phebe Ann. "Maria Mitchell." *Daughters of America*. Boston: B.B. Russell, 1883.

Hawthorne, Julian. *Hawthorne and His Circle*. New York: Harper & Bros., 1903.

———— *The Memoirs of Julian Hawthorne*. edited by Edith G. Hawthorne. New York: MacMillan, 1938.

Hawthorne, Nathaniel. *The Heart of Hawthorne's Journals*, edited by Newton Arvin. Boston: Houghton Mifflin, 1929.

Hoffleit, Dorrit. "Maria Mitchell." *Dictionary of Scientific Biography*, vol. 9. New York: Scribner's, 1974.

———— "Maria Mitchell's Famous Students" and "Comets over Nantucket." American Association of Variable Star Observers, 1983.

Horowitz, Helen Lefkowitz. *Alma Mater*. New York: Alfred A. Knopf, 1984.

Howe, Julia Ward, ed. *Sex in Education: A Reply*. Boston: Roberts Bros., 1874.

———— "Maria Mitchell." *Our Famous Women*. Hartford: A. D. Worthington, 1884.

———— *Reminiscences, 1819-1899*. Boston: Houghton Mifflin, 1899.

Jones, Bessie Zaban, and Lyle Gifford Boyd. *The Harvard College Observatory.* Cambridge, Mass.: Belknap Press of Harvard University Press, 1971.

Jones, Blanche A. "Vassar College." *Leslie's Popular Monthly* 43 (1897): 261.

Keller, Dorothy J. *Maria Mitchell: An Early Woman Academician.* Thesis, University of Rochester, 1974.

Kendall, Phebe Mitchell. *Maria Mitchell: Life, Letters, and Journals* (MMLL). Boston: Lee and Shepard, 1896.

Kohlstedt, Sally Gregory. "Maria Mitchell: The Advancement of Women in Science." *New England Quarterly* 51 (March 1978): 39.

Kronk, Gary W. *Comets: A Descriptive Catalogue.* Hillside, N.J.: Enslow Publishers, 1984.

Linner, Edward R. *Vassar. The Remarkable Growth of a Man and his College, 1855-1866.* Elizabeth A. Daniels, ed., Poughkeepsie. Vassar College Publication Department. 1984.

Loomis, Elias. *Recent Progress of Astronomy.* New York: Harper & Bros., 1850.

Lossing, Benson J. Vassar College and Its Founder. New York: C. Alvord, 1867.

Mack, Pamela E. "Women in Astronomy in the United States, 1875-1920." Senior thesis, Harvard University, 1977.

Macy, Anne Mitchell. "Astronomical Garret." *Wide Awake* (May 1888).

Miriam, Eve. "Maria Mitchell." *Growing up Female in America*: Ten Lives. Garden City, N.Y.: Doubleday, 1971.

Mitchell, Henry. "Biographical Notice of Maria Mitchell." *Proceedings of the American Academy of Arts and Sciences* 25 (1889): 331.

Mitchell, Maria. "The United States Coast Survey." *Christian Examiner* 17 (1852): 77.

——— "Mary Somerville." *Atlantic Monthly* 5 (May 1860): 568.

——— "Observations on Some of the Double Stars." *American Journal of Science and Arts (Silliman's Journal)* 2nd ser. 36 (July 1863): 38.

——— "The Total Eclipse of 1869." *Hours at Home* 9, no. 6 (1869): 555.

——— "Other Worlds Than Ours" [review]. *Hours at Home* (September 1870): 472.

———— "Notes on the Satellites of Jupiter." *American Journal of Science and Arts (Silliman's Journal)* 3rd ser. (June 1871) 96; 26; 5 (1873): 454; 15 (1878): 38.

———— Preface and additions to *Wonders of the Moon* by Amedee Guillemin. New York: Scribner, Armstrong & Co., 1873.

———— "The Higher Education of Women" [pamphlet]. Association for the Advancement of Women, First Congress, 1873.

———— "Need of Women in Science" [pamphlet]. Association for the Advancement of Women, Fourth Congress, 1877.

———— "Notes on the Satellites of Saturn." *American Journal of Science and Arts (Silliman's Journal)* 17 (1879): 430.

———— "Reminiscences of the Herschels." *Century* 38 (1889): 903.

———— [Posthumous] "Astronomical Science of Milton." *Poet Lore* 6 (1894): 312.

———— "The Collegiate Education of Girls." *Women and Higher Education*, edited by Anna C. Brackett. New York: Harper & Bros., 1893.

Mitchell, William. "Autobiography of William Mitchell." Vol. 1, Maria Mitchell Association Archives, Nantucket.

———— "Autobiography of William Mitchell." *Historic Nantucket*. (January 1983): 20; (April 1983): 15.

———— "On the Comet of 10th month, (October 1st,) 1847." *American Journal of Science and Arts (Silliman's Journal)* 5 (January 1848): 83.

[Obituary of Maria Mitchell]. *New York Times*, June 29, 1889.

Pierce, Henry Miller and Joseph Parrish Thompson. *Addresses at the commencement of Rutgers Female College on conferring the honorary degree of Doctor of Laws upon Thomas C. Upham, and of Doctor in Science and Philosophy upon Maria Mitchell.* New York: Cushing, Bardua, 1870.

Plum, Dorothy A., and George B. Dowell. The Great Experiment: A Chronicle of Vassar. Poughkeepsie, N.Y.: Vassar College, 1961.

Raymond, James H. "The Vassar Course of Study." *Godey's Lady's Book* (1870).

[Raymond, Harriet] Life *and Letters of John H. Raymond*. Edited by his eldest daughter. New York: Fords, Howard, & Hulbert, 1881.

[Review of Phebe Mitchell Kendall, *Maria Mitchell: Life, Letters, and Journals*]. *The Nation*, September 24, 1896.

Rossiter, Margaret W. *Woman Scientists in America*. Baltimore: Johns Hopkins University Press, 1982.

Spencer, A. G. "The Birth of the A.A.W. [Association for the Advancement of Women]." *The Council Idea* (1929): 5-7.

Starbuck, Alexander. *The History of Nantucket* [1924]. Rutland, Vt.: Charles E. Tuttle, 1969.

Taylor, James Monroe, and Elizabeth H. Haight. *Before Vassar Opened*. New York: Oxford University Press, 1915.

───── *Vassar* New York: Oxford University Press, 1915.

Townsend, H. A. "Maria Mitchell." *Reminiscences of Famous Women*. Buffalo, Evans-Penfold (1916).

"The Two Educations." *Godey's Lady's Book* (April 1870).

"The Vassar Salutation." *New York Times*, February 5, 1888.

Wall, Duncan. "Maria Mitchell: First Librarian." *The Nantucket Atheneum*, Nantucket, 1996.

Whitney, Mary W. "Maria Mitchell." *Sidereal Messenger* (February 1890): 49.

───── "Maria Mitchell." *Vassar Miscellany* (June 1896): 405.

───── "Founders of Vassar." *Vassar Miscellany* (May 1895): 343.

Wood, Frances A. "Earliest Years at Vassar." *Vassar Miscellany* (January 1909): 158.

Wright, Helen. *Sweeper in the Sky*. New York: Macmillan, 1949. Fourth printing, published by the Nantucket Maria Mitchell Association, 1959; Commemorative Edition, Clinton Corners, New York: College Avenue Press, 1997.

INDEX

We must face the light and not bury our heads in the Earth.
I am hopeful that scientific investigation pushed on and on,
will reveal new ways in which God works and bring to us
deeper revelations of the wholly unknown.
The physical and the spiritual seem to be at present
separated by an impassable gulf, but at any second,
that gulf may be overleapt, possibly a new revelation may come.

Maria Mitchell